THE REVOLUTION OF
——— 1905 ———
IN ODESSA

THE REVOLUTION OF
——1905——
IN ODESSA

BLOOD ON THE STEPS

Robert Weinberg

INDIANA
UNIVERSITY
PRESS
Bloomington • Indianapolis

The paper used in this publication meets the minimum requirements of American
National Standard for Information Sciences—Permanence of Paper for Printed
Library Materials, ANSI Z39.48–1984.

Manufactured in the United States of America

Library of Congress Cataloging-in-Publication Data
Weinberg, Robert.
   The revolution of 1905 in Odessa : blood on the steps / Robert
Weinberg.
     p. cm. — (Indiana-Michigan series in Russian and East
European studies) (Studies of the Harriman Institute)
   Includes bibliographical references and index.
   ISBN 0-253-36381-0
   1. Odessa (Ukraine)—History. 2. Ukraine—History—Revolution,
1905–1907. 3. Labor movement—Ukraine—Odessa—History. 4. Jews—
Ukraine—Odessa—Persecutions. 5. Odessa (Ukraine)—Ethnic
relations. I. Title. II. Series. III. Series: Studies of the
Harriman Institute
DK264.2.O3W45 1993
947'.717—dc20   92-23096

1 2 3 4 5 97 96 95 94 93

In memory of Bill Jacobson,
who made my life much richer

She started dancin' to that fine fine music
You know her life was saved by rock'n'roll
—Lou Reed

CONTENTS

Photographs follow pages 23 and 167

LIST OF TABLES

ACKNOWLEDGMENTS

Like many first books by historians, this one had its origins as a dissertation. I am grateful to two of my teachers at the University of California, Berkeley, Nicholas Riasanovsky and Victoria Bonnell, who guided me through the various stages of my graduate career and provided valuable feedback on my thesis. People familiar with the work of Vicky Bonnell should recognize the imprint her ideas have had on my analysis of Odessa workers and the 1905 revolution. My largest scholarly debt is owed to Reginald Zelnik, my dissertation adviser, who has been a formative force in the study of Russian labor and urban social history. As friend, mentor, critic, and counselor, he has influenced my intellectual development in profound ways. Not only has Reggie provided invaluable comments on various versions of this manuscript, but he has offered timely advice, support, and encouragement at every stage of my fledgling career. It has been a great honor and privilege to work with Reggie, and I am sure that I speak for others when I state that the historical profession is deeply indebted to him for his unstinting generosity, warmth of personality, and dedication to his students and colleagues.

In addition to the persons mentioned above, I have benefited from the advice, support, and insightful criticisms offered by Abraham Ascher, Robert DuPlessis, Michael Hamm, John Klier, Lillian Li, Adele Lindenmeyr, Lynn Mally, Joan Neuberger, Alexander Rabinowitch, Janet Rabinowitch, Hans Rogger, William Rosenberg, Steve Smith, Gerald Surh, and Charters Wynn. My interest in Russian Jewry was first piqued by Alexander Orbach. My parents were instrumental in instilling in me a love for books, and I am grateful for their support of my academic endeavors over the years.

I wish to thank the following institutions and organizations for providing financial support for this project: the University of California, Berkeley; the YIVO Institute for Jewish Research; the Memorial Foundation for Jewish Culture; the International Research and Exchanges Board; the Fulbright-Hays Doctoral Dissertation Research Abroad Program; the Center for Russian and East European Studies at Stanford University; the W. Averell Harriman Institute for Advanced Study of the Soviet Union at Columbia University; and the Swarthmore College Faculty Research Fund. I am also grateful to the Slavic specialists and staffs of the following libraries and archives for their excellent assistance: the University of California, Berkeley; the Hoover Institution on Peace, War, and Revolution at Stanford University; the YIVO Institute for Jewish Research, the New York Public Library; the Bund Archives of the Jewish Labor Movement; the Bakhmeteff Archive of Russian and East European History and Culture at Columbia University; the Alliance Israélite Universelle in Paris; the Lenin Library and Central State Archive of the October Revolution in Moscow; and the Central State Historical Archive in Petersburg. Finally, I want to express how impressed I am with Nick Jackiw for his rendition of the map of Odessa.

I also wish to thank the editors of *The Carl Beck Papers in Russian and East European Studies, Slavic Review,* and *Russian Review* for permission to reprint materials in chapters three, four, and seven.

I dedicate this book to Laurie Bernstein and our son Perry. The love that Laurie has showered on me has helped sustain me throughout the arduous process of first writing a dissertation and then transforming it into a book. She somehow has found the time in her own busy professional and personal schedule to read countless versions of the manuscript and has endured the ravings of a frustrated author. Laurie has put up with my moodiness for much too long, and I thank her from the bottom of my heart. The arrival of Perry in my life has forced me to place my work on Odessa in its proper perspective and realize that the world does not revolve around unearthing why workers in 1905 became politicized. At times Perry's random and indiscriminate pounding on the keyboard of my PC—mind you, he still cannot read and write—has produced sentences that are more elegant than those that emanate from my fingertips. Perry has a vague understanding that his mother and father teach "students," but I suspect that what he likes most about his parents' chosen profession is the opportunity it affords his babysitters to take him to the student cafeteria for dinner.

INTRODUCTION

This book is meant as a contribution to the growing literature on 1905 and the labor movement in late Imperial Russia.[1] In 1905 the government of Tsar Nicholas II faced a crisis of major proportions as peasants, workers, white-collar employees, professionals, intellectuals, soldiers and sailors, and even noble land-owners challenged the time-honored prerogatives of autocratic government. Through widespread political agitation, urban strike actions, and rural rebellions, the various strands of the opposition movement nearly brought the government to its knees. In the end, the regime weathered the crisis by granting timely concessions of political and civil rights. The government benefited from fissures in the opposition movement that began to appear towards the end of the year and relied on the military to restore order in both the city and countryside. Although this policy of giving with one hand and taking back with the other did not satisfy all opposition groups and even drove some of them deeper into the camp of political resistance, the government by the end of 1905 had regained enough confidence to devote the next eighteen months to reconsolidating its power.

Historians have long recognized the crucial role that urban workers played in forcing the government to issue the October Manifesto, the decree, prepared by Sergei Witte and grudgingly approved by Nicholas, that granted fundamental civil and political rights and that promised the establishment of a nationally elected legislative assembly. In recent years non-Soviet scholars have begun to study in detail the 1905 workers' movement, focusing on the aspirations, organizations, and actions of urban workers and uncovering the relationship between labor unrest and the revolutionary situation enveloping Russia. These scholars have been interested in revealing the motive forces of Russia's urban revolution in 1905 and explaining why labor erupted in that year into a jugger-naut that contributed to the near toppling of the autocracy. The crucial issue for these historians has been the radicalization of urban workers during the course of 1905, specifically the politicization of their grievances and actions. They have asked to what extent labor unrest derived from a logic rooted in the daily experiences of workers. They have also examined the influence of the radical and liberal intelligentsia on workers and have sought to ascertain the specific conjuncture of political, social, and economic forces that ignited the workers' movement and led workers to express their economic discontent in the forum of local and national politics. The appearance of trade unions and soviets of workers' deputies by the end of the year marked the culmination of this process, as urban workers throughout the Empire claimed rights of citizenship, chal-lenged superordinate authority, and asserted their right to participate in the running of the workplace. For many workers, 1905 was a contest of power between themselves and their social and political superiors, a struggle to achieve a life of respect, dignity, and freedom.

One aspect of the 1905 revolution that has been overlooked in much of this scholarship is the impact of ethnicity on the course of events. This book focuses on Odessa, the fourth largest city in the Russian Empire at the turn of the century, not only because it experienced as much turmoil in 1905 as any other city in Russia, but also because no other city experienced a pogrom comparable in its violence and destruction to the one suffered by the Jews of Odessa in that year. Odessa, like many other cities, bore little resemblance to the ethnically homogeneous industrial centers of Moscow and St. Petersburg, and it is the city's ethnic heterogeneity that provides us with an opportunity to broaden our understanding of the impact of nationality and ethnicity on the political events of this period. In 1905, Odessa's 139,000 Jews (out of a total city population of half a million) formed an integral part of the economy and society. The ethnic mix of Odessa enables the historian to study the nature of Russian-Jewish relations and anti-Semitism during the last decades of the Romanov dynasty and examine why, how, and when ethno-religious conflicts became potent factors in the life of the country. Since Jews in Odessa figured prominently as workers, examination of the interplay among ethnicity, occupation, and politics contributes to an expanded knowledge of the underpinnings of labor activism and helps reveal how ethnicity affected the labor movement. The bloody October pogrom is startling testimony to the impact of class and ethnicity on events in Odessa.

Soviet scholarship on Odessa suffers from the ideological constraints that had been imposed on the historical profession after Stalin's consolidation of power. The Soviet version of 1905—particularly after the 1920s—has denigrated the autonomy of the workers' movement and overstated the influence of the Bolsheviks as the guiding light in the unrest of 1905. The analysis presented in a limited number of articles and books about the working and living conditions of the labor force, the history of Bolshevism, and the landmark events of 1905 is frequently distorted if not erroneous because of the need to toe the party line on 1905. The selective publication of police reports, government communiqués, socialist pamphlets, and reminiscences of revolutionaries has provided some insight into events, but neither these primary sources nor the secondary scholarship on Odessa reveal in any detailed or systematic fashion the underlying tensions that animated Odessa workers during 1905.

Soviet historians have tended to neglect Odessa because of the socio-economic character of the city, which depended on commerce and lacked a large industrial base. For ideological and political reasons, they have therefore preferred to examine other cities, notably Moscow and St. Petersburg, where the local economies were much more oriented toward manufacturing. Moreover, the domination of the local revolutionary movement by Mensheviks and the large Jewish presence in the city have made Odessa unsuitable for investigation by politically cautious Soviet scholars. To date, no Soviet monograph devoted to the Revolution of 1905 in Odessa exists.[2]

With regard to non-Soviet scholarship, only recently have several Western historians turned their attention to Odessa, but none has yet examined its experience of the Revolution of 1905. With few but significant exceptions, Odessa remains uncharted territory for historians of the Russian labor and revolutionary movements.[3] As a detailed account and analysis of events in a major urban center, this study should expand our understanding of the revolutionary process in 1905 by providing a window through which historians can view the crisis of that year and the general contours of the workers' movement. An examination of Odessa in 1905 enriches our understanding of the intricate and multifaceted dimensions of politics and society and serves as a necessary corrective to the traditional focus on the two capital cities of the Russian Empire.

Because workers played such a preeminent role in shaping and determining the events of 1905 in Odessa, a narrative account of the labor movement forms the core of this book. This provides a basis from which to analyze the tremendous outburst of worker activism in 1905 and the radicalization of certain categories of the Odessa labor force. To state that activist workers were reacting to harsh working and living conditions is to grasp a part, but only a part, of their motivation in 1905. To be sure, workers were responding to economic adversity when they sought higher wages, shorter hours, and other bread-and-butter advances. Yet to ignore the political context of this labor unrest, or to neglect the workers' growing involvement in the political struggle against autocracy, is to give short shrift to the distinguishing feature of the workers' movement 1905: its highly charged and volatile political nature. For many workers the struggle for material improvements was part and parcel of a larger fight for social, economic, and political dignity. Labor activism and the political crisis enveloping the autocracy reinforced each other, impelling workers to embrace more radical stances as the year progressed and forcing the regime against the wall. As one Odessa salesclerk wrote in the early spring of 1905, the shop assistant "is not only a salesclerk but a citizen as well. If he doesn't enjoy rights of citizenship, then he should achieve them. Along with other workers he should strive for basic freedoms of speech, print, conscience, unions, and freedom to strike."[4] Moreover, the influence of the radical intelligentsia, revolutionary socialists in particular, on Odessa workers and the resonance of the socialists' political message in the attitudes and actions of the labor movement were important, if elusive, elements in the unrest of 1905.

Instead of focusing exclusively on the manufacturing sector, this study embraces all working people by adopting a broad categorization of workers that encompasses all those engaged in manual wage labor, including nonmanufacturing workers such as day laborers, sailors, and salesclerks. Casting such a wide net permits examination of the work force in all its diversity and allows us to capture more fully the flavor of the events and to assess the actions of all workers who played a major role in the events of 1905. Focusing on the entire spectrum of the Odessa work force enables us to examine why labor protest was generally restrained in terms of violence and why, on those rare occasions when strikes did become violent, they sometimes turned into bloody riots against Jews. That Jewish-gentile tensions periodically degenerated into pogroms, pitching Russian workers against Jewish ones, illustrates the political consequences of labor violence and reveals how the social, ethnic, and occupational identities of workers engaging in violent actions helped determine whether labor protest and social unrest acquired revolutionary or counterrevolutionary coloration.[5] As Arno Mayer has written: "Counterrevolution is closely interlocked with revolution. In fact, the two are symbiotically related."[6] Events in Odessa during 1905 offer insights into the complex relationship between politics and labor unrest.

The bulk of this book's narrative and analysis utilizes material gleaned from two kinds of sources which, when considered in conjunction with the revolutionary press and memoirs of socialist activists, offer a detailed view of labor activism and political unrest in Odessa in 1905. Russian workers infrequently left behind accounts of their experiences, and therefore the historian must rely on sources filtered through the lens of those educated Russians who observed and assessed the thoughts and behavior of workers. The first source—the daily press—provides a wealth of information about the labor movement in 1905; from editorials and letters to the editors to brief (sometimes one- or two-line) descriptions, as well as extended discussions of workers' grievances, demands, and strikes, Odessa's major newspapers kept abreast of the labor movement and did not shy away from covering those issues affecting social and political stability in the city.

In addition, I had the good fortune to use the holdings of TsGAOR, the Central State Archive of the October Revolution, located in Moscow. In particular, I relied on documents pertaining to the Special Section (*Osobyi otdel*) of the tsarist Ministry of Interior's Department of Police (*fond* 102). The Special Section was formed in 1893 to combat political subversion and worked with the *Okhrana* (tsarist Russia's infamous secret police) and Corps of Gendarmes to carry out intelligence operations and weed out subversives and revolutionaries. The files of the Special Section contain reports from various police officials operating in Odessa and, along with *fond* 124, a repository of judicial proceedings against persons charged with political crimes, offer a detailed look not only into the operations of Russia's police force but, more importantly for our purposes, into the inner workings of the revolutionary movement and the dynamics of labor and political unrest in Odessa from the mid-1890s through 1905. In St. Petersburg I worked in the Central State Historical Archive (TsGIA) where I primarily examined: the factory inspector reports (*fond* 23) on work stoppages, especially in 1903, and general information about factories such as the number of workers, hours of work, and other working conditions after the turn of the century; and judicial records of individuals accused of a variety of crimes, including revolutionary and strike activities (*fond* 1405).

One final note to the reader is in order. Until 1918 Russia used the old Julian calendar, which in the nineteenth century was twelve days and after 1900 thirteen days behind the Gregorian calendar in use throughout the rest of Europe. I have given all dates according to the Russian calendar.

THE REVOLUTION OF
——— 1905 ———
IN ODESSA

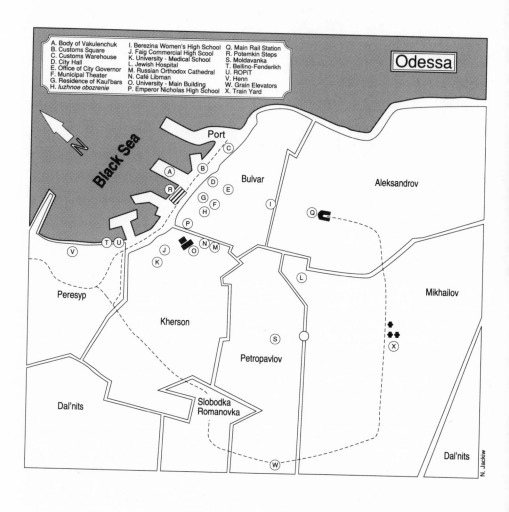

Odessa

A. Body of Vakulenchuk
B. Customs Square
C. Customs Warehouse
D. City Hall
E. Office of City Governor
F. Municipal Theater
G. Residence of Kaul'bars
H. *Iuzhnoe obozrenie*
I. Berezina Women's High School
J. Faig Commercial High Scool
K. University - Medical School
L. Jewish Hospital
M. Russian Orthodox Cathedral
N. Café Libman
O. University - Main Building
P. Emperor Nicholas High School
Q. Main Rail Station
R. Potemkin Steps
S. Moldavanka
T. Bellino-Fenderikh
U. ROPiT
V. Henn
W. Grain Elevators
X. Train Yard

Black Sea

Port

Bulvar

Aleksandrov

Mikhailov

Peresyp

Kherson

Petropavlov

Dal'nits

Slobodka
Romanovka

Dal'nits

N. Jackiw

1

Odessa on the Eve of 1905

THE RUSSIAN EL DORADO?

In Balzac's *Père Goriot,* the protagonist fantasizes about moving to Odessa in order to strike it rich in the grain trade. Financially ruined by the lavish lifestyles of his spoiled and pampered daughters, Père Goriot hopes to amass a new fortune so he can continue supporting them in the regal manner to which they are accustomed. The fact that Balzac selected Odessa as the place about which Goriot dreams of fame and fortune testifies to its reputation by the 1830s as a major commercial center where easy money could be made. The city's distinction as a land of opportunity remained alive through the rest of the nineteenth century and into the twentieth. A chronicler of life among the Russian urban lower classes wrote at the turn of the twentieth century that Odessa still enjoyed prestige as a city where "gold could seemingly be raked in." In a 1903 novella another observer similarly characterized Odessa as a "magical" city "where, it seems, there are no poor people and money, like stones, is scattered about the streets."[1]

This chapter examines how the image of Odessa as a land of opportunity conflicted with the harsh reality of life in the city at the turn of the twentieth century and created conditions ripe for the social and political turmoil of 1905. The unrest of 1905 was shaped as much by the interconnection of local social and economic developments in the decades immediately preceding 1905 as by the political crisis that emerged during that revolutionary year. A composite sociological and economic profile of Odessa on the eve of revolution underscores those aspects of the city's history that made it both similar to and different from other cities in late Imperial Russia and reveals why events in Odessa in 1905 Odessa were in some respects distinct from those elsewhere in the Empire.

Like many other cities of the Empire, Odessa experienced rapid growth during the nineteenth century and underwent significant changes in its economy as the expansion of local and national markets and the industrialization drive of the 1890s stimulated the development of manufacturing. The mushrooming population, caused by the arrival of tens of thousands of migrants

seeking jobs and better lives, created a host of problems for municipal authorities. The challenge of housing, feeding, and educating all these new residents,
let alone providing employment and safeguarding public health, strained the
resources of the city, and the city fathers were hard pressed to accommodate
the rapidly growing population. As in most other cities of the Russian Empire,
the growth of public amenities, including basic sanitary measures, often fell to
the wayside under the sheer magnitude of the problems engendered by the
urban explosion. Odessa's problems were also exacerbated by certain characteristics that the city shared with few other urban areas in the Russian Empire:
the variegated religious, national, cultural, and social backgrounds of its residents; the predominance of foreign commerce and finance in the local economy; and its strong West European flavor. By the turn of the twentieth century,
the hopes and expectations of the vast majority of Odessans had been undermined by a combination of demographic, social, and economic developments.
It took the political crisis of the autocracy in 1905 to stimulate large-scale
unrest in Odessa, but the stage for revolution had already been set by pressing
social and economic problems.

The Rise of Odessa

Odessa's meteoric rise as a center of commercial and financial significance is
all the more startling when we consider that the territory named Odessa in 1795
was nothing more than a small, sleepy trading village adjacent to a Tatar fortress
that the Russians had captured from the Turks a few years earlier. In 1794
Catherine the Great ordered the development of the region in order to stabilize
Russia's conquest of the western littoral of the Black Sea and to promote trade
in the area. A little more than a century later, Odessa was a bustling metropolis
of nearly half a million inhabitants.

Odessa's reputation stemmed from its prominence as a major entrepôt whose
well-being depended on the import and export of manufactured and agricultural
products, in particular grain and other foodstuffs. Odessa ranked as Russia's
number one port for foreign trade by the end of the nineteenth century, handling
the shipment of nearly all the wheat and more than half the other grains exported
from Russia. Grain exports, primarily wheat, comprised approximately 75 percent of the total value of Odessa's exports during the last years of the nineteenth
century. Without a doubt Odessa had become the preeminent port for foreign
commerce, deservedly earning its nickname, *pshenichnyi gorod*—"the city of
wheat."[2]

Odessa's economic rise in the early nineteenth century was made possible by
a favorable mix of geography, government policies, and international and domestic developments.[3] Merchants were attracted to Odessa because it was near
the grain producing regions of southern Russian and lay closer to the markets
of the Mediterranean and Western Europe than did other ports on the Black
and Azov Seas. In the early 1800s, the harbor at Odessa was also sufficiently

deep to accommodate large ships and during the winter did not freeze as readily as other harbors in the region.[4]

The government adopted vigorous policies to spur the growth not only of Odessa but also of New Russia, the territory acquired in the eighteenth century and composed of the provinces of Ekaterinoslav, Taurida, Kherson (in which Odessa was located), and, after 1828, Bessarabia. From the outset, the state offered inducements to promote settlement and investment in Odessa. Runaway serfs were assured their personal freedom and leaseholding status was promised to peasants resettled in New Russia by their landlords. In addition, the government provided incentives to foreign and Russian merchants by offering generous land grants and tax exemptions and promoted the development of Odessa by financing the building of the harbor and port facilities. Municipal authorities were granted sweeping powers to develop the local economy, which they strengthened by allocating customs revenue to the building of the city's infrastructure.[5] Odessa's governor-generals during the first half of the nineteenth century exhibited foresight and vision by regularizing the collection of customs receipts, permitting free storage of imported goods for a period of up to one and a half years, and earmarking funds for the construction of roads, schools, hospitals, and other public work projects.[6]

The disruption of trade by Napoleon's Continental System impelled merchants and industrialists to come to Odessa for grain, raw materials, and manufactured goods, all in abundant supply and cheaper than in Western Europe during these years. As one historian has written, Odessa "could easily attract to its port ships and traders searching for refuge, labor, and profits."[7] Even though Odessa suffered a mild setback after Napoleon's defeat and the revival of trade routes and markets in Western Europe, the city had by then firmly established itself as a center of international commerce. Moreover, unhindered passage for Russian commercial ships on the Black Sea and through the Straits, secured by the Treaty of Adrianople in 1829, enabled Odessa merchants to take advantage of expanding opportunities in the Mediterranean and Western Europe.[8]

It was the conferring of free-port status on Odessa, however, that catapulted the city into its preeminent commercial position. In 1817, Alexander I, convinced of the economic merits of the plan, decreed Odessa a free port, and from 1819 until 1859 Odessa enjoyed special status as a city where goods in transit for countries other than Russia were permitted to enter and leave the city duty-free.[9] In addition to promoting commerce, free-port status prompted foreign and domestic brokerage houses and banks to set up branch offices. It fueled the expansion of Odessa's trade in such luxury items as wine, perfume, and spices and helped establish the city as a major port of entry for goods bound for Russia as well as for those in transit to Western Europe from the Near East and the Caucasus.[10] As Pushkin reportedly quipped, it was cheaper to drink wine than water in Odessa.[11] In fact, the commercial and financial ties between Odessa and foreign markets were so strong that one observer wrote that free-port status "cut off Odessa from the remainder of Russia, creating, as it were, a state within a state, so that the territory of the Odessa port and today's municipality

TABLE 1

Number of Factories under Factory Inspection

Year	Number of Factories
1883	206
1890	332
1898	513

The data for 1890 include only those enterprises with annual production totaling at least 1,000 rubles; the data for 1898 refer to those enterprises under the jurisdiction of the Factory Inspectorate either because they employed at least fifteen workers or utilized engine-powered machinery. Omitted is the output of hundreds of small workshops, regardless of the extent of mechanization. Source: Bronshtein, *Mery k uluchsheniiu*, pp. 30–31; *Statisticheskoe obozrenie Odessy za 1890 g.*, pp. 140–142; Mikulin, *Fabrichno-zavodskaia i remeslennaia promyshlennost' v 1898 godu*, p. 11 and *prilozhenie* 1, sec. 8.

had closer ties with the European and Asiatic ports of the Black and Mediterranean Seas than with the rest of Russia or even New Russia."[12] By the early years of the reign of Nicholas I (1825–1855), Odessa had become the major commercial, administrative, cultural, and educational center of New Russia.

In the post-Emancipation period Odessa's commercial significance was bolstered even further by the expansion of the railway network that, in the 1860s and 1870s, finally linked the city indirectly to the markets located in the interior and the Caucasus. Development of the transport system strengthened Odessa's ties to the increased agricultural production of the fertile Black Earth region and reinforced the city's role as supplier of imported foodstuffs and manufactured items to surrounding provinces. In the course of the thirty years between the mid-1860s and 1894, grain exports from Odessa increased from between 30 and 40 million poods to nearly 160 million poods a year.[13] That most major trading firms in Odessa opened offices throughout Russia in these years underscores the growth of a national market in grain and the important role played by Odessa's merchants in that trade.

The opening of the Suez Canal in 1869, along with the appearance of steam-powered commercial fleets at mid-century and establishment of telegraph links between Odessa and foreign customers, also enhanced Odessa's position. Prior to this Russia obtained most of the Asiatic goods it imported via its Baltic ports. Now Odessa became even more of a center of imported goods, because the canal made it profitable for foreign merchants to ship goods to the city directly and then take advantage of the infant rail system to distribute merchandise in markets located inside Russia.[14]

In order to handle the growing volume of goods that passed through the port each year, city officials undertook efforts to modernize and expand the harbor. Beginning in the mid-1860s, they allotted money to deepen the harbor to permit berthing of larger freighters and to construct new piers, some of them outfitted after 1870 with conveyor belts. A breakwater was added, and both elevated and surface rail lines were built along the piers, facilitating the loading and unloading of ships from freight trains that could now pull right up to dockside. Other improvements, such as the introduction of gas and electric lights and paved roads, made periodically throughout the remainder of the century, added to the port's capacity to handle a larger volume of commerce.[15]

Odessa's economic strength did not rest solely on the grain trade, however. Not all persons engaged in commerce were involved in foreign trade, let alone large-scale import-export operations. Over 30,000 persons made their livings from trade, according to the 1897 census, but only a tenth of them handled the movement of grain products. The rest were middlemen, traders in other agricultural goods, or involved in small retail and petty trade.[16] Odessa also had a sizable and rapidly expanding industrial and manufacturing base. By mid-century machine-construction plants, metalworks, iron foundries, shipyards, steam-powered granaries, a sugar refinery, tanneries, and chemical plants had been established. The number of factories, totaling several dozen at mid-century, shot up to over 100 by the late 1860s, and a workshop economy centering primarily on the apparel and building trades also flourished as the city grew and required the services of thousands of workers.[17]

Factory production in the city expanded even more rapidly during the last two decades of the nineteenth century. As Table 1 indicates, there was a 250 percent jump in the number of factories between 1883 and 1898, with most of the growth occurring in metal processing, machine building, chemical production, teapacking, and sugar refining. The annual value of factory production more than doubled during the century's last two decades, from approximately 26 million to 61 million rubles. This expansion marked Odessa's contribution to the industrialization drive that was occurring in the country as a whole during the last quarter of the nineteenth century and gave the commercially oriented city a more balanced economy.

Much of Odessa's industrial expansion occurred in the outlying areas of the city, where industrialists took advantage of large expanses of undeveloped and unsettled land to establish new plants. During the 1880s and 1890s flour mills, granaries, warehouses, chemical plants, distilleries, wineries, breweries, metal-processing factories, and iron foundries were established in the Mikhailov and Petropavlov districts. Approximately 73 and 83 percent of enterprises under factory inspection in 1898 in Petropavlov and Mikhailov, respectively, had been established after 1880. The number of workers involved in the loading and unloading of grain from freight trains and in warehouses in these two regions also increased dramatically during these years. One sign of the growing significance of Petropavlov and Mikhailov was the decision to erect grain storage elevators near the railway yards in Mikhailov, which was connected by a spur to dockside.[18]

Like Petropavlov and Mikhailov, the districts of Peresyp and Slobodka-Romanovka also underwent rapid growth, particularly in the number of foundries, machine-construction and metalworking enterprises, and chemical plants established there during the last quarter of the nineteenth century. In Peresyp, for example, 84 percent of enterprises registered by the Factory Inspectorate in

1898 had not been operating before 1880.[19] Slobodka-Romanovka and Peresyp were quintessential Russian factory districts, with an abundance of industrial enterprises and overcrowded tenements housing primarily non-Jewish workers. Peresyp occupied the territory along the seashore that extended northward from the port, connected to the city center by a steep incline. Slobodka-Romanovka, situated southwest of the heart of Odessa, was located beyond a wide ravine that divided the district from the rest of Odessa. Described by one inhabitant as "drowning in mud," Slobodka-Romanovka was the poorest district in the city and had the dubious distinction of being the most dangerous, especially at night, when youth gangs roamed the streets.[20]

One notable feature of factory production in Odessa was the smallness of enterprises in terms of work force and output when compared with the manufacturing sector of St. Petersburg. The typical Odessa factory in 1903 annually produced goods valued at less than 100,000 rubles. Slightly over 80 percent of all enterprises surveyed by the Factory Inspectorate in that year employed fewer than 50 people, and 11 percent had work forces of 50 to 100. Thirty-seven enterprises boasted more than 100 employees; of these, only seven employed more than 500 workers. This low concentration of labor per enterprise stands in sharp contrast to the situation in the capital, where one in three factory workers were employed in establishments with more than 1,000 employees.[21]

The commercial nature of Odessa not unexpectedly shaped the city's industrial sector. For the most part, manufacturing either fulfilled the requirements of the port and shipping industry or processed the wide variety of raw materials that funneled into the city. Domestically grown wheat and raw sugar were turned into flour and refined sugar and then sold in both domestic and foreign markets. Imports of jute (used to make rope and burlap sacks, items necessary for the shipping industry), cork, tea, iron, steel, and tin were usually processed for domestic consumption. In addition, a significant share of the manufacturing sector's output satisfied other demands of the local market, such as housing, clothing, and feeding Odessa's burgeoning population.

The factory sector in Odessa was heavily dominated by a few branches of production and, within these sectors, by a small number of enterprises. The processing of foodstuffs was the largest branch of manufacturing, accounting for two-thirds of the ruble value of all factory output in 1903 and employing close to 7,000 workers. Available data for 1903 indicate that two sugar refineries, eight teapacking firms, and twenty-two flour mills accounted for almost 80 percent of the ruble output of this sector and slightly over half the value of all factory production. Sugar production alone comprised nearly one-quarter of manufacturing output in ruble terms.[22]

Metal processing ranked second in terms of production measured in rubles, but employed more workers than the food processing sector. Unlike metal and machine-construction factories in St. Petersburg, where the average number of workers per enterprise was close to 500, metalworking plants in Odessa were relatively small. The typical metal-processing firm in Odessa employed 63 persons, less than half the average for such enterprises in the Empire as a whole.[23]

TABLE 2

Population Growth in Odessa

Year	Population
1795	2,349
1863	120,000
1873	193,513
1892	340,526
1897	403,815
1904	497,395

Source: The 1897 figure includes 400,909 permanent residents as well as 2,906 persons temporarily present in Odessa on the day of the census. It also includes 23,588 men and 1,058 women housed in the military garrison. The 1904 figure is taken from *OOG za 1904 g.*, p. 25. Another source, published in 1914 but also based on 1904 information, indicates that 499,555 people lived in Odessa in that year. See *Goroda Rossii v 1910 godu*, p. 530. Patricia Herlihy (*Odessa: A History*, p. 251) arrives at the somewhat higher figure of 511,000. The differences may be due to the time of year when the data were collected, imprecise methods of counting, and different data bases reflecting whether or not the city's suburban residents were included in the census. Population figures for other years are taken from TsGIA, f. 23, op. 20, d. 1, p. 174; Smol'ianinov, *Istoriia Odessy*, p. 53; *Putevoditel' po Odesse*, pp. 24–25; *Rezul'taty odnodnevnoi perepisi*, pt. 1, pp. 2–3 (Table 1); *Perepis'*, pp. iv and ix.

The processing of animal products, especially leather, and the manufacture of soap and candles ranked third in terms of ruble output, closely followed by the production of chemical products such as paint, lacquer, and gas. Other significant sectors of the factory economy included the production of cork products and the manufacture of rope and burlap sacks. The making of paper goods, cigarette papers in particular, and the printing trade also figured prominently.

By the beginning of the twentieth century, then, the manufacturing sector of Odessa was increasing in importance, though the grain trade still dominated the economy. The city, as one contemporary observer of economic conditions stated, had entered a "noticeable turning point . . . and had ceased living exclusively by the grain trade."[24] The factory sector, this observer noted, possessed a secure and vibrant future and would continue to expand, contributing to the further economic advance of the city. In sum, Odessa recorded impressive economic growth during the nineteenth century, with trade and industrial statistics vividly illustrating its significance to the economic life of Russia and the world.[25]

Population Growth in Odessa

Odessa's economic expansion in the nineteenth century was matched by rapid population growth, as tens of thousands of Russian subjects and foreigners sought to share in the opportunities offered by a dynamic economy. Odessa was only one of many Russian cities that experienced remarkable population growth in the nineteenth century. The population of St. Petersburg, for example, grew from around 539,000 in 1864 to approximately 1.4 million by century's end, and the population of Moscow also rose dramatically, from about 339,000 in the mid-1860s to over 1.1 million by 1902. Similarly, the populations of Riga and Kiev quadrupled during the same period. By the beginning of the twentieth century St. Petersburg, Moscow, and Warsaw were the only cities of the Empire that boasted more inhabitants than Odessa.[26]

As Table 2 shows, the growth of Odessa's population was steady and rapid. Like most Russian cities at the end of the nineteenth century, Odessa was truly a migrant city, serving as the adopted home for tens of thousands of people hailing from all parts of the Empire; at the end of the century, some 56 percent of the its inhabitants had not been born there.[27]

Workers accounted for most of the migration to Odessa, and unlike in other major urban centers where suburbanization and residential segregation by class were more developed, many of them labored, lived, and relaxed in all parts of the city, rubbing shoulders with government bureaucrats, professionals, wealthy landowners, merchants, and industrialists. Yet many of the newly arrived migrants tended to crowd into the poorer neighborhoods that surrounded the wealthier and better-endowed districts of the city center. They occupied the cheap tract housing that sprang up around the new enterprises of the city's industrial suburbs. The districts of Peresyp, Mikhailov, Petropavlov, and Slobod-ka-Romanovka registered rates of population growth far in excess of those experienced by the central districts of the city and became the locus of the lives of the vast majority of Odessa workers.

In addition to permanent settlers, an undetermined number of people flocked to Odessa each year in search of seasonal employment at the docks and construction sites. Still others passed through Odessa as itinerants on their way to other cities, while those with time, leisure, and money frequently enjoyed rest cures at one of the several acclaimed spas for which Odessa was noted. Moreover, peasant men and women from all over Ukraine, hoping to find work as farm hands in the region, made the journey on foot to a local hiring market for agricultural labor that met near Odessa every spring and summer. So many peasants attended the hiring market by the 1890s that city officials, fearing the spread of syphilis and other contagious diseases, set up first-aid clinics and cafeterias and provided lodging in barracks.[28]

Economic opportunity was the primary motivation for migrating to Odessa. From the outset, foreign merchants from Greece, Italy, Galicia, and other parts of Europe established branches of their brokerage houses in Odessa to handle the city's foreign trade. These businessmen, using their family and business connections throughout Western Europe and the Mediterranean, helped transform Odessa into a bustling city. Government policy toward the city was liberal, since officials realized that its prosperity depended on the contributions of foreign subjects seeking a free and open atmosphere in which to pursue profits. The government, seeking to reap the benefit of commerce, encouraged merchants and traders of all religions and nationalities to set up business in Odessa, even at the expense of Russian merchants.

As Odessa began to grow into a budding metropolis, tens of thousands of Great Russians, Ukrainians, Poles, Armenians, Greeks, and Jews from Russia and Poland migrated to the city to take advantage of the opportunities offered by urban growth. The boom economy of Odessa throughout most of the nineteenth century served as a magnet drawing a diverse group of migrants hoping for a piece, however small, of the economic pie. The city needed hired hands to work at dockside, draymen and porters to bring grain arriving from the countryside to the docks, clerks to handle the paperwork, and brokers to procure grain from peasant producers and then sell it to one of the large export firms. Still others were needed to provide the variety of goods and services required by an expanding city that lacked a native labor force. The appearance of a solid manufacturing base in the late nineteenth century also drew migrants to Odessa in search of factory work. This migration in turn fueled further economic growth, since the local economy now had to support and sustain the city's growing population.

As knowledge of its "economic miracle" spread throughout Russia and the rest of Europe, Odessa lured even more people. They perceived life in the city as a chance to escape poverty and create new lives for themselves and their families. I. Fedorov, writing in the late 1860s, likened Odessa to California, another frontier territory where jobs abounded and settlers could give life another try.[29] The attraction of Odessa was particularly powerful for peasants from those provinces of the Russian interior that were experiencing a demographic explosion coupled with severe land shortages and agricultural stagnation. This was especially true in post-Emancipation Russia, when barriers to peasant migration were weakened and peasants could more easily obtain permission to seek employment outside the village. Supplementing those peasants who had fled to southern Russia as serf runaways, army deserters, and drifters in the pre-Emancipation era, these new immigrants—victims of land hunger, rural overpopulation, and deteriorating conditions in the countryside—sought refuge in Odessa. As S. S. Iushkevich writes in *Prolog: Povest'* (*Prologue: A Tale*), peasant migrants were trying to forget the misery of village life. As they journeyed to Odessa, they did not mention the lives they were leaving behind so as not to mar the city's image as a place where there are no "troubles, fear, and suffering."[30]

Jews from the western and northwestern regions of the Pale of Settlement and from those areas of Poland under Austrian domination were also enticed by the promise of Odessa. As problems of overpopulation, economic competition, and impoverishment reached crisis proportions in the shtetls of the Pale, the next best (and cheaper) alternative to emigration to Western Europe or the United States was resettlement in Odessa. As one contemporary observer noted: "If a Jew from the Pale of Settlement doesn't dream about America or Palestine, then you know he'll be in Odessa."[31] Since Odessa was located within the Pale, Jews did not require special permission to move there and, due to special considerations, they were generally exempted from the onerous and discriminatory residency legislation affecting Russian Jewry. For example, a maximum length of stay was never imposed upon Odessa Jews.[32] Odessa, unlike most other cities in Russia, countenanced the presence of a sizable Jewish community and did not hinder its economic activities.

It is not surprising that thousands of Russian and Polish Jews took advantage of the opportunity to leave the stifling atmosphere of the established regions of Jewish settlement for Odessa, where the freshness and dynamism of the city inspired hope and optimism. Many Jewish migrants did not find it difficult to meet the challenges of life in a large city, as Russian Jews in general had long engaged in commerce and petty trade or made their livings as tailors and shoemakers, only two of many pursuits that a growing city could support. The expulsion of Jews from many of the towns and cities of the western borderlands in the 1880s and 1890s, as well as the famine of 1891–1892, accelerated the flow of Jews to Odessa. It was estimated in 1892 that only 38 percent of the city's Jews had been born in Odessa.[33]

For some Russian Jews, however, the appeal of Odessa lay more in the city's psychological and intellectual attraction than in the hope for economic betterment. Unlike regions with long-established Jewish communities, Odessa offered an environment in which the traditional values and norms of Jewish society and culture enjoyed less influence. The newness of the Jewish community in Odessa meant that the restraints and sanctions imposed by older communities were either lacking or severely attenuated. The well-entrenched Jewish communal authority, which based its power and authority on a rabbinic heritage and was generally unwilling to accommodate the demands and pressures generated by more intimate contact with the gentile world, was weak if not entirely absent in Odessa. One indication of communal weakness was the numerous incidents of Jewish youths deliberately snubbing their more religiously minded brethren by holding parties on Yom Kippur without fear of retribution from the Jewish elders. Odessa therefore provided Jews with a setting in which they could engage in new and different intellectual, cultural, and economic pursuits more freely than in areas of traditional Jewish settlement. By 1900 Odessa was home to acculturated Jews; a somewhat smaller proportion of Odessa Jews (89.5 percent) reported Yiddish as their mother tongue than those in the rest of Russia (97 percent).[34]

This "frontier" atmosphere contributed to the rise of Odessa in the course of the nineteenth century as a major center of the *Haskalah* (Jewish Enlightenment). The city could boast that it was a center of Yiddish and Hebrew literature and the home of such Jewish luminaries as Simon Dubnow, Leon Pinsker, Max Lilienblum, and Mendele Mocher Seforim. Moreover, the host society in Odessa, perhaps more than anywhere else in the Pale, was willing to tolerate the economic and political participation of Jews. Jews played a vigorous role in municipal affairs during the nineteenth century, especially after mid-century when substantial local initiative devolved upon Russian municipalities due to the reform legislation of the 1860s and 1870s. Jews served as city councillors, and Osip Rabinovich, a journalist and publisher of *Razsvet* (*Dawn*), the first Jewish newspaper in Russian, was appointed in 1861 to a committee established to draw up a new city charter.[35]

TABLE 3

Nationality in Odessa Based on Language, 1897

Nationality	Numbers	Percent
Russian	183,665	45.5
Jew (by faith)	139,984	34.7
Ukrainian	37,925	9.4
Pole	17,395	4.3
German	10,248	2.5
Greek	5,086	1.3
Other Slavs	2,761	.7
Tatar	1,437	.4
Armenian	1,401	.4
French	1,137	.3
Italian	717	.2
Remaining	2,059	.5
Total	403,815	100.22 (due to rounding)

Source: *Perepis'*, pp. vi–vii and 34–37 (Tables 11–13). The figures refer to the administrative municipality (*odesskoe gradonachal'stvo*) that included the city of Odessa and surrounding suburbs known collectively as Dal'nits. Even though the suburbs possessed a more rural flavor than the city proper, I have chosen to treat the *gradonachal'stvo* in its entirety because the suburbs were under the same administrative jurisdiction and were inextricably linked to the economy of Odessa as both supplier of food and labor and consumer of goods and services.

The following story, recounted by the Jewish writer A. Chivonibar (A. Rabinovich), highlights the appeal of Odessa. "The Bootblack" describes the experiences of a Jewish youth who left his shtetl in Kiev province after hearing of the success of a neighbor's son in Odessa. The neighbor's son, who arrived penniless and alone in Odessa, managed to save 100 rubles by selling matches and polishing shoes and soon married his landlord's daughter. He then joined his father-in-law in opening up a profitable bagel shop and bakery. Upon hearing this success story, the shtetl youth followed in his neighbor's footsteps to Odessa, where he too hoped to find a wife and strike it rich. Unfortunately, when he told this story to Rabinovich, he was still eking out a pitiful living polishing shoes and had little hope for a better life.[36]

True or not, this story stands as a tribute to the reputation of Odessa as a place to make money. Stories such as these lured thousands of poor Jews, who saw the city as a refuge from the deteriorating conditions of village and shtetl life. The hope of rising from penury to relative wealth—which often meant the simple dream of owning a small shop—remained a potent force in the popular imagination. In his autobiography *From the Fair*, Sholom Aleichem records a childhood conversation in which a friend, boasting of his family's impending move from the shtetl to Odessa, tells him: "you'd wish you and I both had the gold that rolls around there during the course of a day." When Aleichem asks the friend what his father will do there, the friend responds: "My father will have granaries full of wheat. . . . My father will have an office with clerks. And money—money will flow into our pockets by the sackful. Odessa? Are you kidding?"[37]

The image of Odessa as a Russian El Dorado did not die easily, even when changing economic conditions at the turn of the century (discussed below) turned the hopes of many newcomers into pipe dreams. Settlement in Odessa in the nineteenth century did not automatically lead to improvements in the lives of the settlers. Many arrived poor and remained poor; for some, conditions even deteriorated. After the turn of the century, circumstances worsened, increasing the likelihood that migrants to Odessa would face a life of unrelieved unemployment, poverty, and hunger. As A. I. Svirskii wrote on the eve of 1905, "Odessa is not a paradise. . . . The army of hungry is growing and spreading."[38] Population growth was outstripping the capacity of the city's economy to provide work for everyone and, as one observer noted in 1900, "The time when Odessa did not have enough workers has already passed." As early as the 1880s Odessa officials, in an effort to stem the influx of migrants, set up checkpoints on roads leading to the city; soldiers would inspect travelers' documents and not allow groups of more than thirty to go on.[39]

Hopeful immigrants nonetheless continued to flock to Odessa. The city governor reported in 1903 that approximately 10,000 migrants from all over the Russian Empire permanently settled in Odessa each year.[40] Perhaps they chose to ignore the gloomy stories and reports or perhaps they were simply ignorant of them. Many may even have reasoned that life in Odessa could be no worse than that which they were prepared to leave behind. Even during slack periods of commercial activity and years of recession, many workers decided not to return to their native villages and towns, preferring to stick it out and weather hardship in Odessa. Their decision to remain indicates a preference for life in the city over that in rural and small-town Russia. Newcomers now considered their new home "Odessa-Mama." Experience would prove her to be a harsh and stern mother.

Nationality in Odessa

To a much larger extent than either the cities of St. Petersburg or Moscow, Odessa attracted a population that was heterogeneous in its ethnic and national composition. According to the 1897 census, the city was home to persons who spoke some fifty-five languages and hailed from over thirty countries, including most European and some Near Eastern nations, the United States, China, and Japan. Nearly 20,000 persons, or 4.8 percent of Odessa's population in 1897, were subjects of foreign governments.[41]

As Table 3 shows, Great Russians comprised the largest national group living in Odessa. Together with other Slavic-speaking peoples such as Ukrainians, White Russians, Poles, Czechs, Slovaks, Serbs, and Bulgars, they accounted for about 60 percent of Odessa's population, while believers in Russian Orthodoxy comprised 56 percent (225,869) of the city's population. Though significant, the Slavic population in Odessa comprised a smaller proportion of the total population than in Moscow and St. Petersburg, where, respectively, nearly all and almost nine-tenths of the residents reported speaking a Slavic language as their mother tongue.[42] It is worth noting that the actual number of Ukrainians may have been masked by the practice of some non-Russians of claiming Russian as their native language in an effort to assimilate.

Jews were the second major group in Odessa, constituting nearly 35 percent of the population. This was a significant increase from the approximately 14,000 Jews (14 percent of the city total) living in Odessa in 1858.[43] My figures refer to those of Jewish faith rather than those recorded as speaking Yiddish as their daily language. Since some 14,568 Jews reported Russian as their language of first choice, the figure for religion provides a more accurate and reliable reckoning of the total number of Jews. For those Jews who reported Russian as their main language, all we can conclude is that they were more acculturated or assimilated (or wanted to be seen as such) than those who continued to rely on Yiddish. It is difficult to determine whether their responses reflected a shift in language use from Yiddish to Russian or the spread of bilingualism. The government nonetheless considered them Jewish by nationality and stamped "Jew" on their passports.

In addition to Slavs and Jews, other national groups in Odessa, as identified by native tongue, accounted for just under 6 percent of the population in 1897. Native-speaking Greeks, who dominated much of the city's economy during the first half-century of Odessa's existence and numbered some 11,500 in 1816, accounted for 5,086 residents by the end of the century.[44] In all, the proportion of citizens from European states living in Odessa had dropped from nearly three-quarters of the population in 1819 to somewhere between 3 and 4 percent by century's end.[45] Thus, Odessa after its first century of existence had become much more Russian and Jewish than it had been at its inception.

The early presence of a large foreign community gave Odessa a sophisticated flavor that other Russian cities, with the exception of St. Petersburg and some of the Baltic seaports, lacked. From its early days, Odessa possessed the cultural and intellectual atmosphere of a major cosmopolitan center. The cultural influence of German, Italian, Greek, French, English, and Swiss residents and visitors permeated Odessa through the import of luxury items, the opening of restaurants and hotels that duplicated the atmosphere of the Continent, and even the hiring of French governesses by both Russians and West European residents in Odessa. Other indications of foreign influence were street signs written in both Italian and Russian in the 1820s and the publication in French of the city's first newspaper. By contrast, the first Russian-language newspapers quickly folded for lack of demand.[46]

The first municipal public library in the Russian Empire had opened in Odessa in 1830, and theater, music, and opera enhanced the city's reputation as a cultural oasis. A perusal of the 1900 edition of a guidebook to Odessa reveals the existence of some two dozen public and private libraries and reading rooms, three museums, several theaters (including a circus), public auditoriums, a university, and nearly 200 public and private schools. Civic life also thrived in the form of seventy-five charitable organizations and social clubs that attracted lovers of drama, literature, sports, yachting, nature, and cycling.[47] In addition, the city was a major resort center that drew thousands of vacationers to the mineral baths of several spas found along nearby estuaries. The Municipal Theater presented opera and drama; this lavish and ornate building rivaled the beauty of opera houses on the Continent. The city center, with its broad boulevards, parks, and rows of buildings designed in the neoclassical style, reminded the visitor to Odessa of Western Europe and testified to the efforts of the city fathers and leading citizens to build a city worthy of praise and equal in grandeur to any European city. Resembling the architectural style and beauty of St. Petersburg and affectionately called by some "the Second Petersburg," "Little Paris," "the Southern Beauty," and "the Southern Palmyra," Odessa was described by one visitor as "a wonderful city. . . . Odessa, like a fairytale beauty, lounges and lolls about by the warm sea and it seems that there is no more fortunate city in the entire Empire."[48]

The cosmopolitan flavor of Odessa was also enhanced by the relatively small proportion of peasants living in the city. Despite the steady influx of peasants into Odessa, the influence of rural Russia was more muted here than in other urban centers for reasons that are not altogether clear. Peasant culture did not smother the elements of a distinctly urban culture and society in Odessa. This state of affairs contrasts sharply with other major urban centers in Russia, where traditional peasant values and customs dominated the urban scene to a far greater extent. Moscow, for example, was known as "the big village" by virtue of its peasant population. In 1897, peasants (based on *soslovie*, or official estate/corporate standing) comprised only 27 percent of Odessa's population, a proportion far smaller than in St. Petersburg or Moscow.[49] In addition, almost three-fifths (approximately 300,000) of the city's residents belonged to the urban estate or *meshchanstvo*, with Jews comprising close to half of this number. While categorization by *soslovie* is a slippery venture and not a clear-cut indicator of social identity or even place of residence, the large presence of *meshchane* suggests that most of Odessa's inhabitants were familiar with city life. This state of affairs attenuated the impact of peasant Russia on Odessa and reduced the importance of ties with the countryside, even among non-Jews. Moreover, of the tens of thousands of peasants and *meshchane* who came to Odessa, many were no doubt attracted by Odessa's reputation as a progressive and open city. They were prepared to jettison much of the cultural baggage that they arrived with and were determined to fit in with the more cosmopolitan world awaiting them.[50]

The large number of Jews residing in Odessa reduced even further whatever impact the peasant element may have had. Jews from small shtetls in the heart of the Pale of Settlement were probably overwhelmed by their initial experience in a cosmopolitan center like Odessa, but it is equally likely that life in Odessa had less of a disorienting impact upon Jewish migrants than upon peasants from the interior. Even though many shtetls resembled peasant villages in terms of material deprivation and poverty, the Jews' greater contact with urban Russia, as well as their more urban occupational patterns, probably made the move to a city less traumatic for them than for a Russian or Ukrainian peasant. They were better prepared than the typical peasant psychologically, culturally, and sociologically for life in the big city.

Ethnic Relations in Odessa

Given the multinational composition of Odessa's population, it is surprising that for many years the traditional suspicion of Russians toward non-Russians was more muted and less visible than in other regions of Russia with ethnically mixed populations. Several factors rooted in the history of Odessa account for this state of affairs. As we have seen, Odessa was a relatively new city where official policy encouraged the settlement of non-Russians. Indeed, the city's first two city governors, the Duc de Richelieu and Alexandre de Langeron, were French subjects whose zeal and energy as administrators during the first quarter of the nineteenth century contributed to the flourishing of Odessa. Moreover, Greeks, Italians, and Jews helped set the tempo of commercial and financial life and assumed active roles in cultural and political affairs. Odessa was an enlightened city that tolerated diversity and innovation and welcomed persons of all nationalities who could contribute to its development.

Unfortunately, official policies clashed with popular prejudices and a Judeophobia prevalent among many gentile Odessans. The veneer of acceptance and toleration of Jews was thin, and Odessa's Jews, like Jews elsewhere in Russia, were no strangers to anti-Jewish animus, sometimes falling victim to anti-Semitic violence. Anti-Semitism generally remained submerged, but it did assume ugly forms several times in the nineteenth century. Serious riots in which Jews were killed and wounded and Jewish houses and businesses suffered substantial damage occurred in 1821, 1859, 1871, 1881, and 1900. Apart from these dramatic outbursts, anti-Jewish sentiment among Odessa's non-Jewish population manifested itself in other ways. Gangs of Jewish and gentile youths often engaged in bloody brawls, and every year at Eastertime rumors of an impending pogrom would circulate through the city's Jewish community, giving rise to anxiety and fear.[51]

Many residents feared that Russian-Jewish tensions could explode in a matter of hours given the right combination of factors. Jews were often scapegoated for such problems as unemployment and other economic difficulties, and organizers of labor demonstrations and strikes had to allay fears among the general public that labor unrest might develop into anti-Jewish pogroms. They exhorted gentile workers not to direct their anger at Jews, but to present a united front of Jews and Russians against employers. The fear that work stoppages would degenerate into anti-Semitic violence dampened labor militance. For example, the 1903 May Day rally never materialized because many potential participants, Jews and Russians alike, had the memory of the recent Kishinev pogrom fresh in their minds and feared that a march through Odessa would spark a similar upheaval. A group of Jewish shopkeepers and property owners, upset by workers gathering in a field to celebrate May Day, informed the police, who arrested some 30 workers.[52] In early 1905, one Russian worker, apparently in response to fear that a pogrom was in the making, assured the Odessa Jewish community that Russian workers were not "wild animals ready to unleash a pogrom." He appealed to Russian workers to recognize as "brothers" other workers "whether they be Jew, Pole, Greek, or German" in order to preserve social calm.[53] Another worker also stated at this time that the "passions" of Russians were aroused during times of social and economic hardship, which stirred up "national hatreds."[54] Employers with ethnically mixed labor forces also understood that Jewish-gentile hostilities could be used to their advantage and sometimes encouraged Russian workers to direct their anger at Jewish coworkers.[55]

Anti-Semitism in Odessa was rooted not only in socio-economic, political, and cultural realities, but also in the perceptions and feelings, more often than not irrational and exaggerated, of gentiles who viewed Odessa Jewry as a danger to the well-being of society. Such was the case in the 1821 pogrom, when Greeks attacked Jews who were accused of aiding the Turks in the killing of the Greek patriarch of Constantinople. After mid-century, religious fanaticism and hatred sometimes mixed with social and economic factors to heighten anti-Jewish sentiments. The increasing prominence of Jews in the commercial life of Odessa, particularly their success in the grain trade, played no small role in fueling anti-Semitism and anti-Jewish violence. In a society that considered agricultural pursuits productive and commerce exploitative, it is not surprising that Jews, who were heavily involved in trade as middlemen and brokers, were regarded as parasitic, unproductive members of society who made their livings at the expense of non-Jews.

Until the Crimean War, Greeks controlled the export of grain from Odessa while Jews dominated the role of middleman. Hostilities disrupted trade routes, however, and forced English importers of Russian grain to turn to American and Canadian producers. Some Greek commercial houses could not absorb their losses and went bankrupt. Many others, although not forced into bankruptcy, realized that the entry of North American grain onto the international market would deflate prices and reduce profit margins. These businessmen, who had branches throughout the world, decided to close their Odessa offices in order to pursue other ventures that promised greater profits. Jewish merchants and traders, accustomed to operating at smaller profit margins, filled the vacuum caused by the departure of Greek merchants and assumed prominent positions in the import-export trade. By the late 1870s, firms owned by Jews comprised slightly over a third of establishments engaged in the export business in Odessa. These companies controlled 56 percent of the export trade in grain, including approximately 70 percent of the trade in flour. Overall, Jews at this time controlled slightly over half the export trade. Jewish domination of the grain trade continued to expand during the next several decades; by 1910 Jewish firms handled nearly 90 percent of the export trade in grain products.[56]

Greek residents started the pogroms of 1859 and 1871. The eclipse of the Greek community and the tendency of Jewish merchants, like other ethnic and religious communities in the city, to give preference in employment to coreligionists had forced many Greeks into straitened economic circumstances. Such actions particularly angered those Greeks, especially sailors and dockworkers, who had been displaced by Jewish workers. The flames of anti-Semitism were further fanned by a false accusation of Jewish ritual murder in 1859 and unfounded rumours that Jews desecrated the Greek Orthodox Church and cemetery in 1871.

Greeks were not the only residents of Odessa who perceived Jews as a threat. Russian resentment and hostility toward Jews came to the fore in the pogrom of 1871, as Russians joined Greeks in attacks against Jews. Thereafter, Russians (and to a lesser extent Ukrainians) filled the ranks of pogromists in 1881, 1900, and as we shall see 1905. The replacement of Greeks by Russians as pogromists reflects the declining Greek presence in Odessa and highlights the tension that was growing between Russians and Jews in the city.

According to some Russian residents, the twin notions of exploitation by and competition with Jews figured prominently in the outbreak of the 1871 pogrom. Some complained that "Jews exploit us." Others, especially the unemployed, blamed increased Jewish settlement in Odessa for reduced employment opportunities and lower wages. In 1871 a Russian cabdriver, referring to the Jews' practice of lending money to Jewish immigrants to enable them to rent or buy a horse and cab, complained: "Several years ago there was one Jewish cabdriver for every 100 Russian cabdrivers, but since then rich Jews have given money to the poor Jews, so that there is now a countless multitude of Jewish cabdrivers."[57] In this account, Jewish competition and the practice of Jews sticking together to help each other contributed to a feeling of oppression among some Russian workers, reinforcing the popular image of Russian Jewry as an alien, parasitic community.

The growing visibility of Jews enhanced this predisposition of Russians to blame Jews for their difficulties. Like elsewhere in Russia and Western Europe, many non-Jews in Odessa perceived Jews as possessing an inordinate amount of wealth, power, and influence. The steady growth of the city's Jewish population during the nineteenth century indicated to some gentiles the seriousness of the Jewish "threat." In addition to their commercial activities, some Jews in Odessa by the end of the century also occupied prominent positions in manufacturing, banking, and the retail sector, thereby leading to Jewish domination of certain sectors of the economy. In 1910, Jews owned slightly over half the large stores, trading firms, and small shops, and thirteen of the eighteen banks operating in Odessa had Jewish board members and directors. They also comprised about half the members of Odessa's three merchant guilds at the turn of the century, up from 38 percent in the mid-1880s. Jews virtually monopolized the production of starch, refined sugar, tin goods, chemicals, and wallpaper, and they competed with Russian and foreign entrepreneurs in the making of flour, cigarettes, beer, wine, leather, cork, and iron products. Although Jews owned in 1887 approximately 35 percent of the factories surveyed, these firms produced 57 percent of the total factory output (in rubles) for that year.[58]

And yet, despite the conspicuous success of many Jews, the common perception that the growing Jewish presence threatened to result in the total Jewish domination of Odessa had little basis in reality and was an unfair representation of Odessa Jewry's role in local life. To be sure, Jews were the fastest growing ethnic and national group in the city: the proportion of Jews in the city's population had risen from about a quarter to slightly over a third during the last quarter of the century, while at the same time the proportion of Orthodox residents dropped from 65 to 56 percent. But the rate of growth leveled out after 1897, with the percentage of Jews actually dropping somewhat by the eve of 1905. According to data assembled by the city governor, the number of Jews residing in Odessa in 1904 was 141,601 (approximately 28 percent of the city's total population), with the proportion of Russian Orthodox residents remaining constant. The reasons for this relative decline of Jews since 1897 are difficult to ascertain (and may be due to imprecise census-taking, since other studies show that the percentage of Jews in Odessa was slightly above 30 percent in 1904),[59] but there is no question that non-Jews continued to hold their own in the economic sphere and were in no danger of being outnumbered, let alone eliminated, by Jews. On the eve of 1905, Odessa was far from being a city whose society, politics, and economy were dominated by Jews.

According to the 1897 census, thousands of Russians and Ukrainians engaged in commercial activities of some sort, especially the marketing of agricultural products, and comprised approximately a third of the total number of individuals listed as earning livings from trade. On the eve of 1905, moreover, about half the licenses granting permission to engage in commercial and industrial activities were given to non-Jews, and in 1910 non-Jews owned slightly under half the large stores and trading firms and 44 percent of small shops in the city. Forty percent of manufacturing enterprises in 1887 were owned by foreigners, with Russians owning another 25 percent; according to 1910 data, Jews owned 43 percent of enterprises under factory inspection. These firms tended to employ Russians, who therefore could not claim that Jews were taking jobs from them. But resentment toward their bosses could nonetheless assume anti-Jewish tones, given the prominence of Jews as employers. Lastly, Jews in 1910 owned only 17 percent of real estate parcels in the city, down from 20 percent a decade earlier.[60]

Jews also did not belong to the the leisured propertied class, nor could they translate their wealth into political influence and power. Despite the presence of an estimated eighteen Jewish millionaires in Odessa in 1900, only a negligible number lived from investments in land, stocks, and bonds, and even fewer—71 in a staff of 3,449—worked for the Imperial government, the judiciary, or the municipal administration.[61] This was due in part to the 1892 municipal reform, which made it more difficult for Jews to occupy government posts and disenfranchised Odessa Jewry. From 1870 until 1892, when the central government limited the number of Jewish representatives to 10 percent of the city council's full membership, Jews had enjoyed the same electoral rights as non-Jewish residents of Odessa. The 1892 statute, however, deprived Jews of the right to elect representatives to the city council, assigning the responsibility for appointing six Jewish councillors to a special office for municipal affairs.[62]

In contrast to the popular perception that Jews enjoyed a stranglehold on Odessa, the vast majority of them eked out meager livings as shopkeepers, second-hand dealers, salesclerks, petty traders, domestic servants, day laborers, workshop employers, and factory hands. Poverty was a way of life for most Jews in Odessa, as it was for most non-Jewish residents. In his study of Jewish poverty in Odessa at the turn of the century, I. Brodovskii estimated that nearly 50,000 Jews were destitute and another 30,000 poverty-stricken. In 1905, nearly 80,000 Jews requested financial assistance from Jewish welfare organizations in order to buy Passover matzo, a telling sign that well over half the Jews in Odessa experienced difficulties making ends meet.[63]

Jews were by no means the only members of the underprivileged, urban lower classes. The overwhelming majority of employed Russians, for example, worked as servants, or as day and unskilled laborers at dockside, railway depots, granaries, and construction sites, or in factories and workshops. Many of them carted and hauled goods around the city, and nearly 12,000 were quartered in the military garrison. Other Slavic-speaking peoples also contributed members to the growing work force. The Ukrainians who settled in Odessa were for the most part poor unmarried males seeking to escape lives of rural poverty. Like many Russians in Odessa, they worked as unskilled laborers and servants or were army conscripts. Some Ukrainians even engaged in agricultural pursuits in the outlying suburbs of the city. Similarly, the majority of Polish inhabitants were either employed as unskilled laborers or stationed as soldiers. By 1900 many Greeks in Odessa, despite the prominence of Greek merchants in the economy earlier in the century, worked as day laborers at dockside and in food and animal processing plants.[64]

At the other end of the occupational ladder, Russians occupied those rungs that bestowed status, prestige, and authority and reflected wealth and power. They dominated the administrative and judicial posts in the city government and, along with foreigners, owned a majority of factories by the 1890s. Russians also accounted for the majority of those who supported themselves from stocks, savings, and land, the latter being one indicator of the extent to which Russian nobles engaged in land speculation in southern Russia.

The magnitude of poverty and the low socio-economic status of the majority of Odessans graphically illustrates that no simple equation of ethnicity and class existed in the multinational Russian Empire. Cleavages of class, power, and status in Odessa were not neatly drawn along ethnic or religious lines, as they tended to be in cities such as Baku and Tiflis.[65] Class divisions and disparities in political and economic power cut across ethnic lines in Odessa; at times ethnicity reinforced class barriers but, as we shall see, it could also transcend divisions of status, power, and money and pit non-Jew against Jew.

Economic Rivalry and the Impact of War

Beneath the vitality of Odessa lay problems that adversely affected the town's social and economic well-being. Despite its economic dynamism throughout the nineteenth century, both short-term events and long-range trends were affecting the economic health of Odessa and hindering industrial and commercial prospects on the eve of 1905. The city's economy faltered during the first half-decade of the twentieth century as it fell victim to fluctuations and uncertainties caused by bad harvests, recession, economic competition, and war. These developments in turn interacted with demographic trends to worsen material conditions for the average Odessa worker. Unemployment became a serious problem after 1900, contributing to the emergence of a permanent core of impoverished and unemployed workers.

One problem confronting Odessa was the fact that the grain trade, the mainstay of the city's economy, had begun to contract by the end of the century. While Odessa remained the major port in southern Russia during the pre-1905 period, it increasingly found itself at a competitive disadvantage with other ports in the region, specifically Nikolaev, Kherson, and Rostov-on-Don. Grain exports from Odessa began to drop after the record-setting year of 1894, and the city's share of the grain trade in the decade or so before 1905 decreased relative to other ports in the region, a trend exacerbated by crop failures and economic recession at the turn of the century. Less grain arrived in Odessa by railroad, both in absolute weight and in the relative share of the total amount shipped to the city, and the appearance in nearby cities of more modern, efficient, and better-equipped harbors, capable of handling a greater volume of trade at lower cost, confounded local grain merchants. During periods of peak activity, loading berths in Nikolaev, Kherson, and Rostov-on-Don were not as congested as in Odessa; ships did not have to wait several weeks, as they often did in Odessa, before receiving permission to enter the harbor. The cost of shipping grain to Odessa from the hinterland increased relative to other ports in southern Russia and in the Baltic due to differential railway tariffs that favored shipment of grain to the northern ports of the Empire and to commercial centers located on the eastern shores of the Black and Azov Seas, which were now closer than Odessa to new centers of grain production. The lack of direct rail connection between Odessa and the interior also hurt local grain merchants, as did the declining role played by southern Russia in supplying wheat and other grains for the world market.[66]

Odessa was paying the price for its role as a pioneering commercial center and hub of the grain trade. Just as those countries that embarked upon the path of industrialization after England benefited from the transfer and application of more advanced technology and production processes that decades of industrialism afforded, so too did the newer port cities of southern Russia enter the grain trade with the most modern facilities of the day. Despite efforts to deepen the harbor and outfit the port with the most up-to-date equipment and facilities, Odessa still lagged behind ports of neighboring cities in terms of efficiency and capacity. It simply lacked the facilities to handle a growing amount of traffic. Some grain may have been transferred into the holds of ships by means of conveyor belts, but the sad truth was that most goods still had to be loaded or unloaded by hand. The elevated railway running from the main rail depot in Mikhailov facilitated the movement of goods to dockside, but even this development did not change the fact that ox-drawn carts carried most grain to the harbor, a distance of some two miles. One observer, writing about Odessa's threatened status as Russia's preeminent port, suggested that its share of exports would increase if the harbor was expanded and modernized and if more rail lines were erected between the port and the main trunk of the South West Railroad.[67] But after the turn of the century the repair and further modernization of port facilities floundered due to the lack of funds. The city fathers now found themselves managing a budget with large deficits and were hard put to allocate funds to renovate the harbor. Customs and tax receipts could no longer cover such expenditures and the central government refused urgent requests for the necessary funds.[68]

Another shortcoming was the still overwhelming importance of commerce in the economic life and welfare of the city. Despite the appearance of a vibrant manufacturing sector, the fact that many major industrial processes were linked to the life of the port did not bode well for the economy. As we have seen, industry in Odessa was weighted in favor of food processing such as sugar refining, teapacking, and flour production. These were processes that either depended upon imports for raw materials, as in the case of tea packing, exported much of the finished product, as in the case of sugar refining, or required a supply of domestically grown wheat, as in the case of flour. These industries were therefore particularly vulnerable to fluctuations in market conditions and disruptions in commerce. The impact of disrupted trade routes due to war and the effects of a bad harvest were immediately felt by Odessa's manufacturers, who cut back production and laid off workers.

Economic conditions continued to deteriorate as 1905 approached. Like other cities in Russia, Odessa in 1903 had begun to recover from the nationwide recession that had begun around 1900, but the recovery was shortlived due to a bad harvest in 1904 and, more importantly, the untimely outbreak of hostilities between Russia and Japan in January 1904. City governor Dmitrii B. Neidhardt, brother-in-law of future prime minister Petr Stolypin, noted that the outbreak of war compounded the city's economic woes because it disrupted commerce between Odessa and the Russian Far East, which was a lucrative market for manufactured goods and foodstuffs funnelled through Odessa.[69] Trade with the Far East and Siberia was not insubstantial; indeed, Odessa dominated Russian trade with Port Arthur and Vladivostok by century's end.[70] I. I. Popov, senior factory inspector of Kherson Province, seconded Neidhardt's concern, reporting that the war deprived local industry of markets in Siberia and the Russian Far East and forced many factory owners to cut production, reduce staffs, and even close down.[71] The war disrupted shipping routes and virtually halted all trade to the easternmost regions of the Empire.

In an economy already weakened by several years of recession, the loss of markets, no matter how small, had adverse consequences on Odessa's business community. Credit, already scarce as a result of the recession, now became even harder to obtain as bankers, investors, and foreign merchants demanded cash in advance before delivering goods and refrained from investing during wartime. In January 1904, the amount of capital in circulation in Odessa had declined 43 percent from previous years. The credit crunch seriously impinged on the activities of import-export firms that depended on credit. Bankruptcies and liquidations ensued as commercial enterprises either failed to receive payment for their goods and services or suffered from a decrease in orders.[72]

In addition to problems of credit and finance, Odessa's business community faced other problems caused by hostilities with Japan. Industrialists and merchants experienced difficulty in obtaining raw materials and distributing finished products by rail because military needs enjoyed priority. Not unexpectedly, the grain trade was especially hard hit, since the disruption of normal commercial activities interfered with the transport of grain to and from Odessa. Grain exports plummeted 33 percent between 1903 and 1904, and the decline continued into 1905; grain exports for the first five months of 1905 were only 56 percent of what they had been for the corresponding months in 1904. Overall, exports of all products, measured in volume, dropped a precipitous 38 percent between 1903 and 1905.[73]

Along with this decline in trade, Odessa's industrial sector entered a period of retrenchment. On the whole, the war affected manufacturing less than commerce, but industry was nonetheless hurt by the hostilities. In some cases, such as metal processing and sugar refining, the difficulties had begun before 1904 and can be attributed to unfavorable market conditions; the war compounded the impact of constricting markets. For example, iron-foundry output dropped 50 percent from the years before the war, and several iron foundries closed their doors due to the lack of credit and business. In other industries, such as food processing, canning, and chemical and rope production, the war had a more direct affect by disrupting the flow of raw materials. To be sure, some branches of the economy benefited from the war and the need to satisfy military demands. Such was the case with the leather industry, which filled government orders for boots. But even here many manufacturers failed to recognize the profitability of military contracts and did not enter into agreements to supply the army.[74]

A telling sign of Odessa's economic woes was the specter of growing unemployment despite the thinning of the work force by the calling up of reservists for the war effort. Construction workers were especially hard hit by the economic crunch caused by the war. As new housing starts drastically dropped in 1904, continuing a trend that had begun several years earlier, hundreds of housepainters, roofers, plasterers, and unskilled laborers were thrown into the ranks of the unemployed. Workers in enterprises that supplied construction materials were also adversely affected by the downturn in the economy, as woodworking shops, brick factories, and lumberyards cut production and laid off workers.[75] A Factory Inspectorate report concluded that, during 1904–1905, over 3,000 workers in a factory labor force of over 20,000 under its jurisdiction were unemployed, with another 2,800 working at half wages. The report blamed the Russo-Japanese War for this dismal state of affairs.[76] Since not all workers and enterprises were covered by the Inspectorate, the number of workers left idle by the economic downturn was undoubtedly higher than these figures indicate.

War and recession combined with structural weaknesses in the local economy to exacerbate the growing pains of Odessa. They sorely strained the resources of the city, whose leaders were unable to respond to the challenge of satisfying the basic needs of the burgeoning population. Workers, who accounted for most of this population growth, felt the brunt of the problems that resulted from rapid urban expansion and the economic downturn after the turn of the century. The next two chapters examine the living and working conditions of the Odessa work force and explore the ways in which Odessa workers responded to these conditions before 1905. Later they responded by organizing, protesting and striking, thereby providing the motive force behind the 1905 revolution in Odessa. The stage for mass labor unrest, however, had been set by how workers responded to the inadequacies of life and work in the years before the revolution.

Views of the harbor at Odessa. (Public Record Office, London)

Street scenes in Odessa. (Public Record Office, London)

Rishel'evskaia Street, with Opera in background. From a centennial volume produced by the Odessa city administration, *Odessa, 1794–1894*. (Odessa: Tipografiia A. Shul'tse, 1895)

Bazaar in Slobodka-Romanovka. (*Odessa, 1794–1894*)

Moskovskaia Street in Peresyp. (*Odessa, 1794–1894*)

Municipal night shelter. (*Odessa, 1794–1894*)

Flea market on Prokhorovskaia Square in the Petropavlovskii District, near Moldavanka. (*Odessa, 1794–1894*)

Jewish meat market. (Public Record Office, London)

Jewish bootblacks. (Public Record Office, London)

Pedlars from the Caucasus. (Public Record Office, London)

2

Workers in Odessa on the Eve of 1905

Workers in Odessa were a highly diverse group, including persons engaged in manual occupations in the manufacturing, construction, transportation, sales-clerical, and service sectors of the economy. They ranged from skilled, well-paid machinists employed in the railway workshops and machine-construction plants to unskilled factory hands, from talented bricklayers and masons to lowly day laborers who dug ditches and hauled dirt at construction sites. For every master tailor who made elegant, custom-made men's suits, dozens of inexperienced teenage girls sewed poor quality trousers and jackets in "sweated" workshops or eked out miserable livings as seamstresses in overcrowded apartments that doubled as living quarters for one or more families. For every woman employed in a candy factory or tobacco processing plant, dozens of children earned paltry wages while sitting at home, wrapping candy or rolling cigarettes for subcon-tractors. For every man who operated the mechanized conveyor belt that carried grain from dockside into the hulls of overseas freighters, hundreds of dock-workers lifted heavy sacks of grain on their shoulders into waiting ships. As the following table shows, at the turn of the twentieth century there were approx-imately 190,000 workers. If we include members of workers' families who were not gainfully employed, then the proportion of inhabitants belonging to the working class was well over half the total residents of Odessa.[1]

It is difficult to present a composite social profile of the Odessa labor force or even to dicuss the "typical" Odessa worker, since differences in nationality, sex, age, skill level, and nature of work accounted for variations in working and living conditions. Yet the heterogeneity of working and living conditions should not mask the commonality of experiences shared by all Odessa workers as underprivileged, exploited second-class citizens. In many ways the lives of Odessa workers differed little from those of workers in other Russian cities: they endured the same long hours, low wages, poor working conditions, and regimen of harsh discipline. Officially, the length of the workday in Odessa averaged between ten and eleven hours for workers in enterprises under the aegis of the Factory

TABLE 4

Size and Distribution of the Odessa Work Force
by Sector on the Eve of 1905
(Rounded to the nearest ten)

Sector	Number of Workers
Manufacturing	
Factory	25,300
Workshop	46,020
Construction	14,760
Transportation	13,860
(including merchant marine)	
Shop Assistants	33,000
Service	38,820
Communication	460
Day Labor	16,210
Total	188,430

The number of factory workers (after 1901 any manufacturing establishment with twenty or more employees was classified as a "factory") includes 21,794 persons counted in 1903 by the Factory Inspectorate and approximately 3,500 employees of the workshops of the South West Railroad, the *Dobrovol'nyi flot*, two state-owned distilleries and liquor warehouses, and the print shop of the Odessa military command. The figure for workshop employees does not include 7,620 master craftworkers who owned their own workshops and employed labor. It does include the 11,962 journeymen and 7,703 apprentices registered in 1903 by the Odessa Board of Artisanal Trades. To these numbers I have added 5,236 employees of relatively large workshops with a limited division of labor and ready-made production and 17,715 other workshop employees whom the Board of Artisanal Trades estimated worked in Odessa but were not registered in any guild. I also include 3,800 bakers who were not recorded by either the Factory Inspectorate or Board of Artisanal Trades. The data for construction workers include 4,000 employees of the stone quarries, 7,758 construction workers recorded in the 1897 census, and 3,000 seasonal workers. This last figure certainly underestimates the number of seasonal laborers, since it is taken from a study completed in 1880. The 704 construction workers who in 1903 belonged to guilds (and were therefore counted as artisanal workers) have been classified with construction workers for the sake of consistency. Sources: *OOKTM za 1903–1905 gg.*, *prilozheniia* 19 and 22; *OOKTM za 1901 g.*, p. 207; *OOORU za 1902–1904 gg.*, p. 8; *KR*, April 5, 1905; TsGIA, f. 23, op. 29, d. 80, p. 23. The figures for transportation, construction, communication, sales-clerical, service, day, and other unskilled workers are taken from *Perepis'*, pp. 88–131; Adamovich, *Chernomorskaia registratsiia*; Bel'for, "Profsoiuzy Odessy v revoliutsii 1905–1907 godov," p. 50; Gudvan, *Prikazchiki v Odesse*, p. 15; *OOKTM za 1900 g.*, p. 168; Bernshtein, *Odessa.*, p. 78.

Inspectorate. In practice, however, it often stretched to twelve, thirteen, and even fifteen or sixteen hours, due to loopholes, lax enforcement of existing legislation, compulsory overtime (often without additional pay), and management's refusal to permit workers to take breaks.[2] In branches of the economy not subject to factory inspection, the average workday was even longer. Employees of workshops and small enterprises as well as construction workers, day laborers, and shop assistants were not covered by the meager labor legislation that existed in the pre-1905 period. Workers in the stone quarries commonly endured eighteen-hour workdays, and even the conductors and drivers of trams found themselves working eighteen hours a day, at times laboring up to twelve hours without interruption. Even pharmacists' assistants, though skilled and literate, worked fourteen-hour days.[3]

Working conditions were arduous, hazardous, and sometimes fatal. Accidents abounded. In one instance a stoker, unaware that a boy hired to scrub off the accumulated scum in the boilers of ships had fallen asleep inside the boiler, filled it with water, boiling the child to death.[4] Even in less dangerous lines of employment, workers suffered from industrial illnesses. Factories and workshops were generally characterized by poor ventilation and lighting, filth, and other unhygienic conditions. Respiratory problems and throat, eye, and stomach ailments were common due to the inhalation of noxious chemicals, fumes, and dust. Workers in paint factories frequently succumbed to tuberculosis after two years of employment, and printers often died from lead poisoning.[5] Shoemakers and tailors generally labored in crowded, damp, dark, and cold basement apartments; poised on low, wooden benches, they would sit long hours hunched over their work. One bootmaker complained that he worked in a workshop that doubled as the kitchen of his employer's apartment. He wrote that "it is filthy—dirt and slop everywhere," with cobwebs covering the entire ceiling.[6]

Workers also endured harsh systems of discipline, fines, and arbitrary deductions from their earnings. For example, two rubles, nearly a quarter of their monthly earnings, were deducted from the salary of new female employees at a teapacking plant. This money went into a marriage fund which the women could touch only after two years of employment. If they quit before two years, they forfeited the money.[7] Workers were at the mercy of foremen who set the rates for piecework. Foremen would lower the rates during rush periods in order to motivate their workers to work harder, only to place workers on reduced schedules when rush periods ended in order to cut costs. A manager in the Restel' Machine Works, who dismissed workers who voiced opposition to this practice, instituted a strict regimen of fines and compensated workers who spied for the owner. Restel' workers were required to pay a "security deposit" but never informed of the reason for this deduction.[8]

Laborers in small workshops and garret-masters were targets of arbitrary rate-setting. Storeowners, middlemen, and workshop owners commonly provided workers with defective or insufficient material to do a proper job. When workers complained, they were told not to worry and to do the best they could. But when workers presented the finished products and demanded payment, their bosses would decry their poor quality and arbitrarily reduce the rate of pay. To make matters worse, payment was often late and subcontractors rarely supplied the raw materials on time. Consequently, workers compensated for the valuable time lost waiting for the material by working longer hours and perhaps less carefully.[9]

Women workers were subject to special forms of abuse and mistreatment. Foremen and male coworkers in factories made unwanted sexual advances and relished the opportunity to heap verbal abuse upon women employees, as well as threaten them with physical and sexual violence. One foreman in the Arps Cork Factory kicked and threatened to fine a woman worker because she had temporarily left her post to talk to another worker. The same foreman summoned another woman with the words, "Hey, you cow, come over here."[10] Women endured humiliating physical searches by male supervisors when they left factory premises, and management also felt free to dismiss women employees on a whim. One factory owner commented that he could "hire blondes this week and brunettes the next."[11] One consequence of the low wages and mistreatment of female workers was the frequency with which women turned to prostitution, which was generally more lucrative (and perhaps less oppressive) than toiling in a factory or workshop. There were an estimated 9,000 prostitutes in Odessa in 1905, many earning from 20 to 50 rubles a month, more than they could earn as factory or workshop employees.[12]

The power of some employers was enhanced by their domination of some workers' mutual-aid societies. Owners and managerial personnel had themselves elected to the administrative boards of mutual-aid societies; although worker contributions funded the treasuries of these associations, governing boards under the aegis of employers determined who was eligible for assistance and how much to give out. Workers resented this state of affairs, especially when benefits were inadequate or not forthcoming. In 1903, the workers of the Pekatoros Leather Factory protested the owner's decision to withhold sick benefits to members of the plant's mutual-aid society. As the director of the factory told the workers, "The treasury is not yours, but the company's."[13] Given their lack of civil and legal rights, the aggrieved leatherworkers had no recourse but to bristle at this insult.

Government authority, mainly in the form of police, frequently intruded into the factory, and not only during times of labor unrest. For example, policemen attached to the Factory Inspectorate could be stationed inside factories to ensure observance of factory regulations as well as maintain the smooth operation of enterprises. Such policemen were instructed to find out the cause of worker discontent and pay special attention to those workers who appeared to be "instigators" of labor unrest.[14]

By the same token, the power and prerogatives of management sometimes extended beyond the factory gate. In early 1902, the female children who worked at the Popov Tobacco Factory refused to assist the adult women for 30 kopecks a day. The women workers, unable to meet their assistants' demand for more money because they themselves earned only 1 ruble a day, asked management for a raise of 10 kopecks a day and threatened to join the work stoppage if management failed to comply. Management rejected the demand and the factory stood idle while most of the women and children struck. Popov believed the workers would return to work after a day or two, but when he realized the strike might drag on for weeks he requested police intervention. The police chief instructed his men to go to the strikers' apartments and order them to return to work. When the striking women greeted them with firm refusals, the police dragged many of them by the hair into the streets and back to the factory. During another work stoppage, Cossacks and police visited the homes of striking tram workers and dragged the men back to work.[15]

Other incidents revealed to workers that government and management worked in tandem. The paternalism that frequently characterized government attitudes toward the problems of factory workers for most of the nineteenth century was giving way to unabashed favoritism toward management. Employers, knowing that the police, city officials, and factory inspectors would support them, repeatedly countered workers' efforts to redress grievances by arbitrarily exercising their power and authority, a practice (known in Russian as *proizvol*) that angered workers throughout the Empire. During the 1903 general strike, for example, the chief of one police district slapped striking dockworkers when they refused to return to work.[16] In another incident, employees of the railway workshops were threatened with dismissal if they did not contribute 2 to 3 percent of their monthly wages to the war effort against Japan.[17] Workers were clearly treated as second-class citizens by the authorities and police. According to a municipal statute from the 1890s, workers in work clothes could not walk on sidewalks and could be barred from trams. As one worker stated, such humiliating experiences confirmed many workers in the belief that "at every step employers crudely assault" (*grubo oskorbliaiut*) their dignity, adding a powerful moral argument to the workers' sense of material deprivation, political helplessness, and indignation.[18]

Besides the nature of their treatment at the hands of superiors, Odessa workers also felt the brunt of inflation, which had a direct effect on every worker in terms of purchasing power. For many workers, the relatively good wages of the industrial expansion of the 1890s were eroded as inflation and unemployment took their toll after the turn of the century. One Soviet historian has estimated that the cost of living in the Ukraine increased approximately 10 percent between 1900 and 1903, with the prices of many staple food items registering a much higher rate of growth. Moreover, urban Russia experienced the largest increases in the cost of living. For most Odessa workers, real wages dropped during the first half-decade of the twentieth century. Between 1897 and 1903–05, machine-construction workers saw their annual wages drop from 340 to 258 rubles.[19]

Living conditions in the workers' districts provided a stark contrast to the boulevards, tree-lined promenades, and fancy shopping streets of the city's central districts. Apartments in workers' neighborhoods were generally poorly equipped with running water, electricity, gas, and ventilation. City officials found in 1892 that about 40 percent of Odessans lived in one-room apartments. Sometimes two or more families inhabited such cramped quarters, with many of the apartments located in dark, damp basements. At least a third of all dwellings lacked stoves for heat and cooking. These living conditions were the norm in working-class districts and could even be found in the workers' apartments in the well-to-do sections of the city center.[20] The differences in material well-being between the industrial suburbs and the districts of the city center led some philanthropists and charitable organizations to address the housing problem by building low-income housing and offering other financial and health services. By 1900 five housing projects for the poor had been built, but the problem of inadequate housing required a more comprehensive plan and approach.[21]

Despite this bleak picture, there were some indications that Odessa was beginning to cope with public health problems. The citywide death rate dropped from approximately 40 per 1,000 inhabitants in 1871 to slightly over 21 per 1,000 by 1903, a rate that compared very favorably with death rates in Moscow, St. Petersburg, and some major industrial cities in Western Europe. The city's well-to-do districts fared better than the poorer neighborhoods, however; mortality rates in Peresyp and Slobodka-Romanovka at the turn of the century remained high, hovering above 30 per 1,000. The mortality rate was especially high in Peresyp, particularly for infants, due in part to the city's decision to construct a system of sewers that after 1890 carried human waste in open conduits from the city center—situated on cliffs above the seashore and Peresyp—down the long incline that joined the central regions of Odessa to Peresyp. The conduits ran through central Peresyp to a "sewage farm" (*pole oresheniia*) located at the outskirts of the district, where refuse was used for agricultural cultivation. The new sewer system, along with a piped supply of pure water, may have improved sanitary conditions in the city's central districts, but it undoubtedly worsened the situation in Peresyp. Overcrowding, the lack of indoor plumbing and public baths, the improper disposal of by-products from Peresyp's animal processing plants, and the presence of garbage strewn in the streets added to the problems created by the sewer system. Rather than transport trash to the city's garbage dump, many trash collectors in Peresyp simply dumped their loads at the nearest barren spot.[22] In late 1904 the city council, ignoring the urgent requests of sanitary inspectors and concerned citizens to finance the building of an adequate sewage disposal system in Peresyp, allocated only 5,000 rubles for a project to study the problem. The city councillors, with a new ten million-ruble foreign loan, chose instead to allot funds for the repavement of streets in the city center, thereby demonstrating to Odessa's underprivileged a lack of concern for their needs.[23]

It is likely that the glaring contrast in the living conditions of rich and poor Odessans promoted feelings of resentment and reinforced the sense that workers in Odessa felt of separateness from well-to-do and educated society. As the workers could plainly see, they lived in a world in which wealth and privilege were unequally distributed. By 1900, little in their lives made workers feel that Odessa was their city, a place where they belonged and could expect a better future for themselves or for their children. The enormous disparities between conditions in workers' neighborhoods and the fashionable districts of the city were visible to all: the one-story tract housing of Peresyp and Slobodka-Romanovka contrasted sharply with the two-, three-, and sometimes four-story, well-maintained, fancy neoclassical buildings of the Bul'var and Aleksandrov districts. Peresyp and Slobodka-Romanovka, like other neglected regions of the city, lagged behind the city center in terms of paved streets, street lights, and other public amenities. The extension of public works projects aimed at upgrading the living conditions of workers may have only served to accentuate the awareness among workers that they benefited less than the city's better situated residents. The self-evident gap between conditions in the industrial suburbs and the fashionable city center convinced many workers that they had little stake in the existing order.

The workers' sense of neglect and isolation was enhanced by the city's inadequate transport system. Public transport in the form of horse-drawn and electric trams was geared to facilitating the movement of people within Odessa's central districts and between the city center and the resorts located outside the city limits rather than toward moving people between the city center and the industrial suburbs.[24] Since most residents of Peresyp and Slobodka-Romanovka tended to work near home and avoided riding trams, which strained their limited budgets, these workers lacked the need and opportunity to venture into other areas of Odessa, thereby compounding their physical and cultural separation.

In the foregoing account I have underscored the features of life and labor that provided Odessa workers with common experiences. Just as important as these shared characteristics, however, were the significant differences in work and work setting that also shaped workers' outlooks and actions and differentiated one category of worker from another. The joint experience of exploitation and mistreatment could be overshadowed by fissures caused by significant differences in a host of factors, such as levels of skill, length of stay in the city, and ethnicity. An examination of selected categories of workers—metalworkers, tailors, and day laborers—provides a glimpse of the living and working conditions of a diverse cross-section of the Odessa labor force. I have selected these occupational groups because, as participants in the events of 1905, their behavior in that year was in large part influenced by their on- and off-the-job experiences as well as by structural changes in Odessa's economy. Whether they worked in factories, workshops, or in other settings was of no small consequence; the various forms of collective action in which they engaged was conditioned in large measure by the nature of their work, work setting, and other job characteristics. Division as well as commonality marked the world of Odessa workers.

Metalworkers: Skill and Community

The number of factory workers in Odessa increased dramatically between the beginning of the 1890s and the early twentieth century, growing from some 10,000 in 1893 to approximately 25,000 by 1903. Much of this increase occurred before the nationwide recession set in at the end of the century and was due to expanded production in already existing enterprises, such as sugar refineries, flour mills, and tobacco-, leather-, and jute-processing plants. In addition, industrialists sought to take advantage of economies of scale by introducing the most technologically advanced equipment and machinery available at that time, opening large metal, machine-construction and animal-processing plants that fostered the growth of the labor force.[25]

Large concentrations of metalworkers and machinists could be found in the factories of Peresyp, the large shipyards and plants of the Port Territory, and the repair shops of the South West Railroad in Mikhailov. These workers were blessed with the one occupational characteristic that truly made them stand apart from all other workers in Odessa: skill. Not only did skilled workers receive higher wages, but they enjoyed greater status, prestige, and authority at work. Skilled workers tended to be male as well as older and literate, factors that enhanced their authority in the workplace. In the words of one worker from the railroad workshops, skilled workers enjoyed great "influence among workers," whereas "less skilled workers did not possess . . . authority."[26]

Possession of skill was an essential element in the Russian worker's self-understanding; it engendered pride, dignity, and self-esteem, in part because it granted its possessor a degree of independence vis-à-vis management on the shop floor.[27] Skilled workers supervised the hiring and training of new workers, transmitted a sense of pride in the job to younger workers, and exercised other controls over the labor force and production process. While it is true that skilled workers in factories were not independent employers of labor and, like all factory workers, were subordinate to management, they did possess some of the same responsibilities and authority that traditional artisanal craftmasters enjoyed.[28] As in the traditional artisanal workshop, many metalworking and machine-construction factories were characterized by a strict hierarchy of labor based on skill acquired through a prolonged period of training, the one major difference being that machinery had replaced hand labor.

Skilled workers enjoyed a strong position in the labor market and commanded relatively high wages due to their indispensability. Even though Odessa workers under factory inspection commanded lower wages than workers in St. Petersburg (who earned on average 314 rubles a year), in 1903 they earned an average of around 260 rubles, a sum that compared favorably with the average annual earnings of 213 rubles in other parts of the Empire (this difference might, however, be due to the fact that Odessa factory workers worked more days per year than workers in many other industrial regions). Many skilled metalworkers and machinists earned substantially more than the Odessa average. In 1903 some of the most qualified workers at the Henn Agricultural Machinery and Equipment Factory in Peresyp, for example, could earn as much as 479 rubles a year. By contrast, unskilled women and children rolling and packaging cigarettes earned only 136 rubles annually, which illustrates that earning power was not only related to skill but also to the sex and age of the worker.[29]

Historians of the Russian and West European labor movements in the nineteenth and early twentieth centuries focus on the role skilled workers played in organized labor activities. The fact that they tended to be literate, that they commanded relatively high wages, and that, as men, they were spared the added burden of housework and child rearing, enabled skilled workers to sustain strikes and devote time to labor organizing and political activities. The skilled metalworkers and machinists from Peresyp and the Port Territory possessed certain other social characteristics that, along with their place in the production process, distinguished them from most other workers elsewhere in the city and fostered cohesion and organization. These were prolonged residency in the city, experience with urban life, and a more developed sense of community and neighborhood.

The residents of the factory district of Peresyp lived in a relatively insular and self-contained community that was administratively and economically connected to the city at large but for the most part did not share in its social, cultural, and political life. As we have seen, this state of affairs was partially due to the districts' physical isolation from the rest of the city: a steep incline separated the center of Odessa from Peresyp, and an inadequate transport system enhanced this geographical separation.

Other outlying workers' districts, including Mikhailov, Petropavlov and Slobodka-Romanovka (which was also cut off from the city center by a ravine) were also relatively isolated and overlooked by the municipal authorities. But Peresyp had an important distinguishing characteristic: its workers were more likely to be natives of Odessa. Unlike other districts of Odessa, where most residents were immigrants to the city, Peresyp had an equal share of native and non-native residents.[30] Moreover, nearly 56 percent (or just about the city average) of Peresyp's inhabitants were inscribed in the *meshchanstvo,* which suggests some familiarity with urban life.[31] Although available censuses and other statistical data do not indicate the length of residency of non-native Odessans, it is obvious that people who were born, reared, and entered adulthood in Odessa had longer exposure to city life than did migrants to the city. They also had more opportunity to develop friendships, loyalties, and bonds rooted in shared experiences at work and in the neighborhood than did newcomers to Odessa, even if the newcomers lived in the city on a permanent basis. Thus inhabitants of Peresyp had time to become integrated into urban life and to establish deeper, more permanent social bonds than migrants in other districts. Odessa may have been a city composed largely of migrants, but there were large numbers of residents who had extended contact with the city and fashioned lives that differed significantly from those of recent arrivals. Prolonged residency, as recent research on Russian workers in Moscow and St. Petersburg in 1905 stresses, could be a crucial factor in determining labor activism.[32]

Other data on Peresyp's residents reinforce our picture of this community. According to the 1897 census, the proportion of Peresyp's men and women aged 20 or older who were married was greater than the citywide percentage. It is true that many married men in Odessa, as in all major urban centers throughout Russia, left families behind in their native villages, yet we must also remember that this practice was reserved primarily for peasant migrants, a minority of Peresyp's inhabitants. Therefore it is reasonable to conclude that men and women in Peresyp tended to marry and live with their spouses; the fact that a third of the district's residents were under fifteen (the citywide average was 28 percent) demonstrates that Peresyp's populace was also raising families, another strong indicator that people were striking roots in the district.[33]

Not only did the working and social lives of Peresyp's workers possess an element of constancy, but coworkers and neighbors were often identical. Most workers of the Paraskov Leather Factory, for example, lived on Peresyp's main thoroughfare, Moscow Street, with many even residing in the same building.[34] The proximity of work and residence facilitated the transmission of news and ideas among inhabitants of Peresyp, enhancing the opportunity of workers in different factories to discuss common problems and develop joint strategies to improve conditions. Striking workers of one enterprise could more easily generate sympathy and support among workers in other plants if they were neighbors and had known each other socially for long periods of time.

Finally, Peresyp was relatively homogeneous in terms of ethnic composition, with Jews accounting for slightly over 20 percent of its residents in 1897. Except for Kherson, Dal'nits, and the Port Territory, the city's other districts had a more equal mix of Jews and gentiles.[35] In a city where ethnic and religious differences frequently acted as divisive forces, Peresyp's relative homogeneity minimized the disruptive effect of ethno-religious tensions among its residents.

This combination of demographic, residential, and occupational characteristics fostered close social and work ties among Peresyp's metalworkers and machinists, contributing to their capacity to organize and act collectively both on and off the job. Because so many shared similar life and work experiences in the same enterprises and neighborhood, they were better able to meet and discuss common grievances. The very fabric of work and life facilitated close social contacts and the circulation of news and information, and thereby enabled workers in Peresyp to act in concert.

Tailors and the Impact of Capitalism on Workshop Production

There were at least 46,000 workshop employees in Odessa at the beginning of the twentieth century, a figure that underestimates the actual number since data collectors failed to record all such workers. Thousands of workshop employees, garret-masters in particular, avoided both the census-taker and police registration procedures so as to avoid paying fees and taxes. In addition, many skilled craftworkers were employed in factories but shared characteristics with traditional workshop artisans in terms of the areas of training, skill, work setting, and control over production. Because these workers fell under the purview of the Factory Inspectorate, they were not counted as workshop employees.

Of the 46,000 or more workshop employees, nearly 20,000 (7,700 apprentices and 12,000 journeymen) belonged to guilds. There were also 7,620 master craftworkers who owned workshops and therefore have not been counted as workers, even though many labored alongside their employees.[36] These workers should properly be called artisans since they presumably entered into formal apprenticeship programs, were required to do stints as journeymen, and had to receive certification from the Board of Artisanal Trades. Yet we must be cautious when drawing conclusions from data regarding guild membership. The Board of Artisanal Trades, for example, admitted that it had certified less than 10 percent of all journeymen, thereby implying that a sizable number of workers recorded as journeymen may not have completed a formal training program or met the standards of craftsmanship established by the guilds. Many other artisans evaded registration in the guilds because they could not afford the requisite fees. Such evasion prompted guild authorities periodically to search out unregistered workers (including garret-masters) and, under the threat of legal proceedings or violence, force them to register and pay fines.[37]

When we compare the number of workers employed in factories with the number employed in workshops, not surprisingly we find that workshop employees were overwhelmingly concentrated in those sectors of the economy that were still unmechanized.[38] A preindustrial production process characterized the manufacture of clothes, shoes, jewelry, watches, and leather goods. Factory workers, on the other hand, tended to be employed in those branches of the economy that used machinery or involved production techniques requiring large numbers of workers or a highly developed division of labor. These included food processing and the manufacturing of chemicals, minerals, and machines. One type of production, woodworking, employed large numbers of both workshop and factory workers, a state of affairs that reflected the transition from workshop to factory production that this particular branch of manufacturing was undergoing.[39]

Thus, along with the expansion of relatively large-scale factory production, workshop manufacturing continued to expand. One measure of the growth in the workshop work force is provided by the Odessa Board of Artisanal Trades, which reported approximately 7,700 journeymen and apprentices as of January 1896; the number of such workers had more than doubled less than a decade later.[40] In the words of Joseph Bradley (referring to Moscow in the same period), "a dual economy" existed in Odessa.[41] That is, commercial and industrial concentration was matched by a parallel expansion in small-scale production and trade.

Yet workshop production was simultaneously undergoing substantial changes as urban markets expanded and workshops became subject to the pressures of capitalist methods of marketing and production. Although the workshop sector continued to dominate local industry in terms of the total number of workers employed, by 1900 it had entered a transitional period in which more and more workshops lost the trappings of traditional artisanal enterprises. The likelihood that apprentices or journeymen would achieve the status of master artisan and open their own workshops grew more remote with the spread of subcontracting, a practice that devalued skill and undermined custom-made production. As in Western Europe in an earlier period, subcontracting arrangements were becoming more widespread as many artisans entered into agreements with wholesale and retail merchants in order to take advantage of the growing demand for ready-made goods. Instead of producing custom-made wares to order, subcontracting workshops used "sweated" labor to manufacture mass-produced, ready-made goods that cost less to produce and commanded a lower price. Patterns of production were reorganized as skills were diluted and a division of labor was introduced. Exploitation of labor intensified, working conditions deteriorated, and earnings for workers involved in ready-made production decreased. Master craftworkers who owned traditionally structured artisanal workshops frequently transformed their establishments by hiring additional staff and introducing a limited division of labor into the production process. Retail stores, wholesale firms, and middlemen would then contract out to these workshops. They would also seek out garret-masters, who were frequently unemployed apprentices, journeymen and, in some instances, master craftworkers who could not afford to hire assistants or had gone bankrupt. At times wholesalers and retailers even opened up their own workshops in order to avoid the cost of paying a middleman and to save themselves the trouble of dealing with an independent artisan.[42]

Trends in the apparel trades best illustrate the structural changes that workshop production was undergoing at the turn of the century. Even though a division of labor in the apparel trades was still uncommon in other regions of Russia, task specialization in workshops had apparently already been introduced in Odessa and by the early 1900s was more prevalent there than in other manufacturing centers.[43] By the mid-1890s, a large local demand for ready-made clothes existed in Odessa, and this market was supplemented by the growth of markets throughout the Russian Empire. Wholesalers and retail storeowners in Odessa provided cloth to middlemen, who would then contract out to a master tailor employing mostly male workers to turn the cloth into a finished product. In order to meet deadlines and keep pace with orders, many garment workshops introduced a limited division of labor. Instead of one worker handling the same piece of fabric from start to finish, each person performed a specialized task: one worker cut the cloth, while a second sewed it together; another made pockets, and still others attached buttons and ironed the finished garment. As one observer noted, "Each part of the garment passes through dozens of hands."[44] According to the 1897 census, slightly over 13,000 residents of Odessa earned a livelihood from the production of clothes, including shoes, hats, gloves, belts, and coats. Since the census did not specify where the respondents worked but only what they did, this figure includes all respondents involved in the making of clothes regardless of whether they worked in workshops or at home (as seamstresses and garret-masters). Jews formed a majority of apparel workers, comprising nearly three-fifths of workers engaged in the making of clothes, shoes, and accessories. Russians accounted for most of the others.[45]

Middlemen undoubtedly benefited from severe competition among tailors, offering contracts to those who were willing to accept the lowest terms. Odessa's swelling population led to a surplus of labor and exerted downward pressure on wages. Jewish workers were hit especially hard, since legal disabilities hindered their geographic mobility and forced them to live and compete for work within the towns and cities of the Pale of Settlement, already suffering from explosive population growth. Subcontractors also undermined the position of the independent tailor by setting up their own workshops and hiring labor directly and cheaply, since task specialization enabled inexperienced workers to perform relatively simple tasks without much training. One result of these developments was the influx of women and children into subcontracting workshops and the amount of work put out to them. This was a phenomenon witnessed in other branches of the industrial sector because women and adolescents provided an untapped source of cheap labor. As factory production expanded and production techniques turned to a division of labor requiring less training and perhaps less physical strength, the demand for unskilled, cheaper labor grew. Employers, hoping to cut their operating expenses, replaced male workers with women and children, who tended to accept lower wages. Moreover, these workers were perceived to be more docile and less likely to strike than adult men. According to data compiled by the Factory Inspectorate in 1903, female factory workers (including teenagers and children) comprised 27 percent of the total factory labor force, an increase from the 22 percent recorded in 1898. Women and children accounted for a large share of workers in the needle trades: women of all ages made up 40 percent of the work force in the apparel trades, with teenage girls under 17 comprising 16 percent of all garment workers.[46]

The spread of subcontracting was therefore altering the complexion of workshop production by reducing the importance of training and expertise. Although traditional workshops still existed in Odessa, producing custom-made wares and requiring relatively high levels of skill acquired through lengthy training programs, the proliferation of subcontracting arrangments was eliminating the need for skills acquired in this manner. This development was also eroding the paternalism that typically characterized artisanal workshops, since labor turnover increased with the gradual deskilling of the work force.

Craft-masters who could expand the productive capacities of their workshops to handle the orders of middlemen and wholesalers could expect to share in the market for ready-made clothing. But many independent tailors could not compete with subcontracting workshops and faced the prospect of bankruptcy as subcontracting destroyed their livelihood. Along with their apprentices and journeymen, many master artisans became garret-masters or hired hands in subcontracting workshops.[47] Artisanal manufacturing was being undercut by a system of production that valued mass production at the lowest cost and paid scant attention to the quality of the finished product. In short, urban growth and emergent industrial capitalism were altering the fabric of Odessa's economy and work force, and the age-old hope of workshop employees someday opening their own shops was becoming little more than a pipe dream.

In subcontracting workshops that catered to the mass market and relied heavily on female and child labor, the typical workday lasted thirteen hours in the larger shops and an hour or two more in the smaller ones. The workday for tailors, dressmakers, seamstresses, and milliners increased during the peak seasons, which occurred at Eastertime, in May (when a series of balls and gala events took place), and then from the end of August until the end of the year. Work at these times frequently lasted well into the night.[48]

Workers in subcontracting shops generally earned substantially less than tailors involved in custom-made production, a reflection of their lower skill level. Tailors who produced ready-made clothes, for example, made 60 percent of what tailors engaged in custom-made production earned. Moreover, many tailors did not work year-round as a result of the seasonality of production. Workers in the apparel trades were frequently hired for only a set period of time, usually for the length of the peak season, and spent the remaining months of the year unemployed or working part-time. Not unexpectedly, common demands of garment workers included guarantees of year-round work and weekly salaries (to replace piece-work) in order to minimize the combined impact of low wages and seasonal employment.[49]

In stark contrast to the situation that prevailed among the metalworkers of Peresyp, the capacity of workshop employees to engage in collective action was constrained by the nature of their work. Workshop employees found themselves in small, isolated establishments scattered throughout the city, with little or no contact with other workers. Compounding this problem were occupational divisions among workshop employees, particularly the garment workers. Over a dozen subdivisions of the tailors' guild existed, with separate organizations depending on the article of clothing made, whether the clothing was custom-made or mass-produced, and whether it was intended for men or women. Such a state of affairs made it difficult for these workers to ascertain their mutual problems and agree upon a common course of action. The fact that many workshop employees, especially in the apparel trades, were women and teenagers who faced a series of barriers to labor organizing rooted in sex, age, and occupational characteristics also militated against labor mobilization and group activism. Nonetheless, workshop employees were a constituent element in the fledgling socialist and organized labor movements that emerged in Odessa during the 1890s. That they did play such a prominent role was due, as we shall see in chapter three, due to the influence of other factors unrelated to the nature and structure of workshop employment.

Day Laborers

If metalworkers and machinists occupied one end of the occupational spectrum of skill, pay, and community, day laborers occupied the other. In the words of one observer, unskilled day laborers, dockworkers in particular, "perpetually curse and are dirty, ragged, drunk, and have almost lost human appearance. . . . Life has passed them by; they have no hope for a better future and are concerned only with finding a piece of bread and a corner in a flophouse."[50] Still another description, by a socialist organizer, states that day laborers, especially dockworkers, rarely married and lived "nestled . . . in gloomy filthy houses, from basements to attics jammed full of the begging poor."[51] Day laborers in Odessa led a precarious social and economic existence, suffering from irregular, impermanent work and low wages. Many were unmarried, male migrants to Odessa, lacking marketable skills and work experience. Large numbers of these day laborers were peasants from the countryside, while others were Jews who moved to Odessa in order to escape the poverty of life in the shtetls and small towns of the Pale of Settlement.

Competition for employment between Jewish and gentile day laborers assumed special importance at dockside and in the railway depots, where thousands of unskilled workers vied for employment during the peak season of commercial activity, which began in spring and lasted well into the fall. According to the 1897 census, slightly over 16,000 workers were unskilled day laborers without permanent jobs or specific occupations who supplemented the city's dockworkers, porters, and carters during the busy season. Precise data do not exist, but most estimates place the number of dockworkers in Odessa at the turn of the century at 4,000 to 7,000. Approximately half of these dockworkers were Jews, and at least 9,000 other Jews found employment as unskilled laborers elsewhere in the city by the end of the century.[52] Thus, somewhere between 11,000 and 12,500 Jews worked as day laborers.

Even during peak periods of port activity, operators of shipping lines, brokerage firms, and warehouses did not require the services of all dockworkers looking for work. In the summer few dockworkers worked more than fifteen days a month; job competition increased during the off-season or periods of slump and recession, when over half of all dockworkers were unemployed. It is estimated that between 1900 and 1903 at least 2,000 dockworkers were unemployed at any given time.[53]

Day laborers had not always found it difficult to find work. From the 1860s to the 1890s, workers often preferred employment at the docks because it often paid more than factory labor and was readily available. But unemployment for longshoremen rose dramatically in the late 1890s and early 1900s, when the labor market began to constrict due to the confluence of adverse economic developments discussed in chapter one. One serious consequence was a surplus of labor, exacerbated by the use of conveyor belts, floating elevators, and cranes at dockside. Although most dock work was still done by hand in 1905, conveyor belts had the unintended effect of reducing employment opportunities for stevedores and exerting downward pressures on wages. The constricting labor market heightened job competition between Jewish and gentile dockworkers and led shipowners, city authorities, and longshoremen to establish a quota system for Jewish and non-Jewish dockworkers in 1906–1907.[54]

Some longshoremen belonged to work gangs that were either hired by subcontractors on a regular basis or employed directly by the shipping lines. Each company generally utilized the services of different work gangs, whose members were hired either by the month or day. For example, the several hundred members of the Moscow Customs Artel were hired by the Customs House to handle the freight of foreign ships, while the First and Fourth Artels worked for the Russian Steam Navigation and Trading Company.

The vast majority of day laborers, however, lacked permanent work, a situation that the hiring process made even more difficult and exploitative. Shipping firms employed the services of subcontractors to provide the necessary labor; they paid the subcontractor a fixed sum and were unconcerned that subcontractors skimmed off a hefty portion of the wages owed the workers. In order to work on a given day, day laborers not belonging to work gangs placed their names on sign-up sheets that subcontractors for shipping lines and import-export firms posted at different taverns and teahouses throughout the city. The prospects of finding work in this manner were slim. Prospective laborers had to arrive early in the morning in order to ensure themselves a place on the lists, and those fortunate to find employment for a day had to give the subcontractor approximately a third of their earnings, leaving them with barely a ruble to take home.

According to 1904 data, day laborers earned an average daily wage of 60 kopecks to a ruble for work that could include hauling heavy sacks of grain from barges and dockside into the holds of ships destined for foreign ports. After a long day's work, they returned to await payment at the tavern or teahouse where their subcontractor conducted business; settling up often took until 10 P.M.[55] Given the extraordinary number of wasted hours and the physical exhaustion after a long day of backbreaking labor, it is not surprising that many day laborers lacked the inclination to work every day. Even if they were highly motivated, competition from other job seekers reduced their chances of finding work.

Another factor reducing employment opportunities for day laborers was their tendency not to work in different parts of Odessa. They preferred to limit the search for employment to a certain district or kind of work that they knew best. A day laborer who carted goods at the harbor would refuse to look for similar work in another part of town. He would also disdain switching job specialities (such as they were), shunning day work at construction sites for his usual practice of loading grain at dockside. Given the nature of hiring practices, day laborers coveted the security of living near the source of their livelihood. If they searched for work outside their specialty or work site, they might loose whatever small foothold they had at their customary work site. Day workers also shunned newcomers to job sites, especially during hard times when unemployed workers from other trades competed for scarce jobs.[56] This low geographical mobility and sense of territoriality were compounded by the cost of public transportation, which only reinforced the habit of day workers to work near their place of residence.

Although some day laborers lived in apartments with their families or other workers, many found their wages inadequate to rent a room or even a "corner" in an apartment. They were forced instead to seek shelter in one of the crowded flophouses (*nochlezhnye doma*) that speckled the harbor area and poor neighborhoods of Odessa. At the turn of the century several thousand people, mostly adult Russian males, but also including a sprinkling of children and teenagers, slept in flophouses, with a sizable majority of them living in such accommodations for over a year and nearly half for over three years. In other words, many day laborers had become permanent denizens of night shelters. Indeed, many frequented the same flophouses day after day and even had their favorite sleeping corners.[57]

While the overwhelming majority of such individuals were unskilled and uneducated, some patrons of flophouses were poverty-stricken students or even persons from well-placed families who had experienced sudden reversals in their fortunes. In 1885, *Odesskii listok* published the tear-jerking, overblown tale of one such ill-fated man, César Pusse. Pusse, an educated French citizen from a wealthy family, wound up in Odessa's night shelters because he could not find work as a translator and his failing health did not permit him to accept any physically demanding employment. In desperation, Pusse lamented, "I am literate and know languages. . . . I can be useful in many lines of work. Just give me, give me, I beg you, God, work!"[58]

Conditions in the night shelters were abominable. Breeding grounds for infectious diseases, night shelters offered the lodger only a wooden plank or a filthy straw mattress on a cold, damp, and hard asphalt floor.[59] Because night shelters frequently lacked heat and washing facilities and since no public baths existed in the port district, their residents generally bathed in a nearby canal filled with the warm run-off water from the municipal electric plant.[60] Of the nine night shelters located in the harbor district, seven were privately owned and two were operated by the city. Conditions in the city-run shelters were generally better than those found in privately owned flophouses, since city shelters provided bathing facilities, free medical care, and cafeterias. In addition, the city ran a day shelter that daily attracted up to 500 persons who took advantage of its showers, kitchen, and lending library, and in 1898 the city opened a medical clinic that served certain categories of dockworkers and employees of the Port Authority.[61]

Like many other workers, day laborers drowned their sorrows in drink, alcoholism being yet another factor contributing to their entry into the world of flophouses. As one twenty-year-old worker explained, he began sleeping in night shelters "because of vodka."[62] Contemporary observers often character-ized residents of flophouses as lacking the resolve to lift themselves out of these degrading surroundings, commenting that many worked only to earn enough money to get drunk. Encouraged by those subcontractors who recruited and paid workers in taverns, drinking diminished the chances of finding work and also robbed day workers of the motivation to work on a permanent basis. Consequently, many could not disengage themselves from the crippling world of vodka. Content to work one or two days a week, they would spend the rest of the week drinking. As one observer from St. Petersburg noted, "Hope has died in their hearts—apathy has replaced it."[63]

Dependent on the activity of the port for their livelihood, day laborers in general and dockworkers in particular were usually the first workers to feel the impact of downturns in the economy. During such times, lacking even the few kopecks that night shelters charged, they often slept under the night sky or in open barrels at dockside, often falling prey to marauding youth gangs who stole their clothing.[64] Hunger was such a constant factor in the day laborers' lives that they used a broad range of colorful phrases to express its intensity. For example, "simple hunger" (*gekokht prostoi*) referred to hunger caused by not eating for one day. "Deadly hunger" (*gekokht smertel'nyi*) lasted somewhat longer, and "hunger with a vengeance" (*gekokht s raspiatiem*), which occurred in the slow winter season when "a deathly silence rules the harbor," was of "indeterminate length, whole weeks, months, in short, hunger which has no foreseeable end."[65] Although it is not known whether these expressions, which are a mixture of Yiddish and Russian, were used exclusively by Jewish day laborers, they nonetheless underscore both the general deprivation experienced by day laborers and the significant presence of Jews at the docks. They also provide some insight into why day laborers resisted working every day. After all, how could they work hard when their stomachs cried out for food?

Some historians of Russian labor question the validity of the view, held by many tsarist authorities and members of the radical intelligentsia, that migrant workers and other members of the laboring population, as "strangers and outsiders" to Russian cities, were more prone than other urban residents to participate in public disorders and violence.[66] It is not my intention to argue that social uprootedness determined such behavior, but it bears noting that many Odessans, particularly those responsible for anti-Jewish pogroms, lived marginal existences. Though some day laborers had lived in Odessa for years and enjoyed the relative comforts and security afforded by permanent housing and fairly steady work via membership in a work gang, others had never developed stable family and social roots and existed on the margins of urban society. For the vast majority of Odessa day laborers, life had an ephemeral quality that made it difficult for them to belong to the world of organized labor which emerged during the course of 1905. The faces of their workmates, employers, and those who slept near them in the night shelter changed frequently, even daily, and the lack of full-time employment and permanent lodgings limited their opportunities to form friendships and establish bonds either at home or at work. Day laborers found it difficult under such circumstances (though not impossible) to promote and defend their interests in an organized and sustained manner like more skilled and urban-rooted workers, such as the metalworkers and machinists in Peresyp. Those day laborers belonging to work artels may have found it easier than the others to act collectively, but they too generally lacked those occupational and social characteristics—skill, decent wages, long-term urban residence—that fostered labor activism and collective action among other categories of the Odessa work force.

Many observers referred to day laborers as "peaceful," carefully distinguishing them from hooligans, who were regarded as troublemakers and a social menace. Some believed that the "day laborer is not terrifying when he's had his fill; when the port is busy, this Odessan is calm."[67] The implication of this comment is clear: day laborers could be less than law-abiding and peaceful during times of economic hardship. In fact, day laborers in general and dockers in particular enjoyed a reputation throughout Russia and Western Europe as rabble-rousers and troublemakers prone to acts of public disorderliness, thereby constituting one element of the swelling social underbelly of Odessa society.

One purpose of the preceding discussion has been to highlight the diversity of the Odessa labor force and provide a context with which to assess the behavior of different groups of workers in 1905. The organizational capacities and activism of Odessa workers were in large measure shaped by a host of occupational and social characteristics that varied from one group to another. Along with divisions related to skill, nature of production, age, and sex, ethnic diversity also influenced the occupational make-up of the work force. An examination of the strong presence of Jews in Odessa provides important insights into the nature of Russian-Jewish relations in the city and offers evidence that the common experiences of labor could be undercut by factors unrelated to the work process itself.

Nationality and the Work Force

Rarely working together in the same enterprise, Jews and Russians were generally not even employed in the same branch of manufacturing. Most factory workers were Russian or Ukrainian, with Jews forming but a small minority. One observer, clearly exaggerating, put it this way: "Make the rounds of all the Odessa factories and you will perhaps find ten or fifteen Jewish metalfitters or lathe operators; some factories don't hire Jews at all."[68] A more accurate estimate placed the number of Jews employed in factory production at between 4,000 and 5,000, but the gist of this comment is nonetheless well taken.[69]

Whereas Russians worked in both Jewish- and Russian-owned factories, Jewish factory workers were mainly found in small enterprises operated by other Jews and only rarely in factories owned by Russians. In the late 1880s, for example, Jewish factory workers comprised only 7 percent of the workers employed in Russian-owned factories, but 40 percent of those in Jewish-owned factories. Only in granaries and match, tobacco, candy, cork, and cigarette-paper factories, enterprises dominated by Jewish entrepreneurs, were there many Jewish workers.[70]

Jews generally found employment in workshops and as salesclerks. Between 65 and 70 percent of shop assistants in Odessa were Jews. As we have seen, Jews also worked as stevedores at the port and as carters and porters throughout the city, often taking on the most poorly paid and arduous tasks that gentiles refused. Jews also dominated shoemaking, printing, and the needle trades, as well as figuring prominently as tinsmiths, jewelers, and gold- and silversmiths.[71] Roughly stated, in Odessa workers in workshops and small factories tended to be Jewish, whereas workers in medium-sized and large factories were usually Russian or Ukrainian.

Historians have offered several explanations, ranging from sociocultural to structural, and focusing on the attitudes and practices of both gentile and Jewish workers and employers, for the small number of Jewish factory workers.[72] First, factory owners wanting to employ both Jews and Russians feared that their plants would remain idle two days per week, since many Jewish and Russian workers refused to work, respectively, on Saturdays and Sundays. This may explain why factory owners preferred to employ either only Russians or only

Jews, but does not address the issue of why many owners tended to have all-Russian work forces; a factory owner, especially a Jewish one, could have hired only Jews and shut down operations on Saturdays. Yet it appears that even some Jewish industrialists preferred to hire non-Jews, leaving themselves open to accusations of discrimination against Jewish workers.

Some have suggested that the small number of Jewish factory workers stemmed from differences in upbringing between Jewish and Russian youths. Russian teenagers were likely to enter an apprenticeship program or enroll in a vocational school at an earlier age than Jewish youths, who sometimes attended—though in Odessa this was true to a lesser extent than in other regions of the Pale—a religious school (*kheder*) until they reached age thirteen. Jews also faced institutionalized anti-Semitism: restrictive admissions policies to technical schools and the unwillingess of non-Jewish workers to accept Jews as apprentices.[73] Russian teenagers, it is argued, possessed a competitive edge on the job market due to their earlier exposure to factory life. Moreover, a fourteen-year-old youth would probably accept a lower wage than someone several years older. Yet a Jew who did manage to enter a vocational institute or a training program and finished at seventeen or eighteen was just as qualified for factory work as a fourteen-year-old Russian teenager who had completed an equivalent course.

Other historians have stressed the reluctance of Jewish parents to thrust their children into the gentile environment of factories. Fearing possible religious conversion of their children and violations of dietary restrictions, especially when room and board were provided, Jewish parents generally refused to entrust the vocational training of their young to Russians.

Another approach goes deeper to the heart of the matter. This is the belief of Jewish industrialists, as Ezra Mendelsohn writes, "that proper employer-employee relationships were impossible when both were of the Jewish faith."[74] The Jewish factory owner wanted to avoid potential conflicts between his role as employer and his position as coreligionist of his workers. Jewish workers often asked their employers to serve as godfathers of their children, and a Jew could not refuse such an honor in good conscience, although acceptance could potentially place the employer in a dilemma if he needed to dismiss his godchild's parent.

Yet another compelling factor limiting factory employment of Jews was the belief, prevalent among many employers, that Russian workers were more docile and reliable, a belief that stemmed from the high incidence of Jews in the strike and revolutionary movements (discussed in chapter three). This perception made employing Jewish workers seem more costly and discouraged both Jewish and gentile factory owners from recruiting Jews. The owner of the Zhako Tin Factory, for example, instructed his foremen not to hire Jews because "they are troublemakers."[75] Employers recognized that tensions between Russian and Jewish workers in enterprises with ethnically mixed labor forces sometimes contributed to conflicts and outbreaks of violence. In November 1903, several dozen Russian workers in a steel mill beat up and tore the clothes of a Jewish coworker after his first day of work. When the Jewish workers complained to the owner, the latter lamented, "Those devils constantly do this whenever I hire a Jew."[76] Russian-Jewish animosity can also be seen in an incident in November 1905, when some Russian teapackers hesitated to join their newly established union because they feared that fellow Jewish unionists would turn the union's funds over to the revolutionaries and oust them from work.[77] The attitudes of Russian workers could be crucial in the formulation of hiring policies in factories, as employers hesitated to antagonize their gentile workers.

The reasons for the refusal by Russian workers to countenance the presence of Jews in factories are difficult to determine. Hard evidence is difficult to come by, and we are forced to rely on informed speculation supported in part by comments found in memoirs and reminiscences. Petr Garvi, the prominent Menshevik who spent his childhood and early adulthood in Odessa, suggests in his memoirs that it may have been due to two factors: anti-Semitism on the part of both Russian employers and workers, and fear of Jewish competition for employment.[78]

Experienced and skilled Russian workers refused to train Jewish youths, preferring to take Russian teenagers under their wings and supervise their training. Russian factory workers, especially those possessing skills, may have resented the employment of Jews, no matter how small the number, and perceived Jews in factories as encroaching on their virtual monopoly of certain factory occupations, especially those requiring high levels of skill. As the prominent socialist Zionist Ber Borochov stated, "Christian workers have come to adopt the opinion that machine work is their exclusive prerogative and privilege, and they systematically prevent Jewish workers from working at the machines."[79] Many Russian workers evidently regarded Jews as an alien, undesirable element and avoided contact. Russian factory workers, motivated by traditional anti-Jewish suspicions, cultural differences, and anxiety over potential job competition, closed ranks and resisted the hiring of Jews. Factory owners seeking to hire only Jews realized that they could not draw upon an adequate reserve of experienced and skilled Jewish factory workers. There were simply not enough Jewish workers possessing the requisite skills, training, and experience to staff Odessa's factories, particularly metalworking and machine-construction plants. Factory employers often had no choice but to overlook Jews as potential employees, thereby reinforcing discriminatory employment practices and ensuring that Jews would not break into the factory labor force in large numbers. The factors militating against Jewish factory employment had come full circle.

While Russian owners of artisanal workshops preferred to hire only Russians (often for the same reasons that motivated Russian factory owners), their Jewish counterparts were generally more willing to hire Jews than were Jewish factory owners. A host of psychological, religious, cultural, and legal factors lay behind the larger presence of Jewish workers in small workshops than in factories. In particular, many workshop owners did not yet perceive labor relations purely from the perspective of employers. For those owners operating traditionally structured artisanal workshops producing custom-made goods, the potential for conflict between their role as employers and position as coreligionists was more muted, since they generally toiled alongside their employees, some of whom were relatives, and saw themselves both as workers and employers. The traditionally low rate of labor turnover in small workshops helped create stronger bonds and loyalties between owners and workers. Paternalism still characterized many workshops, and Jewish craftmasters found themselves in a situation that was very different from that of Jewish factory owners. Considerations of cultural affinity and religious observance also played a role. In those workshops where owner and workers shared meals and even lived under one roof, dietary restrictions and other religious observances encouraged Jewish owners to take on only Jews as apprentices and journeymen. Just as Jews hesitated to apprentice their children to non-Jews, gentiles bristled at the thought of their children working alongside Jews. Furthermore, Jewish artisans were forbidden by law to hire non-Jewish apprentices, though such legal prohibitions were difficult to enforce and easily evaded.

Occupational segregation based on nationality strengthened the dividing line between Jewish and Russian workers, reducing the cohesion of Odessa workers as a whole and enhancing the potential for ethnic strife and conflict. The lack of opportunities to establish on-the-job friendships and solidarities helped widen social distances and made it more difficult to smooth over ethnic antagonisms. Differences in religion, culture, and customs were particularly hard to overcome if there was no contact on the job, and these differences were compounded in those instances where Jewish workers had trouble understanding Russian. As in the Donbass and other regions with ethnically diverse labor forces, the ethnic heterogeneity of Odessa hindered the "creation of community" among Russians and Jews.[80]

Social distance between Jewish and Russian workers was also amplified by residential patterns. To a large extent Jews and gentiles lived in isolation from each other. Although no neighborhood or district could be called wholly Jewish or Russian, areas tended to be populated predominantly by either one or the other. Unlike the Jews of other Russian cities, who were restricted to residency in certain quarters, Odessa Jews were not legally subject to residential restrictions. They were free to settle anywhere in Odessa, and they lived with non-Jews throughout the city, particularly in the central districts, where workshops, retail stores, and small industrial enterprises were located, and in industrial suburbs, such as Petropavlov and Mikhailov. But within these areas of mixed residence, Jews gravitated to their own neighborhoods, such as Moldavanka. Located in Petropavlov, Moldavanka enjoyed a reputation as the quintessential Jewish quarter in Odessa and figures prominently in the stories of Isaac Babel. Commenting on the high concentration of Jews in some neighborhoods of the city center, Garvi writes that "the central part of the city was so populated with Jews . . . that for a long time I considered that Jews comprised the majority of the population of Odessa."[81] The factory districts of Peresyp and Slobodka-Romanovka, however, were inhabited primarily by Russians, many of whom lived and worked in isolation from Jews. While ethnic residential segregation was not as marked in Odessa as in other Russian cities, the fact remains that certain neighborhoods and districts had acquired distinctive tones reflecting the predominant ethnic or national group in residence.[82]

To complete our picture of the separation of the lives of Russians and Jews, it should be noted that large numbers of Russian and Ukrainian migrants to Odessa were from rural backwater regions and had almost no previous contact with Jews. Relying on the time-honored practice of *zemliachestvo,* they arrived in Odessa and sought out relatives, family friends, and fellow villagers, who helped them find housing and work. These migrants, like most Russians in Imperial Russia, carried with them the legacy of popular and legal anti-Semitism that defined Jews as outsiders, a pernicious social element that was best counteracted with isolation and ostracism. Little wonder, then, that popular prejudices and fears influenced the attitudes of many gentile Odessans and fostered a general atmosphere of mistrust and suspicion. For their part, Jewish settlers also gravitated to Jewish neighborhoods and jobs. Jewish and Russian migrants to Odessa followed the practice of most migrant communities and stuck to their own kind, limiting their contact with others to a minimum. Despite the fact that Odessa's Jews were more likely to become acculturated than Jews residing elsewhere in the Pale of Settlement, the social and cultural gap between Jewish and Russian Odessans nonetheless continued to exist on the eve of 1905 and provided the backdrop for the periodic acts of violence perpetrated against the Jewish community. As we shall see in later chapters, it also had significant impact on the cohesion of the labor movement.

3

Labor Organizations and Politics before 1905

In its urban setting, the Revolution of 1905 was distinguished by mass labor unrest that forced the government to issue timely political reforms in order to save the substance of autocratic rule. The organizational basis of labor's collective action can only be understood in the context of associational activities in the years immediately preceding the revolution. In the decade or so before the revolution, many Odessa workers began to act in concert to promote and defend their interests. They joined a variety of legal, semi-legal, and illegal organizations that brought them into contact with members of the revolutionary intelligentsia, providing both exposure to radical political doctrines and valuable organizational experience. Many of these pre-1905 associations still existed during the revolutionary year and furnished an organizational network that workers adapted to their needs and interests. The crucible of revolution in 1905 galvanized workers into challenging the existing status quo and prompted them to build upon the foundations laid by pre-1905 labor and political activism.

Legal Labor Activities

Mutual-Aid Societies and Cooperatives

Odessa workers were attracted to a host of legal labor organizations that emerged during the course of the nineteenth century. Of particular importance were the activities of mutual-aid societies. The formation of mutual-aid societies in Imperial Russia was inhibited by the late development of civil society, stunted due to the government's restrictive policies regarding voluntary associations. Despite these hindrances, mutual-aid societies did emerge among a diverse group of workers—teachers, workshop employees, sales-clerical personnel, factory workers, and other wage laborers—during the course of the nineteenth century. These organizations did not address issues of wages and working conditions, but primarily provided sickness, accident, and funeral benefits. Many mutual-aid societies also offered material assistance to widows and orphans of deceased members, cultural and educational activities, unemployment benefits, and legal assistance. They encompassed either workers of a given occupation or employees of an individual enterprise; in both instances, however, membership also included employers, supervisory personnel, and even prominent community leaders who controlled the affairs and purse strings of the organizations by dominating the governing boards.[1] The notion of an adversarial relationship between employees and employers, the essence of trade unionism, was absent in mutual-aid societies. The paternalism of these organizations was well-suited to the existing state of labor relations in late Imperial Russia, where workers lacked collective bargaining rights and policymakers steadfastly refused to sanction independent labor organizations until 1906.

The first mutual-aid society in Odessa emerged among printers in 1816. It is not known how long this association existed, but since printers established another mutual-aid society in 1884, it is likely that the original association had ceased to exist prior to this date. In the 1860s, both Jewish and gentile salesclerks formed separate mutual-aid societies that remained in operation through 1905. At the turn of the twentieth century, five mutual-aid societies of salesclerks and office workers existed in Odessa; in addition to the organizations of Jewish and gentile shop assistants, expediters at the Custom's House, merchants' agents, and office workers belonged to their own associations. The existence of these five organizations was part of the general phenomenon of labor activism among sales-clerical personnel throughout Russia. In 1898, around 100 mutual-aid societies of sales-clerical workers existed in European Russia, claiming the support of some 20,000 members. In Odessa, mutual-benefit associations also existed among workers of various occupations and crafts: housepainters, woodworkers, shoemakers, bootmakers, tailors, waiters, quarry workers, and sailors.[2]

It is difficult to ascertain the number of Odessa workers who joined mutual-aid societies, since existing sources are silent about membership rolls. The fact that many members of the associations were not employees but employers and prominent members of Odessa society compounds this problem and suggests that the number of actual workers belonging to these organizations was lower than indicated by sparse data regarding membership totals. For example, the Odessa Mutual Aid Society of Jewish Salesclerks (*Odesskoe obshchestvo vzaimnago vspomoshchestvovaniia prikazchikov-evreev*, hereafter OMASJS) enjoyed the largest membership of all the mutual-benefit societies in the city. It boasted a membership of 800 in 1898, whereas the Christian-based association of salesclerks claimed 531 members. By contrast, the Odessa Mutual Aid Society of Printers claimed a membership of only 97 persons during the early 1890s.[3]

A brief examination of the OMASJS throws into relief the major characteristics of mutual-aid societies in Odessa and highlights their fundamental weaknesses as well. It also enables us to examine a major occupational group in Odessa at some length and illustrate the process by which mutual-aid societies failed to promote the interests of their members, thereby providing essential background information for understanding the later politicization of Odessa salesclerks.

There were some 26,000 salesclerks or shop assistants (*prikazchiki*) employed in retail stores in Odessa at the turn of the century, and another 7,000 or so sales-clerical personnel working as bookkeepers, cashiers, clerks, and other office workers. At first glance, salesclerks may seem inappropriate candidates for examination by a historian interested in the politicization of Russian labor in 1905. Although many historians would categorize salesclerks as low-level, white-collar employees or petit bourgeois, it is more appropriate to classify the majority of salesclerks as manual laborers for several reasons. First, shop assistants were distinguished from other sales-clerical personnel such as cashiers, bookkeepers, and office clerks by virtue of their lower levels of education, skill, and training. Second and more important, they devoted a significant portion of their work day to cleaning the store, running errands, delivering goods, and stocking shelves. Finally, salesclerks were often compelled to help in the manufacture of the goods they sold. Many owners of hat stores, for example, operated workshops that produced the caps and hats sold in their stores. Instead of hiring additional workers during busy periods, storeowners cut production costs by having their shop clerks put on trim and lace and make alterations, at no extra remuneration, after a full day behind the sales counter.[4]

Clerks in retail stores ranked among the most exploited and abused workers in the Russian Empire; their working and living conditions left much to be desired. Like employees of workshops and small factories, as well as construction workers and day laborers, salesclerks were subject to the whims of employers who were not restricted by legislation regarding wages, hours, and other terms of employment. Indeed, until 1902 merchants (a legal and social category that included storeowners) possessed the right to punish their young employees with a birch rod. Nor did shop assistants have the option of instituting grievance proceedings with a factory inspector, a privilege enjoyed by many factory workers. The overwhelming majority of salesclerks were male, Jewish, and under thirty years of age; nearly 87 percent of them could, to some extent, read and write, and a third had finished elementary school. Female salesclerks were generally found in the least skilled and poorest paying positions in retail stores, but they also were employed in fashionable pastry shops and bakeries where wages were nonetheless low.[5]

Shop assistants entered the labor force as child apprentices, usually at age nine or ten, and were subjected to a regimen of work and discipline that included work days not infrequently lasting nineteen or twenty hours, during which they cleaned the store, washed dishes, helped cook, and performed all sorts of tasks for their employers. In short, the life of an apprentice salesclerk resembled that of a domestic servant. After three or four years of training, young salesclerks would be promoted to work behind the sales counter, but even then work continued to be physically demanding and exhausting.

According to a 1901 survey of shop assistants in Odessa's retail stores conducted by Andrei Gudvan, the leading authority and defender of salesclerks' interests not only in Odessa but in the Empire as well, nearly half of those surveyed were living in cold, damp basement apartments.[6] In addition, salesclerks were often instructed to drum up business by standing in the street, even in inclement weather, and coaxing potential customers into the store. It was widely believed that many came down with such debilitating illnesses as rheumatism and nervous disorders that forced them into retirement by age thirty.

Teenage and adult salesclerks worked an average of fifteen to sixteen hours a day and were required to stand at all times, even if there were no customers. Gudvan found that nearly four-fifths of Odessa's shop assistants never enjoyed a formal lunch hour and ate standing behind the counter. They were generally forbidden to eat lunch off the store premises. Shop assistants generally had no full days off and worked 350 to 355 days a year. Just under half the surveyed salesclerks earned under 20 rubles a month, with female salesclerks earning on average less than half what men received. Some women claimed it was often necessary to turn to prostitution to make ends meet and to afford the nice clothes they were required to wear in the fashionable shops and patisseries.

Salesclerks were at the mercy of their employers, who often mistreated them and subjected them to verbal abuse. In his study of Odessa salesclerks, L. O. Karmen recorded the story of one salesclerk who complained that his employer's wife had cursed him, yelling that he was "drinking her blood," because he took sugar with his tea. In another incident, a storeowner refused a clerk's request for a pay raise by insisting that it was not his fault that the employee was having difficulty supporting his family. The employer shouted, "Didn't I tell you not to marry? A poor salesclerk should not and does not have the right to marry."[7]

The OMASJS opened operations in early 1863, after a group of Jewish salesclerks decided to establish an organization devoted solely to their needs and interests as shop assistants.[8] The new mutual-aid society had the avowed aim of furnishing mutual aid to all male shop assistants and assisting members in the search for employment. The society furnished loans, pensions, medical assistance, and death benefits, and even provided stipends for the education of members' children. Having established a list of unemployed salesclerks from which it selected eligible candidates for these openings, the governing board requested that merchants and storeowners notify it of all job vacancies. The society was popular among some Jewish shop assistants, many of whom actively participated in the formulation of policy.

In the 1880s, however, the organization began to lose its democratic character and popular foundations due to the changing social composition of its membership. Whereas the majority of members of the OMASJS in the 1860s and 1870s were salesclerks and office workers, by the early 1880s many of the original members had become independent shopowners and employers of labor as they worked their way up the social ladder. Thus, the proportion of members who were salesclerks declined relative to the growing number of employers and non-salesclerks whose money and influence enabled them to assume control of the organization. For example, Samson Bernfel'd, a salesclerk who played a critical role in the establishment of the OMASJS and served as its first president, had become a wealthy merchant by the 1880s but retained his position in the organization. Similarly, Grigorii Tarnopol, who started off as a bookkeeper, remained active in the organization after becoming a successful industrialist.[9]

The policies of the OMASJS governing board in the 1880s and thereafter reflected this transformation in the composition of the society's membership: entry fees and dues were increased in order to convert the organization into a preserve of employers and elite workers of the sales-clerical profession. Predictably, as more members began to join the ranks of the propertied class, the society began to ignore the needs and interests of the average salesclerk. It is indeed ironic that the OMASJS, originally established by shop assistants to embrace as many Jewish members of the occupation as possible, became isolated from its constituency because many of its original members had the wherewithal to raise themselves into the employer class.

From the 1880s onward, the chief beneficiary of the OMASJS, as well as the mutual-aid society of gentile shop assistants which followed suit, was that small minority of the sales-clerical profession who could afford the fees and dues (already 40 rubles a year by 1903). The "aristocrats" of the profession—bookkeepers, cashiers, and other office workers—comprised the overwhelming majority of members. Although the high cost of belonging to the organization would have been well beyond the means of female salesclerks, the OMASJS, like most such organizations, nevertheless saw fit explicitly to exclude women.[10] Board members were more interested in the display of wealth (such as building an elaborate auditorium) and programs of enlightenment and culture than in promoting the economic concerns of the average shop assistant. The association boasted the second largest collection of books and periodicals in Odessa and had exceptionally rich holdings on Jewish philosophy, history, ethics, and religion in Hebrew, Russian, and German. It also sponsored concerts, theatrical performances, lectures, and public readings. As important as these activities may have been to expanding the intellectual horizons of those who took advantage of them, the organization did very little to secure improved working conditions for salesclerks or even provide the traditional sickness and death benefits. As the authors of a history of the OMASJS concluded, the organization had "barricaded itself in every possible way" from the rank-and-file salesclerk.[11] Elitism and isolation from the rank-and-file characterized the shop assistants' mutual-aid societies.

In addition to being members of mutual-aid societies, some Odessa workers, like workers in other parts of the empire, joined consumer and producer cooperatives and credit associations.[12] The Odessa Credit Association of Artisans began operations in 1902 with donations from wealthy patrons and a loan of 2,000 rubles from the State Bank; by the end of 1905 over 300 persons had borrowed over 44,000 rubles from the association.[13] Consumer cooperatives emerged in Odessa at the end of the 1890s. The most significant one before 1905 was Self-Help (*Samopomoshch'*), organized by a group of prominent merchants, bankers, and industrialists. Its organizational and operating principles were based on the Rochdale Consumer Cooperative in England. In 1900 nearly 200 workers from retail stores, factories, and workshops belonged to the cooperative and took advantage of the significant savings it offered on food, clothing, and household items. Individuals and organizations such as schools and artels could join for an entry fee of two rubles. A member was entitled to shop in either of the two stores operated by the cooperative in working-class neighborhoods. Workers were also eligible to buy shares in the cooperative, whose profits were distributed according to the amount of goods purchased and/or shares owned. Members received first-hand experience with democratic procedures when they elected delegates to an assembly of representatives, which in turn selected a governing board. Over half the members of the assembly of representatives were workers; the remaining members were bankers, industrialists, and merchants, who were able to keep worker influence in check and dominate the governing board.[14]

In contrast to Self-Help, another consumer cooperative, Bulwark (*Oplot*), limited membership to only artisans. According to a member of Bulwark's governing board, the organization attempted to unite "all local artisans on the basis of spiritual and material interests."[15] After more than two years of planning and preparation, Bulwark opened in early 1905, the first organization in Russia that entitled artisans of all crafts and trades to be members. In addition to the usual functions of consumer cooperatives, Bulwark issued loans and grants to impoverished members, allocated funds for the education of children of needy members, and established an orphanage for children of deceased members. The governing board also operated a warehouse that provided free or low-priced clothing to members and negotiated with local merchants and businessmen to offer special discounts.[16]

Producer cooperatives, also known as artels, were organizations in which members pooled their resources to establish collectively owned and operated workshops. The driving force behind the formation of producer cooperatives in Odessa was N. V. Levitskii, a Jewish lawyer and social activist who helped form dozens of cooperatives among agricultural laborers throughout Kherson province during the mid-1890s. In 1900, Levitskii turned his attention to urban workers and advocated the establishment of producer cooperatives among male artisans. At the 1900 All-Russian Congress of Artisanal Industry, Levitskii criticized the delegates for devoting too much attention to craft-masters and neglecting the interests of "working artisans" (apprentices, journeymen, and garret-masters). According to Levitskii, workers could best improve their working conditions through independent initiative and activity (*samodeiatel'nost'*). He argued that improvements would not occur "while there is no independent initiative, no consciousness among workers of themselves as a class, [and] no conviction that it is necessary to wake up, work, and develop your inner strengths. It is impossible to seek salvation from without."[17] Producer cooperatives, claimed Levitskii, would assist impoverished and unemployed artisans obtain credit so they could produce and market their wares and thereby enable these workers to avoid exploitation.

Official sanction from the local authorities, most notably city governor Petr Shuvalov, played a crucial role in Levitskii's attempt to establish producer cooperatives. At the opening ceremony of the first artel in 1900, Shuvalov and thirty woodworkers exchanged toasts. The city governor wished the members success and expressed his hope that the new organization would help workers "improve their situation and free them from exploitation."[18] Shuvalov's favorable attitude encouraged more workers to form producer cooperatives. At the openings of other cooperatives, local religious leaders conducted services and public prayers, which were followed by luncheons at which Shuvalov and other government officials delivered short speeches. By the end of 1900, Levitskii had helped establish sixteen producer cooperatives in Odessa; by the beginning of 1902, the number had grown to about forty. They included artels for bakers (a separate one existed for matzo-makers), shoemakers, housepainters, tailors, bookbinders, and other artisans. Membership, which was the preserve of men, was small, usually not exceeding a few persons in each cooperative, though a few boasted memberships of several dozen. Total membership in all artels ranged from 700 to 800 men.[19]

Generally speaking, trades characterized by a high incidence of subcontracting and middlemen formed the core of the membership of the producer cooperatives. Tailors, shoemakers, woodworkers, stonemasons, roofers, and housepainters were especially attracted to artels because the pooling of capital, equipment, tools, and labor in a joint venture offered them an alternative to unemployment and "sweated" labor. Artel members had access to a regular supply of raw materials, tools, and equipment that were beyond their financial means as individuals.

Since many of these crafts and trades were dominated by Jewish workers, it is not surprising that Jews were in the vanguard of the producer cooperative movement. One observer estimated that Jews comprised 60–65 percent of the total membership of producer cooperatives in Odessa, while in some artels, such as the eight cooperatives of bread bakers, virtually all members were Jewish. In 1901 Levitskii reported to the provincial factory inspector that Jews had organized twenty-one of the thirty-two producer cooperatives that he had helped establish in Kherson province during the previous year. Levitskii was proud of the high participation rate of Jews in his organizations, stressing that the formation of cooperatives that included both Jewish and gentile workers played an important role in lessening religious and ethnic tensions. Although Jews and gentiles tended to form separate organizations, Levitskii pointed to the existence of several mixed cooperatives as the first step in eliminating religious and ethnic antagonisms. He believed that the harmony of economic interests exhibited in the principles and operations of producer cooperatives would contribute to social calm and stability.[20]

This sanguine prediction was given credence at a conference of Odessa producer cooperatives in early 1902. Convened by Levitskii with Shuvalov's permission, the meeting attracted some 600 members of thirty-two artels. The conference was marked by a comradely spirit that overshadowed whatever prejudices and tensions may have existed, and the participants exhibited near unanimity on all issues discussed. Virtually all the representatives of the producer cooperatives reiterated their support for the principles of collective production and equal wages to all members in order to preserve the spirit of equality. They also addressed the need to establish a credit association for all artels so that individual producer cooperatives could buy supplies. One Russian woodworker with a communalist bent even suggested that artel members buy a "house where they all could gather and live as brothers."[21]

Despite official approval and Levitskii's efforts, producer cooperatives, like most other legal labor organizations in the pre-1905 period, enjoyed only modest success and did not become a permanent fixture of the organized labor movement. The initial enthusiasm displayed by several hundred workers from 1900 through 1902 flagged in 1903, when no new artels were established and the existing ones began to declare bankruptcy and disband. Membership in the woodworkers' artel, which peaked at eighty men, fell to thirty-eight by the end of 1904. The onset of economic recession and the outbreak of war in 1904 no doubt played a role in these failures. But the producer cooperatives also fell victim to structural problems and weaknesses. They lacked sufficient operating capital and experienced difficulties obtaining credit at reasonable rates. Forced to turn to usurers for financing, several artels went bankrupt by the end of 1902 when their creditors called in debts for the nonpayment of bills. Producer cooperatives also had difficulty competing with subcontracting workshops that produced ready-made merchandise at lower cost. If the artels, notorious for shoddy craftsmanship, had produced high-quality goods, they would have no doubt attracted more business. Artels apparently could not attract the membership of skilled workers, since bankrupt independent craftworkers and experienced journeymen preferred to work as wage earners in someone else's workshop, where they commanded higher wages than they could earn as members of a producer cooperative. The principle of equal wages regardless of expertise and experience did not, as a rule, appeal to skilled workers, especially those who had once owned their own workshops. Hence, the producer cooperatives were dominated by workers whose level of skill was often inadequate.[22]

Finally, many artels underwent transformations that challenged their status as producer cooperatives in the pure sense of the term. A major organizational principle of producer cooperatives was the prohibition of hired labor; employment of nonmembers violated the claim that artels did not exploit labor. For the most part, artels in Odessa adhered to this stricture, but some organizations found it necessary to hire nonmember workers in order to survive. The tailors' and woodworkers' producer cooperatives, for example, employed temporary workers during their respective peak seasons. Otherwise, they would have failed to meet deadlines or would have been forced to refuse work. These artels found it more convenient and profitable to hire additional workers for a specified period of time and rate of pay than recruit new members. Since each new member could mean a corresponding reduction in every member's share of the profits, there was a reluctance to take on new members. The limited consumer market and competition from subcontracting workshops did not justify, from the perspective of artel members, the enlargement of the cooperatives. The use of hired labor altered the character of the cooperatives and undermined their democratic and participatory nature, turning some of them into part-time capitalist enterprises that, as it was put at the time, exploited labor.[23]

If the vast majority of workers remained outside the framework of these short-lived groups, those who did participate learned something about the value of voluntary association and mutual assistance. Self-help and self-activity were indeed essential strategies in a society where government and employer offered little assistance in the event of illness, accident, or unemployment. Mutual-aid societies, producer and consumer cooperatives, and credit associations may have been weakly developed in Odessa, but they did demonstrate the benefits of organization to some workers. In 1905, Odessa workers built upon this awareness when they challenged the prerogatives of management and the autocracy.

Educational Pursuits

The horizons of many workers in Odessa were also broadened by attending the public lectures, discussions, and concerts that philanthropic, educational, and cultural organizations organized in workers' neighborhoods. These events, held in special People's Auditoriums that the city built in the late 1880s and 1890s in Peresyp, Slobodka-Romanovka, and Moldavanka, attracted all kinds of workers. Towards the end of the nineteenth century, growing numbers of workers took advantage of the spread of literacy throughout urban Russia and regarded their attendance at events sponsored by the People's Auditoriums as a means of boosting their self-esteem, enhancing their image in the eyes of both fellow workers and social betters, and reducing the social and cultural distance between workers and educated society. Not surprisingly, it was skilled workers who comprised the bulk of the pupils who enrolled in evening and weekend courses, where they studied literature, history, economics, geography, the physical sciences, and even "cosmography."[24]

Efforts toward self-improvement required dedication and determination on the part of the workers who attended the events at the People's Auditoriums. Not only did they often have to attend classes and lectures after an arduous day of work, but they frequently had to travel long distances in inclement weather to an area that lacked public transportation. Some night classes, for example, were conducted in a building located at the extreme end of Peresyp, where the streets were often impassable because of mud and puddles. It took workers coming on foot from neighborhoods outside Peresyp at least an hour to reach this auditorium. An additional obstacle was the ridicule and scorn of other workers, who sometimes poked fun at these efforts at education and enlightenment.[25]

For those workers who braved the elements and peer pressure, the rewards could be rich. As one survey of Jewish workers attending evening classes found, "They all want to understand more, to learn how to act in life . . . in order not to be 'dark and blind.'"[26] Attending these cultural events exposed workers to a world of ideas from which their less inquisitive coworkers remained isolated. By the end of the nineteenth century, nearly three-fifths of Odessa's residents aged seven or older could read and write, a state of affairs that compared favorably with other Russian cities.[27] As Daniel Brower has written, "The spread of literacy and other manifestations of urban culture played a direct role in forming bonds around new political ideas and political movements."[28] The emergence of a literate urban culture in which an increasing number of workers participated broke down barriers between workers and educated Russian society by facilitating the flow of ideas and information. But at the same time it also enhanced the potential for social and political instability, as radical ideas began to circulate more freely among workers who were breaking free of the cultural isolation that typified lower-class urban life.

Some of these workers began to realize that the world was not immutable. As a one metalfitter wrote of his experience in a People's Auditorium: "At the end of a lecture we left as if we were reborn. We began to gain an understanding that we . . . had every right to a life like the one lived by those who command us. And we began to expound upon our thoughts in words, something which we had not done previously."[29] Workers who attended lectures, Sunday schools, and night classes met radical students and socialists who "pointed them along the political path." Labor organizers in Odessa recognized the role of these educational pursuits in politicizing the workers. As one activist noted, "the conscious workers, the worker-*intelligenty* went to schools, lectures, and courses at the People's Auditoriums."[30] In the words of Iurii Steklov, a leading Odessa Marxist organizer in the 1890s and later a prominent Bolshevik, workers attending public readings threw away the "chaff" and kept the "wheat."[31]

Illegal Labor Activities: Workers and Revolutionary Parties

Odessa workers did not limit their activities to legal organizations. Many were also attracted by the entreaties of local revolutionaries. The revolutionary underground in Odessa had a rich and colorful history, and workers found themselves the object of concerted organizational efforts. Although the number of workers who actually contributed to illegal strike funds and joined clandestine revolutionary circles never amounted to more than several hundred in the decade or so before 1905, participation in one of the various socialist organizations was the most significant expression of political opposition among Odessa workers in this period.

Populist Precursors

Odessa's history as a center of revolutionary activity stretches back to the 1820s, when Greek nationalists established a secret society to help plan their drive for independence from the Turks; in the next half-century, many Bulgarian, Polish, and Ukrainian nationalists centered their operations in Odessa. The lively activity of the port and the steady stream of foreign ships and nationals no doubt proved conducive to the smuggling of all kinds of contraband and stymied efforts by officials to block the entry of unwanted goods and ideas into Russia. Beginning in the 1850s, the city served as a major entry point for the illegal publications of Alexander Herzen. In the early 1870s, a branch of the First International was operating in Odessa, as well as an offshoot of the Chaikovskii Circle, led by the populist Mark Natanson. In one humorous incident, the Odessa police in 1872 arrested an English merchant named Marx after noting that a Karl Marx was on the secret police's list of people forbidden to travel in Russia. During the 1870s and continuing for the next several decades, labor unrest became a perennial problem for employers and officials as disparate groups of workers struck over wages, hours, and other conditions of work and sometimes formed strike funds. Several dozen strikes, most of them shortlived, were recorded from the mid-1860s until century's end.[32]

Odessa was also home of the South Russian Workers' Union, the first political organization in Russia devoted primarily to the interests of urban workers. Established in the mid-1870s by E. O. Zaslavskii, a revolutionary with connections to Petr Lavrov, the Union set out to organize factory workers and artisans throughout southern Russia. In late 1875 its leaders were arrested and its activities suspended, but only after over 100 workers had been organized in several large metalworking plants, the railway workshops, typographies, and other assorted enterprises. Several strikes over wages and hours were conducted and ties with other Black Sea port cities were established.[33] Interestingly, though the organizational life of the South Russian Workers' Union was short, many of the enterprises that fell under the sway of Odessa revolutionaries in the 1870s remained hotbeds of radical political opposition and labor strife for the next several decades. This was particularly true of the railway workshops, the Henn Agricultural Tool and Equipment Factory, the Bellino-Fenderikh Iron Foundry, and the Russian Steam Navigation and Trading Company; workers in these enterprises would play significant roles in strike movements after 1900.

Throughout the remainder of the 1870s and into the 1890s, the South Russian Workers' Union was emulated in Odessa and nearby cities by surviving members and new converts to the revolutionary cause. These revolutionary activists formed new circles, encouraged strikes, and attempted to revive a movement that would embrace the workers of southern Russia. Members of the People's Will, the terrorist organization responsible for the assassination of Tsar Alexander II in 1881, also enjoyed some success among Odessa workers and students during the early 1880s and gained a degree of notoriety after killing a military prosecutor in 1882, despite the decline of the organization on the national level.[34]

Social Democracy

Like many other revolutionaries in Russia in the 1880s and early 1890s, some Odessa socialists slowly but steadily began to lose faith in the principles and tactics of populism and terrorism. In the mid-1880s, radical university students established ties with D. N. Blagoev's Party of Russian Social Democrats, the first avowedly Marxist organization in Russia, and had some contact with the Swiss-based Emancipation of Labor Group led by Georgii Plekhanov and Pavel Axelrod. The first social-democratic circles in Odessa emerged in the late 1880s among university and high school students who gathered in small Marxist study groups. They increasingly embraced Marxism as the most promising political strategy and devoted their time to reading and discussing the works of Marx, Engels, Plekhanov, and Axelrod, along with the more traditional fare of Herzen, Lavrov, Mikhailovskii, and Chernyshevskii. It was not until 1890, however, that Odessa's fledgling Marxist groups succeeded in making contact with workers.[35]

In that year, David Gol'dendakh (later known as the prominent Bolshevik D. B. Riazanov) established the first Marxist circle in Odessa that included workers. Like Social Democrats (SDs) elsewhere in Russia, Gol'dendakh led discussions about the workers' movement in Western Europe and exposed the members of his circle to Marxist concepts of political economy and historical materialism in an effort to train a group of politically conscious students and workers who could then form new circles and propagandize among other workers. According to judicial reports preserved in Soviet archives, these meetings were attended by about twenty workers. The police arrested Gol'dendakh in 1891, but not before he had successfully established a well-stocked library of socialist literature and organized several circles.[36]

If the social-democratic movement in Odessa did not entirely collapse after Gol'dendakh's arrest, this was largely due to the efforts of the students Iurii Steklov (Nakhamkes) and Grigorii Tsyperovich, members of one of Gol'dendakh's circles who had escaped arrest. By 1893, using former contacts with workers and enlisting the support of politically radical students from a Jewish vocational high school, Steklov and Tsyperovich were able to reestablish a network of circles among factory workers and artisans. Circles were formed among machinists and metalfitters of the Russian Steam Navigation and Trading Company, bootmakers, sailors and stokers of various shipping lines, construction workers, and skilled workers of the railway workshops.[37]

Like their predecessors, the circles of Steklov and Tsyperovich enjoyed only modest success. Membership was fluid and attendance at meetings irregular. We should bear in mind that the recruitment of large numbers was not their purpose; the emphasis was on finding and training individuals who demonstrated potential leadership qualities as propagandists and organizers. Steklov and Tsyperovich also prohibited the recruitment of Jews and women, a policy that further limited the size of their circles and helped determine the composition of Odessa Social Democracy for several years to come.

The interdiction against Jews needs explanation, especially since so many organizers and leaders of the early circles in Odessa had been Jews, as was Steklov himself. He and Tsyperovich excluded Jewish workers because they were afraid of alienating Russian workers who might harbor anti-Jewish prejudices. They also hoped to vitiate government claims that the movement was the result of

"Jewish intrigue." Hoping to combat the revolutionaries by playing upon the prejudices of Russian workers, police officials in Odessa tried to discourage Russians from joining revolutionary organizations by promoting anti-Semitism.[38] Whether police tactics corresponded to the workers' sentiments or influenced their behavior cannot be determined, but the fact that both Marxist organizers and government officials acted on the assumption that workers had these biases suggests that gentile workers were indeed reluctant to associate with Jews.

The prohibition against women was based on Steklov's fear that women members would violate the rules of conspiracy by "carelessly blabbing about the affairs of the circle to their neighbors." He insisted that married members conceal their activities from their wives, lest the wives, who were undoubtedly afraid of losing their breadwinners to the police, attempt to prevent their further participation. Steklov readily admits in his memoirs that his reasoning was "noxious and unfounded," and laments the lost opportunity to establish ties with women workers.[39] Both women workers and Jews would be receptive to the efforts of SDs to organize them when these policies were abandoned a few years later.

Steklov, Tsyperovich, and several dozen leading members of their circles were arrested in January 1894, but many others managed to avoid the grasp of the police, and the survivors soon formed new propaganda circles. By the fall of 1894, two noblemen, Boris Okol'skii and Anton Boreisha, along with a train conductor named Ivan Iukhotskii, had formed the nucleus of a new group of circles that claimed membership of some 200 workers, and in early 1895 they established a new South Russian Workers' Union.[40]

The backbone of the new circles was provided by construction workers, many of whom had already been exposed to SD propaganda. Okol'skii, Boreisha, and their comrades now made it a point to address the economic grievances of construction workers by condemning the exploitative practices of subcontractors who served as hiring agents for local construction firms. Subcontractors frequently violated the law, specifically those provisions limiting the length of the workday. Addressing this problem, worker-activists in the circles obtained the signatures of some 1,000 workers on a petition they planned to present to the city governor, requesting him and the Board of Artisanal Trades to enforce the law limiting the length of the workday. Pavel Merkulov, an activist construction worker, told police interrogators that he joined the circles of Okol'skii and Boreisha because he wanted to end exploitation by subcontractors "who force us to work fifteen hours a day and make a profit on our account."[41] It is unknown whether Okol'skii and Boreisha were deliberately following the tactics of Jewish socialists in Vilna who, several years earlier, had used a 1785 statute limiting the workday for artisans as the basis of their campaign against employers, but it is clear that they were laying the groundwork for Vilna SDs who were arriving in Odessa and beginning to reorient the local SD movement toward "mass agitation" (discussed below).

Boreisha and Okol'skii saw themselves as *narodovol'tsy*. They subscribed in part to the views of the People's Will and did not wholly embrace the position of the SDs. In fact, Okol'skii stated that he had not read Marx and Plekhanov until the fall of 1894.[42] With few exceptions, Soviet historians have ignored the complex ideological stance of Boreisha and Okol'skii, since it would be embarrassing to admit that populists were still so active among workers in the mid-1890s, let alone that they organized Odessa's first May Day celebration.[43] Okol'skii, Boreisha, and their followers were not the traditional *narodovol'tsy* of a decade earlier; for example, they relegated acts of political terror and assassination to secondary importance. Instead, they focused on achieving political freedoms and economic reforms, jettisoning the emphasis on the seizure of political power in favor of struggle for a popularly elected, constitutional form of government. Norman Naimark has aptly called such measured adherents of the People's Will "*narodovol'tsy* of a new type," or "young *narodovol'tsy*," in order to distinguish them from their terrorist precursors while stressing the coalescence of political strategy and vision among Marxist and non-Marxist revolutionaries in the 1890s.[44]

The objectives of the new South Russian Workers' Union resembled those of the new-style *narodovol'tsy* and their short-lived Party of People's Rights (formed in 1893). The *narodovol'tsy* of the 1890s tried to ally with the broader Russian liberation movement in the struggle for political change. The union asserted that fundamental civil and political liberties, such as freedom of speech, association, and the press, and a government based on popular representation, were necessary for genuine improvements in the living and working conditions of workers. In the words of the union's charter: "The struggle for economic interests is impossible without political freedom."[45] Rejecting the viability of a frontal assault on the autocracy, the union moved toward the position of those Marxists who emphasized that political propaganda and education better served the cause of revolution.

Narodovol'tsy and Social Democrats did not see each other as archenemies or rivals competing for the loyalty of Odessa workers. In fact, there was a great deal of contact and shifting allegiances between the two groups. According to V. V. Straten, "no sharp differentiation between Marxists and *narodovol'tsy* existed." Some members of the Boreisha and Okol'skii circles, for example, had received their first political exposure under Gol'dendakh a few years earlier. Similarly, Moise Vinokur, who was among those arrested along with Okol'skii and Boreisha in the summer of 1895, reemerged in 1896 to direct his own Marxist workers' circle. This fluidity of boundaries between revolutionary groups is not surprising, given the formative stage of the socialist movement and the fact that most Odessa radicals shared the same heritage of political education, which stemmed from the radical traditions of the 1870s and 1880s. Many SDs active in Odessa during the 1890s acknowledged their intellectual debt to the populists and terrorists, and stressed that the legacy of these movements continued to be felt even after a genuinely Marxist movement had emerged.[46]

Before its dissolution by the government in June 1895, the South Russian Workers' Union succeeded in celebrating May Day twice, first on April 19, in order to to coincide with the May 1 celebrations in Western Europe, and then on the Russian May 1, at the Botanical Gardens, where a worker delivered the keynote address emphasizing international labor solidarity and the struggle for political freedom. In another speech, a worker whose revolutionary career dated back to the early nineties called upon workers to contribute to a recently established strike fund and to participate in work actions against construction subcontractors.[47] Together with the actions of a group of Jewish seamstresses who met separately on May 1 and formed a strike fund,[48] these efforts of the South Russian Union marked the initial phase of the transition from propaganda to mass agitation.

The abandonment of propaganda for mass agitation was one of the most important moments in the history of Marxism and the workers' movement in Russia. Outlined in *Ob agitatsii* (*On Agitation*), the famous pamphlet written in 1893 by the Vilna Marxist Arkadii Kremer, mass agitation was adopted in 1894 and 1895 by Jewish SDs in Lithuania and Belorussia, who were attempting to emulate the success Polish socialists had enjoyed with a similar approach in the late 1880s. Mass agitation was based on the idea that workers, under the guidance of SDs, would acquire revolutionary class consciousness by participating in the daily struggle for economic improvements. Determined to better their lives, workers would engage in mass strikes, during the course of which they would come to recognize that the economic and political struggles were inseparable and that true improvement in their working and living conditions required the overthrow of the autocracy. The tactic proved so successful in the Jewish community that SDs elsewhere in Russia adopted it for use among Russian workers, often with an equal measure of success.[49]

The Jewish SDs who provided the impetus behind mass agitation also formed the nucleus of the General Workers' Union in Russia and Poland (renamed in 1901 the General Jewish Workers' Union in Lithuania, Poland, and Russia, and commonly known as the Bund). Founded in 1897, the Bund played a critical role in the organization of the Russian Social Democratic Workers' Party (RSDWP) in 1898. The activities of Bundist organizers in Russia's northwest and the confrontation between the Bund and *Iskra* (*The Spark*), Lenin, and others, especially at the second congress of the RSDWP in 1903, are well-known chapters in the history of the Russian revolutionary movement. Less well known are the efforts of the Jewish activists who moved from the northwest region of the Pale of Settlement to southern Russia to avoid arrest and police harassment.[50] Once in the south, they applied techniques of mass agitation in cities with sizable Jewish work forces, such as Odessa and Ekaterinoslav. In Odessa, the full transition to mass agitation from propaganda coincided with the arrival of a group of Jewish Marxists and labor activists from Vilna. Drawing upon their past experience, these transplanted activists, along with several recently arrived Polish SDs who were equally well versed in agitation, set out to create strike funds and generate mass opposition to employers and government.

In contrast to their immediate predecessors, the newly arrived Vilna SDs directed their efforts specifically toward Jewish workers. Accustomed to working among Jews, they helped Jewish workers establish strike funds and organize labor unrest. They encouraged local SDs to seek employment in workshops in order to attract workers to the movement, tailoring recruitment tactics to the specific grievances of their coworkers and emphasizing that strike funds were a means of achieving better working conditions. Several women SDs from the northwest provided the impetus behind the May Day celebration of Jewish seamstresses and their decision to create a strike fund.

The efforts of the Vilna SDs in Odessa were fruitful in comparison to earlier socialist efforts. The year 1895 witnessed a flurry of organizational activity and strikes. Strike funds were successfully established among metalfitters, tinsmiths, woodworkers, tobacco workers, seamstresses, tailors, shoemakers, bookbinders, and pursemakers. With the exception of metalfitting, Jewish workers dominated these occupations. Cigarette makers, women tailors, and seamstresses conducted successful strikes, sustained in the case of the cigarette makers by a strike fund of 150 rubles.[51] The strategy of mass agitation, which sought in principle to embrace as many workers as possible, retained its appeal throughout 1896 and 1897 as more workers, frequently following the lead of SD activists, formed strike funds and libraries, debated working and living conditions, and voiced grievances and complaints.

SDs also set out to revive the defunct South Russian Workers' Union, first on Christmas eve 1896, and then again some months later, when they attempted to create a citywide organization that would unify all strike funds and workers' circles. Like its immediate predecessor, the 1896 South Russian Workers' Union did not call for the immediate overthrow of the autocracy, but limited its efforts to making workers aware of the inequities of the existing order and preparing them for political struggle. But unlike the Okol'skii-Boreisha organization, the 1896 union was solidly Marxist in orientation and attempted to affiliate on a regional basis with similar organizations in Kiev, Nikolaev, Elizavetgrad, and Ekaterinoslav. Yet the union managed to incorporate only a few workers' circles in Odessa into a single citywide organization and directed activities among only a small, close-knit group of workers.[52]

According to Boris Witte, procurator of the Odessa Judicial Court and brother of finance minister Sergei Witte, mass agitation "struck a responsive chord among workers."[53] Local officials noted the emergence of well-endowed strike funds, many of which were set up by enthusiastic workers independently of SD leadership. Workers were also more willing to register their grievances with factory inspectors, whose responsibility included adjudication of labor disputes. Not surprisingly, the Odessa strike funds were modeled on their counterparts in the cities of Lithuania and Belorussia. Frequently administered by a committee elected by workers rather than appointed by socialist organizers, strike funds supported workers during work stoppages and provided material assistance to members and their families during times of hunger, illness, and unemployment. Strike funds also paid for a small library, which collected and distributed legal and illegal journals, books, and newspapers in Russian, Yiddish, and Polish.

Odessa labor activists placed special emphasis on organizing workers by craft, insisting that all workers in a given trade belong to a single organization and encouraging each craft to establish its own fund.[54]

In their application of mass agitation among Odessa's Jewish workers, the Vilna revolutionaries, unlike many of their comrades in Lithuania and Belorussia, were not motivated by stirrings of Jewish national feeling or by a desire to create an independent Jewish workers' movement. One prominent Jewish activist in Vilna, according to a recent account of this period, was "never an enthusiast of the nationalist orientation."[55] As Allan Wildman asserts, their orientation "was entirely toward the Russian movement," and though they made use of their experience among Jewish workers in Vilna, "their actions were directed solely toward the construction and solidification of a Russian Social Democratic party."[56]

Specific conditions in southern Russia, and in Odessa in particular, encouraged this approach. First, the language barrier was less formidable in Odessa than in the northwest region of the Pale, where Jewish organizers were often unable to communicate with Lithuanian- and Polish-speaking workers. In Odessa the presence of a sizable Russian-speaking labor force could lead to greater contact between Russian workers and those Jewish SDs who knew Russian. Petr Garvi, an assimilated Jew, writes that he did not know Yiddish very well. It was presumably for this reason that, as one of his first tasks as an SD organizer, he was instructed to organize Russian workers in a small furniture factory.[57] Second, like the SD organizers, Jewish workers in Odessa, despite occupational and residential segregation, were relatively less isolated from Russian culture and more comfortable with the Russian language than their coreligionists in the northwest. Jewish organizers did not need to rely solely on Yiddish when communicating with Jewish workers, although there is some evidence of Russian-speaking SDs being stymied by encounters with Jewish workers who did not understand Russian.[58]

Thus, the need for an independent Jewish labor movement as it developed in Lithuania and Belorussia was somewhat attenuated. The high proportion of Russians in Odessa's work force, relative to the cities of the Pale's northwest, detracted from the appeal and practicality of a strategy designed to create an independent Jewish movement. The cities of southern Russia offered Jewish SDs the opportunity to find a niche in the general Russian revolutionary movement, a prospect that attracted many Jewish Marxists. As a historian of the Jewish workers' movement has written: "The old desire to serve the Russian movement had never died" for these activists.[59]

And yet the Vilna activists, as we have seen, strongly gravitated toward Jewish workers. This is not hard to explain. Given their prior activities among Jewish workers employed in workshops and small factories, the existence in Odessa of a large Jewish work force that was similarly concentrated in small enterprises, and their lack of familiarity and prior experience with non-Jewish, especially Russian, workers, it is not surprising that the transplanted Marxists chose to work among Odessa's Jews, even while refusing to make this work an end in itself. Moreover,

Jewish activists found it difficult to find work in enterprises that hired Russians, thereby restricting contact between Jewish SDs and Russian workers.

The success of the Vilna activists encouraged other organizers who had been working in Odessa for several years and had managed to avoid arrest to rethink their strategy of propaganda and adopt mass agitation. For many propagandists, the emphasis on education and the formation of an elite corps of politicized workers was a slow, tedious, and frequently unrewarding process that isolated them from the majority of workers. Mass agitation, by contrast, offered revolutionaries the exciting prospect of grassroots organizing. It also appealed to workers, who welcomed the chance to organize for improved conditions. Some workers, it will be remembered, had already begun forming strike funds, and the new tactic reinforced their practices. The new organizational technique was designed to attract as many workers as possible, especially those who had been untouched by the study circles. Inspired by the favorable response of Jewish workers, as well as by the successes of the strike movement, the SDs who had been active in Odessa prior to 1895 embraced the new strategy and worked closely with their colleagues from Vilna.

The newly arrived Vilna activists, due to their revolutionary credentials and the vacuum created by the arrest of local activists and organizers in 1894 and 1895, assumed leadership positions.[60] This enabled them to redirect the focus of the workers' movement toward the Jewish workers. As a result, Jewish workers soon formed the backbone of the SD movement in Odessa. To be sure, certain categories of skilled Russian workers, particularly in metalworking and machine-construction plants and in the railway workshops, continued to attract the attention of some veteran labor organizers. Indeed, the railway workshops remained an important object of SD organizational efforts right up to 1905, hosting numerous circles and becoming a socialist stronghold. Nevertheless, in the mid-1890s most strike funds were established by Jewish workers employed in artisanal workshops and other small enterprises.

In late 1896 and early 1897, a group of SDs with experience in both the Odessa propaganda and agitation movements began to reevaluate the focus of mass agitation. Motivated by ideology, these SD activists felt uncomfortable focusing all their energies on workshop employees and neglecting what they regarded as the more proletarian factory workers. They did not want to abandon mass agitation but to alter its focus to draw in as many workers as possible and stimulate widespread labor unrest. These revolutionaries hoped to extend SD influence beyond Jewish workshop employees and revive organizational efforts in factories where workers were concentrated in large numbers and therefore easier to reach.

According to police reports, advocates of these tactical changes clashed with the eighteen-year-old Leon Trotsky, who insisted on retaining primary focus on agitating among workshop employees. Then one of the principal Marxist organizers in nearby Nikolaev, Trotsky frequently spent time in Odessa collecting agitational literature and establishing underground contacts. He and his supporters were outvoted at a meeting in June 1897, after which SDs were supposed to devote their main attention to factory workers. Many activists balked at this shift in tactics, however, and refused to organize factory workers. Nor did the new focus necessarily mean that SDs were now agitating among Russian as opposed to Jewish workers; some found themselves working in match, cork, and rope factories, enterprises that generally employed Jewish women.[61]

By the late 1890s, many Jewish revolutionaries who had operated among Odessa's Russian workers in the pre-agitation period had vanished from the scene as a result of arrest, self-imposed exile, or departure for party work elsewhere in Russia. The SDs who replaced them continued to tailor their organizational methods to the specific characteristics and needs of Jewish workshop employees; having found the tactics successful, they believed that shifting to work among factory workers would be too challenging and difficult. Garvi emphasizes, for instance, the lack of trained organizers and agitators who could approach Russian workers.[62]

This pattern of recruitment continued to characterize the efforts of Odessa SDs after the founding congress of the RSDWP in 1898 and into the next century. As one SD organizer stated in reference to the 1900–1901 plan to establish parallel strike funds in factories and artisanal workshops, "such a division did not come about since the agitators, being more familiar with artisans, would not give up active agitation among them."[63] Writing in 1900, Steklov noted that the SD movement "is still unnoticeable in the factories." He added that the situation among factory workers was "very sad," and concluded that there was very little promise for a strong labor movement among them.[64] The report on the Russian revolutionary movement presented to the 1900 International Socialist Congress stated that workshop employees comprised the bulk of the membership in SD organizations in Odessa.[65] One result of this focus was the continued predominance of Jews in the Odessa social-democratic movement after 1900, and another was the isolation of Odessa's Russian workers from Social Democracy. With few exceptions, SD activists never made a concerted effort to recruit factory workers.[66]

In late 1901 and early 1902, this issue hastened the split of the Odessa Committee of the RSDWP, then under the leadership of several SDs who opposed the positions advocated in *Iskra* by Lenin, Plekhanov, and Iulii Martov. *Iskra*'s supporters, seeking to wrest control from the Odessa Committee, separated from the Committee in late 1901 to form the Iskraite Southern Revolutionary Group of Social Democrats. They attacked the Committee for failing to organize factory workers and, in language reminiscent of the disputes of the mid-1890s, for concentrating efforts so exclusively on artisans. The breakaway group asserted that there were no "special difficulties involved in the organization of factory workers." Its members outlined specific plans to agitate among factory workers, defining their task as the "development of a mass movement among factory workers through written and oral agitation and propaganda."[67]

Far more was at stake than organizing factory workers. The debate between the Committee and Group was a smokescreen for Iskraite leaders, who were really dissatisfied with the focus on strike funds and work actions. At this time

Iskra advocated a political agenda that sought to ally with the student movement and the non-Social Democratic Left. Daniil Novomirskii recalled that when he first became involved with the Odessa Committee he was instructed not to discuss politics or "curse the tsar."[68] Unlike the Iskraites, who distributed revolutionary leaflets on the streets and even disrupted theater performances by tossing socialist literature from balconies, the Committee shied away from open political demonstrations and street rallies, claiming that such actions would invite police reprisals and endanger the party.[69] Following *Iskra*'s lead, the Group hoped the workers' movement in Odessa would link up with the recent upsurge in political opposition among educated society, particularly among students, a strategy that SDs were then adopting in other parts of Russia.

Since the labor movement was quiescent at this time, Lenin and other *Iskra* leaders pinned their hopes for a new wave of revolutionary unrest on the revived radicalism of students and relegated the economic struggle of workers to the background. In the words of the 1902 manifesto of the Southern Revolutionary Union (as the group now called itself), Social Democracy in Odessa must ally "with the most radical wing" of Russian society and devote its "attention to the revolutionary student organizations."[70] The failure to specify urban workers as an object of socialist attention is quite striking, and reflects the belief of Lenin and others that the revolution would be better served by cooperating with left-leaning, non-proletarian groups. By embracing the student movement, the Iskraites were moving scarce resources and manpower away from the labor movement. As a result, they failed to make significant inroads into factories to exploit whatever appeal they may have had for factory workers. That the Southern Revolutionary Union did not protest these policies is indeed curious and not readily explained.

The feud between the two factions of Odessa Social Democracy ended in early 1903 when the Southern Revolutionary Union, heeding the wishes of Lenin and Martov, reunited with the Committee, which acknowledged its "full solidarity with the views of *Iskra*."[71] But this reconciliation, which was brittle at best, did not shift the focus of agitation. Despite the emphasis on factory workers in their rhetoric, Iskraites still found themselves organizing strikes among the same kind of workers, many of them artisans who had been receptive to the Odessa Committee. Tailors, seamstresses, woodworkers, and workers in candy and tobacco factories remained the focus of many organizers. Declared intentions notwithstanding, adherents of factory agitation and organization remained dependent on existing connections with workshop employees and never cut their ties to those workers who had traditionally formed the core of SD support in Odessa. The efforts of Rozalia Zemliachka, then a prominent Iskraite in Odessa, and her comrades to conduct "systematic agitational and propaganda work among the workers of the Peresyp district" are put into question by a report stating that the Party's literature "rarely reaches Russian factory workers," most of it going to students, Jewish artisans, and the general public. Indeed, on the eve of 1905, the Party was still actively concentrating on workshops in the city's central districts, along much the same lines Odessa SDs had pursued in the 1890s and after the turn of the century.[72] By early 1905 Odessa SDs had still not managed to establish firm roots in the outlying factory districts.

Other Socialist Organizations

The SDs were not the only revolutionaries active in Odessa before 1905. Other Marxist and non-Marxist socialist groups competed with the main tendencies of Social Democracy for worker support. Particularly in 1902 and 1903, the SDs had to fight off a range of challenges to their authority. The first major challenge came from adherents of *Rabochaia volia* (Workers' Will), a significant opposition movement within Russian Social Democracy after the turn of the century. *Rabochaia volia* attracted workers who resisted the domination of local SD organizations by the intelligentsia and resented the centralism that characterized Party affairs. Asserting its right to elect Party officials, this workers' opposition group split from the Odessa Committee in the spring of 1902 to form the Odessa Social Democratic Union "Rabochaia Volia" under the leadership of V. Trakhtenberg. For a few months *Rabochaia volia* acted as a separate organization, issuing proclamations and leaflets numbering in the thousands in its own name. Then, in September 1903, the organization's leaders announced their adherence to the views of *Iskra* (now controlled by the Mensheviks) and rejoined the Odessa Committee. The reversal indicated their opposition to the Bund and their recognition of the need for a strong centralized revolutionary organization to lead the workers' movement. *Rabochaia volia* had participated in the general strike of July 1903 (discussed below), but lack of funds and influence among workers convinced them that only a unified social democratic movement under the direction of *Iskra* would lead to "victory over tsarism and the oppression of capital."[73]

In early 1903 the precarious unity of the city's SD movement was further threatened by the establishment of an Odessa branch of the Bund. Though individual Bundist organizers had been active in Odessa since the turn of the century, the Bund had refrained from formally establishing a local branch. Circumstances in Odessa, particularly the fact that Yiddish was less essential as an organizational tool there than in the northwestern region of the Pale, attenuated the need for a special Jewish labor party. In the northwest, because the social democratic movement was led by Jewish activists and had emerged first among Jewish workers, the Bund continued to hold sway among organized workers. But in Odessa and elsewhere in southern Russia, where the presence of SDs predated the formation of the Bund, SD organizations already served the needs of Jewish workers. And, since the labor forces there were more ethnically mixed than in the northwest, fewer workers and activists recognized the need for a separate Jewish socialist movement.

Before 1903, official Bundist party policy had discouraged the formation of local branches in regions where other SD organizations already existed to represent the interests of Jewish workers. This policy remained in force until the

Second RSDWP Congress in 1903, when the Bund, having lost its campaign to maintain autonomy within the Party, withdrew from the RSDWP. But even before this schism, Odessa Bundists, aware of the brewing conflict, had begun to emphasize the need for an independent Jewish SD organization. On January 1, 1903, they held a holiday celebration at which plans for a formal Bund committee were discussed. During the next several months Bundists in Odessa busied themselves with the formation of their local organization. By early 1904, they had affiliated themselves with the Bund's Central Committee and claimed a membership of 400. In early 1905 the Bund, in recognition of the growing significance of its Odessa branch, bestowed rights of full membership on it and recognized it as a full-fledged "committee" (rather than a mere organization). Considered by the Mensheviks to be their most serious competitors, the Bund made significant inroads among Jewish workers, particularly those who had recently settled in Odessa from the northwest and were accustomed to agitation in Yiddish. The Bund was also active in rallies and demonstrations (especially in synagogues), May Day celebrations, and the strike movement (including the 1903 general strike).[74]

Odessa Social Democracy also faced rivalry from the Socialist Revolutionaries (SRs) and anarchists. A local branch of the SR movement was established in Odessa in the fall of 1901 and soon began to vie with the SDs for the support of Odessa workers. Michael Melancon has convincingly demonstrated that the SRs, far from limiting their focus to peasants and the problems confronting rural Russia, developed a program and strategy that had strong resonance among a wide range of urban workers.[75] A serious challenge to SD influence, the SRs organized dozens of branches throughout urban Russia, granting high priority to the establishment of party cells in factories. As late as January 1902, according to a gendarme's report, the Odessa Group of SRs was "still very small in numbers." Indeed, the SRs had not yet built up an efficient organization, going so far as to request assistance from local SDs in distributing their pamphlets.[76] But half a year later, as a full-fledged organization within the SR party, the Odessa SRs stepped up their agitational and propaganda work, winning favor among the workers of several enterprises, including some typographical workers, shop assistants, bakers, and workers in a sugar refinery. The SRs cooperated with local SDs in the February 1902 demonstration commemorating the peasant emancipation as well as in the May Day celebrations of 1902 and 1903. They also played a direct role in a 1903 strike at the Brodskii sugar refinery, a large factory in the Mikhailov district that employed 850 men, most of whom were seasonal peasant migrants particularly attracted to the programmatic appeals of the SRs.

In late 1903, radical elements known as the "Intransigents" (*neprimirimye*) left the parent SR organization and advocated greater reliance on terrorism, forming one strand of Odessa's budding anarchist movement.[77] Although anarchists had begun to appear in Odessa in the spring of 1901, they only became very active in 1904, after the police liquidated a group of Makhaevists. The Makhaevists were followers of the revolutionary Jan Machajski, an opponent of

Marxism who criticized the dominant role of the radical intelligentsia in the labor movement and opposed the involvement of workers in the struggle for "bourgeois-democratic" political reforms. With its emphasis on action and the general strike as appropriate revolutionary tactics, Makhaevism appealed to many youths. The Makhaevist group served as the nucleus of Odessa's anarchist movement, soon giving birth to anarcho-syndicalist and anarcho-communist factions. Novomirskii—who was a member of the Odessa Committee in 1901 and 1902 and who headed the Odessa anarcho-syndicalists in 1905—frowned upon the ineffective "motiveless terror" of anarcho-communists. His group, he later boasted, had been successful among factory workers, dockworkers, merchant marines, and bakers. The activities of anarchists in Odessa alarmed local police, who kept close tabs on known anarchists and executed a series of raids on anarchist circles in 1904 and 1905. It was not until late 1905, however, that anarchists began to play a major role in social and political unrest.[78]

Zubatovism and the 1903 General Strike

Where the SDs and other revolutionaries experienced difficulties, the Zubatov movement saw promise of success. The failure of the Odessa SDs to establish a network of solid party organizations among Russian factory workers helped the Zubatovist trade-union movement of 1902–1903 secure a foothold in the city's factory districts. The famous experiment in police-directed "unions" conducted by Sergei Zubatov, chief of the Moscow Okhrana, was designed to undermine the appeal of revolutionary parties by offering workers the opportunity to organize for their economic and cultural advancement under police supervision. Zubatovist unions offered workers the legal right to form collective associations empowered to seek concessions from their employers. The Zubatov unions were among the largest and most successful workers' organizations in the pre-1905 period, and in Moscow, Odessa, and elsewhere they provided the organizational experience and glue that laid the foundation of many of the trade unions that workers established during 1905.[79] Though the Zubatov unions received official government sanction, their actions were revolutionary in consequence and help illuminate the nature of workers' aspirations, politics, and organizations before 1905.

Agents of Zubatov appeared in Odessa in 1902. The first organizer to test the receptivity of workers to Zubatovism was Meer Kogan, who reported that a cross-section of the labor force was attracted to the Zubatovist program. Iurii Volin, another Zubatovist agent, soon joined Kogan and, after several weeks, concluded that Odessa provided fertile soil for the establishment of Zubatovist unions. Even though he admitted that some 1,500 persons belonged to one of the SD groups active in the city, Volin nevertheless termed this number "insignificant," claiming that the SDs had not succeeded in planting strong roots. Volin deliberately underplayed the existing network of SD strike funds in order to convince his superiors that the time was ripe to organize Odessa workers. Zubatov gave him the green light and, by the end of July 1902, Volin and Kogan had established the Independent Labor Group (later renamed the Independent Labor Committee). By spring 1903, tsarist officials reported a membership of 2,000 in Odessa's Zubatovist unions, although some estimates placed the number of workers involved in the movement at 6,000.[80]

Viewed from the standpoint of ethnicity and locus of organizational strength, the Zubatov experience in Odessa was almost the mirror image of the SD one. In general, Russian factory workers, particularly in the major metalworking and machine-construction plants of Peresyp and the Port Territory, responded enthusiastically to the overtures of Zubatovist organizers. The Zubatovites had little trouble attracting those Russian factory workers who had no contact with SDs before Zubatovist agents made their appearance. One Zubatov organizer wrote that an "enormous gray mass of Russian workers did not know what an 'organization' was" until the Zubatovites began their union activities.[81] The decision by the Zubatovites to locate their headquarters in Peresyp, where thousands of workers remained untouched by Social Democracy and had probably never been exposed to the propaganda of any revolutionary organization, was a calculated move to establish a foothold in a district ignored by the revolutionaries.[82] The Zubatov movement added to the isolation of Odessa SDs from the city's factory workers, impinging on the future organizational efforts of Mensheviks and Bolsheviks alike. In the aftermath of Zubatovism, Odessa SDs experienced their greatest (though by no means insurmountable) difficulties organizing those workers in enterprises where the Zubatovist unions had been most successful.

The union's quasi-official status and police protection undoubtedly assisted the Zubatovites in their organizational efforts. But the real appeal of Zubatovism lay in its emphasis on workers' immediate economic grievances and aggressive strike strategy.[83] As we have just seen, *Iskra* policy at this time had shifted from economic to political agitation and did not exert its full energies in factory districts. Displaying an overwhelming desire to organize in defense of their economic interests, many workers not surprisingly turned to the Zubatovist unions. By the same token, because most Odessa SDs continued to organize in artisanal shops, Jewish workers did not feel compelled to abandon Social Democracy for Zubatovism. The Zubatovites failed to attract Jews to their unions, a failure that stands in stark contrast to the successful recruitment of Jewish workers by Zubatovist unions in some cities of the western and northwestern regions of the Pale. The conspicuous absence of Jewish workers at their organizational meetings prompted one organizer to lament that "it is unusually difficult to work among Jewish workers."[84] Thus, when his agents in Odessa informed Zubatov in July 1902 that "the majority of revolutionary workers are journeymen," they were merely acknowledging a set of circumstances that had been shaped by the tactics of SDs since the mid-1890s.[85]

The Zubatovites also enjoyed a significant following among Russian workers in the railway workshops, brickyards, creameries, and tanneries, and among certain artisans such as woodworkers, printers, watchmakers, tinsmiths, bakers, and housepainters. Sailors, stokers, and longshoremen of various shipping firms also formed Zubatovist unions.[86]

The statutes of the various Zubatovist unions reflected the economic orientation of the movement and help account for their organizational success. The stated aim of the Union of Woodworkers of the City of Odessa was to "improve the material conditions of life and labor of woodworkers and raise the intellectual and spiritual level of its members by reducing the length of the workday, increasing wages, and providing mutual aid in cases of illness and need." The union also organized a lecture series on subjects pertaining to the labor movement and established a treasury to fund strikes, distribute literature, and promote organizational work. Membership was open to any woodworker who "works for wages and leads an honest life." Union affairs were directed by a council that was elected by secret ballot at a general membership meeting. The council had the right to announce a strike directed against a single employer; the right to declare a general industry-wide strike belonged, however, to all union members, and was subject to the approval of the Independent Labor Committee. In addition, each member was required to attend union meetings on a regular basis, pay dues, and submit to all union decisions.[87]

Workers were impressed by the militant, aggressive leadership of the Zubatovites. The acknowledged leader of the unions after January 1903 was Khunia (Genrikh Isaevich) Shaevich, a local Zionist who reportedly possessed a doctorate from Berlin University.[88] Shaevich was a fiery speaker who was said to cause tears to well up in the eyes of his audience when he decried the workers' deplorable working and living conditions. Under his leadership the Zubatovites adopted an uncompromising approach to labor relations and pursued a vigorous campaign of strikes during the spring of 1903. Beginning in March, the Zubatovites struck several machine-construction plants, canneries, and an iron foundry.[89] In their campaign for better working conditions, members of the Zubatov movement revealed their commitment to freedom of organization and went to great lengths to defend their unions, resorting to threats, intimidation, and even physical violence against strikebreakers.

This was especially true of the Zubatov-inspired strike at the Restel' Iron Foundry, which began in April 1903 and was still unresolved when it was subsumed by the July general strike. During the Restel' strike, workers engaged in an orchestrated campaign of violence and terror against the strikebreakers hired by management. Groups of striking Restel' workers and members of other Zubatovist unions would fall upon their replacements and beat them. In some instances workers, many brandishing knives, participated in the violence, with attacks so brutal that many victims required hospitalization. Initially, the attacks occurred after the strikebreakers had left the factory premises and had begun to go home, but when they began leaving work in groups of twenty or thirty, the strikers switched tactics. They decided to gather near the apartments of the strikebreakers before the latter left for work in the morning. There, strikers intimidated the isolated workers, threatened bodily harm, and in many instances meted out beatings to discourage them from going to the factory.[90]

The frightened strikebreakers appealed to I. I. Popov, senior factory inspector for the city, and to the police for protection. Popov vigorously protested the lawlessness of the Zubatovites and even solicited the support of Lieutenant General D. G. Arsen'ev, the new city governor. Arsen'ev ordered the Zubatovites to cease their activities, but the local police and *Okhrana* officials, adhering to instructions from Zubatov to render assistance to the Zubatovites (or at least to follow a policy of benign neglect), never implemented Arsen'ev's directive. In fact, when a group of thirty strikebreakers escaped from the clutches of one angry mob of workers and managed to find their way to the Bul'var police station, the officer in charge "cursed them and kicked them out, saying that it was forbidden to gather in crowds." He also threatened them with imprisonment if they ever again gathered in a group.[91] Another instance of police indifference to the violence of the Zubatovites occurred on May 23, when two teenagers beat a strikebreaker unconscious at the Restel' plant. The on-duty policeman heard the screams of the worker, but failed to come to his aid. He approached the injured worker only after the teenagers had left, and when the worker came to the policeman reportedly "smiled and grinned."[92]

The architects of police "trade unionism" hoped their organizations would weaken the attraction of socialism and strengthen the workers' monarchist loyalties by allowing workers incremental improvements in their material well-being. In his initial assessment of the labor movement in Odessa, Volin stated that workers were "searching for a purely economic form of organization."[93] The spring strikes directed by the Zubatovites bore out his evaluation, since workers limited their demands to purely economic issues of wages and hours. The success of the strikes in winning higher wages encouraged other workers to turn to the Zubatovites for assistance in the formation of unions. Government officials soon became alarmed, however, as the Zubatov movement spiraled out of control and was responsible for inspiring the first massive work stoppages in Odessa's history. By mid-July Odessa was in the midst of a general strike that brought all economic activity in the city to a virtual standstill as tens of thousands of workers walked off the job.[94]

The July strikes—not limited to Odessa, but occurring throughout the major industrial centers and port cities of southern Russia—were spontaneous in origin, with a strike at the railway workshops, where workers were protesting the unjust dismissal of a worker, providing the spark. The walkout at the railway workshops resulted in a partial victory for the workers and prompted dockworkers, the merchant marine, tramworkers, and workers in other enterprises to put forth demands and strike. Employers and government officials prudently pursued a series of negotiations to settle the disputes, which generally concerned wages and working conditions. Fearing a violent response, the government exercised restraint and did not resort to repressive measures to end the walkouts.

Meanwhile the strike was gaining momentum, as workers made the rounds of the city's factories, workshops, and retail stores to encourage workers to join the thousands already on strike. By July 16 and 17, the city was in the grips of a general strike. Tens of thousands of workers attended mass rallies to exchange news, formulate strike demands, and listen to the entreaties of both SD and Zubatovist orators. But efforts by the SDs to persuade workers that a revolution was necessary generally fell on deaf ears; workers tended to adhere closely to the Zubatovist program and eschew the revolutionary politics espoused by SD activists. Zubatovist workers consistently interfered with SD speakers who were trying to channel economic grievances into open opposition to the regime. As Jeremiah Schneiderman writes, "The determination of the workers to confine their demands within economic bounds found expression repeatedly during the July days."[95] Even the SDs recognized that many workers were resisting their political overtures; an *Iskra* correspondent, for example, reported that some workers attending a rally at the height of the general strike denounced the efforts of SDs to speak about politics and revolution. One worker shouted, "We don't need the Social Democrats."[96]

Odessa authorities, who had been watching the events with increasing alarm, finally took steps to restore order on July 18, a day which saw a repetition of mass rallies under the direction of the Independents and socialists. Even though the strikers exercised self-restraint and avoided violent confrontation with the police and soldiers, the military was ordered to disperse the workers and break up the rallies. Given the enormity of the task and the tense atmosphere, the dissolution of the strike was accomplished with few casualties and little bloodshed. The soldiers and Cossacks did their job without resorting to force and violence, largely because most strikers dispersed without resistance. By evening the strike had been broken, and life began to return to normal during the next several days.

Zubatovism had been thoroughly discredited. Its unions were disbanded and Zubatov himself was dismissed. As for the wage and hour concessions granted during the course of the strike, they were negligible and shortlived. For example, several workshops had their workdays shortened by as little as twenty or thirty minutes, and nowhere in Odessa was the eight-hour workday, a major strike demand, granted. Moreover, some 200 workers were arrested and dismissed for their role in the general strike; seventy-five of them were exiled to Siberia.[97]

Concluding Remarks

It is impossible to determine with precision the impact of the radical intelligentsia on the politicization of workers and the effects of socialist propaganda. Exposure to SD agitation and propaganda does not imply that workers either accepted or even understood the political message espoused by organizers. Examination of dozens of leaflets addressed to workers in the half-decade or so before 1905 reveals that revolutionaries made a concerted effort to call attention to the political lessons inherent in workers' economic grievances, specifically the links between oppressive working conditions and the existing order. Yet calls for a constituent assembly or even the right of assembly and trade unions may have rung hollow in the ears of many uneducated and uninformed workers. It is not known how many workers understood SD leaflets proclaiming that the road to a better life was a two-step process, requiring first the overthrow of the autocracy and establishment of political freedom and then a revolution that would lead to the building of socialism. Nevertheless, the values and ideas imparted by labor activists provided those workers involved in both legal and illegal organizations a framework for interpreting their problems and helped them articulate grievances with an empowering strategy, vision, and vocabulary. The involvement of Jewish artisans and Russian factory workers in the pre-1905 labor movement generated an awareness of the problems workers encountered and offered them a range of possible solutions.

On the eve of 1905 Odessa workers had been exposed to a variety of labor organizations and activists. Although only a small fraction of the work force was directly involved in any of these legal and illegal unions, strike funds, and other groups, membership rolls alone do not provide the full measure of workers' exposure to these organizations and their ideas. For every worker who joined a strike fund, attended a meeting organized by a socialist or Zubatovist activist, or went out on strike, dozens of others were undoubtedly partially caught up in these developments. They were bombarded with news of political rallies and demonstrations, and the contents of socialist and Zubatovist pamphlets, proclamations, leaflets, strike demands, and assessments of work stoppages touched the lives of workers who remained aloof yet aware of these organizations and their actions.

Some categories of workers were more likely than others to be the focus of socialist and Zubatovist organizers. In some enterprises, members of the several SD factions as well as SRs and anarchists competed with each other in organizing workers. Bolsheviks, Mensheviks, and Bundists vied for the support of the primarily Jewish work force in tobacco plants, while Bundists and Mensheviks were at loggerheads in candy factories and fought for the support of salesclerks. In bakeries, SDs, Zubatovites, and SRs set up rival organizations, and among printers both Mensheviks and Bolsheviks had appeal.[98]

The labor organizing and political activism after 1890 had mixed results. The revolutionaries enjoyed limited success in radicalizing Odessa workers and creating an organized labor movement, and most Odessa workers before 1905 did not take the giant step of embracing a position that called for the establishment of a new social, political, and economic system. Yet the efforts of revolutionaries and other labor activists did play a role in future developments of the Odessa labor movement. Workers' contact with SD strike funds, Zubatovist unions, mutual-aid societies, and producer cooperatives provided many workers with firsthand experience in conducting strikes, negotiating with employers, formulating grievances, and drawing up demands. Workers elected coworkers to represent their interests and learned the value of collective association. The workers of the Restel' Iron Foundry, for example, recognized that they could never have sustained their three-month strike without the prompt and regular payment of dues by union members. During the strike, workers with families received four and one-half rubles per week and single workers three rubles a week from the union's strike fund.[99]

The pre-1905 labor movement furnished Odessa workers with a common point of reference, furnishing in many instances the building blocks of labor organizations established in 1905 and enriching the workers' movement by providing organizational expertise. Categories of workers that had been part of the organized labor movement before 1905 would again emerge at the forefront of the workers' movement during 1905 as they engaged in work stoppages, formed trade unions, and challenged the existing political order.

4

First Stirrings

THE WORKERS' MOVEMENT FROM
JANUARY TO MAY

Historians traditionally refer to January 9, 1905 (popularly known as Bloody Sunday) as the start of the Russian Revolution of 1905. On this blustry winter day government troops opened fire on several thousand men, women, and children who had marched to the Winter Palace in St. Petersburg to present to Tsar Nicholas II a petition requesting better living and working conditions and fundamental civil liberties. When several hundred of these unarmed petitioners were killed, news of the massacre reverberated throughout the Empire, and Russian society demonstrated its solidarity with the workers of St. Petersburg. The government's rash action sparked work stoppages in many major cities, fueled liberal and revolutionary opposition to the regime, marked the rupture of the popular belief in a beneficent autocrat who defended the interests of the common people, and forced the government to embark on a path of reform.

Public tensions nearly reached the boiling point when news of Bloody Sunday reached Odessa. Local authorities and the general public girded themselves for a general strike almost immediately. On January 11, M. P. Bobrov, chief of the Odessa *Okhrana* or secret police, telegrammed his superiors in St. Petersburg that local revolutionaries were agitating for a general strike, scheduled to commence in the workshops of the South West Railroad. He reported that rumors of a general strike had been circulating since the previous day and that residents had begun preparing for it by stocking up on groceries and other necessities. The local Menshevik and Bolshevik factions, which had formally split during the first week of January, with the Mensheviks setting up the Odessa Group of the Central Committee of the RSDWP, busily issued leaflets and proclamations appealing to workers to protest the killings of January 9. The Bolsheviks called upon workers to prepare for an armed uprising. The Bund and SRs also issued public appeals for a general strike and stepped up their agitational efforts. The police, hoping to forestall the outbreak of unrest, redoubled its surveillance of known revolutionaries by arresting nearly fifty persons for strike agitation and capturing for the second time since the previous November the printing press used by the Mensheviks.[1]

The strike, however, never materialized. Odessa workers proved to be reluctant to join the wave of largely spontaneous work stoppages and protests enveloping many regions of the country, where, according to far from comprehensive official government figures, some 400,000 workers were on strike. Despite the watershed importance of Bloody Sunday in triggering labor unrest unprecedented in terms of its magnitude (over twenty times as many workers walked off the job during the first three months of 1905 as in any year between 1895 and 1905)[2] and that comprised the most potent form of opposition to the government, it must be remembered that workers in many cities remained quiescent in January and failed to confront the government.[3] With the exception of donations collected for the victims of the January 9 shootings, Bloody Sunday failed to strike a responsive chord among workers in Odessa. In some astonishing instances, workers even turned over to police fellow workers and revolutionaries agitating for work stoppages. Odessa workers evidently felt that Bloody Sunday did not merit a concerted, collective protest.

On the morning of January 13, Fridrikh Faifer and V. I. Rogov, both members of the local Bolshevik organization, entered the machine shop of the South West Railroad and sounded the work whistle. Unaccustomed to hearing the whistle at 9 A.M., workers gathered at the entrance of the shop, where Faifer began addressing them about Bloody Sunday and the need to initiate a general strike. Despite the existence of party cells in the workshops, his appeal fell on less than sympathetic ears. Workers not only refused to stop work, but several metalfitters surrounded both agitators and roughed them up. Rogov managed to escape, but Faifer was detained until the police arrived. Five compatriots distributing leaflets outside the workshops in preparation for a rally were also arrested. In another incident that same day, Varvara Salita, a Bolshevik worker in the spinning shop of a cotton-jute factory, assembled a group of fifty workers and exhorted them to demand higher wages and a shorter workday. Several workers, objecting to Salita's efforts to instigate a strike and to distribute socialist leaflets, held her for the police.[4]

The workers' favorable reaction to a patriotic appeal issued by city governor Neidhardt on January 14 provides additional evidence of a wariness to confront employers and the government, let alone engage in direct political action. In a proclamation addressed to the workers of Odessa, published in all the daily newspapers and distributed throughout the city, Neidhardt blamed the current wave of labor unrest in Russia on the Japanese, whose objective in the Russo-Japanese War, he claimed, was to capture Russian markets in the Far East. The city governor acknowledged that "we all want the war to end," but strike actions would "play into the hands of the enemy" by further weakening the economy. He noted that many factories in Odessa were already operating only two or three days a week. He warned that, if these enterprises were forced to close because of work stoppages, they would encounter difficulties obtaining credit to resume operations. The ultimate victim, according to Neidhardt, was the worker, who would "remain without work."[5]

One Odessa newspaper reported that the city governor's appeal stimulated lively discussion among workers who openly expressed their opinions, many seconding its sentiments. Local SDs admitted that Neidhardt's perspective was popular among workers because it appealed to their sense of patriotism and frightened them with the specter of unemployment. Fedor Achkanov, who came from a family of revolutionaries and was himself an SD organizer in the railway workshops, attributed worker resistance to a general strike and sympathy for Neidhardt's proclamation to "a spirit of patriotism that was still quite strong" at the beginning of 1905.[6]

Worker reluctance to engage in overt political opposition and challenge tsarist authority, especially when promoted by revolutionaries, continued into February. During the first two weeks of February, both Bolsheviks and Mensheviks once again agitated in vain for a general strike to coincide with the anniversary of the emancipation of serfs on February 19. As in January, the Bolsheviks found their agitational efforts in the railway workshops so disappointing that they set aside a day to negotiate with representatives of the railway workers in hope of convincing the workers to join the planned work stoppage. The police, however, got wind of this plan and raided the apartment where workers and revolutionaries were meeting. Most in attendance escaped, but some were detained and searched by the police.[7] It is unlikely that this particular police action discouraged workers from striking on February 19. As analysis of incidents later in the year will reveal, if workers had indeed planned to strike, the detention of fellow workers probably would have strengthened their resolve to walk off job. More likely, a February government decision to place the entire rail system under martial law raised doubts in the minds of railway workers about the wisdom of walking off the job. Martial law gave the police the right to detain workers without cause for up to a week; workers who failed to show up for work without a valid excuse faced a possible jail sentence of several months.[8] *Iskra*'s correspondent reported that workers in only ten factories struck on February 19, including those in enterprises closed by owners sympathetic to the workers' cause. Yet even these workers returned to work the next day, as the military stationed troops throughout the city.[9] The inability of SDs to stimulate worker protest supports *Okhrana* chief Bobrov's evaluation that "workers are not very active in the political struggle."[10]

The workers' refusal to respond to the appeals of revolutionaries was not due to the leftover influence of Zubatovism, as some Soviet historians have suggested, but stemmed in part from the unwillingness of workers to protest circumstances they did not regard as relevant to their immediate interests.[11] One worker, Taralenko, wrote a letter to the daily paper of the Odessa *gradonachal'stvo* in order to dispel fears of disorders. Calling most Odessa workers "peaceful," Taralenko hoped to reassure the authorities and society that no trouble was brewing among the workers. Ironically, his soothing words may have had the opposite effect, since he added that "there will be a peaceful resolution of a complex issue, namely the definite emancipation of labor from capitalist influ- ence."[12] Odessa workers exhibited their independence from the would-be tute- lage of socialists, avoiding strikes and political protest when such actions did not suit their interests and desires. It would take other developments to prompt labor unrest among Odessa's workers.

The Opening of the Political Arena and the Radicalization of Labor

Despite their unresponsiveness to the crisis engendered by Bloody Sunday, Odessa workers gradually became engaged in work actions designed to improve their material circumstances. As we noted in chapter one, several years of inflation, recession, a constricting labor market, and war had reduced real income, threw many into the ranks of the unemployed, and threatened others with the specter of partial and permanent layoffs. Yet, as many historians of strike movements have cautioned, low wages and harsh working conditions by themselves are not always sufficient causes of labor unrest. In fact, workers tend to turn away from labor activism during periods of economic downturn. Worker misery, exploitation, and poverty, however, may serve as a backdrop for the open expression of worker discontent, which is then sparked by other events.

A conjuncture of certain political developments ignited the simmering dis- content during the early spring of 1905. In order to understand what fueled this explosion of labor activism and why it slowly assumed political coloration, it is essential to focus on those local and national political events that created a climate ripe for labor unrest and affected the timing and content of worker demands. From the perspective of Odessa workers, Bloody Sunday was too remote a political issue to generate protest, but the overall political climate immediately prior to and after January 9 did combine with immediate economic grievances to stimulate work stoppages during the next several months. Not only did Odessa workers increasingly voice demands for higher wages and shorter workdays, but their struggle also challenged the power structure of the factory order. Workers took their cue from political developments on the national scene, but relied on local events to impel them into acts of defiance.

The emergence of a vocal liberal opposition movement among students and professionals was a crucial factor in motivating workers to express their griev- ances. The heightening of tensions between state and society had already begun to occur before Bloody Sunday as revolutionaries and moderates alike con- demned the war with Japan. Liberal elements centered in the zemstvos (elected organs of self-government in the countryside) and Union of Liberation (pre- cursor of the Western-style, parliamentary, liberal Constitutional Democrats or Kadet party) began to press the government to establish a popularly elected national assembly. The labor movement had been in a period of remission during 1904, as most workers rallied behind the war effort and refrained from striking. Active opposition to the government and calls for political reforms came primarily from liberal professionals, who organized a series of public banquets and lectures in late 1904.[13] A brief examination of this banquet movement will expand our knowledge of political opposition in Odessa on the eve of 1905, as well as provide insight into an issue more central to our concern, the interaction between the liberal professional opposition and the incipient labor movement. The banquet campaign served as a springboard for popular unrest in late 1904 and early 1905 and helped generate open hostility between society and the regime. The actions of various professionals—especially lawyers and doctors—who called for social and political reforms contributed to the emergence of labor protest.

Beginning in November 1904, doctors and lawyers in Odessa held a series of lectures and banquets at which opponents of the government criticized the policies of the regime. As in the rest of urban Russia, the banquets and lectures provided a common setting in which activists of various political persuasions and social backgrounds could voice their concerns about the current state of affairs and suggest possible social and political reforms. This campaign contributed to the opening of the political arena and set a tone for the revolutionary days ahead. Not only did the banquets and lectures reveal that certain professional groups were opposed to the autocracy, but the discussion of political issues in a public forum attracted members of revolutionary parties, workers, and students and developed on several occasions into popular rallies that led to direct confrontations with the authorities.

On November 18, 1904, members of the Odessa Society for the Protection of Public Health met in the auditorium of the city council, ostensibly to hear reports on public health in the city.[14] Times were such, however, that they were joined by an estimated 1,000 spectators in the crowded hall, with another 500 standing outside the building, straining to hear the speeches. Odessa Mayor P. A. Zelenyi opened the meeting by praising public interest in the meeting and commenting that he had never seen "such a gathering." The session was lively, as E. P. Vel'shtein and Mikhail Bogomolets, physicians on the Peresyp Sanitary Commission familiar with workers' living and working conditions, gave speeches that stirred up many in attendance. Although their talks covered seemingly nonpolitical topics like infectious diseases, public hygiene, and the organization of sanitary facilities, both Vel'shtein and Bogomolets used the opportunity to introduce timely political concerns by emphasizing that public health could not be improved without fundamental legal, social, and political reforms.

Vel'shtein called for the introduction of an eight-hour workday and, in a direct reference to a resolution of a recent national zemstvo congress, stressed the need for civil rights. The audience, whose cheers of "Down with the Autocracy," "Long Live Political Freedom," and "Long Live the Russian Social Democratic Workers' Party" filled the auditorium, reacted to Vel'shtein's speech with applause. Bogomolets, a Bolshevik who used his apartment as a delivery point for letters from Krupskaia and Lenin to party agents in Odessa, described in detail the poor living and working conditions of the Russian worker. In the spirit of the minimum program of the Bolsheviks, Bogomolets called upon Nicholas II to convene a constituent assembly based on "four-tail" suffrage, that is, a general, equal, direct, and secret ballot. Bogomolets admitted that such reforms were only the first of a series of changes necessary to cure "all social illnesses," but he also emphasized that they would place Russia on the "course of progress" and enable Russian workers to begin their struggle "to destroy the capitalist system."

The audience responded with more applause and shouted more anti-government slogans. When the moderator hurried to adjourn the meeting, students and SD agitators in attendance started singing the "Marseillaise" and other revolutionary songs while everyone exited into the square outside the building. Then, under the watchful eyes of the police and Cossacks, the demonstrators peacefully dispersed through the streets of the city center.

During the next several months radical students and SDs turned subsequent lectures and banquets into political rallies. But unlike the November 18 banquet, some of the subsequent ones ended in bloodshed. One such meeting occurred just two days later, at a celebration convened by the Odessa Juridical Society to commemorate the fortieth anniversary of the 1864 judicial reform. As Terence Emmons writes, this incident was "the first big street demonstration of the 1905 Revolution."[15] The meeting drew several thousand spectators, who crammed into the Society's headquarters to hear speeches about the significance of the 1864 reform. When the official meeting had adjourned, some radical students pressed on. One seized the rostrum and began an oration with these words: "It is very rare that we have the opportunity to speak about pressing current needs." Most of the audience left, but several hundred workers, students, and SD activists decided to remain in the auditorium, electing a chairman who was instructed to convey to the government demands for the immediate end of the war and formation of a four-tail constituent assembly "in order to secure the peaceful political and cultural development of Russia."[16]

A worker then mounted the stage and invited all those remaining to a demonstration outside another building, where the local chapter of the Union of Liberation was also commemorating the judicial reform. They filed out of the auditorium and began marching through the streets of the city center singing revolutionary songs, shouting antigovernment slogans, and waving red flags. Policemen and Cossacks, displaying less tolerance than they had two days earlier, used rubber sticks to disperse the demonstrators, who by this time numbered several thousand. When a sizable contingent of students, workers, and SDs managed to reassemble, they found themselves once more under attack by police and Cossacks, who now wielded their truncheons more ferociously. Several dozen demonstrators were arrested and wounded; according to the correspondent for *Iskra,* one woman was killed.[17]

Students at Novorossiiskii University also played a role in generating opposition to the autocracy, particularly after Bloody Sunday. The Coalition Council, an illegal organization founded in 1898 by radical students at the university, assumed direction of the student movement after January 9 by issuing a leaflet calling on students to express "in one form or another their protest and solidarity with the bearers of the revolutionary struggle."[18] Students responded quickly:

they stopped attending lectures, hung signs calling for a strike, and disrupted classes and other university events. In one incident on January 16, a group of students interrupted a dissertation defense, shouting "Death to the Tsar" and "Down with the Autocracy" and demanding the erection of a monument commemorating the victims of Bloody Sunday. They then marched into the street, joined now by other students. Their demonstration ended at the student cafeteria with the singing of revolutionary hymns and shouting of antigovernment slogans.[19]

Asserting that students could not study during such "momentous events," the Coalition Council called a student strike until the government implemented fundamental legal and political reforms. The police, fearing disorder at a general meeting of university students scheduled for January 24, arrested the principal student leaders on the evening of January 23. Local authorities were especially concerned that a speech given by a student visiting from St. Petersburg University on January 23 might spark a demonstration. The next day, the rector closed the university for an indeterminate length of time. The authorities also anticipated trouble among students of secondary and vocational high schools and stationed both policemen and soldiers near them. This tactic backfired as students, apparently irritated by the presence of police and soldiers, clashed with them intermittently for several days.[20] But organized opposition soon petered out among university students as the movement, deprived of its leadership and a meeting place, lost its momentum. Many students returned to their native towns and cities after the Council of Ministers confirmed the cancellation of classes until the fall.

The student protestors were joined by their professors. Soon after Bloody Sunday, several dozen university professors and lecturers established a local branch of the All-Russian Academic Union, whose platform included a call for university autonomy and academic freedom. Under the leadership of mathematics professor S. P. Iaroshenko and history professor Evgenii Shchepkin—who had a reputation for making incendiary speeches at banquets, where he frequently stood on chairs in restaurants and broke wine goblets to drive home his point—the Odessa branch supported the student strike. It affirmed that the university should remain closed until fall or until basic educational and political reforms were implemented. Influenced by the Academic Union, on January 22 the faculty-organized University Council (responsible for administering university affairs) blamed "the political frame of mind of the government" for the current wave of student unrest. The University Council also asserted that it would be unthinkable to resume classes given the agitated condition of the students, a state of affairs, it added, which would exist until there were "changes in the existing order and basic reforms."[21] Not all professors agreed with this stance, and a group of conservative professors withdrew from the University Council, leaving it under the control of liberal and radical colleagues who consolidated their positions and set out to make the council a bastion of opposition to the autocracy throughout the remainder of 1905.[22]

In mid-January, in an effort to reduce the likelihood that banquets and lectures would continue to serve as staging grounds for demonstrations, city governor Neidhardt prohibited restaurants from accepting reservations for groups of more than ten persons without his permission. But he was unable to prevent doctors and lawyers from convening meetings of their professional societies, since the statutes governing these organizations did not require them to obtain prior permission.[23] Thus, doctors and lawyers continued to hold lectures that students and revolutionaries frequently transformed into anti-government forums. In one representative incident that occurred in early February, at a lecture entitled "The Social Tasks of the Lawyer," many of the 2,000 students and youths in attendance handed out leaflets, sang revolutionary songs, and shouted anti-government slogans while four social democratic speakers seized the rostrum and delivered speeches about the revolutionary struggle. When the police arrived, the students demanded they doff their caps out of respect for the demonstrators' songs. When the police refused, some students tried to force compliance. The result was a fight between police and students marked by shoving, fistfights, and the throwing of chairs and tables. The protesters finally emptied into the street, only to clash there with a detachment of Cossacks which had surrounded the building.[24] Other public lectures and meetings also ended in violence as radical students, youths, and members of various revolutionary parties—many of whom were reportedly Jews—turned the events into confrontations where government troops exercised little restraint in their attempts to maintain order.[25]

Activity in the city council also reflected the growth of political opposition to the regime among liberal elements in society, which in turn inspired workers. Workers following events in the city council realized that some of the city fathers sympathized with their plight by protesting the government's actions on Bloody Sunday and advocating reforms that would ameliorate working and living conditions. For example, the city council expressed its sympathy and support for the January 9 protesters in St. Petersburg by allocating 5,000 rubles from the city treasury to the families of the victims of Bloody Sunday. Neidhardt, however, blocked the transfer of funds, citing violation of procedural rules, to ensure that none of the allotted money reached Petersburg.[26]

In early 1905, Mikhail Bogomolets reported to the city council on the living and working conditions of workers in the Peresyp district. Well acquainted with the lives of Peresyp workers from his medical work among them, Bogomolets assembled a remarkable array of facts and statistics about health, sanitary conditions, and the lax enforcement of protective labor legislation by the Factory Inspectorate and city officials. He condemned the absence of an adequate sewage system in Peresyp and chastised the city for allocating the "miserly sum of 5,000 rubles" for a feasibility study instead of the anticipated 400,000 rubles needed to construct adequate sewers. Bogomolets blamed such decisions on the self-interested property owners who controlled the city council, accusing them of placing the interests of the well-to-do sections of the city center before the needs of the working class suburbs. The doctor also criticized the Factory Inspectorate for ignoring health and sanitary violations in Peresyp's factories, especially in the municipal slaughterhouse where animal carcasses, left rotting in open fields, attracted vermin. Repeating a resolution of a recent Empire-wide congress of doctors, Bogomolets, in words reminiscent of his November 1904 speech, asserted that the struggle with "illness among workers is possible only under conditions of wide public control of the means of production, with participation by worker representatives in the control as well as in the regulation of factory legislation." He called for the establishment of an eight-hour workday and "toleration" of trade unions and other labor organizations, stressing that the "only guarantee of the full satisfaction of the needs of the population is for local self-government to be widely democratic." In short, he demanded a municipal duma elected by all residents of Odessa regardless of their sex and social, legal, or economic status. Bogomolets advocated the devolution of power to the municipal level and exhorted the city government to pursue a more aggressive and interventionist approach in labor relations by applying legislation already on the books.[27]

These public gatherings help explain the radicalization of Odessa workers in the spring. Even though the opposition movement among students and professionals remained for the most part distinct from the labor movement during the first half of 1905, the activities of educated Odessans raised the hopes of workers, who recognized that other segments of society were defending labor's interests by calling for social and political reforms. Odessa workers realized that they did not have to struggle alone and could depend on others to help press the government and employers for amelioration of their working conditions. In light of the extent to which opposition to the government articulated by educated members of society had spilled over into the streets, workers could not avoid concluding that they too were entitled to voice their grievances and seek redress through public protest. Not only did these public meetings and the accompanying disorders create an atmosphere favorable to the open expression of grievances and encourage workers to defy employers and the government, but workers involved in the unrest came into direct conflict with established authority.

Existing evidence does not permit any solid conclusions regarding the impact of these lectures on workers in attendance. Nor does it allow us to reach any conclusions regarding the political awareness of workers or the extent to which they agreed with or even understood the speakers' political intent. Nevertheless, it is reasonable to infer that the speeches and acts of public defiance had a cumulative effect on workers in attendance, much like the influence socialist and Zubatovist organizers previously had on workers with whom they had contact. The banquets, student unrest, and actions of the city council in late 1904 and early 1905 complemented the political messages expressed by revolutionaries and other labor activists seeking to energize workers. At these events, workers heard activists of various political persuasions call for fundamental reforms such as the convocation of a national assembly, establishment of basic civil rights and liberties, and the immediate end of the Russo-Japanese War. Public discussion of the strategy, tactics, and objectives of the political reform movement filled the lecture halls. For the first time in their lives, many members of the general public, workers in particular, were participating in meetings where issues of immediate and direct concern to them were being discussed. Workers at these meetings were becoming more and more familiar with the concepts of popular sovereignty, a constituent assembly, and civil liberties, and how these notions were intimately connected to their lives as workers and citizens. During the remainder of the year the ideas implanted at these lectures continued to percolate in the minds of workers, influenced their thought and behavior, and ultimately affected the course of events in Odessa.

Finally, government pronouncements in the aftermath of Bloody Sunday also widened the political arena and encouraged workers to discuss, formulate, and present their grievances as well as suggest ways to improve working and living conditions. The government's decision to establish several commissions to explore the causes of labor discontent prompted workers to articulate their grievances. By soliciting society's opinion on pressing issues of the day, the government was essentially inviting its subjects to participate, albeit in a limited and indirect manner, in the formulation of policy.

For the first time in its long history, the Romanov dynasty had found itself confronted with a powerful opposition movement that threatened political stability. Frightened by this independent activity and aware of the erosion of public confidence due to Bloody Sunday and the failing war effort, the government invited additional public discussion in the hope of coopting and ultimately controlling it. Odessa workers welcomed the opportunity to express in formal settings their opinions on issues of immediate concern to them. They were supported by the Mensheviks, who saw in the government's actions an opening wedge in winning significant concessions, particularly fundamental civil liberties. Although the Bolsheviks, viewing such commissions as non-revolutionary and collaborationist, discouraged workers from sending delegates or even petitioning the government, they acknowledged that workers were interested in taking advantage of the expression of the government's good intentions.[28] This altered political atmosphere offered workers a greater opportunity to organize and enhanced their sense of possibilities. Whereas Odessa workers had remained politically passive when the SDs appealed to them, they did become active when tsarist authorities sanctioned workers to address problems of direct interest to themselves.

Two government policies had particular impact. The first was the Imperial ukase and rescript of February 18, 1905, which declared that Russians had the right to send the tsar proposals "for improving the public well-being" and expressed the government's intention to convene a national representative assembly enjoying consultative powers in the legislative process. [29] The ukase and rescript, copies of which were displayed prominently on the walls and at the entrances of Odessa factories, signified the loosening of the political process and encouraged society to organize and voice its opinions. Notwithstanding the fact that details of the proposed assembly, particularly suffrage provisions, were not revealed, the promise of a popularly elected national assembly represented a significant concession by the regime as it attempted to weather the political crisis of early 1905. The second policy was the commission organized in late January by Minister of Finance V. N. Kokovtsov to examine the causes of labor discontent in the Russian Empire. The Kokovtsov Commission was empowered by the Committee of Ministers to consider workers' opinions by inviting individual workers to hearings or permitting workers to submit oral or written proposals through factory inspectors. On March 19 the Minister of Internal Affairs instructed Neidhardt to permit Odessa factory workers to assemble freely and discuss their needs so they could draw up a petition for submission to the commission.[30]

Workers Move into Action

In his review of events in Kherson Province during 1904, written in early 1905, senior factory inspector Popov warned his superiors of the possibility of labor unrest in the months to come. Despite the outward calm, factory workers in Odessa were "nervous and restless" and workshop employees were "agitated and extremely dissatisfied with their lack of rights." As for the dockworkers, they were "exasperated with their constant hunger and the despotism of artel elders and shipowners."[31] Indeed, beginning in February, certain categories of workers participated in intermittent work stoppages designed to extract concessions from their employers. Strikers, following the example of workers elsewhere in the Empire who were winning concessions from employers, at first demanded higher wages, shorter workdays, and the end of compulsory overtime. As the strike movement increasingly embraced a larger part of the work force, snowballing into a massive work stoppage by early May, workers went further by encroaching on the prerogatives of management and challenging the structure of the factory regime. Inspired in part by government intentions to investigate worker grievances, striking workers insisted on their right to elect worker deputies to represent their interests before management and participate in determining some aspects of the internal factory order.

Strikes first occurred in February, when pharmacists' assistants and workers in small enterprises throughout the city, including several tin, tobacco, tailoring, and printing establishments, struck over wages and the length of the workday. These strikes were followed, in turn, by walkouts by several hundred workers from a sugar refinery and by Georgian longshoremen at the end of the month. In some instances, strikers achieved modest victories, such as half-hour reductions in the workday, but in others management refused to accede to workers' demands. Even though these work stoppages were short-lived and episodic and did not prompt other workers to follow their examples, they did signal the beginning of the self-activization of workers and served as the prelude to more widespread labor unrest.

The actions of pharmacists' assistants is a case in point. Assistants in Odessa's pharmacies were among the first to take advantage of the possibilities for independent action and organization that were permissible in the post-January political climate. Even though the number of pharmacy workers in Odessa was very small—perhaps no more than several hundred—their partially successful strike was an early manifestation of revived labor activism. It demonstrated the benefits of collective action and, in light of their demand to share in the making of decisions regarding dismissals of workers, indicated the start of a campaign for an expanded role for labor in the running of the enterprise. Literate and skilled, pharmacists' assistants earned decent wages, but they endured workdays averaging fourteen hours and were required to work fifteen nights per month. Conditions for apprentices were much harsher, with many trainees receiving no salary and required to perform menial, custodial tasks.[32]

Aspiring pharmacists had to go through many years of schooling and practical training, including two years of university courses, before they could receive a license to dispense drugs. Many then opened up their own stores. But at the turn of the century pharmacists' apprentices and assistants found themselves threatened by the proliferation of drugstores (*aptekarskie magaziny*), which exerted downward pressure on wages in the more traditional pharmacies (*apteki*) by reducing the need for skilled pharmacists. Commercialization of the pharmaceutical industry threatened the monopoly enjoyed by pharmacy owners, as drugstores filled the demand of a rapidly expanding urban population for cheap, prepackaged medicine. Insufficient funding rendered police supervision inadequate to prevent the opening of unlicensed drugstores with unqualified workers and left new drugstore owners free to undercut the traditional pharmacists by charging lower prices. Recognizing that their position in the labor market was threatened, pharmacy apprentices and assistants, like so many other workers facing similar situations, attempted to stem the tide of proletarianization by defending their interests.[33]

In January 1905, the apprentices and assistants of twenty-two Odessa pharmacies formed the Committee of Odessa Pharmacists and drew up a list of demands designed to improve conditions. They included the introduction of a double shift so workers did not have to work nights, wages for apprentices with more than six months' experience, and a guarantee that employees would not be dismissed without good cause and the agreement of their coworkers. When the pharmacy owners rejected these demands, a strike ensued. On February 3, eighty workers in some thirty pharmacies failed to show up at work, remaining on strike for several days until employers granted a double shift. The Odessa strike occurred several days before a similar strike of pharmacists' assistants and apprentices in Moscow: together, both job actions set an example for pharmacy employees in other urban centers. As Jonathan Sanders writes, the achievements of the Odessa pharmacy workers "heightened many urban pharmacists' sense of possibilities" and undoubtedly encouraged other workers to follow suit.[34]

The influence of SDs on these work stoppages was limited; only in a few instances did the promptings of revolutionaries have direct impact. At the Valtukh Tin Factory, Mensheviks reportedly initiated a work stoppage, and in March the demands of striking Georgian longshoremen were identical with those circulated in a Menshevik strike leaflet. Tailors in a subcontracting workshop, demanding a pay hike and guaranteed employment for a year, set up a commission with employees of other tailor workshops and invited two Mensheviks to help in preparations for a strike that never materialized. With the exception of these incidents, however, strikers acted upon their own initiative, without any known prodding or assistance from any of the revolutionary parties. It is likely that some of the striking workers, many of whom were Jewish and perhaps belonged to one of the Marxist organizations operating in Odessa, drew upon the legacy of strike funds and labor unrest that dated back to the turn of the century in most of these enterprises.[35] Such connections were particularly strong among railway workers, who walked off the job in early March. Not only did they possess prior exposure to strike funds and Zubatovist unions, but their acknowledged leaders were worker-SDs.

Employees in the workshops of the South West Railroad began to pursue an aggressive strategy in February. Although SDs in January had failed to elicit a response to Bloody Sunday in the railway workshops, railway workers responded to other political developments, particularly those that invited worker input to discussions about terms of employment. They readily organized in defense of matters that they perceived to be of direct and immediate concern to their daily lives. Unrest among railway workers during February and March graphically illustrates how the changed political atmosphere after January 9 affected the mood and actions of workers in Odessa and impelled some of them to pursue vigorous courses of action designed to wrest concessions from employers.

Employees and workers of railway lines and depots elsewhere in Russia had been striking intermittently since early January. In addition to purely workplace demands for improved wages and working conditions, some striking railway workers confronted management with grievances that were primarily political in nature, since they were not wholly oriented to bread-and-butter issues, questioned managerial authority, and might even be directed against the state rather than the enterprise. Such demands included the right to strike without reprisals; recognition of worker-controlled deputies as a permanent feature of labor-management relations; freedom of the press, speech and assembly; formation of a four-tail constituent assembly; and the granting of equal rights to women.[36]

Frightened by the disruptions caused by strikes and the growth of autonomous organizations among railway workers, the government on February 8 issued the Temporary Rules on Worker Deputies in Shops and Engine Depots of State Railways. The framers of the new regulations hoped to undercut the strike movement by granting local managers the right to introduce the nine-hour day, revise piece rates, and permit railway employees and workers to elect management-approved deputies to represent their interests.[37] This last concession extended the *starosta* (factory elder) law of June 1903, which provided for labor representation in the settlement of disputes in factories. The government was pleased with the impact of its concessions since news of the shortened workday prompted many strikers to return to work.

News of strikes on other railways in Russia and in the main workshops, central depot, and administrative offices of the South West Railroad in Kiev stirred up railway workers in Odessa and encouraged them to organize. As other historians have noted, white-collar and administrative personnel played a crucial role in generating the strikes and activism that swept Russia's railways for much of 1905 and served, at least until the fall, as the melding force of a movement that encompassed both blue- and white-collar workers. The mobilization of administrative employees, who tended to be politically attuned and advocates of democratic reforms, energized the organizational and strike efforts among railway workers in general, lending the activism a political coloration that shaded into revolutionary opposition.[38] Events in Odessa followed a similar scenario, as both administrative and manual personnel cooperated and coordinated activities in their rush to take advantage of the Temporary Regulations.

Key in stimulating Odessa's railway workers were the provisions of the Temporary Rules, especially the promise of worker representation. Honoring the intent of the regulations, Klavdii Nemeshaev, the innovative and energetic director of the South West Railroad who became Minister of Communications later in the year, invited white-collar employees of the railway's central depot and branch lines to suggest ways to improve working conditions.[39] The structure and management of the pension plan was of particular concern for these workers, who complained that only a fraction of the money contributed to the retirement plan came back to them in benefits, most of it instead lining the pockets of high-ranking managers and bureaucrats in charge of investing the fund. Like their coworkers throughout Russia, administrative employees of the South West Railroad in Odessa met in mid-February to discuss the reorganization of the pension plan. They forwarded the results of the meeting to Nemeshaev, along with a petition requesting, among other demands, an eight-hour workday and higher wages. Nemeshaev pointed out that he could not authorize an eight-hour workday or substantial wage increases, and noted that the Ministry of Communications had just conceded a nine-hour workday and was preparing to reevaluate wage rates, which were based on a pay schedule dating from the 1860s. Nemeshaev instructed the heads of various Odessa stations and depots to establish a commission of representatives from both management and labor to review employee petitions on ways to improve conditions of work.[40]

Odessa workers responsible for the maintenance, repair, and construction of locomotives and rolling stock—who were, for the most part, exempt from pension plan coverage—followed the lead of the administrative staff. They elected representatives who drew up demands for presentation to the railway administration. The majority of these approximately 2,000 workers were skilled metalworkers and machinists employed in the workshops of the South West Railroad in the Mikhailov district. Railway workers were particularly well-prepared to engage in collective action on both the shop and enterprise levels for several reasons. Not only did they possess a long and vibrant heritage of organization and labor radicalism, but the railway workshops had been the nucleus of the South Russian Workers' Union in the 1870s, a focus of social democratic agitation since the 1890s that gave rise to well-entrenched revolutionary circles, and one center of the Zubatovist movement. Railway workers had been major participants in the unrest of 1903, with many strike leaders still playing a guiding role in the organization and direction of their colleagues in 1905. One such worker, Nikolai Raikh, an SD metalfitter who had been employed in the workshops since the 1890s, enjoyed the esteem of his coworkers and displayed leadership qualities both in 1903 and 1905.[41]

Railway workers also had experience with self-organization, since they frequently elected workers' deputies and established strike committees during labor disputes. Even prior to 1905, management had encouraged the selection of workers' representatives in order to keep abreast of employee needs and grievances. Factory elders selected by owners and managers from a list of candidates drawn up by workers had been serving as intermediaries between management and employees since 1903. Railway workers responded favorably at first, but soon grew annoyed with representatives who were under pressure from the railway administration to work against the workers' interests. This unfavorable experience with managerial interference in the elective process strengthened their resolve to retain exclusive control over the actions of their representatives.[42]

Finally, employees in the railway workshops possessed many of the occupational characteristics that facilitated collective action and labor radicalism among workers in both Russia and Western Europe during the late nineteenth and early twentieth centuries, namely relatively high levels of skill, pay, control over the work process, and independence on the shop floor. As Henry Reichman shows in his study of Russian railway workers in 1905, the railway workshops employed workers whose skills resembled those of metalworkers in machine-construction plants. By virtue of their skill, wages, and job functions, railway workshop employees, like other skilled metalworkers, formed a privileged stratum of workers.[43]

Developments in the organization of production were threatening the special position of skilled workers in the railway workshops. A rapidly expanding work force and more impersonal authority relations in the plant, designed to increase work efficiency, were eroding the work brigade, the heart and soul of the working lives of skilled metalworkers. Combined with inflationary pressures and a drop in real wages, the "decay of an accustomed job situation and threatened losses in perceived status" created a situation rife with tension and potential for conflict. Skilled railway workers were well-suited to respond to these developments in a unified, cohesive and aggressive manner. [44]

In early February, workers in Odessa's railway workshops elected twenty-two representatives, who then presented a grab bag of demands concerning issues inside the factory and out. The list included higher wages, sick pay, an eight-hour day, the abolition of compulsory overtime, free medical care for workers and their families, establishment of an arbitration council to settle disputes among workers, and the formation of a joint labor-management commission to resolve labor conflicts and negotiate a wide range of matters concerning the internal order of the workshops. Other demands were the granting of freedom of speech, press and assembly; the right to form a union; a guarantee of the personal security of elected workers' representatives; the rehiring of all workers dismissed after the 1903 general strike; and establishment of February 19 (the anniversary of the emancipation of serfs) as a holiday.[45]

A demand for permission for workshop employees to meet jointly and discuss common issues and interests was especially important since the physical layout of the workshops hindered links between workers of different shops. Employed in eleven shops located either in separate buildings or in different sections of the same building, workers had difficulty establishing on-the-job contacts with people in other shops. Indeed, workers within the same shop could find it hard to become acquainted, exchange views, and discuss mutual problems. The steam-engine assembly shop, for example, was located in four separate buildings, as were the foundry and the shop responsible for repairing train cars.[46] In order to discuss grievances and formulate demands common to all employees, railway workers clearly needed to hold general meetings.

Many of these demands reflected the influence of two workers, Ivan Avdeev and Fedor Golubkov. Avdeev was a lathe operator and Bolshevik; Golubkov, a joiner, was a Menshevik. Golubkov, in particular, had been pressing his fellow workers to petition for permission to hold a meeting of all workshop employees. Circumstances in the workshops, Golubkov argued, hindered the workers' ability to form a united front against management. They needed to unite in one organization without distinction of craft and shop and without interference by either management or governmental authorities. As one Menshevik leaflet circulated in the workshops exhorted, "Do you want to be worthy members of the common family of workers?" If so, the leaflet continued, railway workers had to stand as one and fight for civil rights and political freedom; without the rights to free assembly, speech, and press, and without a reformed political system based on a constituent assembly, their economic demands would remain "worthless" and impossible to guarantee.[47]

G. Stempkovskii, manager of the workshops, stood firm and refused either to satisfy the economic demands or allow a general meeting of workers. Angered by his intransigence, the workers reiterated their February demands in early March, and Avdeev and Golubkov redoubled their agitational campaign. On March 3, the workers of several shops elected representatives who requested a 20 percent hike in rates for piecework. The workers' deputies buttressed their argument by referring to local newspapers accounts stating that Nemeshaev had granted a wage increase in accordance with the Temporary Rules.[48]

Stempkovskii responded that the workers had misunderstood the Temporary Rules and the newspaper reports about Nemeshaev's wage directive. The railway administration, he told the workers, would raise wages for piecework only after a panel of experts had reviewed wage rates and conditions in each shop. Aware that this process would undoubtedly take several months, the workers threatened to strike the following day if management did not grant a pay increase. The next day both workers and their delegates approached Stempkovskii's office and repeated their demands, although they now insisted on only a 15 percent wage increase. Stempkovskii again explained that he was powerless to grant their demands, but he did agree to telegram Nemeshaev in Kiev requesting authorization for the wage increase. Although many workers then returned to work, some 400 workers waited anxiously outside Stempkovskii's office for the response from the central offices in Kiev that never arrived that day.[49]

The following day, Saturday, March 5, a lathe operator who belonged to one of the railway's SD circles exhorted his fellow workers to join the work stoppage begun the day before. By mid-morning over 800 workers had walked off the job. Later that day, a representative of the railway's main office in Kiev arrived in Odessa to confirm Stempkovskii's contention that Nemeshaev had never issued a directive granting an immediate wage increase. In an effort to console the workers, he reported that management was in the process of reevaluating wage rates and assured the workers that any wage increase would be retroactive. He also offered to pay workers for time lost during the brief work stoppage if they returned to their job on Monday.[50] The words of Nemeshaev's messenger dampened the militant mood among the workers, who reconsidered their position and agreed to return to work.

Authorities in Odessa differed over the appropriate response to the walk-out. *Okhrana* chief Bobrov argued that the work stoppage was not due to economic grievances but the consequence of agitation by "undesirable elements" and suggested arresting twelve of the workers' deputies for fomenting discontent and the strike. But N. M. Kuzubov, head of Odessa's gendarmes, advocated caution and restraint. Because he possessed no "solid information regarding the political intentions" of the strike leaders and accepted at face value one deputy's assertion that the strike had no revolutionary undertones, Kuzubov did not wish to detain them. He feared that the workers would perceive such detentions as a "deprivation of the possibility to request by legal means improvements in their working conditions."[51]

Despite his failure to acknowledge the socialist links of the strike's major leaders, Kuzubov displayed an incisive understanding of the railway workers' mood. He revealed a sensitivity unusual for a police official by recognizing how importantly workers valued the right to organize and select representatives without interference from management or government. Indeed, he sensed that government intransigence and intervention could transform worker discontent into open political protest, regardless of the workers' original motivations. The unexpressed but implied message of Kuzubov's evaluation was that the detention of the railway workers' acknowledged leaders would add insult to injury and trigger additional work stoppages.

Apart from the requests for economic concessions, the call by railway workers for fundamental civil rights and a guarantee that workers' deputies be secure from reprisals indicates that railway workers were beginning to perceive the connection between political reform and the fight to achieve improved working conditions. Employees in the railway workshops recognized that they could not effectively pursue their economic objectives without securing the rights of assembly, speech, and inviolability of person. They realized that economic and political demands could act in tandem to bring about improved working and living conditions. After all, how could workers promote and defend their interests without being able freely to meet and discuss issues of common concern?[52] By early March, then, some workers in Odessa were beginning to understand the importance of political reform in their struggle over bread-and-butter concerns, demonstrating that the distinction between economic and political demands was, at best, an artificial one that did not always correspond to a more complex reality.

Although government officials and revolutionaries alike used the categories of "economic" and "political" demands and strikes to describe the motivations and objectives of workers, these distinctions were not necessarily clear or relevant. To be sure, economic and political concerns varied in terms of content and intent; there is no doubt that demands for higher wages differed significantly from calls for a constituent assembly or a democratic republic. In this sense, there was a difference between the strike movement and political activism. Yet workers themselves paid scant attention to the labels affixed to their behavior by outside observers,[53] and strikes over wages and other material issues often had political ramifications, as they did in the 1903 general strike. Given the close links between autocratic politics and capitalist development in late Imperial Russia, in which government involved itself with the intimate details of labor-management relations, distinctions between demands concerned directly with material conditions at work and those associated with the structure of power in both the enterprise and society at large could be blurred. This was especially true when workers' demands drew the government into the fray. For example, a call for shorter workdays—nominally a bread-and-butter issue—might possess political coloration because it could be addressed to both employer and government and could symbolize the workers' desire to have time to rest and participate in public affairs. Likewise, the right to strike or enjoy collective bargaining rights was an inherently political demand, since employers had to defer to the authority of the central government in deciding these issues. Although concerned with ostensibly workplace issues, the demands to participate in hiring, firing, and settling labor-management disputes were also politically explosive because they challenged existing power relations within the enterprise and affected the broader arena of municipal and national politics.[54]

The Politicization of Odessa Workers:
The Case of Salesclerks

Railway workers were only one among several groups of workers who took advantage of the post-January 9 atmosphere to organize. For the first time, members of Russian society could articulate their grievances publicly. Consequently, the country bristled with the excitement of independent activity by social groups that had never previously expressed themselves politically. A case in point is provided by the behavior of salesclerks, whose political awakening can be gleaned from the pages of *Kommercheskaia Rossiia* (*Commercial Russia*), a local newspaper that served in the spring of 1905 as a forum for debates about the pressing issues of the day.

Kommercheskaia Rossiia catered to commercial and industrial interests and generally published articles about economic conditions. But in response to the budding political opposition movement among industrialists and merchants, beginning in 1905 the editorials of the paper acquired a distinctly leftist slant, with an especially conciliatory attitude toward labor. According to an editorial from mid-March, the newspaper wanted to promote economic development. A strong economy, however, required "stable and just relations between workers and employers" and "respect for labor" on the part of employers.[55] Thus, the first step toward solving the labor problem was to permit the formation of trade unions that would reach agreements with employers over working conditions and help regulate the internal order of enterprises. According to another editorial written several weeks earlier, unions provided a forum from which workers could influence work conditions and alter the existing state of affairs in which factory rules emanated from government ministries and management without input from workers.[56]

Beginning in late winter, the newspaper began publishing articles and letters by workers decrying their deplorable working conditions and discussing the relevance of labor organizations and politics as means of ameliorating these problems. The pages of *Kommercheskaia Rossiia* from mid-February to the end of March are filled with accounts of workers expressing their belief that the solution to their economic woes was linked to the transformation of the economic and political order. Some of the letterwriters even advocated workers taking matters into their own hands and pursuing a course of direct action because they could not wait for the government to take appropriate measures. Such an outpouring of discontent by workers was unprecedented in Odessa; its public expression was faciliated by the relatively lax efforts of censors in the aftermath of Bloody Sunday. Letters to *Kommercheskaia Rossiia* from local salesclerks offer an unusual glimpse into the process of politicization, demonstrating the extent to which some workers in Odessa had become involved in the debate over political issues and the appropriate form that labor activism and organization, particularly in its trade union and socialist variants, should assume.

As we saw in chapter two, salesclerks led especially vulnerable lives, even when compared with the overall poor working and living conditions that characterized late Imperial Russia. In the decade or so before 1905, salesclerks, some mutual-aid societies claiming to represent them, and social activists like Andrei Gudvan attempted to bring salesclerks under the umbrella of protective labor legislation. Central to their campaign were petitions—addressed to various city councils and the Ministry of Finance—for the standardization of working hours, especially on Sundays and holidays. Some merchants and storeowners in Odessa and other cities throughout the Empire, guided more perhaps by a concern with productivity than by humanitarian instincts, even voluntarily decided to restrict hours of operation on Sundays and holidays. Odessa was one of the few cities to adopt measures designed to help shop assistants, but these acts were piecemeal, half-hearted, and virtually unenforceable. The Odessa city council, for example, issued a regulation limiting hours of operations of retail stores to four hours on Sundays and nine on holidays, but compliance with this ordinance was easily avoided, especially if the store was located in an outlying district of the city. The movement to normalize the workday of shop assistants through legislation and good will failed to achieve its intended aims, largely because the central government and local municipalities never committed themselves to such a policy and concerned merchants and storeowners could not enforce compliance with self-imposed restrictions on their competitors.[57] Despite the proddings of social activists, very little substantive progress had been made to standardize the workday by 1905.

As 1905 approached, fewer and fewer Odessa salesclerks had faith in the tactics pursued by the well-meaning social activists, bureaucrats, and mutual-aid societies involved in the petition campaign. In early 1905, frustrated with the failure of existing policies and caught up in the highly charged political atmosphere of the revolutionary crisis, salesclerks assumed a more militant and activist stance, embracing a strategy that was political in orientation and that marked a rupture with the traditional autocratic pattern of labor relations among workers, employers, and government. Their first target was the elitist Odessa Mutual Aid Society of Jewish Salesclerks. Claiming that the presence of employers on the boards of directors undercut the capacity of mutual-aid societies to promote the interests of the average salesclerk, Odessa's salesclerks began to channel their organizational drives into alternative forms of association that more effectively promoted their interests.[58]

This was not the first time the OMASJS had met with criticism. Although evidence is fragmentary and scattered, extant sources suggest that organizational fissures had appeared several years before 1905, with a splinter movement emerging in 1903 to challenge the OMASJS leadership. In that year, a group of salesclerk activists, angry at the lack of concern shown by the mutual-aid societies, began to voice their grievances. Led by Moisei S. Kleiner, an office worker and member of the OMASJS since 1892 as well as a Socialist Revolutionary, these activists gave vent to their democratic leanings by suggesting that the organization establish closer ties with the rank-and-file. They clashed with the better-off salesclerks, merchants, and storeowners who dominated the OMASJS and succeeded in replacing several long-term members of the board of directors with individuals who pledged to represent the interests of the typical salesclerk. One consequence of this confrontation was a reduction in the initiation fee and monthly dues.

SD and SR organizers also challenged the OMASJS's hegemony by stepping up their activities; they circulated leaflets and proclamations and successfully organized small numbers of shop assistants. The socialists even advised and cooperated with Gudvan in the petition campaign to achieve legislation regulating work hours for salesclerks. In early 1903, Odessa SDs organized an illegal union among the rank-and-file commercial and industrial salesclerks without restrictions on sex or nationality of members and used it as a base for establishing ties with sales-clerical workers in other cities of southern Russia. Similar developments occurred in other cities as reformers challenged the power of employers who controlled the mutual-aid societies and revolutionaries tried to recruit shop assistants.[59]

In 1905, salesclerks explored more radical solutions to their problems. Some continued to work with the existing association, but others broke with the OMASJS and called for a new organization embracing as many salesclerks as possible without distinctions of age, sex, or religion. They claimed that it was "the moral responsibility" of the OMASJS to provide initiative, advice, and financial backing for the new organization. The existing board of directors and membership were guilty not only of "ignoring problems confronting the mass of Jewish salesclerks," but of acting indifferently toward their own organization and avoiding their responsibilities to it. A spokesman for this splinter group who went by the initials K. M. pointed out that the board of directors met only once or twice a year—usually without a quorum. How could such a leadership, he asked, be relied upon to undertake substantive reforms? The members were also at fault; by failing to elect new board members, they indicated their acceptance of the status quo. A new society representing the interests of typical salesclerks, argued K. M., would enjoy broad support and loyalty.[60]

Despite its appeal for a more broadly based organization of salesclerks, this proposal nonetheless emphasized the traditional functions of mutual-aid societies. The proposed organization was not innovative in terms of goals and objectives: its primary purpose was to provide death benefits, loans, insurance, and intellectual and cultural activities for members and their families. K. M. steered clear of advocating the establishment of a trade union that would challenge management and seek material concessions by striking and demanding collective bargaining rights. The thrust of his reform proposal was the elimination of employer influence in administrative affairs and the establishment of a mediation process to resolve labor disputes.[61]

Not all salesclerks were of the same mind. Some conceded that the existing organization did not serve the interests of most shop assistants but argued that a new mutual-aid society would be "harmful," since it would divide rather than unify shop assistants. This group of workers, led by Moisei Kleiner, wanted to change the current policies of existing societies, as they already possessed the institutional framework and material foundations to serve the interests and needs of salesclerks. Evidently Kleiner, despite his political predilections, preferred to continue his reform efforts within the existing organization. [62] Other salesclerks, however, forsook the concept of mutual aid altogether, calling for the formation of a trade union and involvement in politics, preferably with a socialist slant.

Two editorials in *Kommercheskaia Rossiia* set the tone for the ensuing debate on the objectives of trade unionism in general and a salesclerk union in particular. On March 8 and 13, the paper's editors declared that before salesclerks—or any workers for that matter—attempted to achieve the ideal goal of "one large workers' party," they first needed to pass through several preliminary stages, such as the establishment of labor organizations based on occupation and locale. According to the editors, unions provided the fundamental solidarity and "discipline of mind and heart" upon which all other forms of workers' organizations, including political parties, were based. They cautioned the salesclerks to maintain organizational independence from all other labor groupings and political parties, because this was the only guarantee against the centralizing tendencies inherent in a workers' party.[63]

This approach satisfied those salesclerks who welcomed the idea of forming a trade union geared only to obtaining improved working conditions through collective bargaining and strikes, but more radical salesclerks condemned the editorials for overlooking the importance of politics and class struggle. In a letter published on March 30, one such radical accused the editors of *Kommercheskaia Rossiia* of focusing on narrow, professional interests, an approach that obscured the salesclerk's vision that he or she "is not only a salesclerk but a citizen as well" who should achieve "rights of citizenship." These radicals urged salesclerks to join forces with other workers in a campaign for basic civil rights and a constituent assembly, without which the pursuit of economic improvements would be futile. The article proclaimed salesclerks "part of the proletarian army" and advised them to form a trade union to defend their "interests not only as salesclerks, since their social conditions make them proletarians."[64]

This energetic plea for a trade union subsumed in an independent workers' party pursuing the class interests of its members was reiterated in other articles. One correspondent, D. O-kii, in a series of articles with distinct socialist tones, condemned political neutrality among trade unions because disengagement from politics did not provide workers with an understanding of the social and economic forces ruling their lives. He challenged the contention of the editors of *Kommercheskaia Rossiia* that a trade union which limited its activities to purely economic issues could achieve substantial improvements in the well-being of its members. Both trade unions and mutual-aid societies were interested only in achieving "temporary and transitory" economic successes within separate enterprises, thereby accepting the salesclerks' status as a "seller of labor on the market of a capitalist society." He faulted his opponents for failing to consider social issues and recognizing the "limit to how much salesclerks can gain by operating within a bourgeois society: there is a limit to improvements that can be achieved."[65]

Similar anticapitalist messages were evident in other letters from salesclerks. These letters supported O-kii's views that improvements within the existing socioeconomic order were mere palliatives; only the transformation of the political order would lead to lasting benefits for salesclerks. One salesclerk asserted that workers were ready to resolve their problems by themselves because they could not wait for society and government to take the necessary action. Still another argued that "exploitation by capital" was the cause of the salesclerks' hardships. The "problem of class" concerned all workers, according to this salesclerk, and required them to organize a labor party since unions were "too narrowly focused to deal with the real cause of exploitation." Yet another wrote that "the salesclerk is not only a clerk but a citizen as well. If he doesn't enjoy rights of citizenship, then he should achieve them. Along with other workers he should strive for basic freedoms of speech, print, conscience, unions, and strike."[66]

The proletarian message of these letters undoubtedly spoke to the interests of the overwhelming majority of salesclerks. By the turn of the century, the hope of rising from the counter to open their own stores was a pipe dream for most salesclerks. Unlike the early members of the OMASJS, who experienced upward mobility and regarded their work behind the counter as a way station to a life of comfort and status, the typical salesclerk by the end of the nineteenth century could not look forward to a life of independence and status. In the words of N. Lialich, there was "no exit" for shop assistants from their situation as hired hands who must "defend their class interests" as workers vis-à-vis storeowners. The emergence of retail firms utilizing large amounts of capital and labor that outcompeted small storeowners had contributed to the deterioration of sales-clerks' conditions, as small-scale employers made ends meet by squeezing their staffs. The salesclerk had to acknowledge, Lialich admonished, that employment in a store no longer resembled a "hotel where he is temporarily staying" until he can open his own store, but a "permanent residence" which needed to be maintained in good condition.[67] These statements throw into relief the basic lesson learned not only by salesclerks but by many other workers in 1905. Starting in the spring of 1905, political liberation gradually became an element in labor's struggle to achieve improved working conditions; more and more workers acknowledged the intimate connection between material gains and political reform and the significance of assuming their rightful place as citizens enjoying full and equal rights.

The sources are silent on how many salesclerks had contact with revolution-aries, let alone how many participated in radical political activities and organi-zations. As mentioned earlier, socialist agitators had been active among Odessa's salesclerks for a few years. Several leaders of the salesclerks' union formed in late 1905 were socialists who had been active among shop assistants for several years, much like the SD leaders of salesclerk unions in Moscow and St. Petersburg. But exposure and contact do not necessarily translate into control and direction, and although many salesclerks were undoubtedly exposed to the ideas and views by socialist activists, caution is required when drawing conclusions about the political understanding and allegiances of rank-and-file shop assistants. In all likelihood socialist, like nonsocialist, leaders of the salesclerks' union occupied prominent positions because they enjoyed status among their constituency and possessed the expertise needed to run a formal organization, not because they espoused specific political platforms.[68] Witness the activities of the SR Kleiner, who advocated internal reform of the OMASJS and continued his affiliation with the mutual-aid society even after a Union of Salesclerks emerged in late 1905.[69] If the political allegiance of an acknowledged leader is such a poor predictor of behavior, then the views of the rank-and-file are certainly more difficult to determine. In early 1905, Gudvan reasonably attributed the politicization of Odessa salesclerks not to the machinations of revolutionaries, but to bureaucrats who failed to standardize hours of work and prevent other abuses of shop assistants.[70]

The existing salesclerks' organizations, aware of discontent among most shop assistants, paid close attention to the debate over the utility of mutual-aid societies, and some responded by offering concessions and advocating political reform. In mid-March, representatives of the five mutual-aid societies of sales-clerks and office workers met to discuss not only strictly economic issues (e.g. establishment of a pension fund financed by both employees and employers), but also clear political ones: freedom to assemble, form unions, and strike. In a display of near unanimity that reflected a new commitment to promoting the interests of their purported constituencies, most of the representatives favored these proposals. Proposals for an arbitration court to resolve labor disputes and civil rights generated the most discussion, but the conference ended with the representatives supporting these demands. As one delegate stated, the suggested reforms, particularly the establishment of an arbitration procedure, possess "moral significance which, by placing moral responsibilities on employers and employees, frees them of . . . unnecessary and tiring judicial red tape."[71] The conferees also advocated ending all residency restrictions and legal disabilities for Jews in order to reduce job competition among sales-clerical personnel in the Pale of Settlement.[72]

Representatives of Odessa's mutual-aid societies voiced similar reformist tend-encies on a government commission created to address some of the problems confronting salesclerks. As part of its conciliatory attitude after January 9, the government took up the plight of salesclerks. Soon after Bloody Sunday, Assis-tant Minister of Finance V. I. Timiriazev requested mutual-benefit societies of salesclerks and office workers throughout Russia to select delegates to his commission investigating the normalization of the workday in retail stores, warehouses, and offices. But in the heated atmosphere of 1905, any discussion of salesclerks' working conditions was guaranteed to open a Pandora's Box and bring up a host of other social, political, and economic matters.

The Timiriazev Commission generated an adamant response from the sales-clerks. As early as April, when news of the planned conference first reached the city, the OMASJS considered not sending a delegate to the commission. Citing the tsar's recent rescript of February 18, the organization's leaders expressed the opinion of most salesclerks when they asserted that it was impossible to improve the working and living conditions of salesclerks without "the funda-mental reconstruction" of the government on the basis of popular representation and civil and political liberties. They also called for the abolition of discriminatory legislation against Jews and supported self-determination for all nationalities.[73] Although the Jewish salesclerks in Odessa had little expectation that the Timiri-azev Commission would improve the lot of Jewish salesclerks, they agreed to send one delegate. Representatives of non-Jewish salesclerks in Odessa also debated the merits of the Timiriazev Commission. Like their Jewish counter-parts, members of the Mutual Aid Society of Christian Salesclerks argued that "the only guarantee for better working conditions for salesclerks is freedom of strikes, person, and assembly."[74]

When the conference opened in late May, it was marked from the start by dissension. Delegates from provincial zemstvos, stock exchanges, the merchantry of Moscow and St. Petersburg, and mutual-aid societies of salesclerks from all over the Empire locked horns. Timiriazev limited the topic of discussion to the length of the workday, but the majority of salesclerks' representatives not surprisingly sought to include other issues on the agenda, such as paid vacations, severance and sick pay, pensions, establishment of arbitration procedures, freedom to assemble, strike and form unions, and the end of discriminatory legislation against Jewish salesclerks.

Angered by restrictions on discussion and the fact that conference decisions were not binding on the government, the majority of salesclerks' representatives walked out. They issued a statement calling for the immediate election of people's representatives who would be responsible for "the reorganization of our entire legal order" and "improvement of the standard of living of salesclerks." Condemning as futile all efforts to address the problems of salesclerks through bureaucratic channels, the representatives vowed to participate in only those commissions established by popular election.[75] Their firm, unrelenting stance vividly testifies to the highly politicized atmosphere among these traditionally conservative and politically passive organizations.

This effort at reform notwithstanding, many rank-and-file salesclerks were unimpressed with the conference. In April, they formed a new organization (named the Society of Employees in Commercial and Industrial Enterprises) under the leadership of Gudvan. It received official sanction by Neidhardt and quickly attracted nearly 1,000 Jewish and non-Jewish salesclerks who could afford the initiation fees and membership dues, which were substantially lower than those charged by the already existing associations and well within the means of most salesclerks, including women, who were now allowed to join.[76] The establishment of an organization embracing both Jews and gentiles, as well as both men and women, marked a break with past practice and highlights the efforts of the organizers of the new mutual-aid society to bridge the separateness that had kept Jewish and Christian salesclerks in different organizations.

Radical salesclerks, however, continued to believe that the new society did not go far enough. For one thing, the local authorities' seal of approval meant that the organization had undergone "a still birth." The radicals claimed that it was "insufficiently proletarian" in its objectives and did not defend workers' interests aggressively, particularly when it came to hours and days off.[77] Yet this criticism was not entirely fair. After all, defenders of the new organization also believed that "the interests of salesclerks and employers are antagonistic, and in the name of liberation from exploitation salesclerks are uniting."[78] More importantly, at least from the perspective of typical salesclerks, this organization was open to all shop assistants and had their interests at heart.

To be sure, the Society of Employees in Commercial and Industrial Enterprises retained the traditional focus of mutual-benefit societies: its stated aim was the promotion of the "material and moral" interests of salesclerks, such as providing legal advice, sickness and death benefits, and low-cost consumer goods. But as we shall see later, the charters of many fledgling trade unions emerging throughout urban Russia during 1905 expressed similar aims and pursued philanthropic concerns along with tactics of strikes and collective bargaining. The new salesclerks' association significantly recognized the need to pursue a more forceful policy of confrontation with employers by establishing an arbitration bureau and creating a strike fund to assist shop assistants in "partial and general strikes" to achieve higher wages. Finally, while available sources do not agree on whether employers and other non-workers were excluded from the new organization, some evidence suggests that only shop assistants themselves were eligible for full membership.[79] If this indeed was the case, then salesclerks were beginning to break with the traditional patterns of mutual assistance by asserting their desire to control their own organization.

The emergence of a new organization of salesclerks highlights the extent to which one stratum of the Odessa work force had become frustrated with existing institutional arrangements and sought new avenues to obtain improved working conditions, especially standardization of hours. The activities of Odessa salesclerks in the spring of 1905 illuminates a debate that raged among Russian historians concerning the origins of trade unions in their country. Bolshevik historians, following the lead set by Lenin, asserted that trade unions emerged primarily from the strike movement of 1905, while other labor historians recognized that workers' experiences in pre-1905 legal organizations such as mutual-aid societies played a key role in the establishment of unions. As Vladimir Sviatlovskii, a liberal professor at St. Petersburg University, asserted, mutual-aid societies were "the precursors . . . of the trade union movement."[80] The evidence presented here supports the position that historians of Russian labor would do well to examine the part played by mutual-aid societies and other legal labor organizations in the genesis of trade unions in 1905.

Salesclerks had broken with the institutional legacy of mutual aid, especially in their readiness to engage in strike actions; in the process, they were expressing the urge for rights of collective bargaining and citizenship so characteristic of the labor movement in Russia in 1905. In the words of Mayor Zelenyi, who addressed the opening session of the new organization, Odessa's salesclerks had set an example for other workers by "democratizing" mutual aid and demonstrating that the populace is socially active and "fully worthy to receive rights of full citizenship," which will transform city government into "a forum for all citizens of all classes."[81]

The Spread of Labor Unrest

The actions of other workers confirm our picture of an increasingly restless, if not radicalized, Odessa work force. In April, representatives from leather, metalworking and machine-construction factories in Peresyp, like their fellow workers in the railway workshops, petitioned city authorities for permission to convene a citywide meeting of workers in accordance with the guidelines established by the Kokovtsov Commission. They approached Mayor Zelenyi to furnish the necessary space for such an assembly, but Kokovtsov, who apparently countermanded the interior minister's directive of March 19, instructed Neidhardt to announce that the issue of workers' meetings was still in "a state of preliminary discussion" by the commission. A general assembly of workers could not take place until the commission made its formal recommendations; this never occurred due to the resistance of industrialists on the commission to Kokovtsov's proposals to legalize certain labor organizations, set up a medical insurance fund, and grant a shorter workday.[82]

In response, the Mensheviks issued a leaflet encouraging local workers to protest the government's reliance on tsarist bureaucrats and capitalists to examine the causes of labor unrest. Condemning the efforts of "propertied men" to resolve the problems of workers, the Mensheviks called upon workers to demand "the right to convene a free and general assembly of all workers in Odessa."[83] Workers applied pressure on local officials to permit such an assembly. The new salesclerk organization, for example, asked Neidhardt to sanction a general meeting to discuss the needs and interests of the city's shop assistants. In addition, forty-six workers of the lathe shop in the railway workshops signed a petition, drawn up by the Menshevik Golubkov, requesting permission to convene a general meeting of Odessa's residents regardless of class and social standing. They invoked the spirit of the February 18 proclamations and expressed their intention to discuss the significance of the tsar's directives as well as to elicit opinion regarding the introduction of civil liberties. It was possible to restore social calm, stated the petition, only if the people could assemble and speak freely about the problems confronting Russian society. On the whole, the petitioners were nonconfrontational. They guaranteed that leaflets, broadsides, and inflammatory speeches would not mar the meeting and emphasized that they would select "the most respected persons, who will have a sacred responsibility to fulfill precisely the solemn promises" given by them. Yet the workers also warned the municipal authorities that "the calm of our city depends on your granting permission." Neither the salesclerks nor the metalworkers received a response; in early May they finally acknowledged the lack of response as a rejection of their request.[84] The reasons for the failure of city authorities to give an answer are unknown, but they are presumably connected with the confusion felt on all levels of the Russian bureaucratic apparatus over whether open meetings of workers were legal and should be countenanced.

Several incidents of labor unrest in April indicate that workers in many key sectors of Odessa's economy were becoming politicized. Strikes by bakers and sailors (that is, the merchant marine) of Odessa's shipping lines, like the unrest among railway workers, exemplify this state of affairs and the challenge posed by workers to managerial prerogatives. The sailors' and bakers' work stoppages spearheaded a wave of actions that culminated in widespread walkouts that paralyzed Odessa in early May. The strikes by sailors and bakers shared several features with that of railway workers. In all three instances, the workers had experience in labor organizations and strikes that predated 1905, and management and city authorities took swift action to resolve the disputes as quickly and peacefully as possible. Finally, workers' demands centered not only on issues such as pay, hours, and working conditions, but also included requests for joint worker-management commissions to settle disputes and to ensure observance of any agreements reached between staff and employers.

Even though the sailors in Odessa's merchant marine had obtained wage concessions as a result of a walkout in July 1903, living and working conditions had nonetheless steadily deteriorated. L. L. Gavrishev, an official intimately involved in the settlement of the brewing conflict between the sailors and shipping lines, pointed to "the extremely difficult conditions" endured by the sailors. He stated that sailors and stokers frequently worked from eighteen to twenty hours a day for wages that lagged far behind the cost of living in southern Russia. The absence of a formal grievance procedure also contributed to the "embitterment of the workers," since shipowners, according to Gavrishev, exacerbated "problems of the workers" by taking advantage of their crews' inability to redress grievances in a formal and organized fashion.[85] In early 1905, the Central Board of Commercial Navigation asked the Odessa Stock Exchange to examine working and living conditions among sailors, and in February the Stock Exchange formed a commission that held hearings at which shipowners and representatives of the crews offered their opinions. The sailors stated that they could not live on their current wages and requested a hefty wage hike of 70 percent, shorter hours, overtime pay, free medical care, and sick pay. In either late February or early March, the Stock Exchange forwarded its findings and suggestions to the Central Board and urged the sailors to wait for a response.[86]

By early April, the patience of many sailors had run out. On April 8, the crews of ships operated by the Russian Steam Navigation and Trading Company held a one-day work stoppage and issued a petition demanding higher wages, a nine-hour workday, and pay for overtime, injury, and illness.[87] They returned to work, but gave management three days to satisfy their demands. The crew of one ship did not even honor the three-day grace period and walked off the job on April 9 because they lacked the strength to continue work. They stated that they would return to their posts only if I. E. Zhirar, director of the company, would meet with them and guarantee a wage hike in writing. The company refused to negotiate and instead dismissed nineteen striking sailors.[88] News of the dismissals spread to other crews as sailors and stokers went from ship to ship, urging their fellow seamen to halt work. In some instances, strikers threatened violence or force against those merchant marines unwilling to join the strike. The port police did nothing to interfere and were helpless to prevent crew members from leaving the ships and joining other sailors on shore. By April 10, ship traffic to and from Odessa had come to a near standstill as sailors throughout the port joined the work stoppage.[89]

Aware that capitulation to the workers' wage demands would cost the company over 100,000 rubles a year, Zhirar was determined to break the strike.[90]

He continued to dismiss workers he deemed "instigators of the strike," and Neidhardt supported this tactic by exiling some of the fired sailors from Odessa. Zhirar even tried to recruit strikebreakers from nearby Nikolaev and Kherson, a strategy that did not succeed because the strikers had sent agents to these cities to agitate against recruitment.[91] Yet not all officials in Odessa were unsympathetic to the sailors; gendarmes chief Kuzubov wrote that the sailors' demands were not excessive, given the high cost of living in Odessa and "inadequate wages."[92]

When the sailors showed no signs of returning to work, Zhirar asked V. P. Pereleshin, chief of the Odessa Port Authority, to act as intermediary in negotiations between crew members and their employees on April 12. Pereleshin reviewed the demands submitted by the sailors and, citing their complexity, told both parties that they warranted careful examination. Negotiations, Pereleshin announced, could be "conducted only during a period of calm and not during a strike." He therefore advised the sailors to return to work and suggested the formation of a joint labor-management commission to study the sailors' demands.

The striking sailors and shipowners accepted Pereleshin's proposal, which was supported by Neidhardt, and within several days the crews of the Russian Steam Navigation and Trading Company and other shipping lines in Odessa had elected twelve delegates to the joint commission. The sailors, for their part, promised to resume work, but only after the dismissal of all strikebreakers hired during the course of the walkout. They also reserved the right to strike again if the commission did not reach a settlement after three months of negotiation.[93] Management agreed to this demand, and the movement of ships in and out of the port quickly resumed. The impact of the strike on the economy, which was in its annual upswing after the dormant winter, had been minimized due to the vigorous action of city authorities to avert a prolonged and potentially damaging strike and the cooperative (albeit belatedly) attitude of both strikers and shipowners.

The establishment of the labor-management commission (which would meet for the next three months under the guidance of Gavrishev) evidently raised the hopes of the sailors that their grievances would be given a fair hearing and encouraged them to air a wide-ranging list of demands. They included, in addition to requests for material concessions, a promise not to reduce the size of any ship's crew, selection and approval of foremen by crew members, immunity of workers' deputies from government retaliation, freedom to assemble and form unions, review of all dismissals by an arbitrator, and the creation of a worker-controlled labor exchange to fill job vacancies from a list of registered sailors.[94] This last demand was clearly an attempt to transform the labor exchange that the employer-dominated Odessa Mutual Aid Society of Sailors had formed in 1904 into a union.[95]

In the case of brewing unrest in the city's bakeries, municipal authorities adopted measures similar to those employed to defuse the sailors' strike. Neidhardt, alarmed by the chaos that a shortage of a staple food item could cause, worked hard to arrange negotiations between bakers and their employers. When bakers finally went out on strike in April, Neidhardt redoubled his efforts to resolve the dispute.

Bakers in Odessa had shown their receptivity to the Zubatov movement by establishing a union that was active in the 1903 general strike. Despite the formal collapse of Zubatovist unions after the summer of 1903, the bakers' union remained alive in skeletal form: the treasury remained intact and veterans of the 1903 strike continued to meet.[96] This organizational heritage, along with the presence in many bakeries of cells set up by various revolutionary parties, particularly the SRs, provided the necessary experience for an organized campaign to win concessions from bakery owners. This history formed the backdrop for the bakers' activism in the spring of 1905.

The structure of work in most bakeries in Odessa resembled that found in traditional workshops. Most of the city's 5,000 bakers, comprised primarily of Russians, Jews, and Greeks, were divided into a strict hierarchy based on skill and experience, with bakeries usually owned by a master baker who employed several journeymen and apprentices. It was still common in 1905 for employers to provide room and board for employees; this held true even in large bakeries such as the Filippov bakery, which employed nearly seventy workers and was a branch of a Moscow-based company. Even though aspects of baking bread products and pastries constituted a skilled craft organized in a variety of guilds, hours were long, pay relatively low, the work arduous, and living conditions restrictive, with workers resenting the close supervision that employers exercised over them during non-working hours.[97]

In late February 1905, bakers formed a Union of Odessa Bakers with the assistance of SR activists. They announced demands for increased wages, standardization of the workday (preferably eight hours, with full and paid Sunday rest and no night work), other improvements in working and living conditions, and an arbitration board of workers and bakery owners to settle disputes. Reflecting its contacts with the SRs, the bakers' union also issued a set of more overtly political demands: a constituent assembly, an immediate end to the war, and freedom of speech, print, assembly, and strike. In those bakeries where the owners refused to accede to these demands, workers walked out. This tactic was only partially successful, however, because many employers preferred to shut down operations rather than satisfy the workers' demands.[98]

Neidhardt was frightened by the prospect of a general work stoppage by bakers and appointed I. V. Vladislavskii-Padalka to chair a commission to standardize working hours for bakery employees. On February 24, Vladislavskii-Padalka met with the heads of the Odessa Board of Artisanal Trades and various guilds of the bakery trade, bakery owners, and fifteen worker representatives. Negotiations continued for the next two months with workers and employers arguing over the length of the workday, night work, the number of shifts, and Sunday rest. In mid-April, with no resolution of the conflict in sight, several hundred bakers walked off the job. None of the revolutionary parties, despite some claims to the contrary, played a role in instigating the work stoppage, but contacts between striking bakers and revolutionaries after the walkout began injected a dose of political rhetoric into the bakers' proclamations. Reminiscent of the sailors' work stoppage, the bakers' strike spread as strikers went from bakery to bakery, exhorting and sometimes coercing others to join them. Hoping that a display of strength would discourage the strikers, police arrested the strike's leaders for violating Neidhardt's recent injunction against unapproved public gatherings. But the bakers were undaunted and the strike grew. By April 21, most bakeries in Odessa had been hit by work stoppages and the price of bread had risen rapidly.[99]

Still trying to settle the dispute, Neidhardt decided in mid-April to permit workers' representatives to meet directly with bakery owners under the supervision of Vladislavskii-Padalka and factory inspector Popov. The bakers repeated their calls for the abolition of night shifts and Sunday work and presented as well several new ones; the abolition of room and board, the use of the polite form of address by employers, the release of all arrested strikers, and establishment of a work norm. The workers also insisted on the creation of a worker-employer commission to settle disputes and the formation of workers' bureaus in each bakery to monitor observance, and they repeated the call for freedom of speech, assembly, press, and strike. One final demand called for the introduction of a qualifying test, to be administered by the breadbakers' guild, which all journeymen had to pass. This measure, similar to that proposed by master artisans in Germany in the decades following the Revolution of 1848, was designed to bolster guild control over the work force and halt the drop in wages caused by the influx of less skilled bakers, not all of whom belonged to one of the bakers' guilds.[100]

Agreement was finally reached in late April, when a ten-hour workday was established, compulsory overtime was ended, and a night shift allowed only when the day shift had not baked enough bread. Sunday work was also eliminated so long as local authorities judged there would not be a shortage of bread. A special commission of worker-elected representatives and two members of the breadbakers' guild became responsible for observance of the terms of the agreement. Even though not all matters of contention had been resolved, bakers were evidently satisfied and returned to work. The price of bread dropped accordingly as the city's bread supply was replenished by the reopening of bakeries.[101]

As in the case of the sailors' strike, the persistent and energetic efforts by city officials, Neidhardt and Vladislavskii-Padalka in particular, had been crucial in resolving the dispute. The strike could have dragged on for weeks had it not been for the perseverance displayed by these two men in convincing both striking bakers and bakery owners to compromise and reach an accord to their mutual satisfaction.

The success of the strikes by sailors and bakers inspired other workers in Odessa to air their grievances and pressure employers by walking off their jobs. During the second half of April, journeymen shoe- and bootmakers, slaughterhouse workers, capmakers, Jewish and Russian tinsmiths at the Levin Tin Factory, workers at a teapacking plant and a salt mill, and photographers' assistants jumped on the bandwagon and struck—primarily for higher wages, shorter workdays, an end of searches, and other improvements in working conditions, including free medical care and better ventilation and hygiene. They also demanded reforms that transcended the boundaries of specifically workplace concerns and were beyond the authority of their employers to grant. For example, employees of the Levin Tin Factory called for a constituent assembly and were followed in suit by workers in other tin factories, who issued in *Kommercheskaia Rossiia* a demand calling for a four-tail constituent assembly and full political freedom as a guarantee of "the successful and fruitful struggle for a better future." Women embroidery workers presented similar demands for full civil and political rights, as well as employer subsidies during the off-season when work was scarce.[102]

Shoe- and bootmakers were experiencing the same problems as the tailors. They understood the value of organization and representation in labor disputes and evidently drew upon the long involvement of many Jewish cobblers in socialist strike funds and job actions. In fact, during the previous month Bundist organizers had issued hundreds of copies of a leaflet urging these workers to strike. Timing their walkout to coincide with the spring season, shoe- and bootmakers insisted that they would negotiate with their employers only if the personal safety of their deputies was assured. In an action that reflected the cumulative impact of years of disillusionment, they—like striking capmakers—refused to present their grievances to the Board of Artisanal Trades for adjudication because they regarded it as conservative and pro-employer. Finally, they supported establishment of a worker-management commission to negotiate a settlement to the strike and all future disputes.[103]

Shoe- and bootmakers also demanded shorter workdays and the abolition of piecework, because employers took advantage of a labor surplus to keep wages low and hours long. In a letter published in *Kommercheskaia Rossiia,* one shoemaker urged his fellow workers to organize for a shorter workday not merely to enhance working conditions but to spread work more evenly among all shoemakers, including those who were unemployed and victims of Odessa's straitened economic conditions. "If we all work eight hours," wrote the anonymous cobbler, "then all the unemployed could find work and let us lead more human lives." Thus, the call for an eight-hour day, in this instance, did not necessarily emerge from a commitment to an abstract political slogan that "was regarded as a symbol of . . . civic equality,"[104] but out of problems rooted in the workers' daily lives, particularly the issue of job security. Striking cobblers and capmakers returned to work in early May after employers conceded to some of their demands, granting higher wages and shorter workdays.

The work stoppages in March and April highlight the way employers and city officials were willing to negotiate settlements in the first half of 1905, thereby displaying the well-known paternalistic approach government officials sometimes adopted toward labor problems. Notwithstanding initial misguided attempts to sabotage the strikes by arresting activists and exhibiting a show of force, employers and city officials responded to workers' demands by negotiating in good faith. Neidhardt and his assistants were determined to reach a modus vivendi with workers by settling labor disputes as quickly as possible, if only to avoid serious economic disruption. Neidhardt urged employers to grant workers' economic demands where feasible and sanctioned the formation of joint labor-management commissions to adjudicate disputes and monitor agreements. His task was made easier because striking workers demonstrated a readiness to compromise as well. He boasted that he was able "to work out compromises and agreements" during these negotiating sessions and ensure that work stoppages were shortlived.[105]

Neidhardt's experience with labor conflict predated 1905. In late 1903, one of his first tasks as city governor had been the attempt to improve employer-employee relations in order to prevent a repeat performance of the 1903 general strike. At that time he recommended strict observance of labor regulations, particularly those establishing ten-hour workdays for workshop employees, and advocated punishing violators; tramway workers received substantial wage increases upon his insistence. Neidhardt also supported a proposal by the Odessa Municipal Bureau on Factory and Mining Affairs to establish a minimum wage for unskilled day laborers, and he organized special conferences between management and labor to settle disputes. This concern continued into 1905. In addition to his efforts during the bakers' and sailors' strikes, he ordered a tailor's workshop to close its doors for a month in April because the owner forced his employees to work longer than permitted by law. In May, he arranged a series of conferences so owners of shoemaking and tailoring workshops and their respective work forces could discuss the standardization of the workday. He also encouraged retail storeowners to establish a twelve-hour day for their clerks.[106]

This is not to suggest that Neidhardt's behavior was due to any moral or principled commitment to accommodate workers' grievances. Rather, it was rooted in his responsibility to maintain public order. As a guardian of the status quo, Neidhardt recognized that state interests were sometimes best protected by means of the carrot rather than the stick. He countenanced the labor movement so long as it did not threaten constituted authority; as soon as workers overstepped what Neidhardt considered legitimate activity (and this did not necessarily include work stoppages), he met them with force, thereby revealing his willingness to apply the stick when necessary.

Concluding Remarks

The pre-May strike movement illustrates that many workers were beginning to recognize the connection between political reform and improvements in working conditions. The workers' grievances were longstanding and were an important feature of earlier strike movements, especially in 1903; the economic discontent that motivated workers in 1903 remained unresolved in 1905, when it again surfaced in the aftermath of Bloody Sunday and gradually began to assume a political coloration. Labor was beginning to assert its right to participate on a permanent and equal basis in the resolution of worker-management disputes and elect representatives from whom the government promised to solicit advice and opinions. Demands for collective bargaining rights sounded the initial salvo in the workers' struggle to win *svoboda* (freedom) and rights of citizenship both in the workplace and society. Taking their cue from workers already on strike and drawing upon the demands issued both by these strikers and by socialist agitators, a larger number of Odessa workers mobilized in order to pursue improved working conditions and stake their claim to participate in the making of decisions at the workplace.

The emphasis on elected worker deputies was the hallmark of the Odessa labor movement in 1905 and often overshadowed other crucial demands and issues, such as higher wages and the eight-hour day. Control over hiring and firing was not only an aggressive assault on traditional managerial prerogatives, but also reflected the workers' desire to end *proizvol* and assume greater control over their lives, especially when the specter of unemployment and hunger loomed large. Even though an unevenness of political awareness characterized the labor movement in the spring, the strikes of March and April set the stage for a contest for power and authority on both the enterprise and municipal level later in the year. It was not until the fall that workers on a mass scale engaged in protest designed to transform society and the political system.

The strikes of early spring also created the building blocks of an organized labor movement that would play a critical role for the remainder of the year. By offering workers first-hand experience with the challenges of labor and political organizing, the meetings, rallies, demonstrations, and strikes of the first months of 1905 fostered a nascent sense of worker solidarity which, though fragile and hardly encompassing all workers, did possess significance, if only because of the lessons workers learned about the difficulties involved in the struggle for improved working and living conditions.

The pre-May labor movement reveals how workers, employers, and city officials tried to settle disputes amicably and peacefully in the aftermath of Bloody Sunday. In May and June, however, the conciliatory atmosphere gave way to confrontation as relations among workers, employers, and government grew more strained. The government and employers then stopped seeking to accommodate workers and pursued instead policies of provocation, repression, and subterfuge. Labor politics in Odessa during the late spring reflected the vacillation in government policy, a swing that led from accommodation to repression as the carrot gave way to the stick. The opposing sides dug in their heels: workers became adamant about the need to meet on a citywide basis to discuss their collective interests, city officials steadfastly refused to sanction such meetings, and employers rejected workers' demands for improved working conditions. The result was widespread labor unrest in May and a bloody confrontation between workers and government troops in June.

5

First Confrontation

POPULAR UNREST IN MAY AND JUNE

Strikes in late April presaged work stoppages in early May among workers in both large and small enterprises throughout Odessa. Catalyzed by the refusal of officials to grant the strikers' urgent demand for a citywide assembly of workers, this round of unrest embraced a much broader spectrum of the work force than earlier strikes. The May walkouts initiated a new phase in the spring strike movement and culminated a month later in a general strike and bloody confrontation between workers and government troops that coincided with the well-known mutiny on the battleship *Potemkin*. These work stoppages reflected the radicalization of the labor movement and posed the most serious threat to social calm since the 1903 general strike. Events in late spring and early summer prefigured work stoppages later in the fall and early winter, when Odessa workers, building upon the organizational and practical experience garnered in the spring, formed trade unions and created a soviet of workers' deputies.

Strikes in May

It was a seemingly innocuous meeting on worker health that helped catalyze the May strikes. In April, Minister of Finance Kokovtsov attempted to placate Russia's workers by convening a commission to study medical assistance to factory workers. Odessa's Mayor Zelenyi received instructions to submit suggestions and proposals only several days before the April 25 deadline. On the day before the deadline, he hastily arranged a meeting with prominent employers, physicians, city officials, and several dozen workers.

From the outset, workers in attendance declared that their opinion had "no significance" because they could not claim to speak on behalf of coworkers who did not have an opportunity to discuss the issue of medical assistance prior to the meeting.[1] Criticizing Zelenyi's failure to arrange preliminary discussions in every factory in the city, they complained of the meeting's eleventh-hour nature and the haphazard manner in which it was convened. How could they regard themselves as worker representatives, they asked, without the express approval of all factory workers in Odessa? Since workers did not serve in city government, it was crucial that each and every worker in Odessa be given the opportunity to express an opinion. Workers also insisted that the city fathers help them win the right to meet and speak freely. In a speech that was the most forceful and direct expression of worker recognition of the connection between material improvements and political reform, one worker asserted:

> We ourselves should have discussed the minister's proposal point by point. If the city government wants to know the opinion of the workers, then it should strive to secure those conditions under which workers themselves could discuss the proposal. But until that time, we should abandon the conference. To give our opinion under such conditions would be dishonest to our comrades. . . . We should demand that the city government achieve for the workers, who comprise a significant part of the population, the right to discuss this vital problem.[2]

Other workers seconded these sentiments by demanding freedom of assembly, speech, and press. Some even drew a connection between the discussion of medical assistance and the problem of worker discontent in general.

The chair of the meeting, Dr. I. F. Sabanev of the city hospital, agreed that worker opinion was not fully represented at the meeting, but he pointed out that the situation could not be otherwise, given the city government's lack of authority to sanction a general assembly of workers. He urged workers present at the meeting to participate and offer advice on medical assistance to workers. For his part, Zelenyi pleaded with the workers to remain calm, emphasizing that they could discuss only the question of medical assistance; all other issues, he stressed, were outside the "competency" of the meeting. He admitted that labor issues could not be discussed in "their entirety" given the nature of the meeting, but concluded "there is nothing else that can be done." After all, Zelenyi stated, he himself had not been given sufficient time to organize the hearing.[3]

Worker opposition grew more vociferous and confrontational. The worker quoted above took the floor again to denounce Zelenyi and voice his concerns regarding freedom of assembly:

> The city administration should struggle to win for workers the right to assemble and discuss the problem. . . . We demand this—I repeat, we demand—since up to now we have requested it too many times. We don't doubt that in the city administration there are good people, but it is impossible to achieve much from them. We know full well how good people exploit workers.[4]

Other workers also harangued Zelenyi, insisting that he tell Kokovtsov that he could not solicit worker input because not all workers in Odessa had the opportunity to voice their opinions. When one worker asked the mayor why workers congregating on the street were not invited to join the meeting, Zelenyi replied that "admittance was conditional upon his approval." Zelenyi, despite his liberal leanings, was unwilling to let in other workers. Upon hearing the mayor's rejoinder, the workers shouted that they would not remain and stomped out, leaving the task of formulating the proposal on medical assistance to Zelenyi and a group of doctors, employers, and bureaucrats.

Neidhardt fueled the workers' ire when he refused another request that Odessa workers be allowed to assemble on a citywide level. On Monday, May 2, representatives of Peresyp workers, who were well aware of the incident with Zelenyi, asked to hold a general assembly of workers to discuss their common needs and interests. They were supported by the Mensheviks, who approved of the idea of a general assembly of workers and worked for its realization.[5] Neidhardt repeated what he had said to similar requests in March and April: a general meeting was "superfluous and unnecessary." Workers should, he insisted, assemble separately by enterprise. (In all fairness to Neidhardt, it is necessary to stress that his hands were tied by the ban imposed by central authorities on any general assembly of workers.) Needless to say, those workers who were now attaching great significance to freedom of assembly were not impressed by this line of argument.

In a move to placate the workers, Neidhardt invited delegates to talk with factory inspector Popov. Although SDs involved with the workers were opposed to the meeting, the workers, surprised by Neidhardt's emphatic rejection of their request, thought that the factory inspector would react more positively. Indeed, Popov greeted the workers cordially and told them that he "had nothing against a general workers' meeting." The matter, however, was beyond his jurisdiction. Boasting that he had "always defended" workers' interests, Popov nevertheless claimed that his function was limited to that of "a liaison between workers and employers"; only the city governor possessed authority to grant them permission to assemble. Angered at the way he patronized them and feeling as though they were being given the run-around, the workers accused Popov of betraying their trust. Now visibly annoyed, Popov instructed them to return with him to Neidhardt's office. He conferred briefly with the city governor in private conference and added insult to injury by leaving without talking again with the workers.

The next day the same worker representatives returned to Neidhardt's office, but the city governor had evidently decided that the issue merited no further discussion; the workers waited in vain for an opportunity to meet with him. On May 4, Neidhardt attempted to iron out his differences with the workers, sending a policeman to advise them to draw up a petition requesting the formation of a commission, to consist of factory owners, the factory inspector, and a worker representative from each enterprise. The workers were irritated with this offer, however, which they considered too little too late, and rejected the proposal.

Feeling driven to the wall, the workers called for work stoppages. By May 6 over 10,000 workers, representing a broad cross-section of the labor force, had walked off the job, as the police tried to prevent striking workers from disrupting work in those enterprises still unaffected. One major exception was the railway workshops, which did not experience any unrest in May except for a one-day work stoppage in the lathe shop in the middle of the month.[6] The hub of the unrest centered in the factories and workshops of Peresyp and the large machine-construction plants and shipyards of the Port Territory.

The magnitude of worker discontent can be gauged by the willingness of workers in many instances to walk off the job without first presenting demands to their employers. Popov reported that workers gave "no warning" and many had not announced demands before walking off the job.[7] Many workers may have been jumping on the bandwagon without much forethought and following in the footsteps of others who were already on strike. Even so, such actions signified an outburst of elemental and unarticulated anger that testifies to the spontaneous nature of the strikes. As Michelle Perrot writes about similar incidents among French workers in the late nineteenth century, the phenomenon of going out on strike without first drawing up demands "suggests a worsening social climate and an underlying discontent, which had very probably been long repressed and which it was no longer possible to express peacefully within the enterprise itself."[8] In Odessa, relations between workers and management in some enterprises were so tense that foremen in at least one factory took to carrying guns during the strike.

Striking workers asked for higher wages, shorter workdays (an eight-hour day in particular), and improved working conditions such as free medical assistance, sickness benefits, and cafeterias. A common demand for an end to body searches when leaving work is particularly revealing of the workers' mood, since it represented an effort to stop a practice that they regarded as demeaning and physically invasive. Also designed to assert the workers' sense of dignity and respect was insistence on polite treatment by plant management, who addressed workers with the informal "thou," a form of speech used by social superiors to address those below them. Workers in many enterprises, evidently paying close attention to the preceding strikes, also attempted to win the beginnings of collective bargaining rights by setting up labor-management arbitration boards to settle disputes and determine wages.

Like worker insistence on freedom of assembly, this demand challenged traditional employer prerogatives to administer enterprises without consultation with labor. Workers of the Russian Steam Navigation and Trading Company, for example, demanded the right to elect foremen and representatives who could meet on company time and premises without fear of retaliation. They also requested strike pay, an eight-hour day, and permanent tenure of employment unless employee representatives consented to the dismissal of a worker. This mix of demands, if satisfied, would have had wide-ranging implications for the nature of power and authority relations in the enterprise. In other plants strikers presented similar demands. Some even called for the end of the war and formation of a four-tailed constituent assembly, demands which imbued the walkouts with political significance since employers lacked the power to grant them. In one incident, workers in a tin factory requested recognition of May 1 as a paid holiday. Municipal employees stood out in their demand that the city set an example for the private sector by acceding to labor's demands. They stressed that workers' needs would be met only when the city council is elected "not by a small group of property owners, but by all residents of Odessa, both rich and poor," thereby revealing a commitment among these workers to a society based on social and economic justice.[9]

Despite the radicalism of these strikers, the May unrest never assumed the scale of a general strike for several reasons. The willingness of management to accede to workers' demands, especially at small-scale and medium-sized enterprises which lacked the stock reserves to withstand work stoppages, helped defuse the situation.[10] More important was the fact that most strikers simply could not afford the financial sacrifice demanded by a prolonged work stoppage, since their meager wages did not allow them either to accumulate individual savings or build up a collective strike fund. Among workers who had the good fortune to have strike funds, the resources were often depleted very quickly. As one newspaper reported, some workers resorted to bartering household goods and valuables for food.[11] Strikers also realized that their employers could not meet their demands without risking bankruptcy.[12]

Other considerations discouraged workers from engaging in prolonged strikes as well. Employers determined to stand their ground frequently adopted a number of tactics designed to intimidate their workers and break the strikes. The threat of hiring strikebreakers or actually shutting down operations was particularly effective in driving workers back to work. Closely related to this was the decision of some less resolute owners to reduce their work force in order to cover the cost of wage increases and the shorter workdays that they granted.[13] In addition, Neidhardt took an active role in helping management by sending troops as strikebreakers and deploying troops at strategic points throughout the city such as the water, gas, and electric works. When employees of the municipal slaughterhouse walked off the job, Neidhardt ordered troops and Cossacks to butcher the livestock in order maintain the city's supply of meat. He bolstered police patrols in factory districts and arrested workers suspected of strike agitation in order to halt contact among workers from different enterprises and the spread of walkouts.[14]

At the same time that Neidhardt displayed a willingness to bully the workers, he continued his policy of conciliation and mediation by encouraging both sides in the conflict to settle their differences at the negotiating table. As we have seen, the city governor in previous months sought to defuse labor unrest by listening to workers' grievances and encouraging meetings between employers and workers. Neidhardt also tried to discourage strikes by assigning policemen to deliver lectures to workers on the impossibility of winning concessions from employers during times of war and recession, and he had his office publish an article on the results of the 1903 summer strikes which argued that the negligible concessions in wages and hours had been outweighed by the loss of wages.[15]

The failure of the May work stoppages to command the allegiance of all workers was another weakness of the walkouts. The refusal of some workers to strike reflected the lack of unity and common purpose and revealed holes in the labor movement. Finding common ground across a broad spectrum of workers is a difficult task, and the lack of a coherent program and plan of action plagued the May work stoppages. From the outset, striking workers in one enterprise visited nearby factories and exhorted workers to join the work stoppage in a display of solidarity, a tactic that may help explain why many workers walked off the job without first formulating demands. When confronted by recalcitrant workers, striking workers often tried to enforce compliance through threats of violence, and in many instances strikers attacked workers who failed to honor picket lines. In one case, eighteen strikers scaled the walls of a leather factory and threatened to throw a bomb if work did not halt immediately. Workers unceremoniously bowed to the threat. The police attempted to break up rallies, often with the use of whips, and tried to disperse striking workers before they could reach the gates of neighboring factories. Frequently, however, they could not prevent clashes between striking and non-striking workers, which resulted in bloodshed, scores of injuries, and even deaths.[16]

Like the peasants of a Russian village who were suspicious of and hostile to outsiders, Odessa workers in one factory were often belligerent and uncooperative when workers from other enterprises approached them. This state of affairs reflected the strikers' localism, rooted in the enterprise, and interfered with the formation of a unified plan of action.[17] Bundists in Odessa noted the tendency of some workers to focus on issues specific to their own enterprise and lose sight of the broader, more general problems confronting all workers. One Bundist account of the May strikes reported that the strikes were uncoordinated and "assumed a partisan character. Each workshop, factory, and plant struck independently—there was no general strike wave. Thus, it was easy for each to wither and exhaust itself." Similar accounts were reported by the SRs.[18] Even when workers from different enterprises agreed to go out on strike, failure to concur on objectives, strategy, and tactics often sapped the walkouts of strength and vitality.

Along with the absence of unity of purpose, the strikes lacked leadership. The revolutionary parties failed to guide and lead the strike movement; in fact, the outbreak of unrest took the social-democratic factions by surprise. The revolutionary parties were in a shambles due to organizational, personnel, and financial problems. In the words of Daniil Novomirskii, the SDs and SRs "could hardly succeed in addressing the strikes with proclamations."[19] Ties with workers were weak if not nonexistent in many districts. One Bolshevik organizer has written that "the percentage of workers in the party in early 1905 was small, and sometimes there were no workers at all."[20] And a Bundist reported that "many levels of the Odessa proletariat are hardly touched, with some not touched at all, by the social democratic parties. . . . There are entire . . . trades in which no or little organizational work of any sort has been conducted up to now. We are talking about the Jewish proletariat here."[21] This was also true among the city's factory workers, a situation that was in large measure due to past SD strategies and the repercussions of the Zubatovist movement. As late as mid-1905, according to several Bolshevik organizers, SDs generally experienced their greatest difficulties in those enterprises where the Zubatovites had been most successful. One exception was the railway workshops—a site of traditional SD organization—where the Bolsheviks enjoyed a solid following. Mensheviks, continuing their practice of their SD predecessors in the city, maintained a presence among Jewish workers.[22] Overall, there were somewhere between 550 and 1,050 Bolsheviks and Mensheviks in the city in mid-1905, with slightly more of the latter than the former.[23]

Contributing to the socialists' lack of influence among the strikers was the tendency of each group to believe that it could assume control of the strikes. Early on in the unrest, the three local social-democratic organizations, at the behest of the Mensheviks, had agreed to form a committee responsible for leading a general strike. Yet almost from the start, Bolshevik and Menshevik members were at each other's throats, denouncing their opponents' tactics and actions. One worker later recalled that SDs and SRs would interrupt each other's speeches at rallies; one such incident ended with an SR shooting an SD rival for calling his organization petty-bourgeois and capitalist. The Bolsheviks eventually withdrew, stating that they would cooperate only at the time of a general strike or uprising and refusing to issue joint leaflets or even announce the existence of an agreement. Because the revolutionaries could not bury their differences and cooperate, their strike committee was stillborn. Factional struggles rather than a desire to generate a general strike sapped their strength, and each faction continued its own agitation independently. Most SD leaders recognized how the precarious state of party affairs in Odessa resulted in weak ties with workers and an inability to influence the labor movement except in isolated instances.[24]

The revolutionaries took advantage of the unrest as best they could, but they did not direct the workers' movement. As participants but not initiators or leaders of the unrest, they exerted a secondary influence in generating work stoppages. Indeed, some SD and SR activists admitted that workers did not always welcome the revolutionaries and resented the latter's efforts to interfere with discussions of workers' grievances. For example, workers at the Henn Agricultural Tool and Equipment Factory (who were to play a crucial role in the labor unrest in June) hooted SD orators who tried to persuade them to include a call for the end of the war in their demands, even though the workers had already approved other strictly political demands such as the release of all political prisoners. Workers at a tobacco plant omitted political demands from their list of grievances, only to reinstate them after their strike committee, which had turned to the Bund and Bolsheviks for assistance, refused to help lead the stoppage. The Bund reported that even in those instances where strikers "voluntarily accepted the leadership of the SD organizations," they did not necessarily accept all the demands drawn up by the revolutionaries and would frequently tear off from strike proclamations the signature of all social democratic literature: "Proletarians of the World, Unite."[25] Such actions reflected the tensions, common throughout the Empire, among conflicting camps within the same enterprise, one group of workers focusing purely on material issues such as wages, the other interested in more overt political concerns. They also indicate that in some instances demands for an end to the war and formation of a constituent assembly may not have reflected strikers' aspirations and were imposed by SD activists. The May strikes testify to the uneven emergence of political awareness among Odessa workers.

The SDs did manage to organize some rallies, distribute leaflets, and send activists to factories, where they assisted in the formulation of demands. And in a few instances party activists did assume leadership roles in strikes, although one report by the Bund boasting that it led all May strikes by Jewish workers, sometimes with the assistance of either the Mensheviks or Bolsheviks, clearly exaggerated its role.[26] A more frequent scenario found workers with party affiliations serving as worker delegates in the formulation and presentation of demands to management. Yet it bears stressing that the work stoppages started independently of social-democratic agitation, and the revolutionary parties never assumed leadership or asserted control of the strike movement, even in Peresyp and workshops with Jewish employees, the traditional bases of social-democratic support in Odessa. It is clear that the radical intelligentsia had little luck mobilizing Odessa workers, who acted independently of the urgings of the revolutionaries.[27]

The strike wave peaked by the end of the first week in May, after which it began to ebb as employers caved into worker demands and workers returned to their jobs. According to the Factory Inspectorate's review of events in 1905, workers primarily from small enterprises emerged victorious in many of the May strikes.[28] Employers granted reduced workdays and substantial pay increases, along with other concessions such as the promise to use the polite form of address and not subject workers to searches at the end of work shifts. In some instances, employers even promised strike pay and agreed not to dismiss workers without the agreement of worker representatives. In printing establishments a nine-hour workday was introduced, along with a 10 percent wage increase, and owners of granaries enticed workers back to work with (an unkept) promise of an eight-hour day. A May 20 report in *Kommercheskaia Rossiia* maintained that work in most enterprises with fewer than 100 employees had resumed.[29]

Workers in the iron foundries and larger machine-construction and metalworking plants of Peresyp and the adjacent Port Territory, however, remained in a deadlock with their employers, who possessed the resources to withstand prolonged work stoppages and believed that the financial hardships imposed by the strikes would force workers back to the job. As of June 3, some 3,700 workers in thirteen enterprises were still on strike, including several large metalworking enterprises such as Bellino-Fenderikh, Restel', Shpolianskii, and Henn.[30] Workers in these enterprises faced employers who were still resisting concessions. The distinguishing feature of the strikes as they developed among metalworkers in Peresyp and the Port Territory was the continuing effort by workers in different enterprises to meet together to discuss issues and strategies. Possessing the resolve and means to engage in prolonged strikes, these workers remained determined not to capitulate, largely because they were angered by their employers' intransigence and Neidhardt's refusal to permit a general assembly. Unlike workshop employees dispersed in tiny enterprises throughout the city, metalworkers and machinists in Peresyp were better able to act on common problems and complaints, with neighborhood and community bonds helping to generate the strikes and meld solidarity. As skilled workers, they were able to rely on well-funded strike treasuries, which permitted them to stay out on strike. It is therefore not surprising that workers from the plants and factories of Peresyp—some belonging to one of the socialist factions or having had experience in the Zubatovist unions—assumed directing roles in the organized labor movement, especially in the district strike committee that became the nerve center of the May work stoppages.

As May wore on, striking workers in Peresyp became more agitated and the atmosphere grew more turbulent. Freed from work because of the work stoppages, workers from different enterprises congregated on street corners and in the inns and teahouses of Peresyp to discuss strike developments and current affairs. Tensions heightened when workers learned of an attempt by factory owners to convince local shopkeepers and grocery storeowners to refuse credit to striking workers. This effort to break the strike failed because the merchants of Peresyp, in a display of community spirit and solidarity reflecting close ties with their working-class customers and the absence of a presumed conflict of interests, rejected the appeals of industrialists.[31] Other efforts to break the resolve of the strikers also failed. The decision by the Restel' Iron Foundry to bring strikebreakers under military guard in late May backfired when strikers beat up two of their replacements and succeeded in closing down operations. The employers' refusal to grant worker demands redoubled the strikers' determination and inspired returned workers in some plants to contribute a percentage of their pay to workers still on strike. The decision of telegraph and telephone operators, municipal hospital employees, longshoremen, and day laborers at one railway depot to strike contributed to the deteriorating state of affairs.[32] By late May, a stalemate had been reached. In the words of a police officer, "both sides were standing firm."[33]

Peresyp workers received strong support from members of the Peresyp Sanitary Inspectorate, a group of physicians assigned by the city to monitor health conditions. In mid-May, the inspectorate asserted that the prolonged work stoppages were caused by poor working conditions. The inspectors requested that the city establish a free cafeteria for families of unemployed workers and insisted that the city council, as part of its civic duty, accede to the workers' demand for a general assembly of deputies. The doctors wrote that, since the causes of strikes are "of a constant and permanent nature," such meetings must be held on a permanent and regular basis.

The platform of the Peresyp doctors created a stir among members of the citywide sanitary commission. A report by E. P. Vel'shtein asserted that the labor unrest was caused by "the abnormal conditions of labor." Because workers lacked faith in factory legislation, the Factory Inspectorate, and government commissions set up to safeguard their interests, the report concluded that workers believed their problems could be resolved only through a fundamental restructuring of the political and economic systems. Workers, according to Vel'shtein, were interested not only in improved working conditions but were also "conscious of human rights." The workers' demand for a general assembly of all Odessa workers indicated their recognition that they needed freedom to discuss common issues and grievances if they were to defend and promote their interests.

Other doctors seconded Vel'shtein's evaluation of the situation. One physician maintained that the "problem of Peresyp is one that confronts all Odessa," since workers throughout the city were striking. He called on the city administration to assume the role of arbitrator in labor disputes, but other members argued that the city could not mediate disputes because it did not enjoy the trust of both workers and employers. Still another noted the political significance of the strikes and the moral obligation of the city to support the workers' protest "against the existing regime."

The city council responded to the discussion by affirming its duty to help settle strikes and admitting that the peaceful resolution of labor disputes required "discussion by workers, individually and with owners, of the causes of strikes." Acknowledging that they did not possess the authority to sanction such meetings, the city fathers promised to petition the appropriate authorities for permission. According to a resolution passed by the city council, the first step in resolving the current wave of labor disputes was recognition of the right to hold a "general meeting of deputies of workers and representatives of factories." By taking a public stand on behalf of workers, the city council lent its moral support to their cause and strengthened their conviction that they did not stand alone.[34]

The June Days

Striking workers, although becoming exasperated, as one activist metalworker recalled two decades later, responded to the recalcitrant stance of their employers with an equally unyielding determination.[35] As strikers grew more frustrated, they discussed measures—including a general strike—to force capitulation. It was therefore deemed imperative that all workers, especially those who had already won their strikes, learn from the shortcomings of the May strikes and establish a united front, with workers back on the job contributing funds to support those workers still out on strike. Such a strike fund would counter the financial assistance furnished by factory owners to fellow industrialists who had not yet settled with their work forces. When, in early June, rumors began circulating at the Henn factory that striking workers in the firm's other, smaller plant in Mikhailov wanted to return to work, workers from the Peresyp plant sent a delegation to convince workers to remain off the job. In early June, striking workers established a citywide committee to bring pressure upon employers still refusing to grant concessions.[36] In this fashion striking workers closed ranks and grew more resolute in their willingness to strike until the owners relented.

According to a report by the Odessa *Okhrana*, workers representing enterprises in Peresyp held a meeting on June 4 at which they discussed not only whether to call a general strike, but whether they should request arms from the SDs. Fearing clashes with police and troops, they did not want to be unprepared.[37] The leader of the workers was Ivan Alekseev, a blacksmith at the Henn Agricultural Tool and Equipment Factory who had been active in workers' politics during the spring. Alekseev, who was unaffiliated with any revolutionary organization, was a major figure in the campaign to win permission for a general workers' assembly and had led the delegation of workers' deputies to Neidhardt and Popov in early May.

In an apparent attempt to counter the workers' growing militancy, the police invited representatives to a negotiating session with factory owners at the Peresyp police station on June 8. But the invitation was a trap: the police had arranged the meeting with the ulterior motive of detaining the thirty-three workers' representatives who showed up at the police station. According to the account in *Iskra,* the strategy backfired because 1,000 workers, after hearing about the arrests, surrounded the police station and demanded their delegates' release. The crowd began to tear down the handrails of the station's courtyard and frightened the police into releasing the detained workers. The crowd, growing in size as bystanders and workers left their jobs to join the demonstration, then marched through the heart of Peresyp singing revolutionary songs and shouting "Down with the Police" and "Long Live the General Strike."[38] Outraged by the tactics of the police, Peresyp workers viewed the arrests as a provocation and a direct challenge to their right to select representatives to promote their interests without government harassment. The arrests confirmed workers in the belief that government officials were on management's side and could not be trusted to serve as impartial mediators in the resolution of labor disputes. Workers saw factory owners as negotiating in bad faith and engaging in subterfuge with the connivance of local officials. Given the enhanced atmosphere of distrust and suspicion, workers became convinced that a more aggressive strategy was needed to exert pressure on recalcitrant employers. They decided upon a general strike and sought the help of local revolutionaries.

On June 10, thirty workers met with Il'ya Levin, a pharmacist's assistant and representative of the Mensheviks. The workers expressed their commitment to a general strike and asked Levin for his organization's support in obtaining weapons in the event the strike turned violent and workers clashed with the police and military. Levin refused to supply the arms, replying that he spoke "in the name of the Social Democrats," and suggested that the workers arm themselves. Not giving up, the Peresyp workers then turned to the SRs in the district, who had been advocating the transformation of the May-June strikes into an armed assault on the government. According to SR sources, the popularity of the SRs, whose strategy seems to have corresponded to the militant mood of the Peresyp workers, grew at the expense of the SDs.[39]

On June 11, Alekseev and two other workers met with an SR representative who agreed to furnish the workers with bombs and revolvers. Later that day the three workers reported the results of the two meetings to the Peresyp workers, whereupon the workers voted to accept the leadership of the SRs in the upcoming general strike. They also instructed their delegates to meet with the SRs on Sunday, June 12, in order to complete plans for the strike.[40] The police learned about the meeting and sent a detachment to arrest the participants. The workers tried to outsmart the police by moving the meeting to a remote beach on the seashore, but they were stymied by the police, who kept abreast of the new plans and surprised the workers by raiding the meeting. Thirty-two persons, including several SDs and SRs, were arrested.[41]

Not surprisingly, this second arrest of worker representatives in four days triggered a new wave of demonstrations and protests. On the morning of Monday, June 13, the day on which the general strike had originally been scheduled, several hundred workers gathered outside the gates of the Henn factory. They anticipated the arrival of strike leaders who were to report the results of the meeting the previous night and issue the call for a general strike. Under the leadership of Alekseev, workers from the Henn plant, who ranked among the best paid workers in Odessa, were an especially militant group and comprised a significant portion of the crowd. They had been on strike since early May, protesting reduced piece rates and a harsh regimen of fines and discipline that included bowing to foremen, and they were growing more and more frustrated with management's refusal to negotiate in good faith. Every morning at six, the striking Henn workers gathered outside the factory gates and spent the day discussing the strike. But on the morning of June 13 they were joined by striking workers from all over Odessa, anticipating the start of a general strike. As news of the arrests spread among the assembled workers and throughout the city, workers, whose numbers were now estimated by some as high as 1,000, became agitated and confrontational.[42]

News of this ominous situation reached Peresyp police chief Parashchenko, who then notified Neidhardt and Aleksandr D. von Hessberg, head of the police in the city. Under orders from Neidhardt and von Hessberg, Parashchenko arrived at the Henn factory at 9 o'clock, accompanied by a detachment of Cossacks, and ordered the workers to disperse. They refused, insisting first on the release of the arrested workers. When Parashchenko suggested they send a delegation to the owner of the Henn factory, the workers scoffed at his proposal but indicated a willingness to avoid direct confrontation by urging him to invite Henn for negotiations. According to Parashchenko, after trying in vain to locate Henn, he again tried to persuade the workers to disperse while he continued his search for the factory owner. But once again the workers rejected Parashchenko's suggestion and remained in place.[43]

Exasperated by his inability to influence the crowd, Parashchenko claimed that he asked the Cossack commander to confer with the workers. It was already noon when the Cossack commander addressed the crowd, and even though his words were barely audible over workers' shouts, catcalls, and whistles, the commander appealed to the workers to go home. Frustrated, he ordered his troops into position, warning the workers that he would give three signals on the trumpet to disperse, after which he would instruct his troops to use force to secure compliance with his order. Parashchenko reported that the workers stood their ground after the first signal. When the trumpeter sounded the second signal, members of the crowd began throwing rocks at the Cossacks, who retreated only to become the targets of more rock throwing by people standing in courtyards of nearby buildings. One rock hit the Cossack commander on his side, knocking him from his horse, while at the same time pistol shots rang out from the crowd. The Cossacks then opened fire on the workers, who finally dispersed after the third volley. When the smoke cleared, dozens were wounded and several young men lay dead.[44]

News of the killings spread rapidly. In response workers walked off their jobs, held impromptu rallies, and marched through the streets of Odessa, ignoring an appeal issued by Neidhardt soon after the shootings to "disperse at the first suggestion of the police."[45] Workers carried one of the bodies to the municipal slaughterhouse, where they announced that government troops had shot "their brothers." Slaughterhouse workers halted work in a display of solidarity, as did workers in other enterprises when news of the shootings reached them. Workers of the Russian Steam Navigation and Trading Company, who had just returned to work after winning their strike, announced a new walkout in protest over the arrests and shootings.[46] The mood of the workers grew more militant as crowds, sometimes numbering as many as 2,000 persons and stretching across several city blocks, roamed the city, attacking policemen and disrupting the movement of trams to the suburbs. In the evening, workers stormed the municipal gas and electric station and cut off the city's power supply. They also blocked rail traffic by seizing four steam engines and one passenger train. At the harbor, workers interfered with port activities. In many instances workers used rocks and guns to counter police efforts to restore order.[47]

By June 14, in the words of Nikolai M. Levchenko, procurator of the Odessa circuit court, the unrest had "assumed a mass character," the full extent of which was "impossible to determine" since workers, many of them armed, were going from enterprise to enterprise urging workers to join the strike.[48] On the whole, workers walked off the job willingly, but in some instances strikers resorted to familiar tactics of threats and violence to coerce hesitant workers to walk off the job. The strike spirit also affected professionals, such as physicians at municipal hospitals who joined other hospital employees on strike after three coworkers were arrested at a rally.[49] As was the case elsewhere in urban Russia at this time, this display of solidarity shown by the physicians illustrates that the challenge to the regime in 1905 was frequently an admixture of cooperation between workers and white-collar employees.

Popov tried to calm down some of the workers in the city center by pleading with them to exercise restraint. He reminded them that confrontation could lead to bloodletting, as events the day before so dramatically illustrated. The factory inspector suggested that workers again approach Neidhardt with a request to hold a citywide assembly, a proposal that not unexpectedly met with derision. At the same time several owners of metalworking and machine-building plants, hoping to cut short the renewed wave of unrest, agreed to a nine-hour workday without lowering wages and to end general searches of workers. They refused to grant strike pay, however, stating that the demand was "illegal and unjust," and reserved the right to search "suspicious-looking individuals." The Henn factory also agreed not to interfere in the selection of worker delegates to negotiations and promised double time for overtime work. These concessions came too late and did not influence workers, whose anger became more manifest as the day wore on. By early afternoon on June 14, virtually all stores in Odessa had shut down and crowds comprised primarily of workers had halted tram traffic. One group of 1,500 even tried to seize the offices of a foreign bank. The next day workers in the railway workshops, who had stood apart from the labor unrest of May and June, decided to join the strike.[49]

Local authorities had clearly miscalculated. The general strike they expected to avert through intimidation and force had materialized as a result of those very tactics. Government action on June 8 and 12 had only served to increase worker discontent; Odessa was now the scene of popular disorders and open conflict between workers and the authorities.

Pitched battles ensued between workers and government forces. Workers, helped by children and teenagers, erected barricades from overturned trams and uprooted telephone poles on several of the city's major thoroughfares. Workers ambushed policemen and soldiers on patrol; they surrounded individual policemen, disarmed them, and savagely beat them, sometimes fatally. By evening, news of bombings and shootings, some reportedly perpetrated by local anarchists and SRs, reached the police. In one incident, a police officer tried to arrest a person suspected of carrying a bomb, but the man detonated it, killing himself and decapitating the policeman. In another, a crowd refused to heed an order to disperse and attacked a policeman, who fell victim to fourteen gunshot wounds. The police had a busy day arresting persons whom they caught on the streets with guns, ammunition, and bombs; they also raided homes suspected of housing bomb laboratories and opened fire on Odessans threatening public calm.[50]

Once again the three social-democratic factions were taken by surprise by the turn of events and never developed a common strategy or plan of action. They were still feuding and contending with the problems of poor finances and police surveillance, which had led some activists to flee Odessa. Those SDs remaining in Odessa went into hiding or left the city at the first sign of trouble on June 13 rather than trying to establish contact with workers. The Bolsheviks supported in principle a general political strike and preparations for an armed uprising, but they stressed that the time was not yet ripe for an uprising or even for open protests. They considered such actions adventuresome and foolish given the workers' lack of organization and weapons. Bolshevik strategy placed less emphasis on a general strike than on armed uprising because the latter tactic promised to deliver a more direct blow to the heart of the autocracy. They therefore withheld support from the workers' movement, even though events in the street clearly indicated that a popular uprising was in the making. The Mensheviks and Bundists, on the other hand, supported a general strike that would lay the basis for an armed uprising.

Despite the frenetic activity of individual SD agitators, who busied themselves distributing leaflets and making speeches, an important reason why SD organizations could not assume direction of the unrest stemmed from their lack of influence and credibility among workers. Not surprisingly, past behavior had seriously discredited them in the workers' eyes. The Menshevik cry for confrontation must have seemed especially ironic in light of their refusal several days earlier to supply guns and ammunition. According to Menshevik accounts, workers criticized the SDs' refusal to furnish arms and excoriated the SRs for failing to deliver the promised number of revolvers and bombs. Local Mensheviks confessed that they were "weak, isolated, unorganized, and cowardly" and lacked "determination and organization," including a willingness "to die." These sentiments were seconded by the Bundist correspondent for *Posledniia izvestiia* (*The Latest News*), who wrote that none of the social-democratic organizations led the strike movement in Peresyp.[51] With the notable exception of the SRs, who supplied a limited amount of weapons to workers and tried to foment insurrection, Odessa's revolutionaries were sending mixed signals; whereas some orators urged workers to rise up and rebel, others pleaded with them to remain calm and refrain from open rebellion. In short, the events of June 13 and 14, as in May, were the result of the initiative of workers who acted on their own without the direction and guidance of the socialist parties.

City officials were helpless to restore order. Even the arrival in the late afternoon of June 14 of four companies from the military garrison failed to quell the unrest, because the police and military refrained from undertaking measures to suppress the disorders. The troops, for example, were stationed primarily at police stations, hardly the most strategic points from which to combat rebellious workers. There were also strong indications that the troops, including the officers, sympathized with the workers and would not shoot at rioters. In some instances, the police used blank cartridges. One Cossack officer justified his refusal to order his troops to open fire on a crowd of workers on the grounds that "they aren't doing anything wrong."[52]

The arrests of workers' deputies on June 8 and 12, along with the shooting of demonstrators on June 13, released accumulated hostility and discontent not only among workers but also among other residents of Odessa. The long-awaited general strike enjoyed widespread support among Odessa's populace and the resultant unrest, which attracted the participation of youths, students, and other members of the general public, threatened to turn into a popular uprising. Stores, shops, and factories were closed and daily life was disrupted. The disorders posed a serious challenge to constituted authority in Odessa, and neither police, military officials, nor even the workers themselves knew where events were heading. Would they snowball into an open rebellion and lead to the overthrow of tsarist authority in Odessa, an objective that was not yet articulated by the workers but nonetheless a possibility? Or would the police and military be able to regain the upper hand and restore order? The outcome was still unknown on the evening of June 14; subsequent events provided answers.

The Battleship *Potemkin* and the Odessa Uprising

On June 14, sailors on the battleship *Potemkin* mutinied, shooting several officers, including the captain, and imprisoning or throwing overboard the rest (events memorialized in Sergi Eisenstein's 1927 film). Trouble on the ship, whose crew and others in the Black Sea fleet had been plotting an insurrection for several months, began when a sailor was shot for protesting a meat ration infested with worms and maggots. Some of the mutineers, long-standing socialists who had operated undetected for several years among the crew, believed that the uprising would inspire similar mutinies on other ships of the Black Sea fleet. The mutineers decided to anchor in Odessa harbor and await the arrival of the rest of the fleet. They intended for the mutinous *Potemkin* to support the Odessa populace by threatening to shell the city if the government attempted to quell street disturbances with force.[53]

During the early morning hours of June 15, the huge battleship arrived in the harbor of Odessa; it altered the complexion of events in several significant ways. While the sailors' mutiny did not trigger social unrest in Odessa, the presence of a naval vessel in open defiance of the government increased the likelihood (particularly in the minds of revolutionaries like Lenin, who sent an emissary to Odessa to direct what he thought was an impending insurrection) that the unrest gripping Odessa would intensify and lead to a successful uprising. As a gendarme's report, dated June 22, stated, "the disorders would undoubtedly not have attained the grand scale that they did if the battleship had not arrived."[54] More importantly, the mutiny overshadowed events in the streets: the entire populace of Odessa turned its attention to the port and battleship, where the outcomes of the naval mutiny and popular disturbances were being determined. Until the departure of the *Potemkin* several days later, all eyes focused on the ship, as civilians and officials anxiously awaited the sailors' next move.

Soon after arriving, a small landing party of sailors deposited the body of their dead comrade, Grigorii Vakulenchuk, on a pier. They placed a note on his chest announcing his murder by the ship's captain and the crew's readiness to support Odessa's populace with armed force. Curious about events in the harbor, thousands of Odessans streamed into the port district as news of the mutiny spread through the city. One observer noted that "the entire port was turned into some kind of sea of lively heads . . . and endless crowds of people kept making their way to the port."[55]

People paid their respects to the dead sailor by placing flowers near him, kissing his hand, and swearing to avenge his death. The ground swell of public mourning revealed the oppositionist mood among Odessans, who welcomed the challenge to the regime posed by the mutiny. The public warmly received the sailors and used launches and rowboats to sail up to the *Potemkin* and provision the crew with food and coal. The detachment of sailors who remained on shore to guard the corpse cautioned the police not to remove the body under risk of immediate retaliation in the form of bombardment by crew members still on the battleship. Some revolutionaries hastened to the harbor to take advantage of the situation by agitating for a general armed uprising.[56]

Police and military officials, lacking a clear, thought-out plan of action, responded to the developments as they unfolded, while remaining careful not to provoke the mutinous sailors. At 6 A.M., before the authorities on shore knew very much about the mutiny, Neidhardt asked General S. V. Kakhanov, commander of the Odessa Military District, to position troops throughout the city in order to stem the influx of civilians already arriving in the port territory to view Vakulenchuk's body. The situation grew more complicated when, several hours later, Neidhardt and Kakhanov learned of the crew's threat to bombard the city if the police or military attempted to interfere with activities in the port. Sometime around 9 o'clock, Neidhardt transferred to the military the authority to restore order in light of the situation's gravity. Kakhanov realized that his troops might have difficulty maintaining law and order given the mood of the people gathering in the harbor, and he now requested reinforcements from other garrisons in the military district, including troops stationed as far as 200 miles away in Ekaterinoslav that could not arrive for at least one or two days.[57]

Kakhanov and his assistant, Major General K. A. Karangozov, took the threat of the sailors to bombard the city seriously, as did hundreds of other Odessans who chose not to go to the port but, in a state of panic, fled the city. The military leaders were in a quandary: they wanted to break up the crowds congregating near Vakulenchuk's body because the demonstrations could escalate into widespread unrest, but they risked incurring the wrath of the sailors if they directed their troops to enter the port to restore order. Neidhardt suggested that troops could furtively make their way into the harbor region on the elevated rail spur that transversed the port, but Kakhanov and Karangozov rejected this proposal as too provocative. Instead, the military preferred to wait it out, thereby giving free rein to the crowds at the harbor. The only decisive measure they took was to surround the port with soldiers during the afternoon, stationing them at both borders of the region and along the bluff overlooking the harbor, to prevent those already gathered at the harbor from exiting and hindering others from entering. This tactic was designed not only to isolate the port from the rest of the city and localize whatever disorders might arise, but, as Karangozov informed Neidhardt, to afford the military easy targets if the decision was made to use force. Although the troops were now under instructions to detain all persons trying to enter the port, it took several hours before the military was properly deployed. Consequently, the crowds grew unimpeded for most of June 15 and numbered several thousand by evening.[58]

Government circles in St. Petersburg, which had been monitoring events in Odessa, were alarmed by this new development. Sometime during the day of June 15, Nicholas II proclaimed martial law in the city and instructed Kakhanov to take "very decisive measures to suppress the uprising in Odessa." However, the pronouncement did not reach Kakhanov until 3 A.M. on June 16. At that time, Kakhanov appointed Karangozov Provisional Governor-General of Odessa, with instructions to restore order.[59]

Despite the proclaimed intentions of the sailors to support the current unrest in Odessa, the crew of the *Potemkin* did not render any assistance and rejected a joint appeal by the city's revolutionary organizations to furnish weapons, shell the city, and send an armed landing force to direct an uprising.[60] Several factors explain this failure to take decisive action and throw the full firepower of the battleship behind the workers of Odessa. Not only did a significant portion of the crew want to avoid additional bloodshed, but a majority of the sailors wanted to confer with crews on other ships of the Black Sea fleet (which were speedily making their way to Odessa with orders to suppress the mutiny) before making any important decisions. The sailors also did not want to weaken the defense of the ship by sending an armed detachment to shore. The ship's crew reasoned that sailors on land are like fish out of water and cannot be as effective a military force as they are on board. Consequently, the sailors refused to fulfill the request for armed assistance made by several SDs who managed to make their way onto the battleship. Instead, the crew suggested the revolutionaries return to shore and tell the crowds to remain calm and patient.

The Bolsheviks, in a sudden change of tactics, joined the Bundists in voicing their disappointment with the sailor's inaction, since they now believed that bombardment of the city center could spark a successful armed offensive on government buildings. The Mensheviks, also changing their thinking on the value of armed uprising, opposed bombardment because they feared too many innocent bystanders would die; they urged the crowds thronging the harbor to disperse peacefully and avoid confrontations with the police and military.[61] As one Soviet historian has written, "Not one of the party organizations rose to the occasion" to lead the rebellious populace.[62] Yet it is highly improbable that the revolutionary parties could have assumed direction of the unrest on either shore or ship given their disunity, indecision, poor organization, understaffing, and, most importantly, the independence of the workers and mutinous sailors. As in May, the SDs were condemned to the role of spectators. Twenty years after the events of June, one Bolshevik participant remembered that the strike was "completely divorced from party leadership."[63]

In retrospect, the sailors' refusal to take decisive action was in all likelihood a missed opportunity to fan the flames of rebellion. A strong display of force by the crew of the *Potemkin* might have harnessed the energy of the public and encouraged further unrest that would seriously have threatened—and perhaps toppled—tsarist authority in Odessa. Moreover, the Peresyp strike committee set up by the workers could have provided the needed direction and command necessary for a successful uprising. Given the paralysis that gripped city officials, disagreements between the police and military, and the initial unwillingness to employ force against the crowd, the possibility existed that the shelling of the city and the presence of an armed landing force might have thrown police and military into such disarray that government buildings could easily have been seized. But inaction and vacillation enabled the police and military to regroup and reassert their control.

While waiting for the sailors to take the next step, workers were distracted from further anti-government demonstrations. Instead of taking the offensive as they had done on the previous two days, Odessa workers ceded center stage to the sailors and were relatively calm until late afternoon on June 15. Several violent and bloody incidents did occur, however, including intermittent shooting throughout the day at the police and military from rooftops and apartment houses, ambushes of police by angry mobs screaming "Beat the police!," and the occasional throwing of bombs.[64]

In the late afternoon and early evening, the crowd in the harbor area began to plunder warehouses. The composition of the looters is difficult to ascertain, since the crowd at the port included men and women of all ages and social groups. But many contemporary accounts attribute the trouble to persons of "undetermined occupations" (*bez opredelennykh zaniatii*) or *bosiaki,* the latter word a catchall term that literally means "barefoot ones" and refers to the urban homeless and downtrodden. In common parlance, *bosiaki* encompassed the lumpenproletariat of urban Russia and could include day laborers and dockworkers as well as vagrants and the homeless, the permanently and gainfully employed as well as the chronically unemployed among the casual labor force. Government officials and members of the educated classes, including the radical intelligentsia, used the word without precision, frequently identifying any troublemaker as a *bosiak* so as to have a ready-made social explanation for public disorders. The preference for simplistic social analyses of urban tensions and unrest reveals the social and cultural prejudices and fears separating educated and middle- and upper-class Russians (*obshchestvo*) from the vast majority of laboring Russians (*narod*). Such was the explanation that gained general currency in many accounts of the June Days, although the vandals included not only *bosiaki* but also a cross-section of Odessa's diverse population: men, women, children, and teenagers of different social groups. Nevertheless, *bosiaki* in the popular sense of the word did comprise a significant portion of the crowd that plundered the docks; a newspaper account of the trial of fifty-two persons accused of vandalism and theft on June 15 indicates that day laborers comprised a significant portion of those arrested.[65]

Fortified by vodka and wine that vandals took from the unguarded storerooms in the port and inspired by inflammatory speeches exhorting them to storm the warehouses, the crowd continued looting warehouses. They carrried off by hand, on horseback, and in rowboats and wagons whatever items they found. Despite the military cordon, many Odessans made their way out of the port into the city center, where they proudly displayed their booty and frequently fell into the hands of the police and military. One dockworker, repeating reports that he had heard at the docks, stated that people in Moldavanka believed that the "tsar has given poor people three days of freedom to take what they want from the port."[66] According to accounts in *Iskra* and *Revoliutsionnaia Rossiia* (*Revolutionary Russia*), some sailors, workers, and members of the general public guarded storerooms of vodka from looting, confiscated liquor from rioters, and threw bottles and cases of alcohol into the Black Sea. As one sailor pleaded with the rioters, "It's freedom we need, not vodka." The rioting continued and took a more destructive bent when the wooden buildings of the harbor were set on fire. The fires lit up the nighttime sky over Odessa and spread steadily and quickly throughout the port. Scores of terrified rioters and onlookers frantically tried to escape from the fire that was consuming the entire harbor region. Nonetheless, these developments did not convince Kakhanov and Karangozov that more vigorous measures were required to stem the disorders or even contain the fire.[67]

Meanwhile, unrest in the center of the city was reaching crisis proportions. Not only were the troops hard-pressed to prevent people from leaving the port, but their efforts to keep out crowds of civilians trying to reach the harbor led to a series of bloody clashes. Around 9:30 P.M. detachments of soldiers and Cossacks found themselves under attack. In one incident, someone detonated a bomb in the downtown section of Odessa, killing a police inspector and injuring several Cossacks. Three civilians were killed and many more wounded by soldiers who subsequently fired upon a crowd of onlookers the authorities claimed were shooting at the soldiers. As the evening wore on, the military found themselves the targets of snipers and bomb throwers elsewhere in the city, and they responded by firing back.[68]

Authorities took official steps to suppress the disorders in the port near midnight, when the fire threatened the liquor storerooms, the Customs House, the ships, and property of foreign governments and companies. Impetus came from a police officer who pleaded with Kakhanov and Karangozov to send reinforcements to the harbor. Although some troops were targets of snipers, the reinforcements did not open fire until their superiors, finally acknowledging the severity of the situation, gave them orders to restore order. What followed was a massacre. Thousands of people, trapped by the cordoning off of the Port Territory, were caught in the crossfire of the soldiers. By the morning of June 16, hundreds—perhaps even a thousand—had died, either from gunshots or from the fire. Many of the casualities perished because they were so drunk they passed out, only to be consumed by flames.[69]

The macabre night of June 15 was a chastening and sobering experience that left the populace of Odessa thunderstruck and frightened scores of people into fleeing the city. As a result of the massacre, worker militance and public disorder petered out. Although the trauma of the bloodletting rivalled the impact of Bloody Sunday in terms of undercutting the legitimacy of tsarist authority and placing the regime in the unenviable position of being responsible for the deaths of hundreds of civilians, this wholesale killing of civilians did not set off another round of unrest. The June uprising, along with the *Potemkin* mutiny, rapidly became part of the myth of the Russian radical movement, and the victims entered the pantheon of revolutionary heroes.

Compared to the preceding days, June 16 was relatively calm and peaceful, although several confrontations between troops and civilians did occur. Even the funeral procession of several thousand mourners for Vakulenchuk—which Kakhanov and Karangozov permitted—was conspicuous for its well-behaved marchers, low-keyed speeches, and determined efforts not to provoke the troops lining the streets between the harbor and cemetery. In the immediate aftermath of the massacre, Odessans were so averse to confrontation that a new wave of protest and violence did not erupt even when soldiers, for unknown reasons, opened fire on the funeral procession when it was returning to the harbor after the burial. Several sailors were either killed, wounded, or arrested in this surprise attack, but the populace did not retaliate.[70]

Despite their initial promise, the crew of the *Potemkin* did not shell the city in response to the massacre. Although the sailors stated that it was too dark to shoot accurately and that they were afraid of killing civilians along with government troops, more compelling reasons explain why they failed to retaliate: the loss of revolutionary zeal, second thoughts about the wisdom of the mutiny among crew members, and the lack of agreement over tactics. The sailors were impelled into action only on the evening of June 16, when they fired several salvos—some of which were blank—out of fear that some harm might have befallen the sailors attending the funeral. One of the shells, targeted for a theater housing a meeting of military officers, missed its objective because a gunner, evidently no longer sympathizing with the mutiny and uprising, deliberately aimed wrong. It is unclear whether the crew at the time of the shelling was aware of the attack on the sailors attending the funeral; it is more probable that crew members were concerned that those sailors were late in returning to the ship and fired the salvos as a warning signal.[71]

The events of June 15 and 16 enabled the government to regroup and reestablish public order. One newspaper on June 16 printed an announcement from the city governor's office instructing the police and military to open fire on public gatherings. The police raided homes and arrested several men caught with bomb laboratories and fake passports. On June 17, Kakhanov announced that groups of twenty or more persons were forbidden to assemble publicly and promised to disperse such gatherings with armed force. His announcement also required homeowners, hotel owners, and innkeepers to report any "suspicious-looking persons" to the police and even threatened landlords with exile if bombs were prepared without their knowledge on their property. Although people flouted the regulation and congregated in the streets, there were no breaches of the peace. Kakhanov also stationed approximately 20,000 troops throughout the city, lending Odessa the atmosphere of an occupied city and ensuring that there would be no additional public disturbances or outbreaks of violence. Funerals of people killed on June 15 and 16 were held on June 18 with no reported trouble. The drama of the *Potemkin* mutiny ended on June 18 when the battleship, accompanied by another ship of the Black Sea fleet whose crew had also defected to the rebel side for one day, weighed anchor and steamed out of Odessa's harbor, heading for Romania.[72]

By June 20, life was returning to normal in Odessa as stores reopened and workers returned to work. Activity at the harbor also resumed, with workers beginning to clear the rubble from dockside and rebuild damaged buildings, piers, and railway tracks. Levchenko wrote that "calm is prevailing once again" and reported two days later that the military had withdrawn from the streets, although "the mood remains extremely anxious" and "a slight provocation could again cause panic and disorders."[73] Many workers on strike since early May reached agreement with employers and were returning to work. In many metalworking, tin, and machine-construction plants, management granted a nine-hour workday and pay hikes and promised improved working conditions, with some enterprises even granting wage increases higher than those requested by the workers. Workers at the Henn plant won the right to elect delegates (although the agreement did not specify their functions and responsibilities) and printers, whose job actions involved participation by Menshevik organizers, achieved a nine-hour workday, higher wages, and formation of a joint management-employee board to resolve disputes. In addition, retail storeowners and owners of shoemaking workshops reached agreement over the price to be paid for shoes, thereby enabling employers to pay their workers higher wages. And Neidhardt, again acting in a conciliatory fashion, ordered the release of the worker representatives who had been languishing in jail for over a week.[74] Yet despite the appearance of normalcy, a tense atmosphere still existed.

The Jewish Question Emerges

Continuing tension was evident in relations between Jews and gentiles, which grew more ominous during times of social and political turmoil. Anti-Jewish feelings ran particularly high throughout Russia during the first half of 1905, with anti-Jewish violence marring the social landscape in several cities. Odessa remained fortunate in that, until June, direct confrontations between Jews and gentiles were avoided. The anti-Jewish disorders in June foreshadowed events in October, when a vicious pogrom would erupt during another period of social and political turmoil.

Two militantly patriotic and pro-tsarist groups, the Holy League and Unity and Strength, had been stirring up anti-Semitic sentiments in Odessa since late 1903, drawing their inspiration from the well-known right-wing politicians V. M. Purishkevich and P. A. Krushevan. The latter's newspaper, *Znamia* (*Banner*), was frequently distributed free throughout the city, especially in the harbor and workers' districts, and was accused by Mayor Zelenyi of fomenting a pogromist atmosphere. Beginning in late January 1905, leaflets circulated blaming the non-Russian nationalities, such as the Georgians, Poles, Armenians, and especially the Jews, for anti-government opposition. The pamphlets called upon Russians to "beat the Jews, students and wicked people who seek to harm our Fatherland" and rid Russia of Jews who "are the cause of evil and grief." The Russian Assembly, the largest right-wing grouping in Russia at the time, also contributed to the anti-Semitic atmosphere by opening a local chapter in early 1905.[75]

Rumors of an impending anti-Jewish pogrom began circulating in February and increased during the Orthodox Holy Week in mid-April. The rumors were nourished by the right-wing belief that Jews were subverting discipline in the military and were therefore responsible for the poor showing of Russian troops in the war. The appearance of pogromist literature inciting Russians to attack

Jews prompted activist Jews to mobilize. Unlike in past years, when they did not take precautions, Jews in Odessa braced themselves for attacks. Building on self-defense groups they had first formed (with the assistance of the Zubatovites) in the aftermath of the 1903 Kishinev pogrom and when fear of a pogrom spread through the city in 1904, Odessa's Jews armed themselves and issued appeals, calling upon non-Jewish residents of Odessa to show restraint and not engage in violent acts against Jews.

Just before Easter Sunday, which fell on April 17, the National Committee of Jewish Self-Defense distributed a series of leaflets threatening non-Jews with armed retaliation in the event of a pogrom. The committee urged all Jews to join self-defense brigades and prepare to counter any attack on Jewish lives and property. Many Jewish residents of Odessa followed the committee's advice to arm themselves with guns, knives, clubs, and whips, and to prepare solutions of sulfuric acid. The Bund, Bolsheviks, and Mensheviks joined in these efforts by reorganizing self-defense brigades they had formed the year before and taking up collections for the stockpiling of weapons and ammunition. The Bund in particular feared that street demonstrations planned for Monday, April 18, to coincide with May Day celebrations in the rest of Europe, would lead to anti-Jewish violence. Despite these preparations, local officials as well as the correspondent of the Bund's newspaper concluded that rumors of a pogrom were unfounded. In fact, the Bund's correspondent wrote that "a pogromist mood was . . . unnoticeable"; Neidhardt's office stated that it had not observed any "pogrom-mongering leaflets," condemned the leaflets of the National Committee of Jewish Self-Defense for "slander" and for giving rise to "alarm among the peaceful residents of our cultured city."[76] April 17 and 18 came and went without serious incident or sign of trouble.

The same could not be said for events in June. During the June unrest, right-wing agitators and pogrom-mongerers appeared in the street. They accused Jews of instigating the current disorders and and encouraged gentiles to attack them. An SR account mentions bicyclists passing out leaflets blaming the Jews for the unrest of June 13, 14, and 15. Similar provocations also occurred during the riot and destruction of the harbor on June 15, resulting in the death of two anti-Semitic rabble rousers: one was shot by Bundists, the other thrown into the Black Sea by furious workers. In one instance a group of workers, at the urging of a Bundist speaker, beat to death a policeman from the Port Authority who had heckled the orator and tried to incite the crowd against her with anti-Semitic remarks.[77]

In the week or so following the massive disorders of mid-June, scattered attacks against Jews were reported as anti-Semitic agitators tried to spark a pogrom among gentiles. On June 20, an anonymous, virulently anti-Semitic, four-page broadside entitled *Odesskie dni* (*Odessa Days*) appeared. It blamed the Jews, in particular the National Committee of Jewish Self-Defense and Jewish secondary school students, for the recent disorders and the tragedy at the port. Accusing Jews of fomenting the unrest and enlisting the support of unwitting Russians, the author of the broadside stated that Jews initiated the shootings of

June 14 and 15 and were responsible for setting fire to the port. The tract ended with a call to hold the Odessa Jewish community collectively responsible for the destruction and demanded compensation for gentiles who suffered property damage and personal loss. In addition, the broadside called for disarming all Jews in Odessa and suggested a general search of all Jewish apartments in the city. Failure to carry out these suggestions, the tract concluded, would make it "impossible for Christians to live in Odessa" and result in a take-over by Jews.[78] Although *Odesskie dni* did not call for acts of anti-Jewish violence and did not lead to any attacks on Jews, its appearance graphically illustrates how in times of social unrest and political crisis, ethnic hostility could come to the fore and threaten further disruption of social calm.

Jews found it difficult to dispel the accusations expressed in *Odesskie dni,* which found their way into the reports of government officials who also held Odessa Jewry responsible for the June unrest.[79] Gendarme chief Kuzubov wrote that the instigators of the unrest and arson were "exclusively Jews," and Count Aleksei P. Ignat'ev, the fiercely reactionary chairman of a government conference set up in 1905 to address the issues of state security and religious minorities, seconded this conclusion in his report on the June disorders in Kherson and Ekaterinoslav provinces. Ignat'ev, who fell victim to an SR assassin in late 1906, accused Jews of setting fire to the port, although he, like most other government officials, furnished no hard evidence or substantiation.[80] These reports highlight the emotionally charged atmosphere of Russian-Jewish relations in Odessa and the extent to which government officials were hard-pressed to make nuanced assessments. In their search for simple explanations and their unwillingness to dig deeper into the root causes of the turmoil in Odessa, bureaucrats and police alike were prepared to affix blame to the Jews. The anti-Jewish campaign in June foreshadowed events in October, when a vicious pogrom would erupt during another period of social and political turmoil.

Concluding Remarks

In sharp contrast to most other cities of the Empire, where the number of work stoppages and strike participants in the spring and early summer tended to decline after the dramatic events of January and February, the labor movement in Odessa heated up in May and June. During the spring of 1905, workers in Odessa not only demanded higher wages, shorter workdays, and other material benefits, but they also insisted on participating on a permanent and equal basis in resolving labor-management disputes and regulating working conditions such as the hiring and firing of personnel. This was not a claim for workers' control, such as emerged in the course of 1917, or an effort to overturn capitalist relations in the factories, but it did mark an attempt to alter the balance of power within enterprises and win workers the right to share in the making of decisions.

The turbulence of the labor unrest in May and June was symptomatic of the general level of discontent felt by Odessa workers, a discontent that infused the strikes with a political significance unanticipated at the outset. The timing of the strikes and their connection to both local circumstances and the crisis enveloping autocratic authority in Odessa as well as the Empire ensured that labor unrest would have serious implications for social and political stability. Odessa workers took the offensive and sought amelioration of working conditions as they became caught up in the spirit of rebellion that had characterized other parts of the Empire since January. Although a specific spark—generally an action that was perceived as deliberately provocative—was necessary to set them into action, by May workers did not need much prodding before walking off the job. The work stoppages of May rested on a foundation of rationality, deliberation, and organization, and they found sustenance in the workers' pent-up anger and frustration. What Abraham Ascher writes about the labor movement throughout Russia at this time applies to the situation in Odessa: "Workers were groping for an effective mode of protest" that stemmed from "an elemental outburst of anger."[81] This is particularly evident in the workers' willingness to walk off the job spontaneously as well as in their efforts to meet on both enterprise and citywide levels to discuss both issues specific to individual plants and trades and concerns affecting all workers in Odessa. They formed strike committees and elected deputies to represent their interests before management, local government, and national authorities. Through these organizations workers challenged the established forms of worker-employer relations and attempted to assume greater control over their lives.

For the workers of Odessa, demands for material concessions and challenges to managerial prerogatives were complementary elements of a strategy based on the workers' belief that they were entitled to a life of dignity and respect. One common demand in these strikes was worker approval of dismissals in enterprises, a clear intrusion into traditional managerial prerogatives. Given the depressed state of the economy and job competition in 1905, workers recognized that job security required at least their partial participation in administrative decisions. Insistence on the right to assemble, select representatives, and participate in the decision-making process was essentially an outgrowth of the struggle for material improvements and not the consequence of an ideological commitment to revolutionary politics. One Soviet historian, writing about the printers, concludes that their June demands showed awareness that "serious improvements in the economic position of the working class could not be realized without fundamental changes in the existing political system."[82] To be sure, some workers, such as radical salesclerks or the printer who wrote in mid-May that "we aren't asking only for a better economic life, but want recognition of our rights as citizens," had acquired a political consciousness that would have pleased Marxist organizers.[83] But it is unlikely that large numbers of workers in May and June would have subscribed to this precise formulation, although it is apparent that a critical mass of workers was beginning, albeit slowly and unevenly, to attach importance to the principles of freedom of assembly and representation, particularly when they had relevance to the workers' struggle for improved working conditions. Thus, a key to understanding the agitated state of workers in May and June and the tenacity with which workers held fast to their position is provided by this admixture of demands.

Workers had been radicalized in large measure by the failure of municipal authorities to sanction a citywide meeting of workers' representatives to discuss first medical insurance and then strike grievances. This refusal stemmed from contradictory government policies that straitjacketed local officials by limiting their options while raising workers' expectations. On the one hand, at the prompting of St. Petersburg, workers had been invited to participate on several commissions to resolve labor disputes. But on the other, government policy forbade workers to assemble on a citywide basis. Because those workers involved in labor disputes were beginning to link improvements in working and living conditions to the right to assemble and discuss their collective needs, the prohibition of a citywide assembly of workers dashed their hopes and generated more work stoppages. Frustration with the government's callous disregard of good-faith bargaining grew into moral outrage in June, when the police deviously arrested workers' deputies invited to negotiate a settlement with industrialists whose workers had been on strike since early May. The arrests antagonized the workers, who perceived these police tactics as a frontal assault on their collective interests and dignity. In response, workers redoubled their resolve to maintain a united front until their demands were met.

Labor unrest in the spring set the stage for developments during the second half of the year. Disorder died down after mid-June largely because employers acceded to some of labor's demands and workers bristled under the combined impact of martial law and memories of the June Days. Workers received valuable organizational and practical experience, which they then parlayed into the formation of trade unions and a soviet of workers' deputies in the fall. The urge to mobilize and organize remained alive, as did the workers' claim to a life of empowerment. In fact, the partial success of the spring strikes and the sense of power that workers experienced in the collective actions of May and June may have contributed to a noticeable sense of confidence, feistiness, and bravado among workers throughout the remaining months of 1905. As the factory inspector for Odessa reported at the end of the year: "After the May and June strikes, which the workers won in the majority of instances, Odessa factory workers continued to be elated . . . and engage without special reason in individual work stoppages and clashes with factory owners."[84]

The dynamics of labor protest in Odessa reveal that the rational pursuit of workers' objectives was punctuated with violence. Although we must be careful to distinguish between the violence that accompanies strikes (such as threats or attacks against strikebreakers) and riots that result from popular passions and discontent, we must acknowledge that force was an integral part of the Odessa labor movement in the spring of 1905 and fed upon years of accumulated tensions, frustrations, and resentments of workers as second-class citizens.

It was the capacity of the labor movement to degenerate into unpredictable outbursts of wanton destruction that made worker protest such a potent and disruptive force in Odessa. In general, workers pursued their goals with self-discipline, but their restraint quickly gave way to violence directed against the government and employers when provoked. The June disorders preceding the arrival of the *Potemkin* therefore fit the pattern of reactive collective action and violence outlined by Charles, Louise and Richard Tilly, since government and employer resistance to what workers regarded as legitimate demands and the arrest of workers' deputies elicited a violent response by Peresyp workers.[85] Other forms of worker violence, however, such as the destruction of the harbor on June 15, do not fit this pattern of reactive collective action and reflect instead a more anarchic expression of labor protest and social discontent. This dual nature of protest in Odessa tended to be rooted in the socio-economic, occupational, and residential characteristics of the workers themselves; workers in metalworking and machine-construction plants, as well as in a variety of workshop settings, generally displayed a high degree of organization; less qualified and poorly paid day workers tended to avoid organized protest and preferred to riot. Yet, as we have seen, even organized workers gave vent to their discontent in hostile ways and resorted to acts of unmediated violence when sufficiently provoked. Several forms of collective action and violence coexisted in Odessa, and during the second half of 1905 this tension—between restraint and organization on the one hand, and violence and fury on the other—continued to characterize the labor movement, with serious consequences for the outcome of worker protest and the revolution.

6

Breathing Spell and Renewed Confrontation

In the wake of the June bloodshed, the labor movement in Odessa entered a period of remission for the duration of the summer. Except for sporadic and short-lived work stoppages, workers were relatively quiescent, much like urban workers elsewhere in the Empire. The number of strikers in the Empire in June and July was well below that for the explosive months of January and February, and the strike movement reached its nadir for the year in August and September. The next wave of labor unrest started in September and swelled to a peak for the year in October, when the Factory Inspectorate estimated some 481,000 workers went on strike.[1] The reemergence of mass unrest in urban Russia crystallized in conjunction with several other developments that affected political stability: the radicalization of the liberal movement after Nicholas II announced plans in August for elections to Russia's first national legislative assembly, the so-called Bulygin Duma; the signing in August of the Treaty of Portsmouth, which marked Russia's humiliating defeat at the hands of Japan; the uprising of peasants and national minorities; military mutinies and the revival of student radicalism after the granting of university autonomy in late August. These developments signaled the faltering of autocratic power. The movement against the autocracy culminated in October with the outbreak of an Empire-wide strike of railway workers and personnel that led to a general strike which paralyzed Russia's cities. Workers in Odessa, along with high school and university students, white-collar workers, professionals, and revolutionaries, formed one element in the loose, broadly based coalition that forced the autocracy to capitulate and issue the October Manifesto, which established a popularly elected legislative assembly and guaranteed fundamental civil liberties.

One of the remarkable aspects of October 1905 was the confluence of divergent social and political movements that directly challenged the autocracy. Workers, like many other politically active forces, eagerly joined in the general revolutionary tide and the upswelling of popular protest against the autocracy. The temporary political alliance, albeit an informal one that not everyone acknowledged or was even conscious of, between blue- and white-collar employees, between professionals and proletarians, between liberals and radicals, held the key to the united front with which Russian society confronted the regime and extracted major concessions. The different strains of the opposition movement—professional, student, and proletarian—came together in October to force Nicholas II to acknowledge to his great dismay that limitations to his power existed. The workers' agenda in October merged for the most part with that of the other opposition groups, which were also calling for fundamental political reform. Despite the presentation of economic demands that were specific to workers in different enterprises, workers were less concerned with issues of wages and hours than with realizing the hopes and ambitions that characterized the liberation movement, in particular rights of citizenship. The October Manifesto was the formal expression of the dilution of autocratic power and authority.

As in June, the labor movement in October was characterized by both organization and violence. On the one hand, workers engaged in a general strike that brought life in Odessa to a standstill and displayed elements of direction and unity. These would link the first half of 1905 with the trade unions and Soviet of Workers' Deputies that emerged in November and December, when the united opposition front of October began to break into its constituent parts. On the other, workers also gave vent to anti-Semitic sentiments and participated in a violent pogrom against the Jews of Odessa. This outburst of wanton and destructive pogromist behavior undercut the solidarity of workers, which had effectively cut across national and religious divisions prior to October. The remaining chapters examine the interplay between the two forces which animated and ultimately divided the labor movement in Odessa, and which led to the defeat of the revolution: the urge to pursue and defend workers' collective interests in a sober and restrained, but nonetheless militant, manner; and the tendency to engage in spasms of rage and fury. This chapter focuses on the situation in Odessa from the immediate aftermath of the June Days to the start of the October pogrom, including the revival of worker and student opposition and the beginning of a general strike in mid-October.

The Quiet before the Storm

The fire on the night of June 15 destroyed almost all the buildings in the port and severely damaged several dozen ships. In an economy already suffering from the effects of war and recession, the destruction of port facilities, property, and stocks of grain and other wares contributed to the further deterioration of the local economy. The fire caused millions of rubles worth of damage and accentuated unemployment among workers whose livelihoods depended on commerce.[2] One newspaper reported that approximately 20,000 dockworkers and day laborers could not find work.[3] This occurred at a time of the year when the port was traditionally most active and the demand for labor at its peak. Partly in response to the depressed state of the economy, porters at the harbor formed an artel in September to facilitate finding work for its members.[4]

The general economic crisis was also made worse by a crisis of confidence that overcame foreign shipping companies and businessmen after the June unrest. Merchants and industrialists doing business in Odessa lost faith in their customers' ability to fulfill contractual obligations, and many foreign shipping firms cut back traffic to Odessa by at least two-thirds. Scores of industrialists from Lodz and Warsaw, who traditionally sent their wares on credit to Odessa merchants, grew wary of extending credit after the disorders. Foreign firms began demanding payment in cash before delivering goods to their Odessa customers, and banks stopped loaning money to Odessa businessmen.[5]

Moreover, the cost of exporting grain from Odessa dramatically increased. Not only were export operations slower due to the destruction of harbor facilities, but wagons, slower and more expensive than rail, were now carrying grain to the harbor due to the disruption of rail service to dockside caused by the fire. This shift in the mode of transportation reinforced the competitive advantages already enjoyed by other nearby ports and led to a transfer of shipping activities to Nikolaev, Kherson, and other Black Sea ports.[6]

The end of the Russo-Japanese War in August gave rise to encouraging signs that the city would pull itself out of the economic doldrums. Demand for Odessa products picked up as orders arrived from cities in the Russian Far East, and in September a ship left Odessa for the region, the first one to do so since the outbreak of the war. By mid-September trade had revived so strongly that Odessa newspapers were reporting that the port lacked sufficient ships to handle revived trade and that goods awaiting shipment to Vladivostok were piling up in the harbor. At the same time, foreign firms were beginning once again to place orders for Odessa-made machine parts and iron goods.[7]

Despite these welcome signs of economic revival, not all sectors of the economy had entered a period of renewed vitality by fall. Sectors like the building trades remained depressed, despite the employment of more than a thousand workers to rebuild the harbor. Many thousands of dockworkers and day laborers remained out of work, and the number of hungry and homeless increased to such alarming proportions that municipal authorities solicited contributions from the Stock Exchange and shipping companies to meet the costs of housing and feeding the needy.[8] Various firms, brokerage houses, petty traders, and merchants also continued to declare bankruptcy as the credit crunch intensified and the money supply dwindled during the summer.

Another consequence of the June Days was the imposition of martial law, a state of affairs that some prominent members of the business community blamed for hindering economic recovery. In a petition authored by A. A. Anatra, chairman of the Odessa Stock Exchange, and sent to officials in St. Petersburg, Odessa's financial and commercial elite complained that martial law contributed to a climate of uncertainty and discouraged merchants and industrialists from conducting business in Odessa. Its continuation during the summer, argued Anatra, "created panic" among businessmen who did not want to engage in trade under such circumstances. Anatra advocated the lifting of martial law so Odessa could project an image of normalcy and stability. Minister of Finance Kokovtsov lent credence to Anatra's analysis when he reported that foreign merchants refused to extend credit to Odessa grain merchants because they lacked faith in the ability of local merchants to fulfill orders.[9]

Not all members of the Odessa business community agreed with Anatra's petition. Many factory owners welcomed martial law, since it permitted them to resume the normal operations fully confident that the army would ensure law and order. Martial law encouraged some industrialists to retaliate against their work forces by reintroducing indiscriminate body searches among workers exiting their plants, a practice many employers had agreed to stop. Owners also began to renege on other terms of agreements reached with workers. For them, martial law was an opportunity to reimpose previous conditions of work and dismiss employees who had been active in the strikes and activism of May and June.[10] Such brazen disregard for the agreements hashed out between employers and workers sowed the seeds of mistrust and contributed to increased friction at the workplace.

Most highranking police and government officials in Odessa also supported retention of martial law. For these officials, martial law facilitated the restoration of public order, enabled them to control the populace, and helped weaken the revolutionary movement. The premature lifting of martial law, they feared, would only encourage a renewal of unrest. As early as June 20, Odessa procurator Levchenko expressed his concern that revolutionary activity would revive as soon as martial law was lifted. Believing that the June disorders were due in large measure to the fact that "a significant portion of the Odessa population is hostile to the police and administration," Levchenko urged that martial law remain in effect until the government had eliminated the possibility of renewed revolutionary activity.[11]

Levchenko's apprehension was seconded in reports by Kakhanov and Karangozov. Both men, relying on information supplied by Bobrov and Kuzubov, stressed that the lifting of martial law would provoke street disorders and give revolutionaries the opportunity to organize a general strike. Indeed, police reports from mid-July asserted that agitators were stirring up workers to strike as soon as martial law was lifted, which they expected to occur within a few days.[12] Kakhanov attributed the social calm after mid-June to martial law and pointed to the disorders continuing in those districts of Kherson province not under martial law as proof of his assertion. According to him, "all rebellious persons are waiting for the lifting of martial law so they can resume their criminal activities." Kakhanov warned that exiled revolutionaries would return immediately to Odessa to resume their seditious activities.[13] Karangozov cited the continued circulation of revolutionary proclamations, the seizure of bombs, weapons, and laboratories, and open public hostility toward the police as evidence that the revolutionary movement in Odessa "is not slowing down, but will burst out again with the same strength as before." He wrote that "the existing calm exists only on the surface, but is no guarantee of genuine calm in the event of a quick end to martial law." Even though worker unrest had died down, Karangozov noted the existence of "uninterrupted agitation" in factories and believed that "trouble is brewing beneath the surface." Joining Kakhanov in his assessment of the situation in Odessa, Karangozov advised keeping martial law in effect indefinitely.[14]

Among local officials only Neidhardt believed that it was time to end martial law. Although he agreed that the potential for renewed disorders was great, the city governor argued that martial law had a constricting effect on trade. Confident that the police could maintain order and angered over his loss of power during martial law, he complained that it "paralyzed" civilian power because the military was not prepared to administer civilian affairs. Consequently, Neidhardt requested restoration of full police authority to his office, especially the right to exile undesirable persons.[15]

Martial law remained in effect until September 30; during its three-and-a-half month tenure, there were few breaches of public order or incidents of labor unrest. Martial law contributed to the restoration of law and order in Odessa because it made it easier for the authorities to round up and exile known and suspected troublemakers. Karangozov, for example, ordered plainclothes policemen to search suspicious-looking individuals for guns and bombs and exiled several hundred workers for participating in the June strikes.[16] The police arrested a group of SRs suspected of plotting to kill local officials during a church service commemorating the birth of the tsar's son.[17] As one Bolshevik organizer reported at the time, martial law "has shattered the organization" by compromising party members and making it very difficult to find secure apartments in which to conduct meetings. He added that "mass arrests, exiles, and searches in the streets . . . have created an oppressive atmosphere" that hurt party work. This disarray continued into the autumn months, and as a result in September and October the Bolsheviks and Mensheviks once again found themselves watching the outbreak of popular unrest from the sidelines, outstripped by the pace of worker radicalization.[18]

Along with martial law as a factor in preventing a new wave of public disorder, we must consider the impact of the June massacre, memories of which no doubt haunted workers. The aftershock and the pained recollection of the hundreds who perished in the fire and shooting had a chilling effect on the workers, who were now less willing to confront management. Moreover, since labor unrest was at a nadir during the summer throughout urban Russia, the likelihood that Odessa workers would be inspired by workers and strikes elsewhere in the Empire was minimized.

The absence of major disorders did not mean, however, that tensions in the city had dissipated. In July and August, civilians and police clashed in several incidents that revealed the volatility of life in Odessa. For example, on August 22 several hundred Jews and gentiles, protesting the brutal murder of a Jew by a Russian, attended a rally organized by Mensheviks and marched through Odessa under the watchful eye of the police. When several marchers unfurled flags with anti-government slogans, a detachment of Cossacks and police swooped down on the demonstrators, injuring and arresting nearly 100 people. In another incident, several hundred Jews pelted police with rocks in an attempt to free a coreligionist detained for attacking a groundskeeper who had ordered a group of Jews congregating in the street to disperse.[19]

In the realm of labor-management relations, workers and their employers settled disputes for the most part amicably. Factory inspector Popov attributed the quick resolution of disputes to the fact that workers could not afford another round of work stoppages.[20] The factories of Peresyp, which were on the cutting edge of the unrest in May and June, escaped open conflict during the summer. Nonetheless, Odessa was not entirely free of labor strife while martial law was in effect and unsettled scores still existed. For the most part, work stoppages in July and August were infrequent, short-lived, and consisted of isolated incidents primarily concerning wage and hour demands among workshop and other nonfactory workers.[21] But some disputes turned violent as tensions in some enterprises reached the breaking point. In one incident, a dozen or so workers at the Bellino-Fenderikh Iron Foundry resorted to a time-worn tradition in labor disputes and carted out in a wheelbarrow a German foreman they accused of crude and abusive treatment.[22]

Workers remained committed to defending the right of workers to select representatives to play a role in resolving labor-management disputes. Several incidents in the summer illustrate the significance that workers placed on institutionalized representation in eliminating the inequities and injustices of the workplace. In some of these disputes, the existence of a grievance procedure, one fruit of the spring strikes, contributed significantly to the settlement of disagreements.

At the Vysotskii Teapacking Plant, where several hundred teenaged girls and women were employed, the introduction of worker deputies played "a visible role in the regulation of relations between workers and employers."[23] In late April, Vysotskii employees won the right to elect six deputies, who then helped defuse situations before they developed into major disputes. These deputies persuaded management not to dock the pay of nine workers who had refused to work on a major religious holiday. In June, they ensured that an April strike agreement would be honored when they verified the financial situation of 150 employees who had requested pay advances of 70–75 rubles each.[24]

Tensions at the plant heightened in late August when the police arrested and exiled a worker for protesting working conditions. Coworkers responded by demanding the immediate reinstatement of the dismissed employee and reaffirmation of the right of workers to elect deputies to oversee conditions in the plant. The workers decided not to stage a long walkout, preferring to heed their representatives' advice and urge the Odessa public to boycott the products of the plant until their demands, drawn up with the help of Mensheviks, were met. The boycott was successful and the fired worker was reinstated.[25]

Negotiations between shipping companies and their crews perhaps best illustrate the significance that worker representation had acquired, not only for employees but for local officials and employers as well. During the merchant marine strike in April, owners of the shipping lines, crews, and local officials had agreed to conduct negotiations for three months. By mid-July, after approximately seventy stormy bargaining sessions during which workers at times threatened to quit negotiations, agreement was reached. In addition to resolving issues of wages and hours, shipowners and their crews agreed to the formation of a "Registration," elected and managed by the sailors themselves; sailors were also given the power to appoint their foremen. Under the terms of the agreement, Registration possessed the authority to settle labor disputes, review decisions relating to the dismissal of workers and, most importantly, operate a labor exchange for filling vacancies on all ships in Odessa. The labor exchange was intended to eliminate the role of labor contractors and inject a measure of order and fairness into the hiring process.[26]

Karangozov provisionally approved the formation of Registration for a period of several months and permitted the election of a ten-member board of directors. The move was enthusiatically received by the sailors; some 2,000 joined the organization during its first months of existence. Not all shipowners welcomed the establishment of an institution that they regarded as impinging on their managerial prerogatives of hiring and firing. When some owners and ship captains tried to evade the terms of the agreement by not notifying the labor exchange about job vacancies, the sailors declared boycotts of these ships in order to secure compliance. Registration enjoyed such strong support among sailors that boycotted ships were unable to hire enough workers to break the boycott. The organization also played a crucial role in maintaining labor peace by adjudicating approximately 600 disputes by October 1. Consequently, city officials ignored the opposition of disgruntled shipowners and granted Registration permanent status.[27] The institutionalization of the sailors' formal participation in labor-management relations highlights the extent to which local officials acknowledged the utility and viability of such arrangements as a means of defusing tensions.

The Storm Breaks: October 1905

The popular unrest and disturbances of October began with the activities of university students, whose mid-September meetings and assemblies served as an impetus for much of the protest that occurred in Odessa one month later. After a silence of more than six months, due to the fact that many students had been away from Odessa while the university was closed, university students reappeared in Odessa in September in expectation of returning to classes. They emerged as active participants in the opposition movement and advocates of radical political reform. More importantly, along with the school's faculty, they opened up the university for popular rallies and meetings. Well attended by thousands of workers, students of all ages, other members of the general public, and even soldiers, these assemblies helped mobilize the Odessa citizenry against local and national authorities and popularized liberal and socialist platforms. The university served as the nerve center of the opposition movement in Odessa as university students, along with their professors, secondary school students, workers, and revolutionaries, used its buildings to hold mass rallies, plan demonstrations, and organize and direct self-defense groups. The student assemblies were noted for their radicalism and marked by the presence of large numbers of workers, who frequently participated in the proceedings; at one gathering, for example, workers from the Henn plant declared themselves in favor of a nationwide general strike. As Senator Aleksandr Kuzminskii, head of the government's investigation of the October pogrom, stated in his final report, "the university was transformed into a place which was accessible to revolutionary mobs."[28]

The government's August 27th declaration of university autonomy provided both faculty and students with the opportunity to use the university as a political forum. Autonomy gave faculty members the right to decide on issues concerning the internal order of the university, such as the organization and conduct of classes, the election of a rector and departmental deans, and the regulation of student life. With the granting of autonomy, discussion of reopening the university for instruction occupied the minds of both students and faculty. Since January the University Council, the governing body of the university, increasingly under the influence of liberal and radical professors in the Academic Union, had used its powers to block the efforts of right-wing colleagues seeking to halt the leftward drift of university policy. The Academic Union not only drafted the politically radical resolutions subsequently adopted by the University Council, but its members also succeeded in electing Ivan Zanchevskii as rector of the university and overturning the election of a right-wing professor as dean of the law faculty.[29]

Although he did not belong to the Academic Union, Zanchevskii openly embraced the liberal views of the organization and sympathized with the objectives of leftist students. Under his direction the faculty adopted a series of measures designed to reopen the university in an atmosphere of academic and personal freedom. The faculty reinstated students expelled for participation in the student strike of February 1904, closed two right-wing student organizations, rehired three professors dismissed for liberal political activity, and ended student inspections. The University Council also agreed to ignore the numerus clausus governing the admission of Jews, Georgians, and other national minorities by enrolling them as auditors in the likely event that the Ministry of Education rejected its petition to admit them as full-time students. In addition, on October 2 and 3, the University Council recognized the right of students to hold assemblies and organize politically so they could actively participate in the liberation movement. The faculty also passed a resolution calling for fundamental political and civil liberties.[30] Senator Kuzminskii no doubt exaggerated the influence of Zanchevskii when he accused the rector of being "the chief disseminator of revolutionary ideas among students," yet there is no denying that Zanchevskii gave his blessing to the political activities of students by sanctioning rallies on university premises and at times even presiding over them.[31] In doing this, he ignored decrees of the Ministry of Education forbidding public assemblies and rallies on school premises.[32]

Students took advantage of university autonomy to hold general assemblies at which they debated conditions for returning to classes. Organized by the Coalition Council, the student assemblies quickly became a forum for opposition to autocracy, with Kadets, SDs, anarchists, SRs, Bundists, and various Zionist groupings debating and delivering incendiary orations about political oppression and the approaching revolution. Originally attended by a sprinkling of secondary school students, these meetings gradually attracted workers, soldiers, and the general public. The first student assembly, held on September 17, attracted approximately 1,500 men and women, mostly students; by October 9, between 8,000 and 10,000 people attended a meeting convened by the Coalition Council. One newspaper account claimed that over 90 percent attending this assembly were non-students.[33]

Karangozov was especially disturbed by the presence of non-students at these meetings. On September 18, he warned Zanchevskii that public meetings were forbidden at the university and demanded that his office be informed of all planned student assemblies. He also urged the rector to prevent non-students from attending meetings. The next day he announced that members of the general public who participated in student assemblies were subject to a fine of up to 3,000 rubles or three months in prison.[34] Despite these admonitions and threats, Karangozov was unable to prevent people not affiliated with the university from attending student assemblies because university officials claimed immunity from Karangozov's instructions. The struggle between Karangozov and university officials intensified with the lifting of martial law on September 30, which encouraged the Coalition Council and Academic Union to act more defiantly. In early October, the university's faculty proclaimed that the university is "not only for science but also for political struggle" and officially welcomed non-students to rallies and assemblies on university premises.[35]

With the end of martial law, university students met more freely to discuss future strategy. One of their first acts was to approve a resolution, recently adopted by the student body of Moscow University, stating that universities should reopen so students could pursue both political activities and education.[36] On the morning of October 4, some 2,000 people (mostly students) listened to professors and fellow students deliver impassioned speeches calling for the overthrow of the autocracy and the establishment of a constituent assembly. It was not the first time such appeals had been heard at a student meeting, but this gathering had a particularly heated and radical tone. During the rally a hat was passed around, inscribed with the slogan, "Contribute for the arming of warriors."[37] As the assembly wore one, the students grew more defiant and aggressive. When the police commanded them to leave the student cafeteria where they had gathered for lunch, only 600 obeyed the directive. The remaining students, supported by their professors and Zanchevskii, refused to disperse, claiming that the assembly was legal and that the police were overstepping their authority.[38]

The mood of the participants grew more elated and jubilant, especially when several hundred students and professors marched to the train station to greet S. P. Iaroshenko, a popular professor and city councillor returning to Odessa after a period of temporary exile for political activities in May and June. They greeted Iaroshenko with shouts of welcome and lifted him on their shoulders. They paraded through the streets of central Odessa, singing songs and shouting anti-government slogans, and some demonstrators appealed to a soldier watching the procession to convince his fellow soldiers not to take repressive measures in the event of an uprising.[39] As Kuzubov wrote in his report about the events of October 4:

> The mood of the professors, university students, and secondary school students, as well as the workers, acquired a tone of confidence regarding the correctness of their demands and the possibility of achieving them. On the whole, the populace was not timid in the streets and theaters and expressed the boldest hopes.[40]

The October 4 meeting was followed by assemblies the next three days at which students and professors continued to discuss pressing academic and political issues and revolutionaries issued appeals for an armed uprising. Students directly challenged Karangozov by removing the sign forbidding non-students to enter the university and by continuing to hold political assemblies. Behaving very much like university students elsewhere in Russia, they called for the abolition of the numerous clauses restricting religious and national minorities and added demands for the admission of women to the university and for the establishment of a Ukrainian studies program with classes taught in Ukrainian. Students also decided to hold a memorial service for the late Prince S. N. Trubetskoi, a prominent liberal and rector of Moscow University. They read aloud a faculty telegram to the Minister of Education which explained that student unrest was continuing because "students are children of society and of the people and clearly react to all events." The students also signaled their support for the faculty's assertion that peaceful and orderly classes could not resume until fundamental civil rights and political liberties were granted. On October 7, when students overwhelmingly approved a Coalition Council resolution calling for elections to a constituent assembly, professors wholeheartedly supported their students' demands.[41] Professor Shchepkin, head of the recently established branch of the Kadets, added to the highly charged atmosphere when he told students: "We professors, your fathers, should first use the remaining means at our disposal to achieve freedom, and if these means don't help, then we'll strike out with you in our own *Potemkin*."[42]

These student assemblies, with their politically charged speeches and appeals, set the tone for a mass rally convened by the Coalition Council on Sunday, October 9. According to police and journalistic accounts, men and women of all social classes and nationalities filled six auditoriums of the university's medical school. Workers, professionals, students, peasants, and soldiers rubbed shoulders as they listened to dozens of speeches by representatives of various student and political organizations. Although some Bolsheviks wanted persons attending the rally to be armed, their more moderate colleagues insisted on a peaceful rally that would not provoke the authorities. Revolutionaries continued to distribute socialist literature and even sold pictures of Marx in order to raise money; representatives of the Coalition Council and revolutionary parties collected over 6,000 rubles for a fund that would be at the disposal of all organizations participating in the rally. The assembly ended in the late afternoon, when student leaders urged the public to go directly home and avoid confrontations with the police.[43]

The revival of labor unrest, not only in Odessa but throughout urban Russia, coincided with the revitalization of the student movement. Walkouts began in September among Moscow printers and soon embraced other workers in the country's second city, as well as sparking sympathy strikes in St. Petersburg and elsewhere. A stoppage by workers on the Moscow-Kazan railroad during the first week of October, concerning pension plan reform and other unfulfilled economic grievances, spread like wildfire to other railways. The walkout by railway workers provided the impetus for a general strike that gripped the Empire by the middle of the month and shook the regime to its very foundations. The strike had spread to Odessa by October 11 and acted to galvanize the opposition movement. It culminated several days later in massive work stoppages and armed clashes between workers, students, and the police. Workers and students were the dominant force in the street fighting, but many white-collar employees, professionals, and members of the city council lent their full support to the general strike. The October walkouts in Odessa were strengthened by the broad coalition of social and political groups seeking to extract concessions from the regime.

On October 11, telegraphers at the South West Railroad's main station announced their sympathies with fellow telegraph agents on strike elsewhere and walked off the job. Following in the footsteps of railway workers in the rest of the Empire, white-collar employees took the initial steps and were immediately joined by other office workers at the station. Over the course of the next several days, engine crews, switchers, couplers, watchmen, and workers in the workshops joined the work stoppage. In an all-too-familiar scenario, the decision to strike was not unanimous; many workers walked off the job only after striking colleagues went from station to station, urging others to join the work stoppage and sometimes threatening violence to secure compliance. At the railway workshops, for example, striking telegraphers and SD activists spent the better part of a day convincing undecided workers to join the walkout already begun by their fellow workers.[44]

Stating that they were reacting to the railway's failure to fulfill a promise to improve working and living conditions, railway workers elected a strike committee consisting of representatives of manual and office workers from all depots, branch lines, and workshops in Odessa. The committee, soon numbering some four dozen delegates, selected the Bolshevik Ivan Avdeev as chair and formulated a set of demands calling for economic concessions, civil rights, and political reforms, including a constituent assembly. This was approved by a general assembly of workers, which then commissioned a dozen or so workers to present the demands to main headquarters in Kiev and, if necessary, to the Minister of Communications himself in St. Petersburg. Despite efforts by military detachments to guard railway buildings and equipment and keep the trains operating, passenger and freight traffic was hopelessly disrupted and had virtually halted by October 15. Hundreds of passengers were stranded at stations that could not handle the needs of travelers who could not afford accommodations. Both Kuzubov and Bobrov expressed apprehension that the strike, which workers vowed to maintain until the return of their delegates, could signal the beginning of a general work stoppage.[45]

At the same, time students at several secondary schools with large numbers of Jewish pupils began their strike. Inspired by the rallies and demands for academic freedom at the university, students at the Emperor Nicholas I Commercial High School requested on October 11 permission to assemble and discuss the current state of affairs in Russia. The school's administration not surprisingly refused, prompting the students to announce a boycott of classes. Two days later, a group of senior students at the Faig Commercial High School also walked out of their classes, joining their fellow students in the streets.[46]

On the morning of October 14, students from the two schools tried to shut down classes at all secondary schools in Odessa. They marched from school to school, disrupting classes, breaking windows, and urging other students to join them. At some schools students simply walked out of classes as soon as the protesters appeared, and in other instances school principals were persuaded to suspend classes. On the whole, students responded enthusiastically to the appeals of the strikers: they unfurled red flags from school windows and joined the procession of students winding its way through the streets of central Odessa. By 2 P.M. some thirty-five schools had been affected by walkouts; the number of student strikers was estimated at approximately 2,000.[47]

Heeding the appeals of many school principals, Neidhardt instructed his police force to guard the city's high schools. Violence finally erupted at the Berezina High School for Women when twenty policemen confronted a crowd of students and began to disperse them with sabres. Several policemen and students were injured, with one student suffering serious head wounds that required extensive surgery. According to some policemen involved in the incident, they were forced to use their sabres because students were throwing rocks. A military doctor, the principal of the Odessa School of Commercial Navigation, and even several policemen, however, testified that the police viciously attacked the demonstrators without warning or provocation. Bobrov concluded in his official report that there was "no indication that students provoked the police attack by throwing rocks."[48]

By late afternoon, several thousand students, workers, and other concerned Odessans (18,000 according to one account) jammed the medical school for a rally, where news of the beatings evoked emotional condemnations of the police. The Coalition Council announced the suspension of all classes, which had been scheduled to resume that very day, and invited all residents of Odessa to discuss "the current state of affairs" at a meeting the next morning. The University Council, in turn, resolved to inform the Minister of Education that it was impossible to resume classes in light of "the barbaric beatings."[49] After the rally a large number of students and others headed for the city council building, where they disrupted a meeting between city councillors, Zanchevskii, and other leading members of the University Council. Shouting "Down with Neidhardt" and "Death to Neidhardt," the crowd demanded the city governor's resignation and his replacement by a provisional civilian administration and militia.[50]

The next day, Saturday, October 15, witnessed further disruption of normal public life. Fearing massive disorders, directors of Odessa's private banks decided at an emergency meeting to close their offices. Many restaurants, stores, and hotels chose not to open for business. In actions reminiscent of January, people began stocking up on food and other necessities in expectation of widespread labor stoppages. The hoarding further raised the prices of sugar and coal, already high as a result of shortages caused by the rail strike. Workers throughout the city also began to walk off the job. Unlike in May and June, when many workers were primarily motivated by issues that concerned them directly, in October larger numbers of workers from a broad cross-section of the labor force reacted to events outside the factory and shop gates, expressing a more generalized discontent with the existing order. All the discontent and anger percolating since June once again boiled over as workers, provoked by the police's mistreatment of the students, took to the streets with students and revolutionaries. Economic grievances, although expressed by many workers who went out on strike, became submerged in the upheaval as the populace of Odessa pitted forces against representatives of the autocracy. One event that illustrates graphically the extent of contact between workers and other members of society in these heady days took place in the afternoon of October 15: when workers from many factories met together, they selected a Jewish university student to preside at the meeting.[51]

Municipal employees, who had recently been guaranteed wage increases, joined the work stoppage, although they promised that the city hospitals, waterworks, bakeries, and slaughterhouse would not be affected. In addition to demands for civil liberties and elections to a four-tail constituent assembly, they called for the formation of a civilian militia and a special committee consisting of workers and city officials to assume control of all municipal affairs. In municipal enterprises still in operation, workers set about to establish collegial boards to supervise and administer plant affairs.[52] In short, municipal workers built upon the fruits of the earlier labor movement and were now claiming an expanded role for themselves, not only in their places of work but in the city as well. These demands encapsulate in a nutshell the political vision of the Odessa labor movement in the fall of 1905—that of a participatory role for workers in controlling their destiny as workers and as citizens.

Nearly 7,000 students (many as young as thirteen), workers, and other members of the general public attended a rally in the main auditorium of the medical school on the morning of October 15. While several women students collected donations for guns and ammunition at the entrance and in the lobby, students, professors, and representatives of revolutionary organizations set about planning a general strike for October 17. Participants sang revolutionary songs and made fiery speeches that resounded throughout the halls and auditoriums of the building. The students decided that striking workers should be armed in the event of police or military attack and arranged for children and students to march at the front of any procession in order to deter policemen and soldiers from shooting.[53]

The rally continued all day as participants—the number growing to 10,000—went from auditorium to auditorium and listened to revolutionaries and student radicals debate whether the time was ripe for a popular uprising. Yet efforts by the various social-democratic organizations to bury factional disputes, especially between Mensheviks and Bolsheviks, were not successful. Representatives of the Bund, anarchists, and SRs appealed to their fellow Menshevik and Bolshevik revolutionaries to work together in preparing and organizing the upcoming general strike, but they were rebuffed by one SD who told his audience not to believe the "honey-coated words" of the SRs and proclaimed that only the SDs should lead the strike.[54]

News of the scheduled general strike spread throughout Odessa, largely due to the efforts of SDs who made the rounds of the city's factories and workshops, where workers were already walking out. Given the fevered atmosphere and reports that students and revolutionaries were contemplating the formation of armed militias, it is indeed surprising that no clashes between the police and populace or any other forms of popular disturbance were reported on October 15.[55] In the words of Baron Aleksandr Kaul'bars, who had returned in August from the Far East to resume his post as commander of the Odessa Military District, "the day in general passed quietly."[56] Even the presence of policemen and soldiers in the streets near the medical school did not spark any confrontations when some 10,000 protestors flooded the streets of downtown Odessa after the rally. Yet city governor Neidhardt was justifiably apprehensive and wary, especially since another rally was scheduled for the following morning. His order to remove ammunition from all stores on the evening of October 15 is evidence of his concern that Odessa was a powderkeg ready to explode.[57]

Explode it did. To workers, students, revolutionaries, government officials, and average citizens, the next day, Sunday, October 16, was the start of the revolution. It began when people arrived at the medical school for the scheduled rally but, instead of enjoying unhampered entry into the building, found it surrounded by policemen and soldiers. Neidhardt, following a recent directive from his superiors in St. Petersburg, had ordered the university closed to all persons except those wearing student uniforms. In order to ensure compliance, he cordoned off the building with troops. In his words, the university possessed "self-government" but not the right "to let outsiders assemble and collect money for weapons."[58]

By this time the meetings at the university had assumed an indispensable role in the lives of Odessans, since persons of all ages, social categories, and liberal and radical persuasions relied on the rallies to provide the latest news about the course of events in the city. It was this mass participation by diverse elements of the Odessa populace—workers, students, and professionals—that allowed the protest to develop into a truly general strike. Outraged by this challenge, and considering the move by Neidhardt deliberate provocation, the steadily growing crowd held a rally in the streets outside the medical building. Students delivered speeches in which they urged their listeners to arm and to build barricades. After several hours of speeches, the highly agitated demonstrators began to march from the medical school in Kherson district toward the city center. They marched spontaneously through downtown Odessa without any set destination, encouraging passersby to join the procession. Some marchers plundered a gun store, seizing revolvers, daggers, pocket knives, brass knuckles, shotguns, and gunpowder.[59]

As the crowd moved through the streets, small groups of demonstrators entered stores and workshops and demanded that sales personnel and shopworkers join the procession. By noon they had stopped the movement of trams and begun to build barricades from overturned trams, wood, wire, material from construction sites, and uprooted telegraph and telephone poles. Fourteen- and fifteen-year-old youths eagerly helped workers erect barricades, much as they had done in June; by mid-afternoon, many of the major thoroughfares of the city center were blocked, affording workers and revolutionaries the opportunity to exhort soldiers not to open fire. Neidhardt, realizing that his police and the troops already stationed in the city could not contain these street actions, requested reinforcements from the garrison.[60]

Government troops encountered fierce resistance when they took action to restore order and dismantle the barricades. Greeted with rocks and gunfire as they approached, soldiers retaliated by returning fire. Military patrols were also targets of snipers positioned in apartments and on rooftops. Although the shooting continued throughout the afternoon, by early evening the violence had subsided as protesters abandoned the barricades. The army once again secured the streets of Odessa while the police disarmed and arrested scores of demonstrators.[61] The exact number of casualties is difficult to determine: Neidhardt reported nine civilians killed and approximately eighty wounded, and seven soldiers and policemen injured. Many injured civilians, however, undoubtedly escaped the count of authorities because they returned home without seeking treatment in hospitals or clinics.[62]

On the whole, the disturbances were neither planned nor coordinated. Neidhardt, however, believed that the street fighting and the organization of emergency medical treatment by students indicated "the careful organization of a popular armed uprising."[63] Unconfirmed reports that students at first-aid stations were distributing ammunition and guns strengthened his conviction, as did information that students were building bombs, establishing self-defense brigades, and smuggling revolvers, ammunition, sabres, and gunpowder into the medical school. A search of the medical school several days later did not reveal any weapons, although the possibility exists that students cleared out incriminating evidence after receiving advanced warning of a police raid.[64] Notwithstanding these signs of preparation and organization, the street disorders themselves were unplanned and clearly resulted from a spontaneous outpouring of popular discontent.

Yet some actions by students on October 16 exhibited signs of organization that suggest, if not a readiness for conflict, at least an expectation of confrontation. As we have noted, students collected money for weapons and ammunition at the rally on October 15. Moreover, in the aftermath of October 14 and 15, students, nurses, and other medical personnel began planning for emergency medical treatment by stockpiling pharmaceuticals and bandages at the university. When street disorders erupted on October 16, students and medical personnel were ready to render assistance to victims of the street fighting. Assisted by hospital attendants, nurses, and members of the Red Cross, students donned Red Cross uniforms and established first-aid posts near barricades. Pharmacy employees who had walked off the job also dispensed medicine to the injured. All these groups spent the day attending to the wounded and transporting the injured and dead to the Jewish Hospital or to the university clinic which they were using to treat the wounded.[65]

Tempers remained high throughout the day and into the evening. In the words of Baron Kaul'bars, "the mood of all residents without exception was heightened and anxious."[66] At the university, a commission of professors composed a heated letter of protest to Neidhardt, blaming him for the day's violence. The professors pointed out that the city governor's directive to close the university to the general public violated the university's autonomous status and forced the students to hold their rally in the streets. "The bloody clashes in the streets of Odessa," concluded the commission, were the direct consequence of Neidhardt's directive, for it "deprived the public of the possibility . . . of meeting peacefully with students at the university." Nowhere in the condemnation was there acknowledgment of the directive ordering Neidhardt to close the university to non-students or of the fact that university autonomy did not extend to them. Nor did the commission concede that civilians may have provoked the soldiers and police by throwing rocks and shooting at them from behind barricades and rooftops.[67] The professors forwarded a copy of the letter to the Minister of Internal Affairs and instructed Zanchevskii and two other colleagues to lodge a protest with Kaul'bars, stressing that the University Council could not guarantee "the restoration of calm among the students."[68] Zanchevskii visited Neidhardt, but failed to prevail upon the city governor to cancel the directive prohibiting non-students from entering university premises.[69]

The city council also met in emergency session on the evening of October 16. It resolved to create an Advisory Committee composed of representatives from various political and civic organizations who would be responsible for undertaking measures necessary to satisfy the needs of the populace and reestablish normal conditions in the city. City councillors also allocated 5,000 rubles to assist the injured and provide relief to families of individuals who were killed. After receiving reports that policemen and soldiers were systematically beating the 214 persons arrested for participating in that day's street disorders, the council instructed six of its members and several justices of the peace to visit police headquarters in the Bul'var district, where the police had already bludgeoned several prisoners into unconsciousness. The councillors interceded on behalf of the prisoners and made sure that some of the more seriously injured received medical attention.[70]

Like the calm before yet another storm, Monday, October 17 passed without any serious disturbances. Although the military, which remained stationed in the city during the night, continued to patrol Odessa, life did not return to normal. Schools and most stores remained closed, and the *Okhrana* reported that 4,000 workers in seventy-eight enterprises did not show up for work. As in past episodes of labor unrest, many of these workers had been coerced to walk out, sometimes at gunpoint, by groups of workers and students who had entered the factories. But most workers joined work stoppages on their own accord. Police accounts, in an effort to affix blame on Jews, reported that enterprises with predominantly Jewish work forces constituted the majority of the enterprises that were shut down, but they glossed over the fact that many plants with Russian workers were also affected.[71] For the most part, workers did not present specific demands, preferring to walk off the job and throw their combined weight behind the swelling movement against the regime. The unrest embraced workers from all sectors of the economy, and it was clear to all involved that workers were acting in an explicitly and self-consciously political fashion.

Groups of workers congregated outside those stores open for business and passed the time discussing current affairs, singing songs, and drinking tea. At the university professors, students, and members of the general public who had managed to evade the military cordon held meetings and discussed the events of the previous day. The University Council listened to the testimony of eyewitnesses to the violence and composed letters of protest to the Ministers of Interior Affairs and Education, requesting an investigation of the beatings of students and Red Cross personnel. Contributions for weapons were once again collected, and students, along with representatives of socialist organizations, began to organize armed militias.[72]

The SDs also continued their agitation. In the early afternoon the Bund held a rally at the Jewish Hospital, where several victims from the previous day had been brought, and invited all local revolutionary groups to participate in a memorial service and funeral procession on October 18 for those killed on October 16. Bundist orators addressed the 700 persons who gathered, emphasizing that an armed detachment would accompany the funeral procession and resist efforts by the police and army to interfere.[73]

The city council building was also the scene of public meetings. People assembled to hear speeches about the beating of prisoners at the Bul'var police station. They listened to P. Kryzhanovskii (who had recently replaced Zelenyi as mayor) request that Odessa residents not congregate in public without first notifying his office and obtaining police permission. Kryzhanovskii feared that impromptu rallies would lead to conflicts with the police and have "deplorable results." Some councillors emphatically expressed their desire to attend the funeral procession scheduled for the next day.[74]

The relative calm of October 17 did not convince officials that the situation was improving. Kuzubov placed his faith in the accuracy of rumors that more factory workers would walk off the job the next day and expressed apprehension that the police force was not adequate to maintain order.[75] Baron Kaul'bars acknowledged that the surface clam of October 17 did not signify a reduction of tensions in the city, and Neidhardt voiced a similar concern that the level of excitement had increased during the day, despite the absence of street crowds and disturbances.[76] One contemprary wrote that "the nervous tension of the residents of Odessa reached its limit. The powers that be were sleeping. Everyone was waiting for mass disorders."[77] Neidhardt was so apprehensive that the scheduled funeral procession might spark another day of violence that he ordered his men to remove the corpses from the Jewish Hospital and bury them in two common graves.

When the storm broke on October 18, events had gone way beyond the control of local officials. The nationwide general strike had succeeded in forcing the hand of the government. News of its reluctant concession—the Manifesto of October 17—had reached Odessa by the morning of October 18, and prompted thousands of people to throng the streets to celebrate the granting of civil liberties and the promise to establish a popularly elected legislative assembly. For Jews living in the Russian Empire, the promised reforms of the Manifesto heralded the initial blow against the legal disabilities they had endured for well over a century. But Jews were not the only Odessans to welcome the concessions of October 17 with open arms; Russians and other non-Jewish national minorities celebrated just as eagerly as the Jews the Manifesto, seeing it as the first step in the long-awaited restructuring of Russian politics. As one university student remarked: "A joyous crowd appeared in the streets—people congratulated each other and a holiday mood was noticeable."[78] According to the report filed by the Odessa correspondent for an American magazine:

> Perfect strangers embraced and congratulated each other, and all walked about the streets with smiles on their faces. Schoolboys and students ran around the streets cheering. Crowds came from the poorer quarters of the centre of the town, mostly composed of Jewish workmen in printing offices, tailor shops, ironmonger-ies, groceries, etc., and swarmed up the main street. At the head of one crowd someone waved a red handkerchief, whereupon like magic other red flags began to appear; crowds rushed up and down the streets crying "Hurrah for freedom!" and singing revolutionary songs.[79]

Indeed, thousands of Odessans sensed the vulnerability of the regime and, drunk with the victory symbolized by the Manifesto, celebrated the tsar's capitulation by unfurling red flags and banners with anti-government slogans. Shouts of "Down with the Autocracy," "Long Live Freedom," and "Down with the Police" pierced the morning air. Apartment dwellers draped red carpets and shawls from balconies and windows, and groups of demonstrators forced pass-ersby to doff their hats or bow before red flags. Neidhardt reported instances (later denied by Jewish groups) of demonstrators tying portraits of the tsar to the tails of dogs, who were then allowed to run freely throughout the city.[80]

One of the day's first confrontations occurred when mourners assembled at the Jewish Hospital and learned of Neidhardt's order to remove the corpses. Angry at the city governor's subterfuge, they threatened to kill the senior doctor if the corpses were not returned. Faced with this volatile situation, Neidhardt relented and ordered the disinterment of the bodies, which were then transferred to the clinic of the medical school. The bodies were embalmed and placed on display, draped with black and red cloth and banners reading "To the Comrade Heroes of the October Revolution" and "To the Fallen Victims of the Struggle for Freedom." The funeral procession was postponed until the next day, Wednesday, October 19.[81]

In late morning, Kaul'bars and Neidhardt greeted a group of celebrants from their apartments. The military commander, trying to abide by the spirit of the newly announced freedoms, instructed his troops not to appear in the streets. He stated that they should "give the populace the possibility to enjoy without interference the freedom . . . granted by the Manifesto."[82] During the next several hours, after crowds of several thousand demonstrators, led by Zanchevskii, went from police station to police station demanding "the liberation of all political prisoners," Neidhardt ordered their release, including all persons arrested on October 16.[83]

Throughout the day orators delivered impromptu speeches on street corners, and thousands of people from all over Odessa assembled in front of the city council building. Excited by all that was transpiring and hoping to inspire the people to strike a deathblow to the autocracy, revolutionaries condemned the Manifesto for its limited suffrage and lack of details concerning the planned State Duma, and they urged their audience to continue the struggle for full political and economic freedom. Osip Piatnitskii, chief Bolshevik organizer among Jewish workers, told the crowd that the Manifesto "was only a trap laid to ensnare all revolutionary elements in Russia" and encouraged Odessans to arm themselves because "the struggle with tsarism had not yet ended." Sergei Gusev, another prominent Bolshevik organizer, also called upon the populace to arm itself and form brigades to fight the government.

In the city council building itself, demonstrators ripped down the portrait of the Tsar, substituted a red flag for the Imperial colors, and once again collected money for weapons. Even Professor Shchepkin admitted trying to obtain weapons for the student militias with city funds. Gusev led a delegation of SDs to the city council, where they requested weapons and money, and students at the university began to barricade the medical clinic and stockpile weapons in an effort to turn the medical school into an armed camp. City councillors also decided to send a telegram to Sergei Witte, urging him to replace Neidhardt, whom they blamed for the recent disturbances, with a new city governor so social calm could be restored in the city.[84]

As its last action, the city council selected eleven of its members to serve on the Advisory Committee. Police reports indicate that officials believed the committee to be a latter-day version of France's revolutionary Committee of Public Safety. Although the Advisory Committee never performed more than limited functions and its demands were not heeded, officials perceived it as a potential challenge to government authority and an effort to devolve power into the hands of locally elected officials. Significantly, after a request from Neidhardt on October 18 to help maintain law and order, the Advisory Committee demanded the removal of police from their posts and permission to establish a municipal militia.[85]

The mood of the celebrants grew angry as the day wore on. Mobs of demonstrators, primarily Jews according to official accounts, viciously attacked and disarmed policemen and began shooting at troops patrolling the city. By mid-afternoon, Neidhardt had received reports that two policemen had been killed, ten wounded, and twenty-two disarmed.[86] The attacks were not limited to policemen; nor were Jews the sole culprits. According to one policeman, shots emanated from the homes of several princes.[87] During the course of the day, tensions between those Odessans heralding the Manifesto and those disapproving of the concessions granted by Nicholas and resenting the flagrant disrespect for the tsar shown by the Manifesto's celebrants had reached a breaking point. Pitched battles occurred in the late afternoon and early evening as groups of armed demonstrators, chiefly Jewish students and workers, clashed with bands of Russians. These incidents of violence marked the beginning of the bloody October pogrom. The pogrom not only reveals the explosive nature of Jewish-gentile relations in Odessa, but illustrates as well the intensification of the social and political turmoil engulfing the city since the beginning of the year.

7

Politics and Pogrom

No other city in the Russian Empire in 1905 experienced a pogrom comparable in its destruction to the one unleashed against the Jews of Odessa. The October pogrom in Odessa was another chapter in the tragic history of Russian Jewry, which suffered the impact of discriminatory government policies, popular prejudices, and at times outbreaks of violence. The first Empire-wide wave of anti-Jewish pogroms occurred in the wake of the assassination of Alexander II in 1881, with the next major outburst taking place in 1905 after Nicholas II issued the October Manifesto. In the weeks following Nicholas II's granting of fundamental civil rights and political liberties, pogroms directed mainly at Jews but also targeting students, intellectuals, and other national minorities, especially Armenians, broke out in hundreds of cities, towns and villages, resulting in deaths and injuries to thousands.[1] In Odessa alone, the police reported that at least 400 Jews and 100 non-Jews were killed and approximately 300 people, mostly Jews, were injured, with slightly over 1,600 Jewish houses, apartments, and stores incurring damage. These official figures undoubtedly underestimate the true extent of the damage, since not all individuals sought medical assistance at hospitals or clinics, preferring to return home or seek sanctuary with friends and family. Other informed sources indicate substantially higher numbers of casualties. For example, Neidhardt estimated the number of casualties at 2,500, and several hospitals and clinics reported treating at least 600 persons for injuries sustained during the pogrom. The Jewish newspaper *Voskhod* reported that over 800 were killed and another several thousand wounded.[2]

The legacy of discrimination against Russian Jewry and governmental tolerance and at times sponsorship of anti-Jewish organizations and propaganda provided fertile ground for a pogrom.[3] When combined with the economic frustrations felt by many Odessans in 1905, as well as timeworn religious prejudices and the alarm sounded by loyalists to the regime, Jews were a convenient target for retaliation. They were seen as the source of the many problems besetting Russia in general and Odessa in particular, from masterminds of the assault on the autocracy to capitalist exploiters of Russian workers. In Odessa, the savage attack against Jews marked a significant break with the course of labor activism and political radicalization, which until fall was noteworthy for the absence of serious ethnic hostilities. Until the outbreak of the pogrom, activist workers had taken care to fashion a united front against their twin enemies, the state and the employer. In the middle of the October general strike, however, labor unrest degenerated into an anti-Jewish pogrom, one indicator of the volatility of ethnic relations in the city. The Odessa pogrom provides an opportunity to examine how ethnic and religious factors affected the labor movement in 1905 and sheds light on the broader issues that interest us here, particularly the character of worker unrest and the dynamics of revolutionary politics. The pogrom left its indelible imprint on the outcome of the 1905 Revolution by bringing to center stage the Jewish question, thereby illustrating how class and ethnic identity could affect political developments.

Analyzing the causes of the pogrom and identifying the pogromists and their motives are difficult tasks, made more complicated by the problem that many available sources tend to be tendentious and filtered through the self-serving eyes of observers and participants with particular axes to grind. Nonetheless, a variety of sources, ranging from eyewitness accounts, memoirs, newspaper reports, and the findings of a governmental inquiry, enables the historian willing to sift through contradictory evidence to piece together a reliable account of the pogrom. Given Odessa's past record of periodic anti-Jewish violence, the fact that a pogrom occurred in 1905 is not surprising. What needs explaining is why the violence surfaced in October and not earlier during other instances of social and political turmoil. Did the eruption of anti-Jewish violence reflect, as one observer suggested, "the release of all the smothered race and class hatreds?"[4] Or, since the pogrom erupted in the midst of general unrest, was its outbreak connected to the political crisis engulfing Odessa in 1905?

The October Pogrom

Most accounts of the October pogroms in Russia assert that they began when members of organized patriotic processions clashed with celebrants of the October Manifesto.[5] But, as we saw in the previous chapter, confrontation between Jews and Russians in Odessa began on October 18, the day before a pro-government march occurred. Armed clashes between supporters and opponents of the monarchy originated near the Jewish district of Moldavanka in the late afternoon and early evening. The fighting started when a group of Jews carrying desecrated portraits of the tsar and red flags to celebrate the October Manifesto tried to force a group of recalcitrant Russian workers, outraged by the sight of the portraits, to doff their caps. Harsh words were exchanged, a scuffle ensued, and shots rang out. Both groups scattered, but quickly reassembled in nearby streets and resumed fighting. The clashes soon turned into an anti-Jewish riot, as Russians indiscriminately attacked Jews and began to vandalize and loot Jewish stores and homes in Moldavanka. The troops who were summoned to quell the disorders were met by gunshots and were equally vigilant in their efforts to restrain both Russian and Jewish rioters. They restored order by early evening, but not before four Russians had been killed, dozens of Russians wounded—including policemen—and twelve Russians arrested. The number of Jews injured or arrested is unknown.[6] Thus what began as a fray between two groups with opposing political views almost immediately transformed itself into an ethnic and religious battle: the Russians did not vent their hostilities against other Russians celebrating in the streets, but rather turned on Jews as the source of Russia's problems. Interestingly, the fact that the rioters also attacked policemen and troops suggests that on October 18 they were not yet fully focused on Jews.

The pogrom began in full force the next day, October 19. In mid-morning, hundreds of Russians—women, men, and children—gathered in various parts of the city for patriotic marches to display their loyalty to the tsar. Like rallies organized by extreme, right-wing organizations (such as the Black Hundreds), these processions enjoyed the blessing of local authorities and were used by advocates of an unreformed autocracy to bolster the government and undermine the concessions of October. Day laborers, especially those employed at the docks, comprised a major element of the crowd that assembled at the harbor. They were joined by Russian factory and construction workers, shopkeepers, salesclerks, workshop employees, and vagrants (*liudi bez opredelennykh zaniatii*).[7] The main contingent of marchers assembled at Customs Square at the harbor, where the procession's organizers distributed flags, icons and portraits of the tsar. Plainclothes policemen reportedly handed out bottles of vodka, along with money and guns, for the marchers to pass around.[8] Onlookers and passersby joined the procession as the demonstrators made their way from the port to the city center. Singing the national anthem and religious hymns and, according to some reports, shouting "Down with the Jews" and "The Jews need a beating," they stopped at the city council building and substituted the Imperial colors for the red flag that demonstrators had raised the previous day. They then headed toward the cathedral in central Odessa, stopping en route at the residences of the city governor and military commander. Kaul'bars, fearing confrontation between the patriotic marchers and left-wing students and revolutionaries, asked them to disperse. Some heeded his request, but most members of the procession continued on. Neidhardt, on the other hand, greeted the marchers enthusiastically and urged them to hold a memorial service at the cathedral. After a brief prayer service, they continued their procession through central Odessa.

Both Neidhardt and Kaul'bars were particularly concerned that the funeral procession scheduled to commemorate the five students killed on October 16 would collide with the patriotic marchers. Kaul'bars extended his decision of October 17 to keep his troops off the streets after receiving assurances from the Advisory Committee that it would help maintain order along the planned route of the procession. Kaul'bars was evidently unaware that the 10,000 persons who had assembled at the medical school on the morning of October 19 for the funeral had already called off the procession when news of the disorders the evening before reached them. Some headed to Moldavanka to render assistance, while many others remained at the medical school, only to clash with groups of armed Russians who had congregated in the streets outside the university.[9]

After the service at the cathedral, the patriotic demonstrators continued to wind their way through the streets of central Odessa. The march was soon marred by a round of gunfire that left a young boy carrying an icon dead. Although some accounts of the incident assert that the shots came from surrounding buildings, probably from the offices of the liberal-leaning newspaper *Iuzhnoe obozrenie* (*The Southern Review*), existing evidence does not allow us to determine who was responsible for the shooting. Some sources suggest that revolutionaries or members of Jewish and student self-defense brigades opened fire. One eyewitness testified, however, that the first shots came from the crowd of patriotic demonstrators. Another eyewitness also reported seeing members of the patriotic procession discharge their revolvers into the air, but whether he is referring to the initial shooting in which the boy was killed is unknown.[10] The immediate consequence of the shooting was panic, as members of the patriotic procession sought to avoid the shots that rang out from rooftops, balconies, and apartment windows. The gunfire was soon joined by homemade bombs thrown by revolutionaries and self-defense units organized by students and Jews. These actions suggest that radicals were lying in wait and seeking confrontation. The stepped-up violence triggered a chain reaction: convinced that Jews were responsible for the shootings, members of the patriotic demonstration began to shout "Beat the Kikes" and "Death to the Kikes" and went on a rampage, attacking Jews and destroying Jewish apartments, houses, and stores.

The course of events was similar in other parts of the city, as radicals and government supporters engaged in fierce streetfighting. Although it is unclear who started the trouble in the city center—radicals or patriotic marchers—in Peresyp, where no patriotic procession took place, the pogrom started only after armed thugs from the city center arrived and began to incite local residents. Mob violence against the Jews was difficult to contain or control once it started. By mid-afternoon a full-fledged pogrom had developed, and it raged until October 22. It resulted in deaths and injuries to thousands of Odessans and caused property damage totalling millions of rubles.[11]

The lurid details of savage atrocities perpetrated against the Jews, the likes of which had never been seen in Odessa, sent shock waves throughout Russia and the international community. Events leading up to the pogrom had evidently touched a visceral nerve among the pogromists and triggered spasms of uncontrollable violence against the Jews. The viciousness of the pogromists was intensified in part by the refuge of anonymity afforded by large rampaging crowds, which enabled people to fall prey to the passion of the moment and engage in a collective act of national or ethnic self-affirmation. The frenzy of the rioting mobs bordered on mass hysteria as pogromists brutally and indiscriminately beat, mutilated, and murdered defenseless Jewish men, women, and children. The terror and savagery were relentless as the pogromists did not let up for several days. They hurled Jews out of windows, tore eyeballs from sockets, discharged guns inside the mouths of victims, raped and cut open the stomachs

Members of a Jewish self-defense unit killed during the October pogrom. (YIVO Institute for Jewish Research)

Mourners at cemetery with victims of October pogrom. (YIVO Institute for Jewish Research)

Mother and child killed during the October pogrom. (YIVO Institute for Jewish Research)

of pregnant women, and slaughtered infants in front of their parents. In one particularly gruesome incident, pogromists hung a woman upside down by her legs and the bodies of her six dead children were arranged on the floor below.[12] Frightened Jews huddled together in their apartments and waited for marauding gangs to break in and set about their business of murder and pillage. One girl who survived the pogrom later recounted her experience, which was undoubtedly shared by thousands of others elsewhere in Odessa:

> The gates to the courtyard of the apartment building were opened and a crowd of people poured into the courtyard and spread out to the apartments. We were sitting in the attic, shaking as we heard banging and shouting. . . . They dragged out one young man—such a neat, delicate person—. . . and broke off a thick leg from an oak table and killed him by smashing in his chest and skull. His murder went on for a long time, and his screams could be heard all over the courtyard.

The girl survived by climbing out of the attic and finding refuge in a storeroom. Others were less fortunate; they were shot by soldiers as they climbed onto the roof from the attic.[13]

Although there were extensive casualties and property damage, self-defense organizations limited the scope of death and destruction. As we have already seen, students and revolutionaries had been stockpiling medical supplies, guns, ammunition, and bombs at the university for several days prior to October 18. When anti-Jewish attacks flared up that afternoon, preparations for the organization of self-defense brigades went into high gear. Two self-defense organizations took shape: one was organized by the Coalition Council and headquartered at the university; the other was established by the National Committee of Jewish Self-Defense, which had been active during the pogrom scare six months earlier. Both groups claimed the support and participation of hundreds of Odessans—both Jewish and gentile—and performed similar functions, namely the protection of Jewish lives and property.

The student militia consisted not only of students from the university, secondary schools, and naval cadet training school, but also workers from the railway workshops, the Henn plant in Peresyp, the shipyard of the Russian Steam Navigation and Trading Company, sailors from Registration, and members of various revolutionary organizations.[14] The student militia played a crucial role in collecting money, distributing weapons, and dispatching brigades to patrol the city and maintain law and order. This last function was especially important on the evening of October 18, when students set up sentry posts and detained suspicious-looking individuals. After the pogrom assumed full force on October 19, the Jewish and student militias, with the help of the Red Cross and Bundists, who coordinated activities with other socialists, organized first-aid stations, fought pogromists, and incarcerated in the university suspected looters and pogromists, who were then interrogated by students and members of the Law Faculty. Pharmacy workers made rounds of the city and rendered medical assistance to victims of the pogrom.[15]

Unfortunately, self-defense groups were inadequately trained and organized.

Woefully ill-equipped to wage a successful battle against the pogromists, at times they mistakenly shot fellow defenders positioned in front of them. In some districts of Odessa, self-defense units did not exist at all. Most significantly, they were far outnumbered and lacked sufficient weapons and ammunition despite the efforts of Professor Shchepkin who, promising compensation from the city council, urged gunstore owners to distribute firearms to the student militia.[16] The Coalition Council tried to coordinate the efforts of all self-defense brigades, but in the final analysis the students, Jews, and revolutionaries were unable to extinguish or even control the rampaging crowds. The militias fought valiantly on October 19 to protect Jewish lives and property, but by the next day it became increasingly clear that they were waging a losing battle. Having suffered severe casualties, the Coalition Council followed the suggestion of the Bolsheviks and decided not to send detachments to fight pogromists; instead it focused its attention on caring for the wounded. Bodies of both dead pogromists and victims were often brought to the medical clinic of the university; corpses of the latter lay in state in a room commemorating them, while the former received less honorific treatment.[17]

The pogrom's unrestrained violence and destructive excesses were in large measure made possible by the failure of authorities to adopt measures to restore law and order. Low-ranking policemen and soldiers refrained from interfering with the pogromists and in many instances participated in the looting and killing. At times policemen, seeking to avenge the attacks of October 16 and 18 on their colleagues, provided protection for pogromists by firing on self-defense units and interfering with the efforts of first-aid groups and the Red Cross. For their part, soldiers, concluding from the actions of the police that the pogrom was sanctioned by higher authorities, stood idly by while pogromists looted stores and murdered unarmed Jews. Some may have reasoned, from their vantage point as upholders of the autocratic order, that shooting pogromists, whom they regarded as honorably defending the regime, would only further the cause of revolution. Such reasoning accords with views of the 1881 pogroms in which rumors, such as that the tsar commanded people to attack Jews as punishment for their participation in the revolutionary movement, incited pogromist activity.[18] Policemen reportedly discharged their weapons into the air and then told rioters that the shots had come from apartments inhabited by Jews, leaving the latter vulnerable to vicious beatings and murder. Eyewitnesses also reported seeing policemen directing pogromists to Jewish-owned stores or Jews' apartments, while steering the rioters away from the property of non-Jews. As the correspondent for *Collier's* reported, "Ikons and crosses were placed in windows and hung outside doors to mark the residences of the Russians, and in almost every case this was a sufficient protection." *Odesskii pogrom i samooborona* (*The Odessa Pogrom and Self-Defense*), an emotional account of the October tragedy published by Labor Zionists in Paris, argues that the police more than any other group in Odessa were responsible for the deaths and pillage.[19]

The evidence indicates that policemen behaved with the knowledge and tacit approval of their superiors. Neither Neidhardt nor Kaul'bars took any decisive action to suppress the pogrom when disorders erupted. Consequently, full responsibility for the savagery of the pogrom must ultimately be placed on them as the two officials responsible for maintaining law and order. As the head of the Odessa gendarmes reported, the military did not apply sufficient energy to end the pogrom. In fact, pogromists greeted soldiers and policemen with shouts of "Hurrah" and then continued their rampage and pillage free of interference.[20]

It was not until the evening of October 20 that troops were ordered to shoot at pogromists as well as self-defense groups. Until then soldiers and police had shot at only self-defense brigades. Whether the directive ordering troops to shoot at pogromists helped restore order is unclear, but it is hard to ignore the effect of the directive, especially since the pogrom began to peter out the next day when met with resistance from the military. Of course, the return to calm may have been due more to the exhaustion of the pogromists than to any military directive and action. Yet it bears stressing that when the military did act to stop public disorders, as they did on October 18 and again on October 21 and 22, pogromists generally stopped their attacks. More immediate and vigorous action by the military, which had some 20,000–25,000 soldiers garrisoned in the city, might have prevented the pogrom from assuming such monstrous proportions.

Neidhardt and Kaul'bars defended the behavior of the police and military by arguing that attacks by student and Jewish militias hampered efforts of policemen and soldiers to contain the pogrom. After all, they maintained, self-defense brigades shot not only at pogromists, but also at police, soldiers, and Cossacks. Thus, the police and military had to contend first with the self-defense groups before turning their attention to pogromists.[21] A commander of an infantry brigade agreed with Neidhardt and Kaul'bars when he told Senator Aleksandr Kuzminskii, who conducted the government inquiry into the pogrom, that "it was hard to stop the pogromists because the soldiers were diverted by revolutionaries who were shooting at them."[22]

The police and military were undoubtedly targets of civilian militias and were rightly concerned about their own safety and security. Yet, as the pogrom gathered momentum, one can hardly blame members of self-defense brigades for continuing to shoot at soldiers and policemen, many of whom were actively participating in the violence. Neidhardt and Kaul'bars reacted as though civilian militias were the only groups involved in the violence and conveniently ignored how the actions of policemen and soldiers after the pogrom began might provoke Jews to defend themselves. Had the police and military genuinely applied their energies even-handedly and not shown preferential treatment, the need for self-defense would have been reduced and attacks on soldiers and policemen would have dropped accordingly. Neidhardt and Kaul'bars were attempting to shift blame for the failure of the police and military to perform their basic law enforcement functions onto the victims of the pogrom.

The work of Hans Rogger and Heinz-Dietrich Löwe has done much to absolve high-ranking government ministers and officials in St. Petersburg of engineering the pogroms and giving a signal to mark their start.[23] But the culpability of local officials is less easy to dismiss. Many contemporaries blamed civilian and military authorities, specifically Neidhardt, for fostering a pogromist atmosphere and for not taking measures to suppress the pogrom. Even Prime Minister Sergei Witte wrote in his memoirs that Neidhardt "made matters worse" due to his arrogance and coarse behavior, making him "thoroughly hated by most Odessans."[24] The standard view of the Odessa pogrom places much of the blame on the encouragement and connivance of local officials, though not all the sources agree on whether the police and military actually planned the pogrom. Members of the city council and the newspaper *Odesskie novosti* (*Odessa News*), angered by Neidhardt's accusation that Odessa's Jews, students, liberals, and radicals provoked the pogrom and deserved what they suffered at the hands of pogromists, placed full responsibility for the bloodletting on the city governor. They particularly stressed his decision to remove the police from their posts on October 18 as the catalyst for the pogrom. One national Jewish paper published in St. Petersburg called for a judicial investigation in order to reveal Neidhardt's responsibility for the pogrom.[25] His dismissal several days after the pogrom did not satisfy demands for the city governor's head.[26]

Despite the accusations lodged against Neidhardt, the Odessa pogrom was not a plot hatched by the highest ranking government officials in the city. But it was also not a spontaneous riot. Politically motivated pogrom-mongerers and rabble-rousers preyed upon the prejudices and anxieties of gentile Odessans and sought to transform their anger into attacks on Jews and other perceived enemies of the state. Certain unidentified local officials may have played an active role in promoting the pogrom. Kuzminskii himself collected evidence pointing to the involvement of low-ranking members of the police force in organizing the patriotic counterdemonstration and pogrom. He stopped short, however, of asserting that either Neidhardt or other local civilian and police officials had planned the disorders,[27] despite the testimony of L. D. Teplitskii, an ensign in the army, who reported that as early as October 15 and 16 policemen were proposing to use force against Jews who were seen as "culprits . . . in the various disorders." As one policeman told Teplitskii, "Jews want freedom—well, we'll kill two or three thousand. Then they'll know what freedom is." Teplitskii also testified to meeting a group of day laborers on the morning of October 18 who told him they had just received instructions at a police station to attack Jews that evening.[28]

Teplitskii's account is supported by additional testimony gathered by Kuzminskii. An army captain stated that a policeman had told him that his superiors had given their permission for three days of violence because Jews had destroyed the tsar's portrait in the city council building.[29] In working-class neighborhoods, policemen and pogromist agitators reportedly went from door to door and, after spreading rumors that Jews were slaughtering Russian families, urged Russian residents to repel the Jews with force. Policemen allegedly compiled lists of Jewish-owned stores and Jews' apartments to facilitate attacks. One Jewish newspaper reported that documents existed revealing how plainclothes policemen, upon instructions from their superiors, paid pogromists from 80 kopecks to 3 rubles per day. Other evidence reveals that policemen were instructed not to interfere with pogromists.[30]

Unfortunately, no evidence has surfaced indicating which police officials were responsible for these directives. Nor is there conclusive evidence linking Neidhardt to pogrom agitation. This is understandable; as a government official entrusted with maintaining law and order, it would have been foolhardy for Neidhardt to have been involved in organizing a major public disturbance. One historian's assessment of the 1881 pogroms pertains as well to the Odessa pogrom: "The government was not free to turn the tap of violence on and off at will. . . . It simply was not powerful enough or competent enough to exercise such control over the population at large."[31] Reluctance to sanction any kind of unrest for fear of events getting out of hand would undoubtedly have been heightened in the midst of the turmoil then engulfing Odessa.

Although Neidhardt may have known about the patriotic procession and even welcomed it, this does not warrant the conclusion drawn by many Odessa residents that the city governor had advance knowledge of the pogrom or that the pro-government march was intended as a prelude to violence. Indeed, he took a few steps to avoid the outbreak of bloodshed between regime loyalists and their opponents. In the morning on October 19, he requested that Kaul'bars cancel permission for the funeral procession in order to avoid violence between mourners and the patriotic counter-demonstration. And soon after he received news of the initial clashes on October 19, the city governor called upon the military commander to adopt measures to prevent the outbreak of anti-Jewish violence and appealed to Odessans for calm.[32] Such actions are reminiscent of his behavior in mid-April, when he ordered extra police patrols to maintain peace when rumors of a pogrom ran high.

Neidhardt was a conscientious defender of law and order, and his actions prior to October indicate that he would not tolerate violations of public peace. The city governor possessed a strong disciplinarian streak, and he was willing to use the stick as well as the carrot to maintain calm. He placed stock in the use of force as an effective deterrent and did not hesitate to employ police measures to counter perceived threats to the social order or to break the will of striking workers. In his report to Minister of Interior Bulygin regarding labor unrest in February, Neidhardt admitted that he feared a general wave of work stoppages arising out of the scattered strikes of February and complained of the distribution of illegal literature, malicious attacks on the military by students, and the growing number of Odessans who were arming themselves.[33] He proposed cracking down on unruly students and revolutionaries and encouraged the formation of right-wing, patriotic organizations among students and the general public.[34]

And yet, once the pogrom began, Neidhardt did not order his men into action. How can we account for his (as well as Kaul'bars's) failure to take vigorous measures to suppress the disorders as soon as the pogrom began in full force on the nineteenth? Why did the two individuals in charge of preserving public peace not order their men to apprehend pogromists and stem the deteriorating situation?

The conspicuous failure of police and soldiers to stop the riot stands in stark contrast to the quickness with which Neidhardt and Kaul'bars coordinated efforts on October 16 and October 18 to suppress street disturbances.

Part of the explanation may have to do with Neidhardt's underlying sympathy with the pogromists. Even though Neidhardt had made sure that anti-Semitic activities stopped short of a pogrom prior to October, he nonetheless attended meetings of right-wing, anti-Semitic organizations, where he presumably approved of the speeches condemning "cosmopolitanism and other socialist teachings" and advocating that "in our country the Russians should consider themselves masters." Neidhardt and conservative professors welcomed these organizations to the university because they saw them as a useful weapon in the struggle against radical students and flagging support of the war with Japan.[35]

In the midst of the pogrom, Neidhardt reportedly told a delegation of Jewish leaders: "You wanted freedom. Well, now you're getting 'Jewish freedom.'"[36] From his perspective, Jews were responsible for the disorders and the pogrom was retribution. Thus, although Neidhardt did not plan the pogrom and did not welcome public disorders, he may have viewed attacks on Jews as an effective method of squelching the revolution, which he believed was due to the machinations of Jews and other revolutionaries. Neidhardt's actions support in modified fashion the notion that officials hoped pogroms would deflect popular hostility and resentment away from the government and its policies. In the case of the Odessa pogrom, however, the anti-Jewish violence was not the result of a plot by local authorities. The willingness of Neidhardt and Kaul'bars to tolerate the pogrom occurred *after* the disorders erupted and points out their negligent approach to stemming the tide of violence.

In his report, Kuzminskii particulary castigated the city governor for withdrawing all police from their posts in the early afternoon on October 18. Instead, Neidhardt instructed them to patrol the city in groups, refusing a request from the police chief to order the police back to their posts once military reinforcements had begun patrolling the streets. The reasons for Neidhardt's action are unclear, since his reports are contradictory and conflict with accounts of other informed police officials and civilian leaders. Although Neidhardt claimed that he was seeking to protect the lives of policemen who were subject to attack by celebrants of the Manifesto, close examination of the testimony indicates that the bulk of attacks on policemen occurred *after* they were removed from their posts. Indeed, many had abandoned their posts even before trouble erupted. Yet the possibility remains that the city governor was acting to protect his men, several of whom had been victimized prior to his directive. There is also evidence that Neidhardt had approved the student militias and hoped they, along with the Advisory Committee, could maintain order in Odessa in the absence of the police.[37] Kuzminskii concluded that the city governor was guilty of dereliction of duty because he had left Odessa defenseless by not ordering the police patrols to take vigorous action to prevent trouble and suppress disorders.[38] The absence of police ready to maintain law and order on October 18 and 19 made for an explosive situation, signifying the surrender of the city to armed bands of pogromists and self-defense brigades.

Neidhardt deserves blame for not preventing his men from participating in the looting and pillaging and for waiting until October 21 before ordering his staff back to work. His callous refusal to heed the pleas of pogrom victims, including a rabbi and bank director who begged him to intercede, highlights his indifference to the tragic consequences of the pogrom.[39] At the same time, he may simply have been unable to control his recalcitrant police force, which was demanding higher wages and even refused to heed his October 21 directive to return to duty.[40] Neidhardt may have realized that he could not depend on a severely underpaid, understaffed and disgruntled police force to maintain order in the city.

The Odessa police resembled most other municipal police forces throughout the Empire in its reputation for corruption. But unlike many others, the Odessa police frequently failed to obey orders and directives. Neidhardt attributed the poor morale of the police to low wages and inadequate training, and he hoped to entice them back to work by promising them a significant wage hike. Local property owners, according to a plan never implemented, were to foot the bill by paying a special tax or face three months in jail and a 500-ruble fine.[41] The city governor had few viable options open to him: his police force was beyond his control and the self-defense brigades which he had sanctioned were an ineffective check against the pogromists. This does not exonerate Neidhardt, but simply brings to the fore some of the concerns that might have limited a more vigorous response on his part. The problem of whether he *wanted* to do so is less easy to determine.

Kaul'bars also shares the burden of responsibility for not acting more promptly to restore order. His failure is not surprising, since he had a reputation for performing poorly during times of crisis. Born in 1844, Kaul'bars was of Baltic German ancestry and had served his entire adult life in the military, including a two-year stint in the early 1880s as minister of war in Bulgaria. He also authored several monographs on the geography of Central Asia, where he was stationed during the early part of his career. He assumed his post as commander of the Odessa garrison in 1903, but in late 1904 he was transferred to the front in Manchuria, where he proved to be an uninspired strategist and field commander. At the crucial Battle at Mukden, Kaul'bars allowed his forces to be outflanked and routed by the Japanese, which led Minister of War Alexei Kuropatkin to cite Kaul'bars's dismal performance as a leading cause of Russia's disastrous defeat. In the fall of 1905, soon after the signing of the Treaty of Portsmouth ending the war, he resumed his duties in Odessa.[42]

Curiously, the military commander was not censured by Kuzminskii. Kaul'bars not only discounted reports that his troops were participating in the pogrom as "unsubstantiated" rumors, but he waited two days before ordering his troops to combat pogromists. Kaul'bars admitted that men wearing military uniforms were part of the pogromist mobs, but he insisted that they already had been discharged from service.[43] Defending his inaction before a delegation of city councillors on October 20, Kaul'bars stated that he could not take more decisive measures because Neidhardt had not explicitly requested the use of force to stem the disorders; Kaul'bars took action to confront the pogromists only on the evening of the twentieth, after Neidhardt reiterated a day-old request to adopt measures to prevent the outbreak of a pogrom.[44] Evidence suggests that Kaul'bars did not act until compelled to do so by his superiors.

One question that Kuzminskii attempted to answer centered on who had ultimate responsibility, Neidhardt or Kaul'bars, in suppressing the disorders. In their respective defenses, Neidhardt and Kaul'bars bitterly accused each other of dereliction of duty and claimed that the other was responsible for maintaining order. According to the chain of command, civil authorities were to request the assistance of military units when the police concluded that they were unable to maintain control. Thus, the prerogative to determine whether force should be employed resided with the city governor. But once he made such a decision, the military commander assumed independent control until the end of operations. As one historian has recently written, "This law on the use of force seemed designed to permit both civilians and the military to pass the blame for shedding Russian blood to one another. Arms could not be used without civilian authorization, but orders to fire must come from the troop commander."[45] In Odessa the military commander claimed he lacked authorization to deploy his troops, while the city governor asserted that he had in fact given Kaul'bars the green light to use arms. In an ironic bureaucratic stalemate, both men were adamant that they had followed regulations to the letter.[46]

Kuzminskii ruled that Neidhardt was at fault for not following proper channels when requesting military assistance; he accused the city governor of failing to make a determination of whether the situation required the use of arms. Thus, Kuzminskii concluded that Neidhardt remained responsible for ensuring law and order, and Kaul'bars was justified in looking to the city governor to restore order.[47] Yet Kaul'bars's claim that he could not interfere in "civilian administration" was a feeble excuse for his inaction, as was Neidhardt's half-hearted abdication of responsibility to the military. After all, the army was permitted in such situations to take action without instruction from civilian authorities in order to defend itself or protect human life.

The sad truth of the matter is that both police and troops were in position to act. That soldiers and police used their weapons on the side of the pogromists is a fact that Kuzminskii conveniently ignored in his assessment. The bloody excesses of the pogrom were in large measure due to the poor communication between the two men responsible for law and order in the city. The tragic consequences in terms of human life makes the dispute over jurisdiction and responsibility a mockery of bureaucratic procedure and legal formalism. Conflicting lines of command may have confused Neidhardt and Kaul'bars, but this does not absolve them of their guilt for not taking more vigorous measures. As of October 19, when Neidhardt had written Kaul'bars a note asking him to take measures to prevent a pogrom, the military commander should have directed his troops to restore order. As we have seen, Kaul'bars had responded promptly to the city governor's prior requests for military assistance, but this time he did nothing to prevent the unrest until the evening of the twentieth, when he announced efforts to stem the disorders. Such inaction hints at a joint decision by the police and military to let the pogrom run its course, but no evidence has been uncovered to confirm this suspicion.

Like Neidhardt, Kaul'bars was torn between his personal views and official durites. On October 21, he remarked to an assembly of Odessa policemen that "all of us sympathize in our souls with the pogrom." But Kaul'bars, who somewhat later openly patronized and even supplied arms to the right-wing Union of Russian People, tempered his remarks by acknowledging that neither his personal sympathies nor those of the police and military relieved these groups of the responsibility to maintain law and order and protect Jews.[48] Unfortunately, his remarks came after almost two full days of unrestrained violence and savagery. This conflict between personal values and official duty, between sympathy for the pogromists and the obligation to preserve social peace, helps account for the failure of Kaul'bars and Neidhardt to act more decisively. Undoubtedly they were galled at the prospect of ordering their men to interfere with the pogromists, who, in their eyes, were the only loyal subjects of autocracy in Odessa. How could they justify shooting defenders of the tsar and autocratic order? Such logic and attitudes led both men to shirk their duties and allowed Odessa's Jews to fall victim to the pogromist mobs.

Explaining the Pogrom

Like many other officials, Senator Kuzminskii concluded that the Jews themselves had provoked this display of rage since the pogrom "was only the sad consequence of the armed struggle of revolutionaries trying to seize power."[49] Kuzminskii attributed previous pogroms to national hatred and economic exploitation by Jews. But the October disorders, according to him, were the result of Jews "playing the dominant role in the revolutionary movement" and insulting "the national sentiments of the Russians." According to government officials, then, patriotic Russians were justified in punishing Jews for such treasonous behavior as desecrating portraits of the tsar and forcing bystanders to pay tribute to revolutionary flags.[50] They had trouble condemning those participants in the patriotic procession, especially members of the Black Hundreds and other organized right-wing groups, who tried to incite other Odessans by appealing to age-old fears and suspicions that Jews threatened the purity of Russian Orthodoxy, contaminated the social fabric, and subverted the political order. Kuzminskii characterized the pogrom as an unplanned offshoot of the patriotic procession; its "horrible dimensions" resulted from Neidhardt's failure to adopt adequate countermeasures, and he called for a criminal investigation of Neidhardt's conduct, particularly in regard to the October 18 decision to withdraw police from their posts.[51]

In short, Kuzminskii joined the city governor, Kaul'bars, and other authorities in blaming the pogrom on its victims. Such tortuous reasoning dated back to the 1880s, when government apologists seeking to explain the anti-Jewish pogroms of 1881–1882 blamed the Jews for being exploiters of the peasantry as well as visible members of the revolutionary movement.[52] Given the heritage of anti-Semitism and the complex set of legal disabilities endured by Jews in Russia, it is not suprising that Odessa officials were predisposed to view Jews as the source of troubles besetting society. In addition, actions by Jews during the course of 1905 confirmed many officials and right-wing journalists in their belief that Jews were a seditious element. They blamed Jews for the June disorders and pointed to the stockpiling of weapons and medical supplies at the university and the organization of student militias in the days immediately before the issuance of the October Manifesto as evidence of a revolutionary conspiracy engineered by Jews, students, and radical city councillors. In the words of *Okhrana* chief Bobrov, Jews were responsible for the pogromist attacks since they were spearheading a revolutionary assault on the autocracy in an effort to establish their "own tsardom."[53]

Despite the exaggerated nature of reports of Jewish revolutionary activity, there is an element of truth in some of the conclusions drawn by officials. Jews *were* behind some—though certainly not all—of the radical activity in Odessa. Throughout 1905, Jews engaged in acts of anti-government violence, such as assassination attempts on police officials and the making and stockpiling of bombs. Jews were active in the various revolutionary parties operating in Odessa and figured prominently among the people arrested and exiled after the June unrest.[54] They also helped organize rallies at the university and direct student strikes and public demonstrations in the fall. Jewish youths, students, and workers filled the ranks of the crowds that attended the rallies at the university in September and October, and Jews actively participated in the wave of work stoppages, demonstrations, and street disorders that broke out in mid-October. On October 16, 197 of the 214 individuals arrested were Jews.[55] Moreover, they eagerly celebrated the political concessions offered in the October Manifesto, seeing them as the first step in the civil and political emancipation of Russian Jewry and terrifying those Odessans who believed that the Jews were planning to destroy the Orthodox faith and place one of their own on the throne. Rumors abounded that Jews were planning to establish a "Danubian-Black Sea Republic" with Odessa as the capital, ruled by Jews who would seize land for themselves.[56]

Although Kuzminskii and others were essentially correct to note the connection between the outbreak of the pogrom and the revolutionary crisis, politics alone do not explain the motives of many pogromists. It took a conjuncture of social and economic factors to transform the political confrontation of October 18 into a full-blown, anti-Jewish pogrom. In Odessa, pogromist behavior had both an ethnic and a class basis that reflected the complex relationship of long-term ethnic antagonisms, the structure of Odessa's economy, and short-term political catalysts. The heritage of anti-Semitism made Odessa particularly ripe for a pogrom: the legal disabilities and mistreatment endured by the Jews of Russia engendered an attitude that accepted anti-Semitism and tolerated anti-Jewish violence. But it took the specific circumstances of October 1905 to trigger the pogrom.

The depressed state of the Odessa economy helped set the stage for the pogrom's outbreak. The straitened economic circumstances of 1905 produced a volatile situation in which many workers were unemployed and, owing to their lack of skills, unlikely to find jobs. Unemployment and economic competition contributed to a growing sense of frustration and despair among many pogromists and helped channel their anger against Jews. Available sources do not allow a precise determination of the composition of the pogromist crowds, but they do reveal that male, unskilled, non-Jewish day laborers and dockworkers, perhaps more than any other group (including the police), dominated the ranks of the mobs that attacked the Jews and destroyed property. As one Menshevik asserted in language that reveals the disdain that the radical intelligentsia all too frequently felt toward the people they were seeking to help, the pogrom drew its sustenance from "the wild, dark ignorant masses of the dregs of society . . . the hungry throngs of *bosiaki.*" [57]

This was neither the first nor the last time that day laborers and dockworkers would release their anger in fits of rage, but Jews were not always their targets. In 1900, at the height of the Boxer Rebellion, dockers, resentful of the fact that soldiers were being used to load ships destined for the Russian Far East, reacted by attacking not only Jews and their property but also by looting and destroying stores owned by gentiles.[58] And in June 1905, when day laborers and dockworkers participated in the unrest that led to the burning down of the port, Jews were not singled out. Quite clearly, then, these workers were not inherently predisposed to anti-Jewish actions; sometimes their anger acquired class coloration, as they attacked persons possessing wealth and property regardless of ethnic or religious background.

Like other workers, some dockworkers involved themselves in efforts to win improved working conditions. In May, several hundred of them conducted an orderly and successful strike for higher wages and shorter workdays, and in November dockworkers again struck over pay, hours, housing allowances, and the right to select deputies who would have the final say in the levying of fines. In mid-1906, these same workers again announced demands for increased pay, an eight-hour day, free medical care, and employee participation in the determination of dismissals and fines.[59]

The domination of the grain trade by Jewish merchants, however, predisposed many dockworkers and day laborers against Jews, whom they conveniently saw as the source of their troubles. Consequently, when unemployed, unskilled Russian workers sought an outlet for their frustrations and problems, they generally focused on Jews. But without taking into account the hostile, anti-Jewish atmosphere in Odessa and the acceptance of anti-Jewish violence as an appropriate way to vent anger, we cannot understand why Russian day laborers at times of economic distress chose not to attack other Russian workers who competed with them for scarce jobs or Russian employers. Instead, they indiscriminately lashed out at *all* Jews, regardless of whether they were job competitors or employers. Thus, the pogrom was as much a component of the trajectory of labor unrest as it was an anti-Jewish riot rooted in the complex reality of Odessa society.

But economic problems alone do not explain why these financially strapped Russian workers decided to attack Jews in October 1905. Otherwise, we might expect them to have turned on Jews in June, when material conditions were not all that different from those in the fall. What had changed since the June disorders was the political atmosphere, which had become more polarized. The breakdown of government authority and the retreat of the autocracy by mid-October created a power vacuum that left Odessans of all social and political stripes unsure whether the new political arrangement had altered class and social relations. The revolutionary climate of mid-October allowed the airing of all sorts of economic and political resentments in a relatively unrestrained atmosphere. The words of one SD activist speaking about the labor movement in 1903 also applies to the situation in 1905: some workers feared that "they would be replaced by Jews and be left without work" in the event of political revolution. Economic insecurity and political turmoil tend to heighten interethnic tensions as members of one aggrieved social group seek to affirm their self-worth by attacking persons perceived as outsiders. The tensions between Jews and Russians that had been percolating throughout the year in the form of pogrommongering finally boiled over. Many undoubtedly seconded the opinion of one Odessan who said the disgraceful anti-government celebrations of October 18 had brought "tears to his eyes."[60]

However, many day laborers and dockworkers were less interested in the political turn of events than by the vodka and money that policemen involved in the patriotic procession reportedly offered. Not all pogromists necessarily stood on the extreme right of the political spectrum, as the dockworkers' and day laborers' riot in June demonstrates. For the politically apathetic and unaware, the struggle between revolution and reaction which inspired the more politically conscious played a secondary if not negligible role; they were simply caught up in the general tenor of events and behaved in a manner reminiscent of their actions during the destruction of the harbor in June. Even at the height of the pogrom, non-Jewish property fell victim to the onslaught of the rioters. As *Collier's* reported:

> After having looted Jewish shops and dwellings, and massacred the residents who could not escape them, the crowd turned its attention to the drinking places. Wine cellars were broken into and casks of wine were broached. Men, women, and even boys were soon standing knee deep in the cellars drinking wine, and before long the drunken hordes were tearing about the streets attacking any passer-by they would meet. Even Russian houses were attacked and plundered."[61]

These pogromists were clearly not acting with malice aforethought; rather, they were responding in a spontaneous manner to events that tended to channel their violence toward the Jews.

Other participants may not have intended to assault Jews and destroy their property, but the shooting and bombthrowing of the revolutionaries and self-defense brigades provoked them to anti-Jewish violence. These actions help explain the virulence and intensity of the pogromists' attack—especially by the police—on their victims. Still others may have welcomed the pogrom simply because it afforded them the opportunity to vent some steam and, perhaps, acquire some booty. Thus, whatever the specific motivations of the various individuals involved in the pogrom, popular and official anti-Semitism and depressed economic circumstances set the stage by providing the necessary psychological and material preconditions; the highly charged political atmosphere of Odessa in 1905 helped trigger and channel the pogrom.

By no means did all Russian workers participate or even sympathize with the bloodletting. One letter to *Kommercheskaia Rossiia,* signed by S. D-t., alleged that only "*bosiaki* and the dregs of capitalist society, the most worthless part of the darkest workers" participated in the pogroms, whereas "the Russian proletariat" from industrial enterprises did what they could to subdue pogromists.[62] While this assertion overlooks the diversity of the pogromist mobs, it is true that many Russian factory workers enlisted in self-defense units and sheltered Jewish neighbors and friends. Russians from a variety of enterprises patrolled the harbor to protect Jewish property, seized pogromists, and organized self-defense units. After the pogrom, Russian self-defense groups provided financial aid to pogrom victims and took vigorous action to punish pogromists and to ensure that another round of anti-Jewish violence would not occur.[63] Significantly, many of the Russian self-defense brigades were skilled workers from the same metalworking and machine-construction plants that had been active in the organization of strikes and the formation of district and city strike committees, trade unions and, in December, the Odessa Soviet of Workers' Deputies.

One reason for the reluctance of these workers to join ranks with pogromists had to do with the simple fact that skilled metalworkers and machinists did not face serious employment competition from Jews, who rarely worked in these industries. Perhaps more important was the fact that many of these enterprises had a history of labor activism and organization as well as a close association with Zubatovism and Social Democracy, the latter of which took a strong stand against ethnic prejudice. The presence of political organizers and propagandists may have muted the anti-Jewish sentiment of the Russian workers in these plants and imparted an appreciation of workers' solidarity that transcended ethnic and religious divisions. As Ivan Avdeev told a meeting of his coworkers in the railway workshops, they had formed a self-defense group during the pogrom in order to demonstrate that "the Russian worker values civil freedom and liberty and does not become a Black Hundred or a hooligan. On the contrary, he is capable not only of protecting his own interests but those of other citizens."[64]

To sum up, the social composition of the work force influenced the form and content of popular unrest. At one end of the occupational spectrum stood the unskilled day laborers who were wont to engage in untargeted campaigns of violence and destruction. At the other end were the skilled, more economically secure Russian metalworkers and machinists, who tended not to participate in the pogrom and who were more inclined than the unskilled to channel their protest and discontent in an organized fashion. Even though skilled and unskilled workers in Odessa frequently resorted to violence as a way to achieve their objectives, they used violence differently. Violence served the cause of revolution or counterrevolution when it occurred in conjunction with other factors. The violence and public disorder that often accompanied strikes by skilled workers, as in June, could radicalize the participants and pose a revolutionary threat. But worker militance and social unrest also had reactionary consequences, as when Jews became the object of workers' outrage and hostility. Charters Wynn, in his work on Ekaterinoslav, where a pogrom also occurred in October 1905, has reached similar conclusions.[65]

It is a commonplace that the most politically militant and radical workers in both Western Europe and Russia during the late-nineteenth and early-twentieth centuries were generally not found among the poorest and most disadvantaged segments of the work force. Yet the unskilled and least integrated workers were very prone to violence—perhaps to a much greater extent than the better skilled, politically aware, and mobilized workers—and this violence could contribute to or impede the revolutionary cause. In June, a riot by unskilled workers posed a serious threat to the authorities, but in October unrest among these same workers effectively undercut the force of the revolution. The pogrom served the purposes of the threatened regime because it defused the revolutionary situation; the counterrevolutionary cause was strengthened when the target of the workers' wrath was no longer the autocracy but the Jews, an object of popular hatred and resentment. The October 1905 pogrom in Odessa illustrates how potent ethnic hostility was in workers' politics and how it served as a centrifugal force that diminished the capacity of Odessa workers to act in a unified fashion. The pogrom dampened the workers' militance and, as we shall see, despite a resurgence of labor unrest in December, the fear of more bloodletting dissuaded workers from vigorously challenging their employers and the government as Moscow workers would during their abortive December uprising.

The Aftermath of the Pogrom

Not unexpectedly, the Jewish community of Odessa quickly mobilized its resources to help the victims of the pogrom. Various Jewish civic and charitable organizations set up a "Central Jewish Committee to Help Pogrom Victims" which assumed responsibility for providing assistance to pogrom victims. The Committee set up a bureau to handle inquiries and process requests for assistance, spending several hundred thousand rubles to feed, clothe, and shelter needy Jews. An estimated 20,000 persons received daily meals at one of the many soup kitchens established by the Committee. The Committee also offered unemployment assistance to pogrom victims who were out of work because pogromists had destroyed their places of employment.

In an effort to attend to the needs of ruined Jewish shopkeepers and craft-workers, the Committee set up two commissions to survey Jewish stores and workshops in order to assign funds for the repair and replacement of damaged machinery, equipment, and property. The Committee also provided sewing machines to several dozen tailors. In addition, Jewish merchants appealed to the Odessa Stock Exchange to extend credit to those Jews whose businesses were destroyed during the pogrom.[66] The international Jewish community also came to the aid of its coreligionists in Odessa. From Paris, the Alliance Israélite Universelle sent several hundred thousand rubles in relief aid.[67]

Notwithstanding these efforts to help fellow Jews, the Committee faced formidable obstacles in its efforts to put Jewish workers and small tradespeople back on their feet. The October unrest, both in Odessa and elsewhere in the Empire, sent shock waves throughout the Empire, crippling the national and local economies for a short time and curtailing the demand for goods and services from Jewish shopkeepers and workshops. Soon after its establishment, the Committee acknowledged this state of affairs and resigned itself to granting unemployment compensation to more workers than it had originally planned.[68]

Many non-Jewish residents of the city also pitched in. The city council appropriated funds to help pogrom victims, regardless of nationality. Several newspapers and the student body and faculty of the university collected clothing and money to establish soup kitchens and provide temporary lodging for the needy. The Vysotskii Teapacking Plant, upon orders from company headquarters in Moscow, contributed food for the needy and donated 10,000 rubles to the Central Jewish Committee.

Besides providing financial assistance, concerned Odessans organized fact-finding commissions to help in the investigation of the pogrom. The city council appointed a commission of justices of the peace and lawyers to examine the reasons for the pogrom and bring to justice those individuals responsible for the killing and looting. Nikolai Levchenko headed the commission and took out newspaper advertisements urging persons who possessed knowledge of the pogrom, especially of the identity of pogromists, to come forward. The Law Faculty of the university extended legal assistance to pogrom victims, and students and lawyers helped Levchenko collect testimony about the disorders. The Odessa branch of the All-Russian Union of Lawyers formed a special commission to collect evidence to use in criminal proceedings against Neidhardt and other police personnel. Indeed, over the course of the next several months, several suspected pogromists were brought to trial. Although some cases were dismissed for lack of evidence, a handful of persons were convicted of pogromist activity and received jail sentences. Several police officers also lost their jobs for their role in the pogrom.[69]

In various factories in the city, Jewish and gentile workers also decided to contribute portions of their wages to help pogrom victims: employees of Vysotskii, the Shpolianskii Iron Foundry, and the Russian Steam Navigation and Trading Company collected over 1,000 rubles for distribution to needy Jewish families, and employees of the Weinstein Granary assigned 2 percent of their weekly wages to pogrom victims. Even the Board of Artisanal Trades agreed to help pay for new sewing machines for those tailors and seamstresses whose equipment had been destroyed in the pogrom. The Board also assigned 12,000 rubles to assist all suffering artisans, establishing a ten-person committee, consisting of five Jews and five Russians, to administer the funds.[70]

Workers in many enterprises were not content to limit their efforts to only financial contributions and legal testimony. Many non-Jewish workers, embarrassed that many pogromists were their coworkers, took vigorous action to punish them and ensure that another pogrom would not occur. One tactic was to refuse to shake hands with known pogromists. In early November, thirty-five representatives from Peresyp's major metalworking and machine-construction plants discussed punitive measures. Some delegates insisted on following the example of those workers in several enterprises who had already demanded the immediate dismissal of all known pogromists. Others argued that such civic-minded revolutionary justice (samosud) would unjustly punish those pogromists who were not genuine anti-Semites, but merely ignorant dupes whom the pogrom's organizers had led astray. Advocates of an alternative approach suggested adopting a two-pronged policy: individuals who had willingly participated in the pogrom with full awareness of their actions were to be dismissed or have their names printed in newspapers so they could be bound over for prosecution. "Naive" or unwilling pogromists, on the other hand, were to be required to return all stolen goods and acknowledge their guilt in writing. After lengthy debate, the delegates decided to encourage coworkers to reveal the names of pogromists, write letters expressing indignation over the pogrom, and render material assistance to pogrom victims. They left the issue of additional punitive measures unresolved until a general meeting of all workers could take place.[71]

Workers in various enterprises took heart from this meeting and set about circulating lists of pogromists whom they sought to blacklist; employees of two teapacking firms and a printing house obtained dismissals of workers who admitted to participating in the pogrom, and at the Shpolianskii Iron Foundry workers circulated lists of pogromists and demanded their immediate dismissal. In addition, Shpolianskii workers insisted that pogromists return all stolen property acquired during the looting. In a factory that made parquet floors, workers struck after management refused to dismiss a supervisor and janitor accused of participating in the pogrom. The proliferation of Black Hundred literature also annoyed many workers and led to boycotts of factories where anti-Semitic and reactionary leaflets and pamphlets were being distributed.[72] The effectiveness of peer pressure can be measured in terms of the scores of accused workers who recanted and "begged for forgiveness."[73]

Some workers believed that blacklisting was inadequate retribution. In one incident, a group of twenty-five Peresyp workers marched to a small village located just outside the city in search of a gang of thieves they believed had participated in the pogrom and had looted Jewish stores and homes. They beat a hasty retreat after being fired upon as they approached the village. Returning to Peresyp, they notified the district police chief, who dispatched a patrol to investigate. In another incident, workers from the Henn factory and other Peresyp factories shot a man suspected of participating in the pogrom. Bands of armed Jews also conducted searches of apartments of persons suspected of possessing stolen property acquired during the pogrom. The Jews claimed they were acting under the instruction of the Central Jewish Committee, but the head of that organization condemned the raids and denied responsibility, asserting they were being carried out without police participation or court permission.[74]

Other workers went beyond these acts of revolutionary justice and adopted measures designed to prevent future outbursts of anti-Jewish violence. For some workers, the horrors of October were due to the inadequate organization of Odessa's workers. In a strongly worded letter published in *Kommercheskaia Rossiia* on October 30, workers of the Russian Steam Navigation and Trading Company blamed themselves for not having formed a workers' militia to resist the pogromist mobs. The events of October, they wrote, revealed that "unorganized workers can be used by dark forces for personal advantage and to the harm of all workers." Thus, they planned to form a trade union of metalworkers and machinists because they believed that membership in a union would prevent Black Hundreds and other reactionary forces from using workers as unwilling pawns in future pogroms and counterrevolutionary activities. Grigorii Achkanov, a Bolshevik activist in the plant, recalled twenty years later how the pogrom "opened the eyes of many . . . workers," encouraging a number to join the revolutionary parties. Two weeks later, Shpolianskii workers published a similarly worded letter: "insufficient worker organization" contributed to the outbreak of the pogrom. Following the lead of workers of the Russian Steam Navigation and Trading Company, they were going to join the newly established union of machine construction workers.[75]

Such responses illustrate the politicizing influence of recent national and local events and reflect the extent to which certain categories of workers in Odessa viewed organization as a way to safeguard their political interests and preserve social peace. This tendency to organize matured in the last two months of 1905, when workers expressed their economic and political aspirations in the form of trade unions and a soviet of workers' deputies.

8

Final Confrontation

The general strike and popular unrest of October brought politics to the fore as the struggle for workplace improvements became subsumed in the broader movement for reform of the autocracy. By year's end the struggle to enjoy participatory rights in the running of the enterprise had expanded to embrace demands for a share in the exercise of local and national power. Odessa workers had learned valuable lessons about the contest for political power as a result of events earlier in the year: the struggle for a life of dignity entailed organizing and fighting for a reformed factory regime, although this did not necessarily include a fundamental challenge to the capitalist order. The fall general strike had a radicalizing impact on workers throughout the Empire, whose actions became more political, even when they were ostensibly acting to promote their material interests.

As it did elsewhere in Russia, the workers' struggle in Odessa to win the right to organize in defense of their collective interests, as well as to acquire greater control over their lives as workers and citizens, found its truest expression in trade unions and the quintessential labor organization formed by Russian workers in 1905, the Soviet of Workers' Deputies. Odessa workers viewed these twin organizations as the means to consolidate the gains of October 17 and the revolution. Essentially, they were talking about nothing less than rights of citizenship, or as T. H. Marshall has written, civil, political, and social equality on both an individual and collective basis.[1] Their experience parallels that of workers in the two capital cities of Moscow and St. Petersburg, where, in the words of Victoria Bonnell, they struggled for "citizenship in the broadest sense and for dignity and respectability in the polity and in society."[2] It was the capacity of the soviet and trade unions to fulfill workers' aspirations that gave these preeminent working-class organizations their power, authority, and appeal.

The Emergence of Trade Unions

During November and December, virtually every category of worker in Odessa either established a trade union or initiated efforts to form one. Motivations varied from one category of workers to another, but all attest to the desire of workers to claim their rights to associate and achieve, both as individual citizens and members of the working class, improvements in their social, economic, and political standing. Even workers who limited their union's stated objectives to bread-and-butter issues linked unionization to the cause of political reform. When the management of Levenson Typography refused to permit its predominantly Jewish employees to hold a union meeting, the workers defied management and held a rally in the plant's courtyard, where orators discussed the class struggle and the need for political reform. How could Odessa workers, they argued, defend their economic interests without the right of collective association? Other workers valued unions because they believed organized labor would prevent the government and employers from backsliding. At an organizational meeting of the granary workers' union, one speaker emphasized that workers had to fight for political rights. Otherwise, he warned, "Any victories will be temporary. They can be taken back." He then encouraged granary workers not to limit their struggle to only economic issues but to include political concerns.[3]

Others, especially those engaged in the apparel trades, wanted to defend themselves against the proliferation of the subcontracting system. Realizing that their dispersal among hundreds of small workshops robbed them of clout, tailors, shoemakers, and hatmakers acknowledged the importance of collective association by forming craft unions. Still other workers agitated for unions in order to counteract the actions of employers who were forming employers' associations. Some workers in female-dominated occupations hoped to achieve, among other demands, more respectful treatment, largely in the form of polite address, from their employers. Since the spring, some women workers had been urging the formation of all-women unions. In the fall women workers embraced the opportunity to form unions, with laundresses, domestic servants, and cooks considering mass strike actions to win material improvements. Lastly, many workers, such as apartment building groundskeepers (*dvorniki*), simply picked up cues from more organized workers and followed their example of forming unions.[4]

Regardless of their motivation, Odessa workers recognized that trade unions offered an institutionized power base. As a male ironer of clothes commented in an appeal to his coworkers, "Remember that our strength is in unity and that only by uniting in an union can we carry out a struggle with our employers and the existing order."[5] *Kommercheskaia Rossiia* is filled with letters urging workers to form unions. "The freedom of unions," wrote one worker, "is one of the most powerful ways to struggle with the dying regime and employer exploitation."[6] A domestic servant, in one of those rare instances when women workers made their voice public, argued, "We are powerless to help ourselves unless we organize." Her sentiments were seconded by a chambermaid who insisted that all domestic servants, chambermaids, and cooks unionize in order to "dictate the terms of work to our employees" and demonstrate to them that "we are all for one and one for all."[7] Similar expressions of belief in the power of trade unions were made by workers of nearly every craft and occupation in Odessa. These calls for unity and cooperation were translated into a labor movement that, surprisingly given the sorry state of affairs between Jews and non-Jews, generally included both Jews and gentiles in the same unions.

Labor activism after October combined elements of both an offensive and defensive posture designed to safeguard as well as assert workers' interests. Collective association and other fundamental civil freedoms clearly had assumed tremendous importance for Odessa workers. Whereas prior to October efforts to organize had been limited to certain categories of workers, the wave of organizational activity after October—during the so-called "Days of Freedom"—was a widespread, broadly based phenomenon which, in large measure, owed its vibrancy to the relatively open atmosphere created by the October Manifesto.

The October Manifesto provided a framework within which Odessa workers could defend their interests during the last two months of 1905. Before October, many workers in Odessa hesitated to organize for fear of government reprisal. But after Nicholas II guaranteed freedom of speech, assembly, and association on October 17, workers who had been previously wary took advantage of the changed political climate. In the heady weeks following the Tsar's proclamation, workers for the first time could organize relatively free of government interference. Although government approval was, at best, tacit and ambiguous (unions were still illegal and would remain so until March 1906), workers perceived the failure to meddle with their organizational efforts as a sign that the autocracy had acknowledged their collective rights of association. As one compositor explained, "what seemed illegal earlier and to many even dangerous is now legal." Indeed, many printers opposed the formation of a trade union before October, but wholeheartedly supported the creation of one after October 17.[8] The October Manifesto released the pent-up desires of Odessa workers, many of whom had long been frustrated in their efforts to secure what Marshall has termed the "collective civil rights" of labor.

The view that trade unionism in 1905 was limited to bread-and-butter issues, whereas soviets and factory committees more genuinely reflected the class consciousness and political aspirations of labor, overlooks the paramount place that issues of power in the workplace and in society as a whole played in the trade-union movement. After all, the struggle for trade-union recognition concerned the fundamental arrangement of power and authority in late Imperial Russia, both on the enterprise level, where workers challenged traditional employer prerogatives, and in the broader polity, where the autocratic regime resisted the workers' right to organize on an independent basis. Union formation was more than a tactic adopted by workers employed in small enterprises dispersed throughout the city who could not exert pressure on employers without combining outside the workplace; it was a microcosm of the contest for political power that was occurring between state and society throughout urban Russia in 1905.[9]

Some observers noted that "trade unions sprang up like mushrooms" after the announcement of the October Manifesto.[10] One of the Odessa representatives to the February 1906 Second All-Russian Conference of Trade Unions estimated the total number of trade unions at approximately thirty, a figure that Soviet historians consequently accepted. My own reading of the Odessa daily press, memoirs, and secondary literature indicates that the number of trade unions formed during November and December was closer to fifty. This total includes unions for which workers had elected governing boards and approved charters, as well as those instances where workers met to discuss creating a union but where it is unknown whether one was formally established.[11] Even if plans for a union never got off the ground, the list of unions that workers either established or wanted to form after October clearly reveals that male and female workers from all positions on the occupational spectrum, ranging from the unskilled and underpaid to the most highly skilled and best paid, were caught up in the drive to unionize. Categories of workers usually absent from the ranks of organized labor, women in particular, participated in factory meetings, helped form and administer unions, and even served as deputies to the Soviet of Workers' Deputies. The unionization drive of November and December is graphic testimony of how the organizational urge captivated Odessa workers and reflected a genuine grassroots movement.

Numbers of workers who joined unions during November and December are even harder to determine. Accounts of union activity for these months allow a rough approximation of 5,000, with printers, machine builders, bakers, candymakers, teapackers, housepainters, and roofers comprising a substantial contingent of unionized workers.[12] But membership rolls, as Victoria Bonnell has pointed out, provide only one measure of worker attitudes toward the organized labor movement, since many workers who attended union meetings did not enroll or pay membership fees and union dues. Some workers were reluctant to join unions due to the lack of money or fear of reprisals, but they would attend union meetings, especially if they did not have to make any financial commitment or assume any responsibility toward the union. Moreover, the trade union movement was in its infancy and some workers may not have grasped the purpose of union membership. Thus, whereas only seventy tailors of men's clothes joined their union by the end of 1905, over 1,500 attended the meeting at which the union charter was drawn up, discussed, and approved. Similarly, less than half of the 800 persons attending the December 4 meeting of the Union of Housepainters, Roofers, Plasterers, and Wallpaper Hangers were members of this organization, and although over 2,500 apartment building groundskeepers attended the constituent session of their union, only a third saw fit to join and pay membership dues.[13] This indicates that large numbers of nonunion workers were exposed to the organized labor movement, whose influence and impact exceeded the smaller circle of persons who made the financial and personal commitment to unions.

Consequently, membership rolls, assuming they were available, would underestimate the extent of union influence and the degree of contact between workers and the organized labor movement. It is true that membership in a union and its concomitant financial and sometimes personal obligations represent a deeper commitment than simple attendance at meetings, but the presence of nonunion workers at union gatherings enabled the organized labor movement to touch the lives of large numbers of Odessa workers. By attending meetings and participating in discussions, nonunion workers demonstrated their interest in unions as well as their tacit support of these organizations. In the process, these workers were exposed to the wide range of political, social, and economic issues raised by union activists.

Trade unions emerged first and most vigorously among those workers who had prior experience with the organized labor movement and had been active in the strike movement. The pre-October labor organizations served as training grounds for cadres of workers to acquire the valuable skills, expertise, and experience necessary for union activity. They also provided the institutional framework in which workers could build trade unions. For example, the factory and strike committees in the railway workshops and many Peresyp metalworking factories provided the leaders and institutional building blocks of the machine-construction and railway unions.[14] Jewish workers in trades where SDs had successfully set up strike funds at the turn of the century were quick to establish unions after October (although not exclusively for Jews), as were workers who had formed Zubatov unions in 1903 and factory and strike committees during the first half of 1905. Workers with a long history of involvement in mutual-aid societies or participation in formal guild organizations were also eager to establish labor unions in November and December. In many instances, the same individuals who participated in social-democratic strike funds, the Zubatov movement, or factory and strike committees played crucial roles in union formation after October 17.

Before October, efforts at unionization usually resulted in incomplete and unstable organizations; it was not until after the Manifesto was issued that workers were able to form more stable trade unions. Thus, workers who had already formed unions during the spring redoubled efforts to strengthen these organizations after October. It will be recalled that bakers had established a trade union in February and achieved significant concessions from their employers in the spring; after October 17, they launched an active campaign to unionize all bakers in order to ensure that bakery owners would not renege on the terms of the agreement.[15] Similarly, sailors decided to transform the Registration into a trade union that was entirely free of ties to the shipping lines and municipal authorities.[16]

For their part, salesclerks who had expressed their frustration with the limitations and essentially nonconfrontational tactics of mutual-aid societies in the spring now engaged in a full-fledged campaign to form a trade union. In November, shop assistants, who had joined most other workers in Odessa in the walkouts of May-June and October, formed a union. In December the more skilled and better paid bookkeepers, officeworkers, and clerks—who regarded themselves as a cut above the typical shop assistant—established their own organization, the "Union of Office Workers," after rejecting an invitation to join the Union of Salesclerks. As in the spring, activist shop assistants delivered speeches and wrote letters to *Kommercheskaia Rossiia* about rights of citizenship, political liberation, proletarian solidarity, and the struggle against capitalist exploitation.[17]

The Union of Salesclerks struck a serious blow to its major competitors, the Mutual Aid Society of Jewish Salesclerks and the Society of Employees in Commercial and Industrial Enterprises, robbing them of their rank-and-file support and overwhelming these more tradition-bound labor associations. Confident that they could extract concessions from their employers, shop assistants chose the adversarial employer-employee relationship implicit in the activities of a trade union. For them, the union offered a sense of greater possibility and promise than did mutual-aid societies mired in the reliance on a regime that had done little to ameliorate their conditions. One measure of the union's appeal was the attendance of thousands of shop assistants, who jammed the auditoriums in November to listen to and participate in initial discussions concerning its formation.

Workers who had not participated in the strikes of May and June and who lacked prior experience with collective associations had a more difficult time forming unions than did workers who had elected strike committees and were active in the spring unrest.[18] Nonetheless, they also set about establishing unions. This phenomenon can be attributed both to the "bandwagon" effect of simply following the example of others and, perhaps more important, to the autocracy's momentary retreat, which inspired workers to experiment with collective association. Thus, domestic servants, groundskeepers, and workers in dining and drinking establishments followed in the footsteps of the more organizationally experienced apparel workers, printers, sailors, shop assistants, and metalworkers in forming trade unions.

As in other parts of the Russian Empire, Odessa workers exhibited a strong tendency to form craft unions, a predilection largely explained by the significance of craft identity and solidarity. Workplace experiences and skill clearly played crucial roles in the capacity and desire of workers to organize by craft. The tendency to organize along occupational lines before 1905 helped condition workers who, when given the opportunity to form trade unions in 1905, reacted by organizing on the basis of craft.

Fragmentation by craft was often so pronounced in Odessa that workers in the needle trades formed separate unions differentiated by whether they produced clothes for men or women and whether they engaged in ready- or custom-made manufacture. Although such *tsekhovshchina* or craft exclusiveness (sometimes termed "shopism") was condemned by some labor organizers, especially SD activists, the apparel workers paid little heed and remained organizationally subdivided. Separate unions existed for hatmakers, capmakers, and milliners, and for shoe- and bootmakers as well. *Tsekhovshchina* also extended to other crafts. Not all tinsmiths belonged to the same union, butchers organized separately from sausagemakers, and pastrymakers affiliated with bakers rather than with their most common coworkers, the candymakers.[19] Even among unskilled workers, who are generally regarded as not possessing craft solidarities and allegiances, an emphasis on occupation marked their organizational efforts. For example, restaurant employees organized independently of waiters and cooks of the steamship lines.[20] Such narrow craft identity undoubtedly made it difficult for workers to mold effective strategies and establish cohesive unions that could overcome differences among workers in similar occupations.

Even in unions that were amalgams of workers from closely related but essentially different trades, the craft principle was nonetheless retained by the organizational autonomy of the constituent crafts. Thus, the metalfitters' union included tinsmiths, bedmakers, carriagemakers, and roofers, but in elections to the union's board of directors workers voted as a bloc based on craft divisions rather than as individuals.[21] Even the few industrial unions which tried to organize all workers in a given industry suffered from centrifugal tendencies largely caused by craft loyalties and by the lack of uniformity in working conditions, which gave rise to different concerns. Electrotechnical workers, for example, fearful that their specific needs would be overlooked if they affiliated with other metalworkers and machinists, preferred instead to form a separate union in December.[22]

Just as workers had different motives when they formed unions, so too did the paths of unionization vary. One common route involved representatives from various enterprises in the same line of production getting together and agreeing to create a trade union. After drawing up a union charter and setting up headquarters, the delegates would then return to their respective workplaces and lobby coworkers to sanction their actions. Events at the Bellino-Fenderikh Iron Foundry followed this pattern in late November, when workers held a general meeting and agreed to join the metalworkers' union. Formal approval came several weeks after these same workers had sent representatives to meetings where delegates from the city's metalworking and machine-building plants had agreed to form a union. Printers followed a similar path in their post-October organizing.[23] Not infrequently, workers of industrial enterprises would meet independently and agree to form a union or to affiliate with an existing one. They would then select delegates to draw up a union charter or establish contact with union activists from other enterprises.

The Politics of Trade Unions

At the beginning of 1905, both Bolsheviks and Mensheviks were wary of trade unionism for practical and ideological reasons. However, developments after Bloody Sunday led both groups to involve themselves in union formation. By the fall they had recognized the usefulness of the budding organized labor movement, because the radicalism of the workers was outstripping the expectations of the revolutionaries themselves and accelerating "the revolutionary process."[24] This embrace of trade unions was easier for the Mensheviks than for the Bolsheviks, since the former were inclined to pin the hopes of a successful socialist revolution on the development of a mass, legal labor movement.

The shift in Bolshevik attitudes first required deemphasizing the Leninist view of trade unions as reformist organizations that diverted workers from more important political tasks. Acknowledging that the mass movement to form unions could not be ignored without risking further alienation from the workers, the Odessa Bolsheviks in October began to advocate the establishment of party-affiliated unions. They formed a special bureau called the Commission for the Organization of Trade Unions (COTU) to assist in a campaign to form such groups in Odessa and undercut growing Menshevik influence in the fledgling organized labor movement. In an effort to assume general leadership of Odessa's union movmeent, COTU instructed party members to organize informational meetings, create union cells in individual enterprises, and compose model charters in order to facilitate union formation, particularly in the case of industrial unions. Bundists participated in COTU after receiving an invitation to send representatives. COTU also soon found itself working with Mensheviks after the Bolshevik and Menshevik factions in Odessa united in early November (discussed below). At that point, it was superseded by the Central Bureau of Trade Unions, which acted as an umbrella association assisting trade unions in organizational, educational, and administrative matters. Whether joint direction of COTU by the Mensheviks and Bolsheviks entailed a shift in policy regarding party-affiliated unions is unknown.[25]

One of COTU's many tasks involved the problem of which language—Yiddish or Russian—union organizers should use when addressing mixed groups of Jewish and gentile workers. Bundists claimed that many Jewish workers possessed an unsure grasp of the Russian language and therefore demanded the right to speak Yiddish or at least a mixture of Russian and Yiddish. But Bolsheviks and Mensheviks strongly opposed this tactic unless some of the workers present did not understand Russian at all. This issue had particular resonance in the central district of Odessa, where there were large numbers of Jewish workers and where some Bolshevik agitators even agreed with the Bund's tactic of conducting work and issuing literature in Yiddish. Here Bundists could buttress their case with specific references to instances when Jewish workers were at a linguistic disadvantage due to their poor understanding of Russian-speaking orators. Although the branch of COTU in this region devised several schemes to satisfy the demands of Yiddish-speaking union members, no solution was found. The issue was apparently never brought before the citywide commission, and the outcome of the dispute is unknown. But the very existence of such a debate once again highlights the organizational difficulties arising from the ethnic heterogeneity of the Odessa work force.[26]

While it is difficult to gauge the extent of socialist influence on trade unions, it is reasonable to assume that the number of union members who also belonged to the Bolsheviks and Mensheviks was well below the parties' estimated fall membership of 1,000–1,500.[27] Most unions and their members avoided formal ties with any of the socialist parties. They reasoned that party affiliation would limit the sphere of union influence and hinder the unionization of the politically indifferent and unmotivated. Although formal independence from the socialist parties provided unions greater flexibility and maneuverability in the conduct of their affairs, it did not spell the absence of party influence. In forming unions and managing union affairs, Odessa workers frequently depended upon experienced worker-activists, many with affiliations to one of the various revolutionary parties, particularly the SDs.[28] A prime example is Ivan Avdeev, who played a leading part in the strike movement during the first half of 1905 and then headed the Union of Railway Workers in November and December. Joining Avdeev in his efforts were other railway activists, such as Fedor Golubkov and Nikolai Raikh, the latter having a history of labor organizing and socialist involvement stretching back to the turn of the century. Similar patterns characterized workers of other occupations. For example, a man named Klimovitskii, having spent four years in prison and exile for organizing a strike fund among Odessa's tailors at the beginning of the decade, was urged by some tailors to resume his union activities upon his return to Odessa in 1905.[29] In early November, it was Menshevik printers who took the first steps to form a union. Among metalworkers, a group of active Mensheviks and Bolsheviks representing workers from the major machine-building and metalworking enterprises of Peresyp were the ones to draw up a union charter in early November.[30]

In light of the immaturity of the organized labor movement in Odessa and the workers' lack of experience in these matters, workers quite naturally turned to those who had already established and managed formal organizations. Individual worker-socialists assumed leading roles in the unions (as well as in the Soviet of Workers' Deputies) precisely because they had earned the esteem of their coworkers and could be relied on to promote workers' interests. Already enjoying status among their fellow workers, these union activists were seen as leaders by those workers who had been radicalized by the events of 1905 and who in late fall envisioned consolidating the gains of October and, perhaps, achieving additional reforms. In the aftermath of October, workers, flushed with victory and sensing the beginning of a new era, turned to the revolutionary organizations—the same groups which had turned their backs on labor in June—for help, which was now forthcoming. As a result, the socialist parties were able to exert an influence on the labor movement that had been lacking before October.

Workers also turned to SDs outside the ranks of labor. Some revolutionaries, recently returned to Odessa from exile for their participation in the unrest of May and June, assumed leadership roles in unions as well, often at the behest of the workers, who looked to the radical intelligentsia for guidance in these matters. This was especially true among those workers who lacked experienced worker-activists and an organizational heritage. When Nina Grokhol'skaia, a domestic servant, appealed to party activists for assistance, she wrote, "Unite us, help us stand on our own two feet, and then we . . . shall break our chains and liberate ourselves from our slavery."[31] Granary workers asked the Menshevik activists who had initiated organizing efforts to assume direction of their fledgling union; sausagemakers were assisted in their union efforts by Mikhail Bogomolets, the socialist physician, and Petr Starostin, a Bolshevik metalworker who had arrived in Odessa from St. Petersburg in the summer. Bolsheviks were influential in the establishment of the union of teapackers, and an SD helped groundskeepers organize the constituent meeting of their union. In addition, workers at cork factories and even some dockworkers, bakers, and pastrymakers adopted union charters based on the models suggested by COTU.[32]

Bolsheviks and Mensheviks were not the only members of the radical intelligentsia involved in the union movement. SRs, Bundists, Labor Zionists, and Socialist Zionists (the last two of whom mixed the tenets of Marxism and Zionism) also participated in the formation of unions, either by invitation or on their own initiative.[33] Socialist Zionists, for example, shared the Menshevik preference for nonparty unions, but local Bundists, having cooperated with the Bolsheviks in COTU, presumably advocated the formation of party-affiliated unions.[34] Competition among the various revolutionary parties for worker allegiance often turned union meetings into battlegrounds where members of rival parties hurled insults at each other and engaged in shouting matches. The SRs, who had enjoyed some support among bakers in the spring and were also popular among woodworkers and construction workers, took to disrupting union meetings in an effort to counteract the growing influence of the SDs. Such encounters usually ended with the SDs, who generally controlled the union meetings, expelling SRs from the halls.[35] Interparty disputes were not limited to clashes between SRs and SDs; at a meeting of jewelers convened by Socialist Zionists, a group of SDs seized the rostrum and convinced the jewelers to elect an SD as chair.[36]

Liberals also became involved in the organization of unions. This is not surprising given their commitment to a reformed political order that guaranteed fundamental civil liberties. Evgenii Shchepkin presided over the first meeting of the Union of Office Workers, and another prominent Odessa liberal, Professor R. M. Orzhentskii, was invited by restaurant workers to help organize their union and was also instrumental in promoting unions among cabdrivers, groundskeepers, and domestic servants.[37] Again, workers seeking to establish unions turned to politically experienced activists who could bestow respectability on their organizations as well as offer practical advice and guidance.

The charters of several unions representing a cross-section of the Odessa work force attest to the influence of the revolutionaries and illuminate the interests, goals, and strategies of organized workers and their leaders.[38] Remarkable similarity exists among the eight extant union charters examined here. In some instances, the wording is identical, either because workers followed the model charters distributed by COTU or because, not knowing how to go about drafting a union charter, they copied the charters of unions that had already been formed, sometimes neglecting to tailor them to the specific needs of their trade.[39] Although such practices detract from the value of union charters as clear statements of members' precise aspirations, we must remember that union members, ostensibly voicing their support of the charters' contents, approved these documents.

According to the charters, the goal of unions was "to protect the economic and legal interests" of their members, "improve working conditions," and win greater control over the administration of the enterprise. To achieve these aims, union members agreed, among other things, to establish legal assistance and employment bureaus, enter into contracts with employers in order to standardize working conditions, ensure observance of agreements, organize arbitration boards to resolve labor-management disputes, and settle all disagreements among union members. The unions also assumed the responsibility to provide unemployment, sickness, and death benefits to members and their families. Emphasizing the need to raise the "intellectual and moral" standards of members, the charters planned to establish libraries and reading rooms, publish newspapers, and organize public lectures. Furthermore, the charters stressed that the strike was the most potent weapon in the struggle to achieve improved working conditions. "The union considers the general strike," wrote the railway workers in their charter, "as the most serious and extreme means of struggle."[40]

Although talk of the class struggle and political freedom was surprisingly absent from the model charter distributed by COTU,[41] several of the actual union charters referred, in good socialist style, to the development of class solidarity, the irreconcilable conflict between labor and capital, and the need for political rights. The woodworkers' charter stated its aim as "the development of the class consciousness" of its members. The printers combined class and professional concerns when they wrote that their union's goal was "to conduct uninterrupted agitation to elucidate their class, legal and professional needs." Railway workers and office employees neglected to say something explicitly about class struggle in their charters, but they did stress the need to expand the political rights of all workers. Evidently, many workers in Odessa unions were not entirely dependent on the SDs for the form and content of their charters. As we have seen time and time again in 1905, some Odessa workers, when it came to assessing their situation as members of Russia's exploited underclass, were capable of formulating their own grievances with both employers and government.[42]

The radical intelligentsia's contribution to the organized labor movement was not limited to assistance in establishing unions. The full extent of socialist influence on workers after October can be gleaned from an examination of the activities of unions and the behavior of revolutionaries at union meetings, worker rallies, and assemblies. The union movement served as a conduit for the spread of radical political ideas. In the wake of the October Manifesto, radical activists reached a wider audience of workers than ever before. Although workers did not join the various socialist parties or even trade unions on a mass scale, by attending meetings and other worker gatherings they were exposed to socialist ideas. Many workers, in their capacities as union representatives, supported elements of party platforms, especially those which expressed the rank-and-file's aspirations for participation, democracy, and equality in economic, social, and political relations.

Socialist speakers had no shortage of opportunities to speak to workers at union meetings, factory assemblies, public lectures, and rallies in working-class neighborhoods, where they reached a broad spectrum of workers. Mass meetings served as schools of political education, where workers were drawn into the world of politics and were exposed to a variety of ideologies. At these forums, some of which were attended by thousands of workers, a variety of revolution-aries decried capitalist exploitation and stressed the need for workers to further political reform. They pointed out the pros and cons of the October Manifesto and of the promised State Duma and, emphasizing that the guarantees of the October Manifesto were not yet realized, urged workers to apply unrelenting pressure on the regime until it assured in law full civil rights and liberties. Finally, socialist orators encouraged workers to struggle for a constituent assembly, which represented a political order that truly signified the end of autocracy.[43]

In one representative instance, Mikhail Bogomolets, addressing a group of workers at a neighborhood gathering on November 19, started his speech by railing against the insufficiencies of the October Manifesto and ended with demands for a constituent assembly, abolition of the death penalty, and full amnesty for all political prisoners. He also encouraged workers to boycott the wealthy merchants who "controlled the city council" and "exploited the poor" of Odessa.[44] At another rally several days later, Bogomolets characterized trade unions as "a political weapon in the struggle with capitalism." But he also noted that unions by themselves could not end capitalist exploitation and emphasized that workers must develop class consciousness and use the general strike as a weapon in the struggle to overturn the existing socio-economic system, replacing it with one which transfers "the means of production" to labor.[45] At other rallies held on November 20 in Peresyp, socialist activists condemned the limited suffrage of the planned State Duma and demanded convocation of a constituent assembly and implementation of the terms of the October Manifesto.

University professors also spoke at assemblies of workers, describing the importance of trade unions and political activism in promoting the welfare of workers. At one such meeting, held in early November, two professors discussed with 700 workers the impending strike of postal-telegraph employees, whose efforts to form a trade union were being undermined by the government. The two men emphasized that workers had a "moral right" to achieve better eco-nomic conditions by means of trade union activity. After reviewing the history of the Union of Unions, the umbrella organization that coordinated the actions of unions representing professional and white-collar groups and some manual workers as well, they urged the postal-telegraph workers to unite with other organizations of white-collar employees and professionals in the struggle for political reform.[46]

The exact nature of the workers' response to these ideas and sentiments is impossible to measure, but gauging by what Odessa workers and unions said and did, it is fair to conclude that the intelligentsia left its mark. The ideas of these activists meshed with those of many workers, who had arrived at a similar understanding of events as a result of personal observation, reflection, and experience. The political messages of revolutionary socialists resonated within labor's ranks, since they helped workers to articulate their own economic and political grievances. Organized labor in Odessa may have insisted on formal political neutrality, but this should not obscure the fact that many workers embraced the general tenor of the socialist message, even if they did not always understand or accept the particulars of a Marxist analysis.

Workers speaking at rallies clearly showed their affinity with the views expressed by socialist orators. The content of workers' speeches indicates that radical sentiments—including open rebellion—had seized the hearts and minds of many Odessans, not just a small circle of revolutionaries. At one meeting organized by the Union of Writers and held in Slobodka-Romanovka, workers along with SD representatives called for the transfer of all land to the peasants, the immediate introduction of the eight-hour workday, free health insurance, free general education, the establishment of a constituent assembly based on four-tail suffrage, and full amnesty for all political and religious prisoners—in sum, many of the demands that had been made throughout the year and that were included in the political and economic program of the RSDWP. At a rally organized by the sanitary commission for the harbor region and held in a night shelter for day laborers, 300 dockworkers listened to various speeches by workers; one focused on the political significance of the October Manifesto, while another blamed the police for inciting workers to attack Jews during the pogrom. Another rally attracted some 2,000 people, many of whom criticized the "liberal prattle" of a Kadet speaker who failed to offer any concrete suggestions on how political freedom could be attained. When the Kadet grew disconcerted in response to a question about whether he supported an armed uprising, the audience intensified its heckling. At still another rally, workers discussed the viability of armed struggle, with many participants exhorting their fellow workers to arm themselves despite warnings by some that the regime's current military strength would render engagement with the army futile and unwise.[47]

During November, union leaders focused on consolidating the organized labor movement rather than spearheading a strike campaign. With the exception of the postal-telegraph employees, whose national union had called a strike in mid-November to protest the firing of several union leaders, and a few other incidents of shortlived work stoppages, labor unrest in Odessa died down in November.[48] The "Days of Freedom" ushered in by the October Manifesto gave union organizers an opportunity to devote their time and energy to practical matters like union organization. Once trade unions were in place, organized workers could set out to lead other workers in the struggle for improved working conditions.

When we turn from stated intentions to the realm of practice, we find that unions repeated demands made earlier in the year. Some unions claimed the right to hire and fire workers and challenged management's prerogative to settle labor disputes without the participation of union representatives. Even workers who had not yet formed unions demanded that all shop floor disagreements and fines be settled by deputies elected by workers: for example, the non-unionized stevedores of the Moscow Customs Artel struck for one day in November over working conditions and the right to elect delegates who would have the power to approve all fines and dismissals. As economic conditions continued to deteriorate as a result of the October unrest and the onset of the winter dead season, some unions decided to spread the impact of increased layoffs more equitably by asking members to reduce voluntarily the number of hours worked, thereby saving jobs for coworkers threatened with unemployment.[49]

One striking aspect of union activity was that, by the end of 1905, a broad spectrum of the Odessa work force had become aware of the importance to them of political developments elsewhere in Russia and the symbolic and practical significance of worker solidarity. Unionized workers in Odessa understood that the course of events outside the confines of their respective enterprises and even outside the city strongly affected the outcome of their own struggles. If, for example, workers in St. Petersburg were subject to arrest and imprisonment for union activities, then did not Odessa workers also face the prospect of a government backlash? Odessa workers therefore adopted a variety of measures designed to support the job actions of workers in other parts of Russia, especially once it became evident that the government had regained its confidence and was intent on undoing the concessions granted in October. In this respect, then, union activism can be seen as a measure to protect workers from the very real threat of an aggressive regime on the rebound. Already by the beginning of November, the government's policy of compromise and reform had given way to one of intransigence and provocation as Prime Minister Sergei Witte orchestrated a frontal assault on workers by harassing the organized labor movement, arresting trade-union activists, breaking up politically vociferous unions, and declaring martial law in Poland. The last action, coupled with the court martial of several mutinous Kronstadt sailors, prompted the St. Petersburg Soviet of Workers' Deputies to call a work stoppage in early November. The response by workers in the capital was overwhelming: over 100,000 struck in protest against government policy.[50]

Odessa workers from various unions responded in a display of sympathy. In an effort to hurt the imperial treasury, they vowed not to buy vodka, and the railway workers' union levied fines on workers who violated this prohibition. When Georgii Khrustalev-Nosar, the leftist lawyer who headed the St. Petersburg Soviet of Workers' Deputies, was arrested, and the government began to suppress workers' political activities in the capital, Odessa workers vehemently protested. They also demanded full amnesty for political and religious prisoners. On November 20, 3,000 persons, many of them workers, attended a rally protesting martial law in Poland and calling for the granting of autonomy to the Poles. The crews of several ships also refused to transport military personnel and supplies, and railway workers threatened to strike if the death sentences of several leaders of a recent railway strike in Samara were not commuted. The government caved in to the pressure of the public outcry against its plans to execute the Samara workers, thereby averting a potentially costly and disruptive walkout.[51]

In sum, many Odessa workers saw trade unions as the means by which they could extract material concessions, acquire greater control over the workplace, and press for political reforms that they regarded as indispensable preconditions for the collective improvement of their lives. They realized that they had to engage in a concerted campaign to win legislative approval of the right to assemble and organize collectively. Without such legislative guarantees of civil liberties and freedoms, the fledgling union movement could not be ensured of survival. Thus, even though workers and union activists viewed themselves as under assault from a hostile government, they also advocated aggressive tactics to win additional concessions. As one Menshevik told granary workers seeking to form a union: "At the present time it's no secret that it's impossible to limit your struggle to economic matters; you need to struggle for your political rights, for your civil rights." To the granary workers in attendance the message was clear: unionization was necessary to safeguard as well as to promote their economic and political well-being in a capitalist society.[52] As Steve Smith has recently observed, "citizenship implied raising workers as a group to a position of equality with the rest of society; and whilst this was deemed to entail the realization of certain individual liberties, it was through the *collective* upgrading of workers that true citizenship would be achieved. This necessarily required . . . the reform of the political system."[53]

According to the Menshevik Semen O. Portugeis, editor-in-chief of *Kommercheskaia Rossiia* when it was aligned with the SDs during the final weeks of 1905, workers had learned through day-to-day experience, socialist agitation, and observation of the national political scene that the appropriate arena of trade union activity was politics. Political activism had forced Nicholas to issue the October Manifesto and would secure and extend the freedoms granted on October 17. In the words of Portugeis, "Politics achieved the October Manifesto, and politics will guarantee it." Since unions defended the interests of workers, workers needed legislative assurances of the freedom of assembly, speech, press, and strike in order to ensure the vitality of the organized labor movement. Workers could patiently wait until government officials granted this legislation or, in the words of Portugeis, they could "engage in open struggle" to pressure the government for these freedoms. The very survival of Odessa's fledgling unions depended on the "unceasing political struggle of workers."[54] In the eyes of unionized workers and socialist activists, politics was the ultimate arbiter of their economic grievances.

The Soviet of Workers' Deputies

By establishing a Soviet of Workers' Deputies, Odessa workers attempted to overcome what Reinhard Bendix has described as the "experience of *political alienation,* a sense of not having a recognized position in the civic community of an emerging industrial society."[55] The soviet went further than the trade-union movement in its effort to create a democratic alternative to the society and polity of autocratic Russia. Like soviets elsewhere in the Empire, the Odessa soviet was the institutionalized forum of Russian labor's attempt to control Russian society and politics; in the soviet, the workers' claim for proletarian self-government and control extended beyond the workplace to encompass society as a whole. The experience of the Odessa soviet in 1905 presaged the Dual Power arrangement that characterized the political landscape of Russia after the collapse of the dynasty twelve years later in February 1917. Of more immediate importance, however, was the coalescence in the soviet of a nascent class awareness among Odessa's workers, who were beginning to realize that they belonged to a social group whose interests were in conflict with those of Russia's other social classes, particularly the industrial and commercial classes. The soviet provided more unity and cohesion to the Odessa labor movement than had the unionization campaign, and it embodied the workers' struggle for a life of dignity, security and control. The Odessa soviet was a lesson in grassroots democracy and initiative that reflected the workers enthusiasm for direct, unmediated political participation. One salesclerk displayed his grasp of the direct connection between political emancipation and the workers' economic welfare when he wrote of the soviet: "We shall discuss issues that concern us first of all as citizens and then as salesclerks."[56] He was echoing the sentiments of a compositor who half a year earlier stated; "We aren't asking only for a better life, we also want recognition of our rights as citizens."[57]

The Odessa soviet fashioned itself after similar organizations that had already sprung up elsewhere in urban Russia. Soviets (councils) evolved out of strike committees representing workers from different enterprises and trades in one geographic region, then becoming revolutionary institutions that spearheaded the campaign for economic and political reform. The first organization considered to be a soviet appeared in mid-May in Ivanovo-Voznesensk, a textile center located some 200 miles northeast of Moscow, during a strike which saw every factory in the city of 80,000 shut down. The soviet emerged when workers agreed to hold elections—at the behest of the factory inspector—for deputies from individual enterprises to conduct negotiations. The Ivanovo-Voznesensk Assembly of Deputies, as it was formally called, was at first concerned with bread-and-butter issues, but soon began to press for political concessions such as freedom of assembly and speech and the convocation of a constituent assembly. More importantly, it attempted to assume local police powers by forming a workers' militia and instituting price controls. Although the Assembly disbanded after a two-month strike in which most of its objectives had not been met, its significance lay primarily in the example it provided for workers throughout the Empire for the remaining months of 1905. When Russia was rocked by the October general strike, workers followed that precedent, turning their strike committees into full-fledged soviets of workers' deputies that were in the forefront of the challenge to the autocracy. As one historian has written, the Assembly was the first organization that "was later to become a powerful revolutionary institution . . . that arrogated political power."[58] During the "Days of Freedom," soviets emerged throughout urban Russia, operating in open defiance of the government and representing labor's desire to assume control over municipal affairs.

The flush and excitement of organizational activism among Odessa workers in the weeks following the pogrom should not obscure the fact that the soviet was also a response to the collapse of public order in the city. City authorities had not reasserted full control, and although there were no major disorders after mid-October, public calm still had not been reestablished. The daily press from late October until the end of November was filled with reports of gangs of thugs preying upon peaceful Odessans; the public was so alarmed that most people were afraid to leave their homes or walk the streets after dark. The fact that *Odesskie novosti* (*Odessa News*) started a new column entitled "Hooligans" is telling evidence of the extent of public uneasiness and the continued existence of a pogromist atmosphere. As the Bolshevik newspaper *Novaia zhizn'* (*New Life*) reported in late November, "After 6 P.M. life in the city comes to a standstill, stores close, and the streets are empty."[59] Incidents abounded in which youth gangs wandering the harbor viciously attacked workers at the docks and looted warehouses. At one railway depot, thugs threatened to beat up Jewish workers. Elsewhere they damaged the stores of merchants and small retailers who refused requests for free merchandise and services; the streets of the city were so unsafe that doctors reportedly refused to make housecalls.[60]

According to local newspapers, the authorities themselves contributed to the breakdown of law and order. Police and military patrols frequently threatened, robbed, and sometimes beat hapless pedestrians. In one incident, two policemen mugged a man and made off with slightly more than a ruble. When the victim pleaded with them to return this paltry sum, one retorted, "Thank God that we are making a present of your life to you."[61] In other instances, the police extorted protection money from frightened Odessans, Jews in particular. Even when the police did not actually perpetrate these crimes, they were generally guilty of inaction and of turning a sympathetic ear to the thugs. When two Jews informed a patrolman that a gang of twelve youths had just mugged them, he snapped it was not his affair. "I am posted here," he noted, "to make sure that traffic moves smoothly."[62]

A. G. Grigor'ev, a longtime resident of Odessa and an army general who had replaced Neidhardt as city governor, tried to allay fears and restore public trust and confidence in the police. His task was made all the more difficult by rumors of an impending pogrom in late October and the persistence of social and political unease. In his first interview with the press, Grigor'ev pledged to undertake "all measures to restore order and calm in the city" and promised to rein in those policemen who were abusing civilians.[63] Toward these ends, the new city governor issued a directive instructing the police to honor the terms of the October Manifesto, which, he emphasized, granted civil rights to every Odessan, regardless of nationality, religion, and social position. Stating that he did not "recognize differences between peoples of different nationalities," he commanded the police to treat every resident with courtesy and ordered them to fulfill their legal obligations and duties. Grigor'ev also abolished night searches of pedestrians, initiated judicial proceedings against one police officer for participating in the pogrom, and promised to investigate other instances of suspected pogromist activity by members of the police force.[64]

But Grigor'ev's efforts were not wholly successful. Even after he tried to restore order and regain public confidence, foreign consul generals stationed steamers flying their respective national colors in the harbor and offered sanctuary to foreign nationals.[65] More significantly, the city council, like those in other urban centers, showed its skepticism by campaigning to establish a civilian militia that would supersede the police. This idea was first voiced in the spring when city councillors, upset at their lack of control over the police, argued that a civilian militia would defend the public from "possible attacks by thieves and hooligans and actual attacks by the police."[66] In late October, the city council once again broached the subject of municipalizing the police, asserting that the police had lost the trust of the populace due to their "shameful and unlawful behavior" during the pogrom. One councillor proposed that they assume control over the police and approve the establishment of a temporary civilian militia until the issue of police reorganization had been resolved.[67] In the end, the city council realized that the government would never permit an armed civilian militia or relinquish control over the police, and they decided not to press the issue further.[68]

Some public-spirited Odessans, however, following the example of Moscow and Petersburg workers and public agencies, created self-defense brigades to patrol working-class neighborhoods and safeguard life and property.[69] In Peresyp, one such detachment chased a mugger onto a tram and dragged him off for a sound thrashing. Homeowners, businessmen, storeowners, and factory owners in Slobodka-Romanovka and Moldavanka agreed to fund a special unit of guards to patrol the districts with regular policemen or night watchmen. In the heart of Mikhailov district, sixteen posts of three men each—two civilians and one policeman—were set up, as was a detachment of eight men ready to assist in the event of trouble. Posts were planned for other streets as soon as the local homeowners agreed to fund them.[70]

Into this breach of public calm stepped the Odessa Soviet of Workers' Deputies. The attempt ¹ ⁄ workers to devolve local power into their own hands is evident in the soviet's concern with both the broad issues of political reform and the more immediate problems of unemployment, pogrom scares, and the maintenance of public order. Efforts to form the soviet began in early November, when thirty-five representatives from the major metalworking and machine-building plants of Peresyp met at the behest of the Mensheviks to discuss the establishment of a council representing the interests of all Odessa workers.[71] As in the capital cities of Moscow and Petersburg, the Mensheviks initiated efforts to establish soviets, while Bolsheviks at first hesitated to endorse an organization that "might easily elude party control and succumb to the 'spontaneity' of the masses."[72] The process by which the Odessa soviet was established varied slightly from what occurred in St. Petersburg, Moscow, and other cities, where soviets emerged from strike committees set up during the October general strike. Workers from many of the enterprises which had been the backbone of various strike committees in May and June (Henn, Bellino-Fenderikh, Shpolianskii, and the Russian Steam Navigation and Trading Company) provided the core of delegates to the meeting. In fact, many of the workers arrested on June 12 went on to become deputies to the Soviet.[73]

At this early November meeting, eight speakers urged their listeners to organize a soviet similar to ones already established in other cities. Emphasizing that Odessa workers were fighting a two-front battle against the government and the capitalists, the speakers told the assembled workers that only a citywide organization encompassing all workers could meet the challenge of defending the economic and political interests of Odessa's working class. The speakers also outlined the soviet's major tasks; these included the organization of trade unions and clubs, leadership of strikes, establishment of a workers' militia, preparation for elections to the State Duma, and the continued struggle for a constituent assembly.[74] The soviet would be an umbrella organization or clearinghouse whose task was the coordination of the various activities and initiatives designed to promote the workers' economic, social, political, and legal interests and to resist counterrevolutionary efforts to turn back the achievements of October. The meeting concluded with a request to the Mensheviks to convene a meeting of representatives from all Odessa's workshops and factories, at which time the issue of a citywide soviet would be discussed.

This second meeting took place several days later, on November 6. Some 200 workers were invited, representing a broad cross-section of manufacturing enterprises throughout Odessa, but nearly 1,000 workers filled the auditorium. The meeting was officially organized by the Bund and the United Committee of the Odessa RSDWP, the name of the newly merged organization of Mensheviks and Bolsheviks. The warring factions of Russian Social Democracy in Odessa, as in many other cities of the Empire including Moscow and St. Petersburg, succeeded in temporarily rejoining forces after October; the process in Odessa was facilitated by the fact that Bolsheviks and Mensheviks had received prodding from both workers active in anti-pogromist activities and party organizers with close ties to workers. Many workers and party activists had bitterly complained about the divisiveness caused by the factional squabbles and welcomed the merger because they saw it as an essential step in the building of a united labor front. Although the merger glossed over rather than resolved the fundamental differences between the two parties, the establishment of the United Committee in November convinced workers that the revolutionaries considered the day-to-day struggle of the labor movement more important than ideological and organizational disagreements, which many workers considered petty if not incomprehensible. The merger enhanced the SDs' reputation among workers and paved the way to an expanded role of the revolutionary intelligentsia in the fledgling trade-union movement and soviet. The Bolsheviks and Mensheviks refrained from pursuing independent courses of action during these months and maintained their alliance into 1906, when the United Committee sent delegates from both factions to the Fourth (Unification) Party Congress in Stockholm.[75]

The delegates agreed to form three district soviets along geographic lines—

one for Peresyp and the Port Territory, another for the central districts of the city, and a third for the outlying districts of Mikhailov, Petropavlov, and Slobodka-Romanovka. Following the bottom-up organizational pattern found in some other cities, notably Moscow, these three district councils emerged before the city soviet and were its organizational underpinning. Each district soviet elected a five-person executive committee, whose members were to sit jointly on the executive committee of the citywide soviet. The delegates also agreed to establish a special bureau of eight workers responsible for organizing rallies at which speakers would urge workers to elect representatives to the district soviets.[76]

In the weeks following this meeting, workers throughout Odessa met in their factories and workshops and selected delegates to the district soviets. Like the unionization drive, which was occurring simultaneously, the movement to form the councils included a broad spectrum of the Odessa labor force, spanning occupational, ethnic, and sexual divisions and affecting virtually every category of worker in the city. Voters included workers from metalworking and machine-building plants; from small workshops, such as tailors, bootmakers and woodworkers; and the unskilled workers of cork, match, and teapacking factories, as well as granary workers. In addition, tinsmiths and workers from the municipal tramway, sugar refineries, and railway workshops and depots met to elect representatives to district soviets. The delegates to the district soviets then met separately as well as in joint session for two organizational meetings of the citywide Soviet of Workers' Deputies on November 24 and 25.[77]

The first plenary session of the Odessa soviet, chaired by Ivan Avdeev, was held on November 28 in the Odessa municipal auditorium. It was attended by 391 delegates of both sexes; approximately 300 had been directly elected by workers of Odessa's factories and workshops, and another eighty represented the city's trade unions (including professional organizations). This number probably underestimates the number of union members who served as soviet deputies, since it does not take into account those members of the soviet who both belonged to trade unions and represented their enterprises. Various revolutionary and liberal organizations sent 16 representatives.[78]

Since a complete list of the deputies does not exist, it is impossible to offer a detailed breakdown of the participants by occupation, sex, ethnic identity, and political affiliation. However, a partial list of 154 deputies has survived and permits us to make some tentative generalizations about the social and political composition of the soviet.[79] The majority of these deputies worked in factories and workshops. They were joined by a sprinkling of students, city employees, professionals, and white-collar employees, postal-telegraph workers, zemstvo employees, representatives of nearby villages, and delegates of political parties. In addition, two members of the St. Petersburg Soviet of Workers' Deputies and one from the Kiev soviet were listed as deputies, despite the fact that one of the St. Petersburg deputies had returned to the capital a week earlier, on November 20. Of these 154 deputies, at least seven were women—primarily workers in teapacking, tobacco, and millinery enterprises—and approximately thirty-three were Jews.[80] The high incidence of soviet deputies belonging to political parties is striking. Eighty-one of the 154 deputies were members of the United Committee of the RSDWP; of these, only three were listed as Bolsheviks, a figure that testifies to the greater appeal of the Mensheviks. The Bund claimed the loyalty of two deputies, and the Ukrainian Social Democratic Party, one deputy. The SRs had twelve party members represented in the soviet, the Kadets five, the Ukrainian Democrats one, and the Anarcho-Communists five. Another five deputies declared themselves unaffiliated with any political party, and the political allegiances—if any—of the remaining forty-two deputies are not recorded. In sum, about 100 deputies belonged to one of the several revolutionary parties operating in Odessa. Within the Executive Committee of the soviet, however, nearly all fifteen members were SDs.[81]

The Soviet and Politics

Like the budding trade unions, the soviet had to determine its relationship with the socialist parties. At the initial organizational meetings of the soviet the issue of whether only SDs should be elected as deputies was raised. The press did not report the details of these discussions, but after considering the membership of nonparty deputies at the first plenum in late November, the organizers resolved not to require deputies to belong to a socialist party. Some worker deputies even went so far as to express openly their general hostility to the representatives of the socialist parties, especially those with tenuous or nonexistent connections to the working class. Participation by members of various revolutionary parties, they feared, would transform the soviet into "a party organization" and negate its standing as a "supra-party" institution. For example, on November 14 some deputies to the Peresyp district soviet insisted on reviewing the proposed charter because it had been drawn up by "*intelligenty* and party representatives." Two weeks later, a speaker told his audience at a workers' rally "not to listen to any party but to make up its mind itself." Some deputies also took offense to the fact that, in violation of the supposed political neutrality of the organization, a Menshevik who was not from the ranks of the workers was elected to chair the November 24 meeting of the soviet.[82]

Whether the soviet should affiliate with any of the socialist parties was also discussed. S. I. Fainberg, a Menshevik and one of the two deputies from the St. Petersburg soviet (the other being Mikhail Zborovskii, a Menshevik who had been active several years earlier in Odessa) who spent several weeks in November assisting in the organization of the Odessa soviet, towed his party's line and advocated political neutrality. Citing the experience of the nonaffiliated St. Petersburg soviet, Fainberg argued that the soviet could not enjoy officials ties with the SDs (or any party for that matter) if it wanted to represent the interests of all workers and direct them in their struggle against both employers and government. He explained the high proportion of SD deputies as the result of the workers' tendency to elect "the most conscious workers." But since not all workers were SDs, it was the responsibility of the soviet to represent the interests of nonparty workers as well. Thus, according to Fainberg, it should function autonomously and "in no instance be a party organization."[83] A majority of delegates supported Fainberg's point of view, reasoning that nonparty workers would see a soviet with official ties to the SDs as a party organ representing the narrow interests of only SD workers and not as a broadly based proletarian organization.[84] Despite the political loyalties of most of its deputies, the soviet, like many of its counterparts elsewhere in the Empire, rigorously maintained formal political neutrality.

As in the case of trade unions, formal neutrality did not translate into a lack of concern with politics; it simply facilitated the recruitment of workers unaffiliated with any political party. Politics was the soviet's raison d'etre, a sentiment embodied in its statutes, which affirmed its responsibility to organize strikes and trade unions and conduct the struggle for workers' individual and collective political, civil, and economic rights.[85] A November 26 editorial in *Kommercheskaia Rossiia* stated that the soviet must "gather around itself all the proletarian elements of the city and become the center of political life in Odessa."[86] The soviet, in an effort to represent the class interests of Odessa workers and promote the aims of the revolution, necessarily pursued a strategy of political activism.

The Soviet, even more than trade unions, bore the indelible imprint of the SDs, particularly the Mensheviks, in its outlook, program, and actions. Given the large number of deputies who were also members of revolutionary parties and the feverish political atmosphere of November and December, it could not avoid viewing issues from the perspective of socialists, who used the city and district soviets as sounding boards for their ideas and tactics. The soviet brought workers into closer contact with the revolutionary parties; from its inception, the soviet and its members enjoyed a close working relationship with the various socialist parties and often issued joint resolutions and proclamations with the United Committee, Bund, and SRs. It was commonplace for representatives of the revolutionary parties to deliver speeches, and each of the major socialist parties was entitled to send one delegate each to meetings of the Executive Committee.[87] Mensheviks, perhaps because of their stronger roots in the Odessa labor force, not only dominated the soviet's executive organ, but the ideology and activity of the soviet adhered closely to those of the Mensheviks.

An examination of the soviet's pronouncements, policies, and actions illustrates its radical character. Although it did not advocate the end of private ownership of the means of production, it must be remembered that the Bolsheviks and Mensheviks generally relegated this tenet of Marxism to a later stage of the revolution. Instead, worker deputies to the Soviet were drawn to the more moderate call by socialists in fall 1905 for bourgeois democratic reform, namely the convocation of a constituent assembly, overthrow of the autocracy, and social security. The precise details of the future society and polity were left unformulated, but the workers shared the revolutionaries' vision of a reformed social and political order.[88]

During its brief existence from late November to early January 1906, the soviet and its Executive Committee made a concerted effort to address a series of pressing concerns that drew Odessa workers more and more into the orbit of local and national politics. It directed strikes and boycotts of enterprises accused of unfair labor practices, organized free cafeterias for the unemployed, set prices for staple foods, arranged boycotts of stores which violated these price guidelines, established a legal aid bureau for workers who had been cheated or dismissed by their employers, and published a newspaper. The Soviet also mobilized workers to resist a rumored pogrom and directed a general strike in mid-December.[89] Like many of its counterparts elsewhere in Russia, the Odessa soviet, reflecting both its Menshevik orientation and the inclination of the workers, sought to act as an organ of "revolutionary self-government," that is, as an institution of local administrative and municipal power that would pave the way for the next stage of the revolution.

The effort to alleviate the problems of the unemployed in Odessa shows how the soviet tried to assume the reins of local government. It established an unemployment bureau consisting of fifteen persons, including two representatives each from the SRs, Bund, and United Committee. The soviet also sanctioned three district unemployment bureaus of five members each, which collected data on the number and needs of the unemployed in their districts. Members of these bureaus would then meet with the Executive Committee and jointly determine the allocation of funds to the district bureaus. Between December 8 and 22, unemployed workers received some 2,400 rubles in benefits from the soviet.[90]

In order to meet the financial needs of all the unemployed in Odessa, the Executive Committee in early December attempted to raise funds by demanding contributions from the city council, which had recently allotted 100,000 rubles to help the jobless, and the Central Jewish Committee, which had just received foreign donations amounting to 50,000 rubles to help Jewish pogrom victims. The Executive Committee demanded that the Jewish organization transfer these funds in full to the soviet but requested only half of the 100,000 rubles from the city council, since some of the funds had been earmarked to help storekeepers whose businesses had been destroyed during the pogrom. The Executive Committee acknowledged that these Odessans were entitled to material assistance, but concluded that since they were not workers the soviet should not assume responsibility for them in order to maintain "proletarian purity."[91]

When the Executive Committee asked the full membership to approve this policy at the December 5 plenum, several deputies questioned its legality. One deputy insisted that the soviet did not have the right to expropriate money contributed by foreigners. Another speaker called the demand "unjust"; the funds of the Central Jewish Committee had a special purpose and the soviet had no right to interfere. Members of the Executive Committee responded to these objections by saying that special funds for separate use by Jews, Armenians, and Poles should not exist; it was the soviet's responsibility to help *all* hungry workers, regardless of nationality. Indeed, as a proletarian organization, the soviet considered itself the most competent institution to organize the relief.

"The Soviet of Workers' Deputies is an internationalist institution," said the Executive Committee chairman, "and, as such, it will help hungry people and not only hungry Jews, hungry Poles, and hungry Russians." Because the Soviet represented all workers, went the argument, it knew better the needs of its constituency than the city council and the Central Jewish Committee.[92] The Executive Committee refused to consider the possibility of administering unemployment benefits jointly with the city council and the Central Jewish Council, dismissing these organizations as bourgeois institutions. Although the Executive Committee convinced the members of the soviet, who voted to approve the transfer of funds, the money was never received: Grigor'ev refused to release city funds to the soviet and the Central Jewish Committee made it known that it had no intention of acceding to the demand.[93]

The failure of the soviet to raise additional funds for unemployment benefits reveals its inability to impose its will on the city council and administration. Unable to dominate the city government and other public organizations, the soviet found itself competing with city officials for power. It commanded the loyalty of workers and enjoyed authority among them, but it lacked the wherewithal to force the city council and city governor to bow to its demands. Still, its very effort to force the city council and Central Jewish Committee to relinquish control over unemployment benefits highlights how it tried to claim authority over matters concerning workers and was prepared to usurp the prerogatives of the tsarist government in Odessa.

Even though the city council had played a prominent role in the opposition movement throughout the year, liberal councillors sympathetic to workers now viewed any effort by labor to undermine the power and authority of the council with suspicion. The city council was beginning to dissociate itself from the workers' movement, since its members sensed that the soviet, in deed as well as in speech, was advocating a program designed to restructure social and political authority in much too radical a fashion. The controversy over the unemployment funds was, from the perspective of the city councillors, a dangerous first step toward the realization of the soviet's vision of a society and polity dominated by workers.

The actions of the soviet with respect to a rumored pogrom in early December provide additional clues about its political bent and the unabated tensions between Jews and gentiles. Black Hundred and other reactionary forces continued to enflame the passions of ethnic and religious hatred by disseminating anti-Semitic leaflets. Reports circulated of Russian workers forcing factory owners to dismiss Jewish coworkers, and in some instances of Russian workers objecting to Jewish membership in their unions. In a curious turn of events, gentile workers in one factory demanded the dismissal of Jewish coworkers as punishment for Jewish participation in the October street disorders.[94] Moreover, in late November gendarmes chief Kuzubov sensed that Russians resented newspaper accounts blaming gentiles for the oppression of Jews and might seek vengeance by attacking them "at the first suitable instance."[95]

We have already seen how workers in late October and early November adopted a series of measures designed to root out and punish pogromists as well as to restore law and order in Odessa. Thus, when rumors of a pogrom (scheduled to occur after a patriotic parade and ceremonial mass marking the Tsar's name day on December 6) began to circulate, workers throughout the city, under the direction of the soviet, readied themselves to prevent another outburst of violence against Jews, students, and socialists.

Soviet officials adhered to the popular belief that the police helped orchestrate the October pogrom and argued that the police were again encouraging *bosiaki* and other ruffian elements to rise up. At its December 5 session, Varlaam Shavdiia, a Georgian Menshevik student and chairman of the Executive Committee, presented evidence implicating the police in the planning of a pogrom. He cited the case of two police officers who made the rounds of the harbor and urged dockworkers to attack Jews on December 6. Shavdiia also stated that police chief Aleksandr von Hessberg had visited the port territory, where he told a group of workers, "Your Russia is being destroyed by seditious elements." Von Hessberg, it was reported, then gave six kopecks to each worker. In addition, pogromist pamphlets were circulating freely at the docks and pogromist agitation had also spread to the military garrison, where officers of one regiment delivered anti-Semitic speeches.[96]

Convinced that the city was reliving the days before the October pogrom and that the planned procession was intended to degenerate into violence, many workers, soviet members, and SDs undertook precautionary measures. One district soviet, for example, instructed all workers to arm themselves, assemble at their respective places of employment on the morning of December 6, and prepare to repel the pogromists. Workers who failed to appear were subject to disciplinary action. Similarly, 1,200 workers of Slobodka-Romanovka vowed to arm themselves and employ all means at their disposal to ensure that "a vile, beastly slaughter of defenseless people" would not occur again. Viewing the pogrom as a government tool to weaken the labor movement, these workers promised to resist any attempt to instigate anti-Jewish violence.[97]

Rallies and meetings were held throughout the city on the evening of December 5, as workers armed themselves and organized battle detachments. Student militias also assembled at the university to await instructions in the event of violence. Grigor'ev tried to defuse the situation by announcing that the police were not planning a pogrom and assured the public that he would use "armed force if necessary" to prevent one from occurring. Some liberal-leaning officers of the military garrison issued a similarly worded warning: they would not "permit the administration and police to delude them" as they claimed had happened in October. They also promised "that any violence against the peaceful citizens of Odessa will be halted with armed force," cautioned that the police would be "unmercifully beaten" if they participated in the pogrom, and vowed to take strict action against those who tried "to stir up one segment of the populace against another."[98]

The Executive Committee also made preparations for decisive action. It issued a brief announcement that "the proletariat of Odessa will come to the defense of the populace at the first attempt by the police and hooligans to start a pogrom." According to police reports, the soviet also announced a boycott of the right-wing newspaper *Russkaia rech'* (*Russian Speech*), the first issue of which had just appeared in Odessa, and organized detachments of youths to seize copies of the paper. By appealing to Odessans to organize and arm themselves, the Executive Committee made it crystal clear that the soviet was ready to use armed force to maintain order and social peace.[99]

Such precautions may have been unnecessary, since the available evidence indicates that rumors of an impending pogrom were false. When a group of SDs made the rounds of taverns frequented by dockworkers and day laborers, they found, contrary to what Shavdiia had reported, no evidence of preparations to launch an assault on Odessa's Jews. Nor does any concrete evidence exist that a patriotic procession was even planned. On December 6, no such gathering occurred; workers assembled at their places of employment, ready to clash with pogromists who never appeared. Although it is possible that the preventive measures taken by the soviet, workers, and Grigor'ev frightened the organizers into cancelling the march, it should be noted that the workers, along with the soviet and SDs, had promised not to interfere with a patriotic procession so long as it remained peaceful.[100] Thus, the fact that there were no signs at all of a patriotic procession on December 6 strongly suggests that the anticipated parade and pogrom were ungrounded rumors, and merely reveals that fears of renewed ethnic violence remained high well over a month after the October pogrom. It is important to note that workers and soviets in other cities, especially Moscow, also feared Black Hundred mobilization on December 6, in keeping with the popular view that pogroms were ventures organized by the authorities.

To the workers and soviet, as well as to the city governor, the threat of a pogrom seemed real and required resolute measures. Whether or not the procession and pogrom were cancelled as a result of the mobilization by the workers is less significant than the determination of the soviet to prevent a second pogrom and its ability to command the obedience of the thousands of workers who willingly prepared themselves in anticipation of violence. The soviet saw its role as the keeper of law and order, and the readiness of Odessa workers to marshal their forces and confront right-wing elements was an impressive display of solidarity and unity of purpose. As an editorial in *Kommercheskaia Rossiia* proclaimed, "December 6 has passed without incident. The lessons of October were not ignored. . . . The public was silent in October, but now it has mobilized itself. The proletariat of Odessa after the pogrom felt all the horror of its silence . . . and decided not to permit it to happen again. . . . We can be sure that we won't have any more pogroms in Odessa."[101]

The December Strike

The Odessa soviet directed a general strike from December 11 to December 18, and its decision to call a strike coincided with work stoppages elsewhere in

Russia. On December 7, Moscow workers walked off the job; Petersburg workers followed suit the next day. Within the week, workers all over the Empire had joined in a general strike, throwing the country into the throes of massive work stoppages for the second time in two months. Paralyzing Odessa's economy and bringing normal life to a standstill, the Odessa general strike in December was a protest against the repressive measures taken by government officials against the workers and soviet of St. Petersburg. Workers throughout Russia saw the arrest of Georgii Khrustalev-Nosar and government reprisals against the All-Russian Peasants' Union, postal-telegraph and railway workers' unions, and St. Petersburg newspapers as stark evidence of autocracy's effort to undo the gains of October. "Pacification" of the rebellious peasantry entailed the meting out of summary punishment to those held responsible for the disorders that rocked the countryside during the fall. The government was sending a clear message that the old order had not rolled over and died without a whimper; in fact, it was demonstrating that it still had the strength and wherewithal to launch counteroffensive against the forces of revolution and reform. In solidarity with its besieged comrades elsewhere in the Empire, the Odessa soviet was hitching its fate with that of workers in cities far from Odessa. Nationwide political concerns were viewed as having direct and immediate consequences for the fate of the local revolution.

As the government continued to recoup its forces and strike back at troublesome workers, Odessa workers and the soviet recognized that the situation demanded immediate action. The pronouncements of Odessa railway workers from mid-November to early December underscore the effect government policy had on radicalizing the labor movement and point to the political crisis that still gripped not only Odessa but all Russia by the end of 1905. In mid-November, railway workers gathered to voice their solidarity with Petersburg workers, stating they were "fully prepared at the first summons of the Soviet to enter into combat with the enemy." They also protested the government's intention to execute several leaders of a recent strike on the Trans-Caspian Military Railroad.[102]

At the end of the month, Odessa railway workers again assembled to support preparation for the "last onslaught to achieve a Constituent Assembly," demanding full amnesty for all political prisoners and the release of all arrested strikers. Several days after this meeting, they declared that the arrest of Khrustalev-Nosar was an effort "to take back from the people the civil rights won by the proletariat" in October; they now called for preparations for an all-Russian political strike and an armed uprising at the first signal from the St. Petersburg soviet.[103] Other workers also expressed outrage in late November and early December at government attempts to suppress the labor movement in St. Petersburg. At a December 4 rally in Slobodka-Romanovka, workers condemned the arrest of Khrustalev-Nosar as an effort to "deprive the people of its civil rights" and force the workers of St. Petersburg into a premature uprising; they expressed their willingness to engage "in the final battle with the autocracy."[104] In addition, workers from the Russian Steam Navigation and Trading Company and Bellino-Fenderikh Iron Foundry protested the arrest and agreed to donate half-a-day's wages to an unemployment fund for St. Petersburg workers. Employees at the city's largest printing firm, in an aggressive and uncompromising appeal, pledged to offer "material and moral support to the St. Petersburg Soviet in order to rally the entire proletariat for the final blow against the obsolete regime."[105]

Discussion of a general strike occurred at the first organizational meeting of the Odessa soviet on November 24. At this meeting, where deputies decided to contribute 1 percent of their wages to help the unemployed in the capital, representatives of the Peresyp district soviet proclaimed that a general strike would be a "sign of solidarity with Petersburg strikers."[106] At the second session of the Executive Committee, held on December 2, it was resolved that "a political strike is inevitable and necessary at the given time," and it was recommended that the soviet collect money for the arming of workers.[107] On December 5, the date of the secondary plenary session of the soviet, workers began to clamor for immediate and effective action, with one worker deputy insisting that "the struggle against the government requires deeds, not resolutions." He appealed to members to arm Odessa workers. The full membership of the soviet resolved to send a letter to the St. Petersburg soviet expressing their indignation at the arrest of Khrustalev-Nosar. Echoing the sentiments voiced at earlier rallies, the soviet declared that the government was attempting to provoke the workers and "spill workers' blood." It assured the St. Petersburg soviet that local workers were being armed for "joint action with the proletariat of all Russia" against the regime.[108] These remarks adhered closely to the curious Menshevik line that preparation for an armed insurrection should be encouraged although an uprising would be impractical at the current time.

Before this letter was approved, the soviet hotly debated the issue of a general political strike. On the one hand, deputies of the district soviet representing workers from Mikhailov, Petropavlov, and Slobodka-Romanovka stated that their constituency supported a general strike. But representatives of the district soviets from Peresyp and the city center emphasized that a decision to call a general strike would be hasty and unwise, since Odessa workers would run the risk of exhausting themselves in a partial walkout before the rest of the country took part. In order to settle the debate, the deputies telegrammed the St. Petersburg Soviet: "A political strike is in the air. What's going on with you?" They insisted that they would not take action until they received a response, but they reiterated their intention to arm workers.[109]

On December 7, the Executive Committee began to organize a general strike (whether or not the St. Petersburg Soviet answered the telegram is unknown). It decided: (1) to hold a series of rallies on December 8, where speakers would explain the significance of the general strike; (2) to organize a strike commission consisting of the Executive Committee and two members each from the United Committee, the Bund, and the SRs; (3) to convene meetings of the boards of directors of trade unions and members of the Union of Unions; and (4) to issue a strike declaration by December 9. The Executive Committee appealed to all political parties and worker organizations to subordinate themselves to the strike commission.[110]

In Odessa, the days after December 7 witnessed a flurry of organizational activity and preparation for a general strike. Nearly 100 representatives from twenty-seven trade unions, meeting on December 9, expressed their full support for a general strike as soon as the soviet gave the signal. One union delegate predicted that "these were the last days of absolutism, and it is the proletariat . . . who will strike the final blow against absolutism." The same speaker went on to add that the unions would take no action without the knowledge of the soviet. Another speaker, concerned that workers lacked the material means for a strike, nonetheless emphasized that he wholeheartedly supported it. Still others urged cooperation among the revolutionary parties for the sake of solidarity. For its part, the Central Bureau of Trade Unions pledged to carry out whatever tasks the Executive Committee assigned.[111] Delegates from the Union of Unions similarly condemned the tactics of the government and requested that all union members and residents of Odessa join the general strike. They also asked members of their organizations to contribute money for use by the soviet in its conduct of the general strike, a clear indication that workers in Odessa had the support of some politically active nonproletarian groups.[112]

Elsewhere in the city, the Kadets resolved to support "a peaceful, general political strike by legal means" and encouraged all members of the party to donate one day's wages to the striking workers.[113] The united front of liberal intelligentsia and workers that had forced the government's hand in October had already broken down in St. Petersburg and was fracturing in Moscow, but in Odessa the spirit of cooperation remained intact well into December, notwithstanding the conflict between the city council and the soviet regarding unemployment funds. It is hard to account for the longer durability of this largely unspoken alliance in Odessa, but the effort of concerned citizens of all classes to band together in the aftermath of the pogrom may have made Odessa workers feel less isolated and betrayed than did their counterparts in the capital. The later breakdown of the coalition in Odessa may reflect the persistence of cooperation between labor and the liberal intelligentsia.

Rallies were held in factories and workshops, and workers began to organize armed detachments called "Red Hundreds." Workers at Bellino-Fenderikh and Shpolianskii in particular assembled a cache of sabres, knives, and daggers and collected money to buy additional guns and ammunition. In addition, armed militias from the various revolutionary parties joined forces in a united militia under the direction of the soviet's strike committee, thereby sacrificing their freedom of action to the coordinating efforts of the Odessa Soviet of Workers' Deputies.[114]

Despite this backdrop of support and determination, the Executive Committee, which concluded that a strike was imminent and requested workers to prepare for a possible walkout, moved cautiously and refrained from calling a general strike on December 9. It wrote a strike declaration but, in order not to outstrip the actions of workers, it decided to distribute the declaration only if workers on their own initiative had begun to strike by the morning of December 11, a strategy one Soviet historian has condemned as "tailism."[115]

Once again, railway workers set things in motion by walking off the job on December 10. Fearful that efforts by union leaders—many of whom were also soviet deputies, SDs, and SRs—to foment a political strike among railway workers would succeed, the police on December 9 arrested a dozen or so major activists from the railway workshops. Included were Ivan Avdeev, chair of the first plenary session of the soviet and president of the railway workers' union, and Fedor Golubkov, another longtime SD activist who was involved with the organization of railway workers during the spring. Several of the arrested activists had organized the October strike; according to police records, they were advocating an armed uprising and possessed revolutionary literature and revolvers when taken into custody.[116]

The police released several of those arrested for lack of evidence the same day. The next morning, two of them showed up at the railway workshops and urged their fellow workers to throw down their tools and walk off the job in protest over workers who still remained behind bars. The railway workers complied, since they considered the arrest of their union and soviet representatives as a blatant violation of the October Manifesto.[117] As in June, when the arrest of workers' representatives sparked a round of street demonstrations and work stoppages, the December arrests provoked a similar response and triggered a new wave of labor unrest.

Now that the workers themselves had made the first move, the Executive Committee, in conjunction with the major revolutionary parties, announced a general political strike for the following day, Sunday, December 11. The soviet announced that the general strike was being carried out in "the name of popular freedom" in order to achieve a constituent assembly based on four-tailed suffrage and to further the cause of socialism.[118] News of the strike spread quickly, and by Monday virtually all factories and workshops remained quiet; most retail, wholesale, and commercial stores and enterprises, especially in worker neighborhoods, kept their doors closed. As in earlier strike waves, many workers put down their tools only after prodding—sometimes in the nature of threats—from revolutionaries and other workers already on strike. Yet the majority of workers went on strike voluntarily in a spirit of solidarity and with a sense of political purpose.

During the strike, the Executive Committee assumed many of the functions and responsibilities of the local government. In order to ensure that essential services were not disrupted, the Executive Committee asked employees of the municipal waterworks, slaughterhouse, cafeterias, hospitals, and medical clinics to remain on the job. It also appealed to bakers to return to work in order to avoid a drastic increase in the price of bread and instructed the district soviets to monitor prices of bread and other food products. The Executive Committee permitted a factory to maintain yeast production so as to ensure the bread supply, but it insisted that all profits from the sale of yeast revert to the soviet. It made similar arrangements with five pharmacies; they were allowed to remain open and profits went into the coffers of the soviet. The Executive Committee prohibited the sale of alcoholic beverages and, in defiance of Provisional Governor-General Karangozov's directive that retail stores remain open into the evening, ordered that stores close their doors at 11 A.M. Sanitation workers were asked not to strike and a tax to support the strike was levied on the well-to-do residents of the city, although it is unlikely that such funds were ever collected.[119]

The Bolshevik Osip Piatnitskii, recalling the December strike in his memoirs, writes that it "seemed as if all life had stopped."[120] As in June and October, the strike shut down normal operations in the city. Activity in the harbor came to a standstill, with the exception of one steamship laden with food and medical supplies that the Executive Committee permitted to sail to Nikolaev.[121] For the most part, stores remained closed, and the movement of trams and passenger trains was sporadic and limited, since there were not enough supervisory personnel to take the place of striking workers. Despite efforts to maintain service under military guard, the trams had largely stopped running by early afternoon due to the pressure of strikers and the lack of riders. For several nights darkness enveloped the city, as the employees of the gas workers and lantern lighters struck. During the strike, armed bands of workers made their way into the premises of several newspapers and typographies and printed proclamations, pamphlets, and the first two issues of the *Izvestiia Soveta rabochikh deputatov g. Odessy* (*News of the Odessa Soviet of Workers' Deputies*), the soviet's official newspaper.[122]

The December strike was remarkable for the absence of open conflict and confrontation between the workers and government forces. In fact, things were so calm that the head of the gendarmes remarked that "the strike is rather sluggish, without violence and clashes with the police and military."[123] The peaceful nature of the December strike stands in stark contrast to the strikes of June and October, when Odessa was turned into a battlefield with students, revolutionaries, and workers engaging in pitched combat with the police and military. It was a strange sight indeed to see soldiers patrolling the city while thousands of Odessans peacefully congregated in the streets, discussing politics and exhorting each other to continue the strike.

In contrast to similar situations earlier in the year, in December both workers and government forces exercised restraint and worked hard to avoid bloodshed. When striking workers pressured storeowners to shut down or prevented the tramway's managerial personnel from working, the police and military did not resort to force or coercion to break up the crowds. Even when martial law was declared on December 15 and defiant crowds continued to fill the streets of Odessa on the following day, everyone remained calm and order prevailed.[124] The police and military continued to search out and detain potential troublemakers, but they also countenanced orderly and peaceful meetings of the soviet, worker rallies, and assemblies, some of which attracted several thousand participants and were held in the municipal auditorium. Perhaps this tolerant approach was due to the attitude of Grigor'ev and Kaul'bars, who did not want another bloodbath on their hands. That the October Manifesto guaranteed freedom of speech and assembly undoubtedly also made it difficult for officials to prohibit such meetings, as did the authorities' realization that they lacked the moral authority to break up these meetings without recourse to violence.

The efforts of the authorities to keep a lid on events were matched by those of the strike leaders. Indeed, the avowed strategy of the Executive Committee was to avoid any actions that might provoke the authorities. Notwithstanding its prior declaration about arming workers, the Executive Committee was determined to maintain peace. On December 10, it resolved "to suggest that all workers avoid clashes of any sort" for the first two days of the strike, lest the government use such incidents to justify full-scale retaliation and repression. The Executive Committee and revolutionary parties issued a joint proclamation calling on workers to refrain from gathering in large crowds, forcibly halting the movement of trams, or engaging in any other actions that would provoke police and military reprisals. The proclamation also instructed workers to ignore anti-Semitic publications and not try to close down the typographies where they were printed. The Executive Committee also recommended that striking workers persuade— rather than bully and menace—other workers to walk off their jobs.[125]

To be sure, opinion was not unanimous within the Executive Committee. One faction, consisting primarily of Mensheviks, pointed to reports from the district soviets suggesting that "a militant mood among workers is not noticeable." Emphasizing that only "the conscious and organized workers" would attend rallies and demonstrations, events that were bound to precipitate "an attack by Cossacks," these members of the Executive Committee argued that the strike should remain peaceful and focus on organizing factory rallies. The other faction, led by Bolsheviks, noted that some workers were demanding guns and reached the opposite conclusion: a peaceful strike was possible for "only two or three days," after which it would be necessary either to take more vigorous action or risk the spread of boredom and disillusionment. The first (and preferable) option, according to the Bolsheviks, required the organization of street rallies as a means of escalating the pace of confrontation and the procurement of weapons as a preparatory step for an armed uprising. The second option, the continuation of non-violence, would eventually lead to calling off the strike. After a lengthy discussion, a majority voted to continue the strike on a peaceful basis.[126] Thus, unlike in Moscow, where workers under the leadership of that city's soviet were bloodily suppressed in an uprising that lasted several days in mid-December, Odessa joined the St. Petersburg soviet in not issuing a call for armed insurrection. Although the Executive Committee had recommended that the soviet "busy itself with the arming" of workers, this was not, at least in their eyes, the same as calling for an armed uprising.[127] In short, the soviet, all bluster in regard to armed confrontation, was unwilling to challenge the government militarily.[128] Soviet historians place too much importance on Menshevik domination in explaining the policies and actions of the soviet; differences of opinion may have existed, but they did not prevent Bolsheviks and Mensheviks, along with the Bund and the SRs, from closing ranks over the issue of armed confrontation.

As the Bolsheviks predicted, the Executive Committee received more and more reports that workers were becoming bored and were considering returning to work. Workers from various enterprises dealt a blow to the solidarity of the general strike by calling off their work stoppages. On December 15, martial law was reimposed, encouraging city employees to return to work and banks and many stores to resume full operations. Efforts to infuse the strike with more aggressive tactics fell on unsympathetic ears in the Executive Committee. By December 16, the Executive Committee recognized that it was no longer feasible to continue the strike since "the workers were tired from inaction" and the approach of the holiday season was distracting many of them.[129] On that day, the Executive Committee decided to call off the strike, effective December 18. Workers in Odessa had "shown the entire world our organization and our discipline, but this time we did not demonstrate our readiness for battle."[130] In fact, most workers had already resumed work before this official pronouncement.[131]

The Executive Committee correctly read the situation. Aware that tsarist troops had just bloodily suppressed an abortive uprising by Moscow workers, the soviet realized that armed confrontation would be foolhardy given the government's resolute stance elsewhere in Russia. This led it to take a firm stand against insurrection. On a more fundamental level, the soviet's decision also reflected a sober assessment of its limited capacity to challenge the autocracy, especially under conditions of martial law. In short, the soviet adhered closely to what Ziva Galili calls the Menshevik tactic of "proletarian self-restraint" in order to prevent the workers from derailing the revolution and isolating themselves from other oppositional forces.[132] It is difficult to agree with those Soviet historians who argue that workers would have joined an armed uprising if only the Menshevik-dominated soviet had so commanded. Most Soviet historians deny workers the capacity of independent action without Bolshevik tutelage, but time and time again in 1905 Odessa workers acted without socialist prompting.[133]

It is unlikely that the workers avoided armed confrontation merely because the soviet wished to keep the strike peaceful. Workers had consistently demonstrated throughout 1905 that they themselves would decide what course of action to pursue. In June, they did not shy away from armed conflict, and there is no reason to conclude that they avoided violence in December merely in response to instructions from their appointed leaders. Although leadership, direction, and organization are hallmark features of successful urban uprisings, Odessa workers were nonetheless capable of mounting an assault on the government had they been willing, with or without the assistance of the organized revolutionary parties or the soviet. In light of what we know about the workers' movement in 1905, it is hard to imagine the workers in December pursuing—or avoiding, for that matter—a course of violent confrontation simply at the request of the soviet. The record indicates that workers in Odessa were too independent and strong-willed to restrain themselves at the behest of an organization, albeit one they professed loyalty to as the embodiment of their collective interests.

Nor can we support the police's contention that an uprising did not occur due to the workers' inadequate supply of weapons.[134] While it is true that the soviet urged restraint and did not make a concerted effort to supply workers with weapons, such behavior does not explain the reluctance of those workers who did possess guns, and who before December 11 pledged to use them, from launching an armed uprising. Nor does it offer insight into why workers did not recoil from armed confrontation in June and October, when they were just as underequipped as in December.

A much more satisfactory explanation for the lack of violence in December is that workers were no longer in a combative mood. The issue was not the lack of leadership and direction; rather, the enthusiasm for confrontation was noticeably absent.[135] Two general strikes in June and October, both of which ended in the deaths of hundreds, militated against the likelihood that the December general strike would degenerate into violence. The soviet pursued a policy of nonviolence because the mood of the workers indicated that they would not engage in open conflict. In June and October, workers had willingly risked the truncheons, sabres, and bullets of the police and soldiers; in December, by contrast, remembering the violence of the previous months, the strikers were eager to avoid another round of armed confrontation. Despite the workers' anger and their commitment to the general strike, their spirit flagged when confronted with the prospect of bloodletting. Even the Social Democrats recognized this state of affairs, when they wrote in a broadside in early January 1906 that the masses did not display "a militant spirit."[136] The mood of the workers significantly affected the style and conduct of the strike. As *Okhrana* chief Bobrov wrote in his assessment, "the desire to conduct a peaceful strike is, for the moment, keeping the strikers from taking more active measures."[137] Fear of provoking government reprisals and repression undoubtedly discouraged labor in Odessa from conducting a more aggressive strike.[138]

Although city authorities were relieved that the general strike ended several days after the declaration of martial law, they nonetheless remained concerned about the continued activities of the soviet. Life began to return to normal with the resumption of business, commerce, and industry, but the soviet did not interpret the end of the strike as a signal to halt its activities, since it did not perceive its task as limited only to strike leadership.[139] Instead, the Executive Committee turned its attention to other matters that were regarded as integral aspects of the mandate given it by Odessa workers. It redoubled its efforts to enhance its authority and to implement its decisions by seeking to convene meetings of the district soviets. The Executive Committee also decided to expand the organizational apparatus of the soviet by establishing a separate district soviet for the harbor region and by devoting more energy to the problem of unemployment assistance. Moreover, members readied themselves for a new round of elections and busily prepared the third issue of the soviet's newspaper.[140]

It was the goal of city authorities to suppress the soviet, and they found ready allies among many businessmen, industrialists, and intellectuals who had begun to fear the workers, especially after news of the bloody suppression of the abortive uprising in Moscow. Although public opinion favored the objectives of the workers at the outset of the strike, with some factory owners even providing strike pay and supplying tea, sugar, and flour to their striking employees,[141] after several days non-worker sentiment began turning against the soviet and the general strike. That the broad social and political coalition that had brought about the October general strike had stayed together until this time may help account for labor's moderate stance in December. Odessa workers had not yet been confronted with the backlash of those liberals and centrists content with the regime's political concessions.

Many employers now joined forces with those industrialists who had been steadfastly resisting the labor movement since November, either dismissing or threatening workers involved in the organization and administration of trade unions and the soviet. Still others refused to accede to worker demands for strike pay and called upon the Cossacks and police to prevent workers from shutting down operations. The management of the railway workshops, after condemning efforts by employees to discuss the issue of pensions, dismissed the entire work force and announced that it would rehire only those who pledged not to strike or join the union. Several tobacco factories refused to grant their workers strike pay and decided to fire several dozen striking workers, a tactic that prompted workers to walk off the job and the soviet to initiate a boycott of these firms. Employers also began to band together in associations, and although no citywide employer association yet existed, the editors of *Kommercheskaia Rossiia* believed that the formation of such an organization was imminent.[142] The political vision of the soviet threatened the supremacy of Odessa's nonproletarian elite, which, if it was not stepping back into the government's camp, at least no longer supported all the goals of labor. Economic self-interest came to the fore and overshadowed the joint struggle against the autocracy.

The enthusiasm of many upper- and middle-class liberals who had at first welcomed the general strike ebbed after several days. The entry from a diary of one Odessan who sympathized with "the workers as a symbol of the liberation of Russia" provides insight into the growing disillusionment of nonworkers. The author of this diary wrote that he was "excited" by the strike on December 10 and 11, but had "lost interest" by December 17. Although he hoped the strike would extract concrete concessions from the government, his excitement flagged when he realized that the regime would not capitulate. In an admission that clearly highlights the different assessment workers and liberals had of the revolution by mid-December, the diary writer wondered "for what end are these disorders," since the workers had already received significant concessions in October. The following day, he concluded that "the strike is counterproductive because it will lead to repression" and that "order and calm should be the slogan of all honest-thinking citizens," who should exert pressure through peaceful means to consolidate the gains of October.[143] This Odessan, then, lost interest in the strike when it became clear that the government had the upper hand and would not bow to the pressures of the workers, who should be content with what the revolution had already achieved. Odessa workers, however, regarded the Manifesto as a means of advancing the aims of the revolution. A *Kommercheskaia Rossiia* editorial blamed the lack of liberal support for the collapse of the strike: "For the liberals the revolution and December strike were about personal satisfaction, but for the proletarian masses, they were an issue of life, a pledge to the forthcoming liberation from capitalist enslavement, the one and only way out of their current situation."[144]

This diarist's change of mind may have also been brought about by a rash of armed robberies and the bombing of the fashionable Café Libman by anarcho-communists on the evening of December 17. These incidents frightened most middle-class Odessans, some of whom curiously equated anarchists with pogromists. The attack on the cafe caused extensive damage, injuring the owner and a patron and killing the bomb-throwers and several passersby and policemen.[145] Thus it is not surprising to learn that our diarist was perturbed by "these disorders" and concluded that "we should begin . . . to struggle against anarchy."[146]

Local authorities found it relatively easy to reassert themselves, at least against the organized labor movement. This was in no small measure due to the fact that the police had retained their freedom of action and power during the strike. Despite its proclaimed intention of establishing a civilian police force, the soviet took no serious steps to municipalize or disarm the police.[147] Moreover, the military garrison in Odessa was not rocked by serious unrest in November and December, a state of affairs that must have been envied by military commanders experiencing a rash of mutinies elsewhere in Russia. Although there were several minor incidents of insubordination and failure to obey orders, the Odessa soldiers' traditional psychology of submission and obedience, described so well by John Bushnell, did not give way to a mood of insurrection, presumably because the peasant-soldiers did not perceive that the prerogatives of constituted authority had been sufficiently eroded or effectively challenged. The fact that soldiers patrolled the city and carried out searches and arrests during the strike without provoking violent responses indicates that the local authorities still felt they were in command. When, on December 23, Karangozov ordered the removal of the corpses of the five students slain on October 16 which had been lying in state in the medical school since then, no one opposed him. This lack of student concern about a symbol of the October unrest was yet another sign that the united revolutionary front was breaking up.[148]

Officials in St. Petersburg were especially disturbed that Odessa officials had not taken vigorous and timely action to rout the soviet and other revolutionary organizations. On December 17, Bobrov's superiors inquired why he had not "liquidated the Executive Committee." They directed him to destroy the soviet and other revolutionary organizations before "new disorders occurred."[149] On December 20, Minister of Interior Petr Durnovo instructed Grigor'ev to shut down the typographies where the soviet had published its newspaper. Ten days later the police closed the Registration, claiming that the sailors' delegates were revolutionaries ignoring the needs of the membership. Governor-general Karangozov also suspended publication of *Kommercheskaia Rossiia* until the end of martial law because he deemed the SD-run newspaper harmful to "social calm and peace."[150] This last action symbolized the regime's flagrant disregard of the guarantees of the October Manifesto and choked off an important source of news and information about the local and national labor movements and political events.

Finally, on January 2, the police arrested the fifteen members of the Executive Committee. Two days later they captured nearly two dozen other members of the soviet who were meeting to discuss arrangements for a demonstration commemorating Bloody Sunday and to elect a new chairman to replace Shavdiia, who had been arrested.[151] Combined with arrests of leading SDs and SRs, the collapse of the Bolshevik and Menshevik organizations, and reprisals against trade unions, the arrest of the Soviet officials robbed the workers of the last of their representatives and leaders. This move marked the death of the Odessa Soviet of Workers' Deputies.[152] In the wake of the workers' unwillingness to confront the police and military and the evaporation of their militance, even this direct assault on the soviet did not impel Odessa workers into action. Instead, they accepted with resignation the destruction of the "workers' parliament," the institutional and spiritual embodiment of labor's struggle for the creation of a more equitable social, political, and economic order. The workers' waning enthusiasm was no match for the renewed vigor of the government's counter-offensive. They stood by and watched as the government dismantled the quin-tessential workers' organization. In Odessa, the Revolution of 1905 had come to an end.

Conclusion

Odessa workers left an indelible imprint on political developments in 1905, as they shifted from a seeming indifference toward national politics in January to a militant defense of political goals by the end of the year. Having begun the year with a refusal to protest the massacre of Bloody Sunday, Odessa workers ended it by striking in support of the besieged St. Petersburg workers and challenging tsarist authority by forming their own Soviet of Workers' Deputies. In November and December, politics was clearly on the minds of Odessa workers, who were taking matters into their own hands to reform the autocracy. Drawn into—and just as importantly contributing to—the unfolding drama of revolution, they learned valuable lessons about the connection between autocratic politics on the Empire-wide level and the struggle over workplace grievances. As the political arena in Russia expanded and new possibilities emerged during the year, workers in Odessa realized that the granting of civil liberties and political reforms would be needed if they were to attain and preserve improved conditions of work. Political liberation became an integral element in their struggle for a better life, served as the driving force behind much of the organized activity of labor during 1905, and brought them into direct conflict with the government and employers. As one Soviet historian wrote to commemorate the 1905 Revolution in Odessa, "Workers may have started off uninterested in politics, but they came to the realization that politics were necessary, that economics and politics were connected."[1] While many of the strikes in Odessa may have been unplanned and focused primarily on material issues, the strike movement, as the year wore on, reflected a crystallization of political awareness which was generated by the contentious atmosphere of 1905.

Odessa workers shared with other opposition groups such as liberals, socialists, and even some reformist gentry activists the goal of winning fundamental civil liberties and democratic freedoms, particularly the right to elect a constituent assembly. Although many of the demands of workers and the liberal intelligentsia were remarkably similar, workers had a different understanding of why they were struggling for political reform. Unlike many of their erstwhile political allies, Odessa workers were not necessarily ideologically committed to abstract notions of civil and political emancipation. Rather, they embraced their own brand of class-based labor politics, less out of intellectual conviction and more as an expression of their disillusionment with the contemporary social and economic order. Labor radicalism and the workers' struggle for political reform were embedded in the experience of both work and daily life and reflected, in the words of Steve Smith, "that *svoboda* (freedom) was perceived to be a multidimensional condition in which political rights were inextricably tied up with economic and social betterment." Linda Edmondson adds: "Political awareness was all the sharper for arising out of a growing dissatisfaction with the immediate working environment."[2] That is why Odessa workers, like workers in other cities, found the concessions of October inadequate, pressed for additional reforms, and continued to challenge the regime by forming trade unions and the soviet.

Like their counterparts in St. Petersburg and elsewhere, Odessa workers sought to expand their power in both the workplace and society as civic, political, and economic concerns melded into a concerted struggle for a reformed polity with greater participation by workers. What Joan Scott writes about late-nineteenth century French workers also applies to Odessa workers in 1905: the struggle between labor and employers was a contest for power that demonstrated to workers "the connections between their work and politics, making it clear that to win a measure of economic control also meant wresting political control from their employers. For this reason politics became a facet of union activity" and strikes involved control of the municipality in which they lived.[3] Neither the spontaneity of strikes nor the occasional lack of programmatic and organizational unity, nor the unevenness of political awareness among Odessa workers detract from the conclusion that, by the end of 1905, attention to Russia's political future took precedence over all of labor's concerns.

One indication of the workers' politicization is the similarity of demands made by different workers on their employees and the regime. Repeatedly, workers demanded the right to enjoy some control on the enterprise level; they sought to acquire participatory rights on a permanent and equal basis in the administration of their places of work by challenging managerial prerogatives, especially in regard to hiring and firing and the settlement of labor-management disputes. As the workers' movement became more political in 1905, workers extended these workplace concerns beyond the factory gates and workshop doors to include demands for civil rights and political liberation in the broader arena of municipal and national politics. Labor militancy entered a new stage after the October Manifesto, as workers pursued other avenues of organization and activity. Workers' claims to share in the decision-making process at work found their most eloquent and expanded political expression in the Soviet of Workers' Deputies, which embodied the workers' class-based demand for authority over both their political and economic lives. In the words of a pamphlet issued by the soviet, "Long Live the Struggle for Democratic Freedom!" and "Long Live the Future Struggle for Socialism."[4] A budding class consciousness characterized the workers' struggle for liberation from an oppressive social and political system, a struggle that in 1905 could find labor straddling both the liberal and socialist camps in its effort to achieve political liberty and social justice.

The development of political activism was neither preordained nor a simple outgrowth of the struggle over bread-and-butter concerns. The precise path which workers traveled to the world of political activism needs to be viewed in light of the interaction between the general crisis of the autocracy in 1905 and specific developments in Odessa. The emergence of political awareness among Odessa workers did not stem from the inevitable evolution of workers' class consciousness, but rather from the workers' experience of the events of 1905; it must be understood with reference to their understanding of and reaction to developments on both the local and national levels. The confrontation with superordinate authority, and the workers' anger at a life of oppression and exclusion, helped mold their political behavior.

The nature of autocratic politics and economic development ensured that even seemingly straightforward grievances over wages and hours could easily grow into confrontation with the political authorities, since some of these demands required resolution on the national level. Similarly, the desire for workplace representation and trade union recognition was essentially a political question, because it involved the issue of power and authority in both the enterprise and society and made the autocratic regime the ultimate arbiter of labor-management relations. Furthermore, the use of police and soldiers to break a strike made it likely that, during times of strife, a localized labor dispute would escalate into a clash between workers and government.

Alexis de Tocqueville noted that political revolution occurs precisely when a troubled government tries to implement reforms. A government in retreat finds itself in a paradoxical predicament, because its reform strategy undercuts its authority, erodes its power, and spurs on the political opposition which, sensing that the regime is a wounded prey, closes in for the kill.[5] Such a scenario occurred in Russia in the aftermath of Bloody Sunday, when the autocracy, recognizing the need to implement political reforms, set out to stave off revolution and in the process moved large portions of Russian society into action.

In 1905, government efforts to reform itself impelled workers in Odessa to adopt an increasingly militant posture vis-à-vis employers and the regime. This was largely due to the contradictory policies adopted by the autocracy in regard to the labor question. On the one hand, the Tsar's promise to convene a popularly elected, consultative assembly and the formation of various commissions to investigate the sources of labor discontent indicated to workers that the government was openly soliciting their opinion and advice. On the other hand, government officials time and again stymied efforts by Odessa workers to meet on a citywide basis. Seeking to discuss interests and grievances common to all workers in Odessa, they were frustrated by the refusal of city governor Neidhardt and other local officials to permit such assemblies.

This frustration turned into open outrage and violence when the police, in an effort to thwart the organized labor movement, arrested the members of the strike committee in June. Several months later, the government's decision to renege on the provisions of the October Manifesto, first by arresting members of the St. Petersburg Soviet and then by turning its attention to politically active Odessa workers in December, signaled the start of an orchestrated government campaign to block workers' efforts to organize and elect representatives. As in June, the arrests in December served as a catalyst for increased labor militancy.

By interfering, the government transformed worker demands into political protest, regardless of the workers' original motivations. In short, workers' attitudes and actions—their decision to act and think politically—were shaped by the local and national political crisis of 1905 and the ensuing confrontation between workers and an autocracy whose half-hearted reform efforts sent mixed and confused messages. Although tempted by the concessions of October, workers grew increasingly bitter when the regime began to chip away at the guarantees and promises of the Manifesto. By the end of November and early December, Odessa workers had come to perceive the government's action in October for what it precisely was: an expedient, stop-gap measure designed to buy the regime a breathing spell before it could muster its forces and roll back the revolution. The actions of Odessa workers in November and December were designed to fend off the counterrevolution as well as to press ahead for the realization of their transformative vision of a new social and political order. Workers defended the revolution while simultaneously pursuing aggressive tactics that challenged constituted authority.

The behavior of Odessa workers resembled that of workers in other Russian cities, particulary Moscow and St. Petersburg, although the periodization of events and details in Odessa differed. The behavior of Odessa workers in 1905 represents a variation of the general pattern of activism exhibited by workers in other cities of the Russian Empire. Throughout urban Russia, workers were key participants in the rallies, demonstrations, strikes, and unrest that challenged tsarist authority. Workers, as much as any other social group in Russia, agitated for the transformation of the political order, both in the workplace and in society at large. Despite variations in the behavior of different categories of workers, there was an undeniable trend toward involvement by a broad spectrum of Odessa workers in radical politics. The details of the story in Odessa differ from those in other cities, but on the whole workers there joined the common struggle of workers throughout Russia by demanding—and at times seizing through direct action—greater control over their lives as workers and citizens. Claims for social, economic, and political justice involved Odessa workers in a struggle against both employers and government officials, who resisted any encroachments on traditional managerial and autocratic prerogatives and engaged the workers in a yearlong conflict to stave off changes in the structure of Russian society and politics. Ultimately, recognizing that it could not preserve the status quo without risking revolution, the regime caved in by issuing the October Manifesto. But the regime's policies after October, and continuing through the remaining decade or so of Nicholas II's reign, poignantly reveal that the government regretted the concessions granted in 1905 and sought to avail itself of any opportunity to limit the application of the October Manifesto.

The 1905 revolution in Odessa was perhaps more purely a workers' revolution than in Russia's two capital cities, where the liberal opposition movement played a more visible and crucial role. Drawing upon a rich legacy of pre-1905 organizational experience, many workers in Odessa engaged in a flurry of activities (factory councils, trade unions, district and city strike committees, and the soviet) that demonstrated a resolve to promote and defend their interests in an organized, rational, and at times aggressive manner. The simultaneous emergence of trade unions and the Soviet of Workers' Deputies underscored the extent to which many workers, despite their strong sense of craft awareness and identity, did not confine themselves purely to problems of craft and shop, but also participated in the more extensive political struggle that cut across craft, enterprise, and other divisions. The formation of trade unions along craft lines and the creation of the soviet, which embraced workers of many occupations and enterprises, illustrates how particularistic interests commingled with universalistic concerns in the actions of Odessa workers.

As in the two capital cities, skilled workers figured prominently in the organized labor movement, provided the initiative and direction of the strikes in June and December, and were critical in the formation of the soviet. The activities of Odessa workers in 1905—from political demonstrations and the creation of the soviet, to mass strikes and the formation of strike committees—found their most ardent and vociferous supporters, and usually their leaders as well, in the railway workshops and in Peresyp's metalworking factories. These relatively large enterprises served as the hub of the strike movements and political mobilization in May and June and again towards the end of the year. Political radicalism may be generated by certain occupational and social characteristics factors such as skill, pay, and nature of authority and work in an industrial factory setting. But the experience of Peresyp metalworkers indicates that a sense of neighborhood, which depends in large measure upon long-term residence, also helps explain the capacity to act in a collective fashion. For Peresyp workers, the distinction between factory and home, between work and residence, was blurred, with the neighborhood, situated in the city's periphery and enjoying a relatively isolated existence, providing the setting of some of the most militant labor conflict and political activism. The coterminous nature of their experiences at home and at work enabled these workers to apprehend their status as exploited, second-class citizens more acutely than other workers, and formed the basis of their political resistance.

Another feature common to the organized labor movements in Odessa, Moscow, and St. Petersburg was the role played by the organized revolutionary parties. The link between workers and the revolutionary intelligentsia is notoriously difficult to assess, but one conclusion supported by events in Odessa in 1905 is that of the revolutionary as a source of radical ideas, a catalyst in creating cells of politicized workers who frequently led strikes and labor organizations, and an eloquent voice for articulating the grievances of workers. In their leaflets, brochures, and speeches, SDs in particular reinforced the workers' growing awareness of the connection between bread-and-butter issues with ostensibly noneconomic concerns such as the lack of civil liberties and political freedom. Contact with the entreaties of revolutionaries exposed workers to the world of political ideas, laying bare the ties between grievances rising out of working conditions and the broader and more distant arena of national politics.

Reginald Zelnik, in his examination of the interaction between Russian workers and the socialist intelligentsia, suggests that "the educated bearers of a more universalistic language" helped endow workers with new values that provided an alternative vision of Russian society and politics.[6] Revolutionary agitation often struck a responsive chord precisely because the message of socialist activists and labor organizers received confirmation in the daily experiences of workers. Workers and socialists played distinct but complementary roles in the revolutionary process, with the socialist intelligentsia furnishing the ideological framework and sometimes the organizational expertise, and disgruntled workers— radicalized by their material circumstances and the events of 1905, and building upon the foundations created by the pre-1905 labor movement—serving as the motive force in the unrest that enveloped urban Russia. As Abraham Ascher writes, by October,

> the industrial proletariat emerged as an organized—and for a time also the most dynamic—force in the revolution. It was not the only class to go on the offensive against the government, but it clearly initiated the strike, kept it going, and provided most of the cannon fodder for the assault on the old order. . . . if workers had not taken the lead, there would have been no general strike in the first place."[7]

Yet the SDs did not generate or direct labor protest. Despite the presence of worker-socialists in many workshops and factories throughout the city, Odessa workers maintained their autonomy and infrequently responded to the appeals of the revolutionaries to demonstrate or strike. Indeed, Odessa workers ignored the entreaties of SDs to stage protests several times during the year and preferred to pursue tactics of their own device and corresponding to their own perceptions of the problems confronting them. The revolutionary intelligentsia was not necessary in motivating labor unrest precisely because Odessa workers, relying on their day-to-day experiences with employers and government officials, assessed their conditions and reached their own conclusions regarding appropriate tactics. Above all, the very act of walking off the job in a collective, organized fashion without promptings from the intelligentsia helped generate additional unrest and radicalism.

As in St. Petersburg and Moscow, the impact of the Odessa SDs on the labor movement was evident only in those instances where the parties' policies and expertise coincided with the particular needs of the workers. But autonomy did not preclude the acceptance or even solicitation of assistance. In such a fashion, much of the mistrust and suspicion that characterized worker-intelligentsia relations during the first half of the year was overcome or at least muted for the time being. But even then the revolutionaries did not control the labor movement; on the contrary, on most occasions the workers held the upper hand and took the initiative. Odessa workers in 1905 acted politically without necessarily following the lead of socialist activists, although at times the interests and actions of workers converged with those of the revolutionary parties. Gerald Surh's comments on party-worker relationships in St. Petersburg also apply to events in Odessa: "At no time during the year was the party able to bring off a strike, demonstration, or protest without substantial prior initiative on the part of the workers themselves. . . . The Social Democrats had the greatest impact on workers . . . when they seconded movements already undertaken by the workers."[8]

The limited impact of the revolutionaries can also be judged from the fact that the militance of Peresyp workers often outstripped that of Jewish workers who had a history of exposure to social-democratic organization. While it is true that certain occupations dominated by Jews played significant roles in the movement to establish unions, and Jewish workers certainly generated some of the unrest that occurred in 1905, Odessa's Jewish workers did not play as significant a role as Russian metalworkers in the organization and leadership of the May-June and December strikes and the creation of the soviet. Although many of the worker-activists in Peresyp were indeed Mensheviks and Bolsheviks, the locus of SD strength and organization in the city was among Jewish workers who were not in the forefront of the workers' opposition movement. Clearly, then, factors other than political affiliation accounted for the differences between Jewish workers on the whole and Peresyp metalworkers. Of prime importance was the dispersal of Jewish workers in hundreds of small workshops and enterprises throughout the city, while the proximity of residence and work, neighborhood ties and experience as skilled laborers in relatively large factory settings, facilitated the radicalization and mobilization of Peresyp workers.

The high point of social-democratic influence on the Odessa labor movement occurred in November and December, when workers busily established trade unions and the soviet. The inroads made by the SDs among workers took place precisely because the actions of the SDs were congruent with the specific needs, aspirations, and goals of Odessa workers at that time. As in June, when Peresyp workers turned to the revolutionary parties for guns because they could not arm themselves, in November and December, Odessa workers accepted socialist influence in the soviet and trade unions because they needed the assistance of persons well-versed in organizational matters. The workers insisted on formal independence from the revolutionary parties, however, and it is unlikely that they would have countenanced social-democratic influence in their organizations if they first did not acknowledge the need for experienced organizers and activists whose views corresponded to their own.

One notable feature of labor activism, not only in Odessa but in other urban centers of the Empire, was the impetus displayed by workers to organize in their struggle over enterprise grievances. Frequently, particularly in the case of district and city strike committees and the soviet, this organizational impetus cut across craft, occupational, enterprise, and even ethnic divisions and brought all kinds of workers into joint action. It was this commitment to joint collective action by a broad spectrum of Odessa's workers that constituted the power of organized labor in 1905.

In general, organized Odessa workers pursued their goals with self-discipline and restraint, but sometimes they resorted to rioting and violence in order to express their frustration. It is important to distinguish between the different kinds of violence that characterized the workers' movement in Odessa, since labor unrest had a double-edged quality that affected the course of events in 1905. For example, the violence which accompanied strikes reflected the radicalization of the participants and posed a revolutionary threat to municipal authorities. This occurred in June, when arrests and shootings provoked an even more violent round of public unrest directed against employers, officials, and soldiers. From the government's perspective, the arrival of the *Potemkin* fortunately diverted the populace's attention and permitted local authorities to regroup and plan a counterattack, which effectively drowned the strike movement and protest of May and June in a pool of blood. Similarly, public unrest and violence in mid-October again challenged the regime, when government action against student protesters led to uncontrollable street demonstrations and attacks on police officers. The issuance of the October Manifesto whipped the political opposition into a frenzy as public sentiment against the regime reached a new level. But, as in June, local authorities weathered the October crisis by the timely outbreak of an anti-Jewish pogrom. Thus, public disorders could acquire reactionary overtones when Jews became the object of workers' outrage and hostility. The pogrom revealed how a potentially revolutionary situation could quickly be defused when the target of labor unrest was no longer the autocracy but a group of people that has served for centuries as scapegoats for a variety of social, economic, and political ills.

The ethnic and occupational heterogeneity of the Odessa work force helps explain this dual nature of labor unrest by revealing that powerful centrifugal forces counteracted the unifying forces of the organized labor movement. At one end of the occupational spectrum were thousands of unskilled dockworkers, day laborers, and homeless vagrants who were marginal members of society, relatively untouched by the mediating influence of organized labor, and not integrated into mainstream working-class life and society. Although the most down-and-out workers were rarely politically militant and radical in Russian and West European labor protest in the late nineteenth and early twentieth centuries, these workers were nonetheless prone to express their discontent in unpredictable ways, which turned out to have serious impact on the fate of revolutions. In Odessa, their behavior meant the destruction of the harbor district in June as well as the barbaric pogrom in October; the former incident challenged the autocracy, but the latter enabled the regime to weather the crisis.

The other end of the spectrum was occupied by skilled metalworkers and machinists who displayed a remarkably high degree of organization, self-discipline, and sense of purpose. When these workers resorted at times to violence and rioting, they consistently directed their rage against employers and government officials and refrained from the anti-Semitic excesses that characterized the behavior of the unskilled and largely unorganized dockworkers and day laborers. In other words, no one form of collective action and violence characterized the behavior of Odessa workers in 1905. Historians of labor protest would do well to pay attention to the varying nature of worker violence, particularly the political contexts in which it occurs, its social and political consequences, and the socio-occupational characteristics of the workers participating in it. The alternation between spontaneity and organization, between violence and restraint, is one key to understanding labor unrest in late Imperial Russia, particularly in ethnically mixed regions.

The ethnic heterogeneity of the Odessa work force ensured that events in Odessa would take a different direction from those in more homogeneous cities such as St. Petersburg and Moscow. The large Jewish presence in Odessa, the long history of anti-Semitism and pogromist activity, and the socio-economic structure of Odessa society served as centrifugal forces that made ties among workers fragile and solidarities across ethnic groups and occupations difficult to build and maintain. Insofar as all Odessa workers experienced similar grievances which impelled them into common action, ethnic diversity—a significant dividing line in the Odessa labor force—made the unity forged in the course of confrontation difficult to sustain, although the experience of the unions and the soviet indicates that workers were able to do so at times. The ethnic composition of the laboring population and the specifics of the local economy created conditions favorable to the outbreak of anti-Jewish violence and hostility. The occurrence of the pogrom in October, much like the destruction of the harbor in June, indicated that popular protest could readily degenerate into unpredictable outbursts of wanton violence and rage. But whether or not Jews were targeted as the specific object of rioting depended in large measure upon broader socio-political and cultural factors affecting the behavior of the populace and developments in the city.

Although the regime suppressed the workers' movement throughout the Empire in December 1905, the government did not completely squelch the activities of organized labor in Odessa and other urban centers. The disappearance of fledgling trade unions and the collapse of soviets throughout Russia by year's end marked the end of the first phase of the urban crisis confronting the autocracy during the early years of this century. The counterrevolution against urban workers gained strength during the next eighteenth months, but in the meantime workers in Odessa and elsewhere in the Empire drew upon the experiences of 1905 and demonstrated that they had learned their lessons well. According to the Odessa Factory Inspector's Report for 1906, "The general workers' movement of last year affected the situation of workers and raised their awareness of the commonality of their class interests."[9] Indeed, one can speak of a revival of labor radicalism in the wake of the March 4, 1906 law legalizing trade unions. During this second phase of activism, workers mobilized to reestablish trade unions and walked off the job in an effort to win improved working conditions and to participate in the administration of their enterprises. It was not until mid-1907, when workers finally felt the full brunt of the government's counteroffensive, that labor unrest subsided. Just as importantly, the labor movement was still plagued by the problems of ethnic hostilities, which continued to flare up and play a role in labor unrest as they did in 1905. In 1906 and 1907, anti-Jewish tensions were in evidence in factories, workshops, and on the streets, and once again hindered workers from confronting their employers in a united fashion.

However short-lived some of the fruits of the 1905 revolution may have been, the lessons learned about the significance of labor organization and political opposition were in the hearts and minds of many workers. 1905 marked the political awakening of Odessa workers and shaped their subsequent struggle for a life of dignity. It took another twelve years and even greater cataclysmic events brought on by war, economic disintegration, and social and political polarization before workers would again seize the day and seek to establish soviet power. The patterns of labor's political activism first witnessed during the 1905 revolution paved the way in 1917 for a vast upheaval that promised workers a democratic polity, expanded authority at work, and a society free of ethnic and national strife.

APPENDIX

Size and Composition of the Work Force

The data used to compute the number of workers have been drawn primarily from two pre-1905 sources, since relatively little information is available on 1905 itself. The sources are the 1897 census of the Russian Empire, the first of its kind, and the report of the Odessa Committee of Trade and Manufacture for the years 1903–1905. Available sources on the number of Russian workers before 1905 are generally limited in terms of accuracy, reliability, and comprehensiveness, and this is especially true for the data on workers in Odessa for several reasons. First, unlike the city governments of St. Petersburg and Moscow, which took censuses in 1900 and 1902 respectively, the city fathers of Odessa did not undertake a similar project between 1897 and 1905. Since the population of the city increased nearly 25 percent during these years, the 1897 figures do not give an accurate count of the labor force eight years later. In addition, the census was taken in January 1897; the number of workers in those branches of the economy that were most active in late spring and summer, such as transportation, dockwork, and construction, are grossly underreported because these sectors attracted many temporary migrant workers who did not live in Odessa year-round.

At first glance, the report of the Odessa Committee of Trade and Manufacture would therefore seem to offer a more reliable reckoning of the size of the Odessa work force on the eve of 1905. This report suffers from several serious deficiencies, however, that detract from its value as a reliable and comprehensive measure. In contrast to the 1897 census, which furnishes the most detailed data regarding the occupational structure of Odessa's population in the pre–1905 era but does not indicate the type of enterprise in which workers were employed, the report of the Odessa Committee of Trade and Manufacture provides information only on the size and composition of the work force under the jurisdiction of the Factory Inspectorate. Before 1901, the Factory Inspectorate exercised jurisdiction only over those manufacturing enterprises that employed fifteen or more workers or used engine-powered machinery. In 1901 the Factory Inspectorate modified its system of classification to include as a "factory" any manufacturing establishment with twenty or more employees, regardless of the type of machinery used. Their data exclude all workers employed in enterprises that were not subsumed under its definition, and therefore leave uncounted tens of thousands of manufacturing workers. Workers in state-owned factories, those in enterprises subject to the excise tax, and all workers not employed in factories, such as workshop employees, those working at home, construction workers, and day laborers, were not under the purview of the Inspectorate.

Another inadequacy of the data compiled by the Factory Inspectorate is the method of classifying workers. Whereas the 1897 census grouped workers according to work actually performed, the Inspectorate categorized workers by the type of enterprise in which they worked. Thus, all workers in a textile mill were considered textile workers, even if some of these workers were machinists. Similarly, an unskilled janitor in a machine-construction plant or printshop was classified respectively as a metalworker or printer by the Inspectorate, even though such a worker shared none of the occupational characteristics of a skilled lathe operator or typesetter.

The Factory Inspectorate also did not distinguish consistently between factory and workshop due to the arbitrary and imprecise definitions given by Russian statisticians to these two kinds of enterprises. For example, workers in an unmechanized workshop were often counted as factory workers in one year because they worked with twenty or more workers. But at the time of the next census by the Factory Inspectorate, these same workers were dropped from the roll of factory workers if fewer than twenty workers were employed. This failure to draw consistent boundaries between factory and workshop plagued statisticians during tsarist times and continues to hinder today the efforts of historians of Russian workers.

The changing structure of nonfactory manufacturing compounded the difficulty of determining the size of the labor force engaged in workshop production, or what is traditionally known as artisanal production. Workshop production in Odessa was characterized by both skilled and unskilled workers involved in a wide variety of work settings and production techniques, not all of whom fit the definition of artisan. The word artisan connotes a skilled craftworker who has gone through a lengthy training program and works in a small workshop where production of custom-made goods is performed primarily by hand with little division of labor. The work force in these establishments was hierarchically divided into apprentices, journeymen, and master craftworkers (who also owned the workshops) and was the preserve of men, with virtually no women entering its ranks. By the beginning of the twentieth century, however, many employees of small, unmechanized workshops were unskilled and had never finished, or even entered, an apprenticeship program. Some workshop employees found themselves working in relatively large establishments that produced for the mass market, where skill had been undercut due to the introduction of a division of labor in the work process, subcontracting, and putting out. In addition, an undetermined number of handworkers labored alone at home as garret-masters (*odinochki*).

Russian statisticians (at least in Odessa) were sometimes sloppy in their collection and computation of data. This is especially true in the case of the 1903 report of the Odessa Committee of Trade and Manufacture. In addition, the publication quality of this source leaves much to be desired, thereby making it difficult for the reader to distinguish among numerals in some of the tables. Finally, the fact that the sources employed date from different years at the turn of the century—years when Odessa's population continued to skyrocket—raises the very real possibility of underestimating the total number of workers in the city.

These shortcomings of the sources notwithstanding, we have no alternative but to use the data provided by the 1897 census and Factory Inspectorate. These enable us to estimate the number of workers in Odessa at the beginning of the twentieth century.

ABBREVIATIONS USED IN
NOTES AND BIBLIOGRAPHY

For brevity's sake, the following abbreviations have been used in the notes. In addition, I have abbreviated the citations of many works in the notes; full references are provided in the bibliography.

ch.	*chast'*
EE	*Evreiskaia entsiklopediia*
d.	*delo*
delopr.	*deloproizvodstvo*
ES	*Entsiklopedicheskii slovar'*
f.	*fond*
IO	*Iuzhnoe obozrenie*
IOGD	*Izvestiia Odesskoi gorodskoi dumy*
ISRD	*Izvestiia Soveta rabochikh deputatov g. Odessy*
JE	*The Jewish Encyclopedia*
KhEZ	*Khronika evreiskoi zhizni*
Khronika	*Khronika revoliutsionnykh sobytii na Odesshchine v gody pervoi russkoi revoliutsii, 1905–1907*
KR	*Kommercheskaia Rossia*
Kuzminskii Report	*Materialy k istorii russkoi kontr-revoliutsii*
NPRR	Trusova, *Nachalo pervoi russkoi revoliutsii: ianvar'-mart 1905 goda*
1905 god	*1905 god. Revoliutsionnoe dvizhenie v Odesse i Odesschine*
ob.	*oborotnaia storona*
Obzor za 35 let	*Obzor deiatel'nosti Odesskago obshchestva vzaimnago vspomoshchestvovaniia prikazchikov-evreev za 35 let*
Ocherk za 50 let	*Ocherk deiatel'nosti Odesskago obshchestva vzaimnago vspomoshchestvovaniia prikazchikov-evreev za 50 let*
OL	*Odesskii listok*
ON	*Odesskie novosti*
OO	*Osobyi otdel*
OOG	*Obzor Odesskago gradonachal'stva*
OOKTM	*Otchet Odesskago komiteta torgovli i manufaktur*
OOORU	*Otchet Odesskoi obshchei remeslennoi upravy*
op.	*opis'*
OPIRKP	Nevskii, *Ocherki po istorii rossiiskoi kommunisticheskoi partii*
PD	*Proletarskoe delo*
Perepis'	*Pervaia vseobshchaia perepis' naseleniia Rossiiskoi imperii, 1897 g.* Vol. 47, *Gorod Odessa*
PI	*Posledniia izvestiia*
PR	*Proletarskaia revoliutsiia*
RBNU	Los', *Revoliutsionnaia bor'ba na Ukraine v period pervoi russkoi revoliutsii, 1905 g.*
RDVL	Trusova, *Revoliutsionnoe dvizhenie v Rossi vesnoi i letom 1905 goda: aprel'-sentiabr'*
RR	*Revoliutsionnaia Rossiia*

SD	*Sotsial-demokrat*
TsGAOR	*Tsentral'nyi gosudarstvennyi arkhiv oktiabr'skoi revoliutsii SSSR*
TsGIA	*Tsentral'nyi gosudarstvennyi istoricheskii arkhiv SSSR*
TsGVIA	*Tsentral'nyi gosudarstvennyi voenno-istoricheskii arkhiv SSSR*
VOG	*Vedomosti Odesskago gradonachal'stva*
VPR	Sidorov, *Vyshii pod"em revoliutsii 1905–1907 gg. Vooruzhenne vosstaniia: noiabr'-dekabr' 1905 goda*
VtPR	Derenkovskii, *Vtoroi period revoliutsii, 1906–1907 gody: ianvar'-aprel' 1906 goda*

NOTES

Introduction

1. See the works of the following authors listed in the bibliography: Victoria Bonnell, Francois-Xavier Coquin and Céline Gervais-Francelle, Laura Engelstein, William Gard, Kathleen Prevo, Henry Reichman, Jonathan Sanders, Solomon Schwarz, Gerald Surh, and Charters Wynn. For general treatments of 1905, see the works by Abraham Ascher and Sidney Harcave. For a valuable Soviet work on the subject, see U. A. Shuster, *Peterburgskie rabochie v 1905–1907 gg.*

2. See the writings of the following Soviet authors for a representative sampling: D. S. Bel'for, S. Ia. Borovoi, V. G. Konovalov, K. S. Kovalenko, S. M. Kovbasiuk, S. K. Mel'nik, and A. M. Shternshtein.

3. Both Frederick Skinner and Patricia Herlihy examine the meteoric growth of Odessa during the nineteenth century from the perspective of urban history. They offer valuable insights regarding social and economic conditions in the city, but neither devotes much attention to the workers' movement and the Revolution of 1905. Their relevant works are listed in the bibliography.

4. *KR*, March 30, 1905.

5. The issue of labor violence is laden with theoretical and practical implications for the understanding of labor activism and politics in the late Imperial period. For one recent discussion, see Brower et al., "Labor Violence in Russia in the Late Nineteenth Century," and the responses the article elicited in *Slavic Review* 41, no. 3 (Fall 1982): 417–453.

6. Mayer, *Dynamics of Counterrevolution in Europe, 1870–1956*, p. 9. See also Charters Wynn, *Workers, Strikes, and Pogroms*, for an analysis of the link between revolution and counterrevolution in 1905 Ekaterinoslav.

1. Odessa on the Eve of 1905

1. Svirskii, *Trushchoby*, p. 181; Iushkevich, *Prolog: Povest'*, p. 6.

2. By century's end more than twice the value of exports passed through the port of Odessa than the harbor of St. Petersburg, which still handled more imports. Overall, Odessa's share in the foreign trade of the Empire in the 1890s hovered between 10 and 16 percent of the total value of imports and exports. *Odessa, 1794–1894*, pp. 198, 208 and 792; Skinner, "Trends in Planning Practices," p. 139; Lazarovich, "Ekonomicheskaia zhizn' g. Odessy," pp. 5–6; Herlihy, "Odessa: Staple Trade and Urbanization in New Russia," pp. 184–185; Siegelbaum, "The Odessa Grain Trade," pp. 136–137; Zagoruiko, *Po stranitsam istorii Odessy i Odesshchiny*, vol. 2, p. 31.

3. The reader interested in the general history of Odessa from its founding in the late eighteenth century until the end of the nineteenth century should refer to the studies by Zipperstein, *The Jews of Odessa: A Cultural History*, Skinner, "City Planning in Russia," and Herlihy, *Odessa: A History*.

4. Siegelbaum, p. 115; Fox, "Odessa," pp. 6–7.

5. Skal'kovskii, *Pervoe tridtsatiletie istorii goroda Odessy*, p. 132 and *Istoriko-statisticheskii opyt*, pp. 50–51; Orlov, *Istoricheskii ocherk Odessy s 1794 po 1803 god*, p. xxi; Skinner, "City Planning in Russia," pp. 110–112; *Odessa, 1794–1894*, pp. 65 and 172–173; Zipperstein, *The Jews of Odessa*, pp. 22–23.

6. For a summary of the activities of Odessa's first several governor-generals, see

Skinner, "City Planning in Russia," pp. 113–165 and Herlihy, *Odessa: A History,* pp. 21–48 and 114–122.

7. Skal'kovskii, *Istoriko-statisticheskii opyt,* pp. 12–13 and 57–58.

8. Puryear, "Odessa: Its Rise and International Importance, 1815–1850," pp. 193–194; Herlihy, *Odessa: A History,* p. 99.

9. Skinner, "City Planning in Russia," pp. 147–148; Plaksin, *Kommerchesko-promyshlennaia Odessa,* pp. 22–23 and 84; *Odessa, 1794–1894,* pp. 174–179; Skal'kovksii, *Istoriko-statisticheskii opyt,* pp. 60–62; Smol'ianinov, *Istoriia Odessy,* pp. 175–177.

10. "Odessa," *ES,* p. 727; Siegelbaum, p. 116.

11. The Pushkin reference is from Skinner, "Trends in Planning Practices," p. 147.

12. *Putevoditel' po Odesse,* p. 9.

13. A pood is equivalent to 36.1 pounds. Zagoruiko, vol. 2, pp. 24–29.

14. Bernshtein, *Odessa,* pp. 73–74; Herlihy, *Odessa: A History,* p. 107.

15. Skinner, "City Planning in Russia," pp. 296–304; "Odessa," *ES,* p. 731.

16. *Perepis',* pp. xviii and 134–149.

17. Skal'kovskii, "Nachalo razvitiia zavodskoi promyshlennosti," p. 152.

18. Mikulin, *Fabrichno-zavodskaia i remeslennaia promyshlennost' v 1898 godu, prilozhenie* 1.

19. Ibid.

20. *KR,* January 16, 1905; Avdenko, *Noveishii putevoditel',* p. 52.

21. *OOKTM za 1903–1905 gg.,* p. 125; Surh, *1905 in St. Petersburg,* p. 22. These data include the workshops and repair yards of the South West Railroad, which was not under the jurisdiction of the Factory Inspectorate.

22. Food processing enterprises turned grain into flour and macaroni, refined sugar, packed tea, baked bread, and manufactured candy, beer, vodka, cognac, sausage, mineral water, canned goods, and halvah. See *OOKTM za 1903–1905 gg.,* pp. 122–125 and *prilozheniia* 19 and 20 and *Odessa, 1794–1894,* p. 151 for Factory Inspectorate data on the size of the factory labor force, number of enterprises and ruble value of output by branch of production.

23. Overall, the average number of workers in the 252 enterprises under the jurisdiction of the Factory Inspectorate in 1895 was 22. Mikulin, *Strakhovanie rabochikh ot neschastnykh sluchaev,* p. 1; *OOKTM za 1903–1905 gg.,* p. 125; Surh, *1905 in St. Petersburg,* p. 23.

24. Lazarovich, "Ekonomicheskie usloviia g. Odessy," p. 2.

25. See Joseph Bradley, *Muzhik and Muscovite,* chap. 1; Daniel Brower, *The Russian City between Tradition and Modernity, 1850–1900;* and Michael F. Hamm, ed., *The City in Late Imperial Russia* for recent discussions of the population explosion during the late nineteenth century.

26. Surh, "Petersburg Workers in 1905," p. 3; Bonnell, *Roots of Rebellion,* p. 21; Hamm, "The Modern Russian City," p. 41; Rashin, *Naselenie Rossii za 100 let (1811–1913 gg.),* p. 93.

27. *Perepis',* p. ix.

28. See N. I. Teziakov, *Rynki naima sel'sko-khoziaistvennykh rabochikh,* pp. 76–78, "Sel'sko-khoziaistvennye rabochie," pp. 8, 26, 29, and 79 and *Sel'sko-khoziaistvennye rabochie,* pp. 27–29, 36, 58, 83, 112, 120, 123, and 129.

29. Fedorov, "O polozhenii rabochago klassa v Odesse," p. 89.

30. Iushkevich, p. 10.

31. Svirskii, "Iz putevogo dnevnika," p. 169.

32. Anderson, *Internal Migration During Modernization in Late Nineteenth-Century Russia,* pp. 174–175.

33. Zipperstein, *The Jews of Odessa,* p. 32.

34. Brutskus, *Statistika evreiskago naseleniia,* p. 37.

35. "Odessa," *JE,* pp. 378–379; "Odessa," *EE,* pp. 56–57; Zipperstein, *The Jews of Odessa,* pp. 37–39 and "Jewish Enlightenment in Odessa," pp. 26–29.

36. Chivonibar "Chistil'shchik sapog," pp. 54–62.

37. Aleichem, *From the Fair,* pp. 43 and 45.

38. Svirskii, "Iz putevogo dnevnika," p. 169. See also Brodovskii, *Evreiskaia nishcheta v Odesse,* p. 10. For one of the first efforts to counteract Odessa's reputation as a city of unbounded wealth and opportunity, see L. N. Samsonov's *The Golden City.* Published in 1870, the book focuses on the poverty and misery endured by so many settlers in Odessa.

39. Lazarovich, "Ekonomicheskaia zhizn' g. Odessy," p. 11; Kleinbort, *Istoriia bezrabotitsy v Rossii,* p. 54.

40. TsGIA, f. 23, op. 20, d. 1, p. 174.

41. *Perepis',* pp. viii–ix, 34–35 (Table 11) and 36–37 (Table 13). See Herlihy, "The Ethnic Composition of the City of Odessa in the Nineteenth Century," for an in-depth discussion of this issue.

42. *Pervaia vseobshchaia perepis' naseleniia Rossiiskoi imperii, 1897 g.,* vol. 24, pt. 2, *Gorod Moskva* (St. Petersburg, 1904), pp. 2–3 and vol. 37, pt. 2, *Gorod S.-Peterburg* (St. Petersburg, 1903), pp. 2–3.

43. For the 1858 figure, see Skal'kovskii, *Zapiski o torgovykh i promyshlennykh silakh Odessay,* p. 12.

44. Of these, 4,400 were Greek nationals. Herlihy, "Greek Merchants in Odessa in the Nineteenth Century," p. 399; *Perepis',* pp. 36–37 (Table 13).

45. *Perepis',* pp. 34–35 (Table 11); Zipperstein, *The Jews of Odessa,* pp. 29–30.

46. *Odessa, 1794–1894,* pp. 584–585; Herlihy, *Odessa: A History,* pp. 42–44 and 141–144.

47. Vanner, *Illiustrirovannyi putevoditel' 'Odessa'.*

48. Svirskii, "Iz putevogo dnevnika," p. 166. Other nicknames included the Golden City, Little Venice, Queen of the Black Sea, Capital of South Russia.

49. *Perepis',* p. viii. Peasants made up 63 and 67 percent of the inhabitants of St. Petersburg and Moscow, respectively. See Surh, "Petersburg Workers in 1905," p. 4 and Johnson, *Peasant and Proletarian,* p. 31.

50. *Perepis',* pp. 152–153.

51. English-language accounts of pogroms in Odessa are provided in Zipperstein, *The Jews of Odessa,* chap. 5, Lambroza, "The Pogrom Movement in Russia, 1903–1906," pp. 275–277, and Herlihy, *Odessa: A History,* pp. 301–304. For accounts in Russian, see Kogan, "Pervye desiatiletiia evreiskoi obshchiny v Odesse i pogrom 1821 goda," pp. 260–267, Morgulis, "Bezporiadki 1871 goda v Odesse," pp. 42–66, and *Opisanie odesskikh ulichnykh bezporiadkov v dni sv. Paskhi 1871 goda.* The 1900 pogrom is described in "Khronika vnutrennei zhizni," *Russkoe bogatstvo,* no. 8 (1900), pp. 159–162 and *Budushchnost',* July 28, 1900 and August 25, 1900. See *PI,* April 6/March 24, 1904, p. 1 and May 5/April 27, 1904, p. 1 and *Voskhod,* March 17, 1904, pp. 25–26 for material on pogrom-mongering in that year.

52. *PI,* June 3/May 21, 1903, pp. 1–2; *RR,* May 15, 1903, p. 14, June 1, 1903, pp. 16–17 and July 1, 1903, p. 19. See the 1904 report of the Odessa factory inspector who observed that workers refrained from striking because they feared worker militance "could lead to a Jewish pogrom." TsGIA, f. 23, op. 29, d. 80, pp. 14–14 ob.

53. *KR,* February 19, 1905.

54. *KR,* February 21, 1905.

55. *KR,* 241, November 2, 1905; *PD,* October 10, 1905.

56. Subbotin, *V cherte evreiskoi osedlosti,* pp. 218–219; Herlihy, "Greek Merchants in Odessa in the Nineteenth Century," p. 419; Bliumenfel'd, "Torgovo-promyshlennaia deiatel'nost' evreev v Odesse," *Voskhod* no. 4 (April 1884), pp. 5–9 and no. 5 (May 1884), pp. 2–3; "Odessa," *EE,* p. 60.

57. *Opisanie odesskikh ulichnykh bezporiadkov,* pp. 10–11.

58. "Odessa," *JE,* pp. 379–380; "Odessa," *EE,* pp. 60–62; Subbotin, pp. 213 and 225–227.

59. *OOG za 1904 g.*, p. 25. A government publication published in 1914 but relying on data from 1904 places the number of Jews in Odessa at 152,364, or 30.5 percent of the population. Patricia Herlihy estimates the number of Jews at 160,000, or 31.3 percent of the population. The discrepancies are evidently due to different data bases. *Goroda Rossii v 1910 god*, pp. 530 and 558–559; Herlihy, *Odessa: A History*, pp. 251 and 256.

60. *Perepis'*, pp. 134–149; "Odessa," *JE*, pp. 379–380; "Odessa," *EE*, pp. 59–61; Subbotin, p. 225.

61. Brodovskii, p. 6; *Perepis'*, pp. 134–149.

62. Zipperstein, *The Jews of Odessa*, p. 75; *Voskhod*, January 29, 1904, pp. 23–26, February 5, 1904, pp. 1–5, and January 27, 1905, pp. 15–16.

63. Brodovskii, pp. 5–6; *IU*, March 22, 1905.

64. *Perepis'*, pp. 134–149.

65. For an excellent discussion of the political implications of class and nationality in Transcaucasia, see Suny, "Nationalism and Social Class in the Russian Revolution."

66. Hamburg, *Politics of the Russian Nobility*, pp. 166–174; Lazarovich, "Ekonomicheskaia zhizn' g. Odessy," pp. 3–5 and 11 and "Ekonomicheskie usloviia g. Odessy," pp. 2–5; Knuzhevitskii, *Obzor kommercheskoi deiatel'nosti iuzhno-russkikh portov*, pp. 35, 49–51 and 72; Kitanina, *Khlebnaia torgovlia Rossii*, pp. 127–128; Markevich, "Zheleznye dorogi," pp. 6–28; *OOKTM za 1903–1905 gg.*, pp. 16–18; Herlihy, *Odessa: A History*, pp. 217–220 and 227–230; *Putevoditel' po Odesse*, p. 233; *OL*, July 23, 1905.

67. *Putevoditel' po Odesse*, p. 223. See also *Doklad Odesskago birzhevago komiteta* and Herlihy, *Odessa: A History*, pp. 224–225.

68. Skinner, "City Planning in Russia," pp. 335–336 and 339.

69. TsGIA, f. 1284, op. 194, d. 53, 1905, p. 2. See *OOKTM za 1903–1905 gg.*, pp. 198–228 and Levin, "Krizis i bezrabotitsa (Pis'mo iz Odessy)" for discussions of the impact of the Russo-Japanese War on Odessa's economy.

70. Herlihy, *Odessa: A History*, p. 203; *OOKTM za 1903–1905 gg.*, p. 207; *ON*, August 18, 1905.

71. TsGIA, f. 23, op. 29, d. 80, p. 14.

72. Levin, pp. 187–193; *KR*, January 1, 1905 and March 25, 1905; *ON*, January 1, 1905; *Voskhod*, January 22, 1905, pp. 17–18.

73. *OOKTM za 1903–1905 gg.*, pp. 19, 102, 198–199, and *prilozheniia* 1–3.

74. Ibid., pp. 131–165.

75. Skinner, "Trends in Building Practices," p. 155 and "City Planning in Russia," p. 338; Levin, pp. 187–193; *KR*, January 1, 1905 and March 25, 1905; *ON*, January 1, 1905; *Voskhod*, January 16, 1904, p. 31 and January 22, 1905, pp. 17–18.

76. *IO*, June 25, 1905.

2. Workers in Odessa on the Eve of 1905

1. See Appendix for a discussion of the problems involved in determining the size and composition of the Odessa work force.

2. *OOKTM za 1903–1905 gg.*, p. 129; Mikulin, *Fabrichno-zavodskaia i remeslennaia promyshlennost' v 1897 godu*, pp. 23–24; TsGIA, f. 23, op. 30, d. 45, p. 78; Parasun'ko, *Polozhenie i bor'ba rabochego klassa Ukrainy*, p. 91.

3. Borovoi, "Ekonomicheskoe polozhenie trudiashchegosia," p. 192; TsGAOR, f. 102, OO, d. 2409, 1903, pp. 129–130; Zil'berg, *Professional'noe dvizhenie sluzhashchikh farmatsevtov*, p. 5.

4. *OL*, April 12, 1900 and April 25, 1900.

5. *SD*, September 30, 1905, p. 8; *KR*, March 23, 1905, April 1, 1905 and April 29, 1905; Bogomolets, "Fabriki spichek g. Brodskago na Peresypi," p. 127.

6. TsGAOR, f. 102, OO, d. 5, ch. 4, lit. B, 1905, p. 4; *KR*, March 18, 1905.

7. Borovoi, "Polozhenie rabochego klassa Odessy," p. 317.

8. *Vpered,* March 30, 1905, p. 16.

9. In one incident at a cork factory, workers had their wages docked after cutting cork on a defective machine. The fine was all the more vexing since the supervisor had rejected an earlier request by workers to fix the machine. See TsGAOR, f. 102, OO, d. 5, ch. 4, lit. B, p. 4; TsGIA, f. 1405, op. 530, d. 87, p. 6.

10. Gorokhovksaia, "Zhenshchiny v revoliutsionnom dvizhenii 1905," pp. 82–83.

11. *PD,* October 10, 1905; TsGIA, f. 1405, op. 530, d. 110, p. 15; "K 40-letiiu 'Iskry,'" p. 35.

12. Gudvan, *Ocherki po istorii dvizheniia sluzhashchikh v Rossii,* pp. 137–138; "Protokoly zasedanii gorodskoi sanitarnoi komissii," *IOGD,* February 1905, *prilozhenie,* pp. 52–56 and April 1905, p. 950; Skinner, "Odessa and the Problem of Modernization," p. 217; Balaban, p. 37; *OOKTM za 1903–1905 gg.,* pp. 127–129.

13. *Iskra,* December 15, 1903.

14. TsGIA, f. 23, op. 30, d. 45, p. 120.

15. *Iskra,* February 1902; *PI,* May 21, 1903, p. 1. In a strike at a sugar refinery in late 1902, police and Cossacks grabbed striking workers and asked them, "What do you want—do you want to go to jail or to work?" Those who refused to return to work were beaten. TsGIA, f. 1405, op. 530, d. 87, p. 8.

16. TsGAOR, f. 102, OO, d. 4, ch. 10, lit. G, vol. 1, 1898, p. 8.

17. *Iskra,* March 15, 1904.

18. When a 70-year-old worker was fired for failing to bow to the manager of the railway workshops, the aggrieved worker took the matter to court, but the judge ruled against him. Evdomikov, "90-ye gody. Kak my bastovali," p. 64; Aleksandrovskii, "Artel'nye rabochie v g. Odesse," p. 246; TsGAOR, f. 102, OO, d. 5, ch. 4, lit. B, 1905, p. 4.

19. Nesterenko, *Ocherki istorii promyshlennosti,* p. 175. On the drop of real wages, see Mikulin, *Fabrichno-zavodskaia i remeslennaia promyshlennost' v 1897 godu,* pp. 25–26 and *OOKTM za 1903–1905 gg.,* pp. 128–129. See also Borovoi, "Polozhenie rabochego klassa Odessy," p. 316 and "Ekonomicheskoe polozhenie trudiashchegosia naseleniia," pp. 194–195; Reichman, *Railwaymen and Revolution,* pp. 85–86

20. Brodovskii, pp. 39 and 43–45; *Odessa, 1794–1894,* pp. 53, 63–64 and 433–470; Vasil'evskii, *Ocherk sanitarnago polozheniia g. Odessy,* pp. 6–17; *IOGD,* May 1899, pp. 1595–1600; Diatroptov, *Narodnoe zdravie.*

21. *Budushchnost',* April 28, 1900.

22. Skinner, "City Planning in Russia," pp. 318–320 and 322; Vasil'evskii, pp. 6–17; *Obzor sanitarnago sostoianiia g. Odessy,* pp. 13–14 and 25; Bogomolets, "Peresypskoe sanitarnoe popechitel'stvo," *Odessa, 1794–1894,* p. 442; Zuev, "Gorodskoe blagoustroistvo," p. 129; Herlihy, *Odessa: A History,* p. 239.

23. Bogomolets, "Peresypskoe sanitarnoe popechitel'stvo," pp. 1–29.

24. See *Putevoditel' po Odesse,* pp. 36–38, for a description of tram routes.

25. See Lazarovich, "Ekonomicheskie usloviia g. Odessy," p. 6, for Factory Inspectorate data on the number of factory workers in 1893. In 1898 there were twenty-nine joint-stock companies operating in Odessa. Nineteen were owned by Russians; the remainder had been set up by West Europeans, with Belgians controlling eight of these ten firms. See Mikulin, *Fabrichno-zavodskaia i remeslennaia promyshlennost' v 1898 godu,* pp. 11, 22–23 and *prilozhenie* 1, sec. 8.

26. Achkanov, "Nasha rabota v glavnykh zheleznodorozhnykh masterskikh," p. 98.

27. For an analysis of the importance of skill among Russian workers on the eve of 1905, see Bonnell, *Roots of Rebellion,* chap. 1.

28. For a discussion of this issue in its wider European context, see Joan Scott, *The Glassworkers of Carmaux.*

29. *OOKTM za 1903–1905 gg.,* p. 128; Surh, *1905 in St. Petersburg,* p. 24.

30. One exception was the district of Dal'nits, which was composed of settlements

that lay outside city limits but were part of the Odessa *gradonachal'stvo* for administrative purposes. The majority of its inhabitants had been born in Odessa. Summer residences were located in these suburbs and year-round residents raised vegetables, livestock and other food and animal products for sale in the city. The 1897 census recorded slightly over 23,000 residents, almost all of whom were Great and White Russians or Ukrainians who hailed from Odessa. *Perepis'*, pp. 2–3.

31. Ibid., pp. 2–3.

32. Bonnell, *Roots of Rebellion*; Engelstein, *Moscow, 1905*; Surh, *1905 in St. Petersburg.*

33. *Perepis'*, pp. 10–13 (Table 5).

34. Volkov, *Opyt ankety o domashnei zhizni*, p. 17.

35. See *Perepis'*, pp. 2–3.

36. A greater proportion of workshop employees in Odessa belonged to guilds (42 percent) than in either St. Petersburg (28 percent) or Moscow (16 percent). See Bonnell, *Roots of Rebellion*, p. 28 and Table 4, above.

37. *Remeslenniki i remeslennoe upravlenie v Rossii*, p. 23; *Voskhod*, May 31, 1901, pp. 3–5.

38. For the distribution of factory and workshop employees by branch of production in 1903, see *OOKTM za 1903–1905 gg.*, *prilozheniia* 19 and 22.

39. Certain aspects of woodworking, such as furniture making, were still taking place in small workshops, whereas cork manufacturing had already shifted to factories. There were over 1,400 factory workers involved in the making of cork products. By contrast, the Board of Artisanal Trades recorded no journeymen or apprentices engaged in cork production. Nearly 3,000 people were employed in furniture workshops; the Factory Inspectorate recorded only 366 such workers. *OOKTM za 1903–1905 gg.*, *prilozheniia* 19 and 22.

40. "Spravochnye svedeniia po g. Odesse," p. 154.

41. Bradley, *Muzhik and Muscovite*, especially chap. 3.

42. For an excellent discussion of these developments, see the articles by Margolin listed in the bibliography. See also Alymov, "Remeslennye fabriki v Odesskom gradonachal'stve." On similar developments in France, see Christopher Johnson, "Economic Growth and Artisan Discontent: The Tailors' History: 1800–1848."

43. Dargol'ts, "Beglye zametki," p. 116; Oliunina, *Portnovskii promysel*, p. 6. Brodovskii, p. 14, also notes that Odessa was a center for ready-made dresses, whose production depended on a division of labor.

44. Garvi, *Vospominaniia sotsial-demokrata*, p. 80.

45. *Perepis'*, pp. 134–137.

46. *Perepis'*, pp. 98–99; Mikulin, *Fabrichno-zavodskaia i remeslennaia promyshlennost' v 1898 godu*, pp. 13–17; *OOKTM za 1903–1905 gg.*, pp. 127–128 and *prilozhenie* 19.

47. Alymov, "K voprosu o polozhenii truda v remeslennom proizvodstve," p. 20; *Iskra*, October 1901.

48. Alymov, "Remeslennye fabriki v Odesskom gradonachal'stve," sec. 4; Zagoruiko, vol. 2, p. 80.

49. *Iskra*, October 1901; Alymov, "Remeslennye fabriki v Odesskom gradonachal'stve," sec. 7; Margolin, "Usloviia truda v remeslennoi i domashnei promyshlennosti," p. 50; TsGIA, f. 23, op. 30, d. 45, pp. 128–129 and 165–167 and op. 29, d. 78, pp. 135 ob., 143–143 ob. and 178–181; Brodovskii, pp. 14–15; Steklov, *Iz rabochago dvizheniia v Odesse i Nikolaeve*, p. 5; Borovoi, "Ekonomicheskoe polozhenie trudiashchegosia," p. 197.

50. Moskvich, *Illiustirovannyi prakticheskii putevoditel'*, p. 177.

51. Sushkin, *Besvestnye*, p. 3.

52. TsGIA, f. 23, op. 20, d. 1, p. 173; TsGAOR, f. 102, d. 2409, 1903, p. 74 and 4th delopr., d. 84, ch. 12, vol. 12, 1907, p. 279; *Perepis'*, pp. 88–131 and 134–149; Adamov, "Rabochie i moriaki odesskogo porta," p.69; Shternshtein, *Morskie vorota*

Ukrainy, p. 19; Vasil'evskaia, "Polozhenie portovykh rabochikh v Odesse," 37; Tsetterbaum, *Klassovye protivorechiia v evreiskom obshchestve*, p. 27; Vasil'evskii, *Ocherk sanitarnago polozheniia g. Odessy*, p. 6; Subbotin, p. 230.

53. One observer of the Odessa port stated that dockworkers worked an average of 120 days per year. Shelgunov, *Ocherk russkoi zhizni*, p. 470. See also Adamov, p. 70; Vasil'evskaia, p. 44; *Opisanie odesskago porta*, p. 40; Shternshtein, *Morskie vorota Ukrainy*, p. 24.

54. Vasil'evskaia, pp. 41 and 44; *Opisanie odesskago porta*, p. 40; *KR*, October 7, 1905 and October 14, 1905; *IO*, February 12, 1905; *OOKTM za 1906 g.*, p. 31; Brodovskii, p. 13; TsGAOR, f. 102, OO, d. 4, ch. 19, lit. A, 1905, p. 62, 4th delopr., d. 84, ch. 12, vol. 2, 1907, pp 273, 275 and 279, and 4th delopr., d. 84, ch. 12, vol. 3, 1907, pp. 147–147 ob., 224 and 349; *ON*, May 4, 1905 and October 4, 1905; Mel'nikov, *O sostoianii i razvitii tekhnicheskikh proizvodstv na iuge Rossii*, p. 12; Bronshtein, p. 16.

55. TsGAOR, f. 102, OO, d. 4, ch. 10, lit. G, vol. 1, 1898, p. 6; Narkevich, "K voprosu o polozhenii bezdomnykh rabochikh v odesskom portu," pp. 111–113; Shternshtein, *Morskie vorota Ukrainy*, p. 26; *ON*, February 17, 1905; *KR*, March 12, 1905; *Goroda Rossii v 1910 godu*, p. 605.

56. Shelgunov, p. 470; Borovoi, "Ekonomicheskoe polozhenie trudiashchegosia," pp. 200–201.

57. On day laborers in flophouses, see Narkevich, pp. 103–131, Vasil'evskaia, pp. 36–49, and *Otchety rasporiaditel'nago komiteta nochlezhnykh priiutov* for the years 1880–1904.

58. *OL*, December 13, 1885.

59. For descriptions of the appalling conditions, see Vasil'evskaia, pp. 47–48; Lazarovich, "Materialy k voprosu o nochlezhnykh domakh v g. Odessy," pp. 214–217; Narkevich, pp. 104–105; Chivonibar, "Dikari"; *OL*, December 1, 1885; *Odesskii vestnik*, no. 295, November 16, 1892.

60. Karmen, *V rodnom gnezde*, p. iii.

61. *Putevoditel' po Odesse*, p. 219; Erazul'skii, *Organizatsiia meditsinskoi pomoshchi*, p. 3.

62. Chivonibar, "Dikari," p. 46. The lyrics of songs popular among day laborers underscore the importance of drink in their lives. See Tiazheloispytannyi, *Pesni odesskikh bosiakov* and *KR*, February 8, 1905.

63. *OL*, December 1, 1885. See also Narkevich, p. 107.

64. Pershina, "Nachalo rabochego dvizheniia," p. 9; *KR*, February 10, 1905.

65. *KR*, February 6, 1905 and February 8, 1905.

66. Brower, *The Russian City between Tradition and Modernity*, pp. 203–204.

67. *Peterburgskii listok*, June 29, 1905. I thank Joan Neuberger for this reference.

68. *Iuzhnoe obozrenie*, December 2, 1905.

69. TsGIA, f. 23, op. 29, d. 80, p. 23.

70. Subbotin, p. 226; TsGIA, f. 23, op. 29, d. 80, p. 23. Data from later years are unavailable.

71. On Jewish salesclerks, see *Voskhod*, January 16, 1905 and February 12, 1904, p. 8. The 1897 census stated that Jews comprised nearly 60 percent of the workers in the needle trades and over half of those in the printing industry. *Perepis'*, pp. 134–149.

72. The following discussion is heavily based on Mendelsohn, *Class Struggle in the Pale*, pp. 19–23, Kahan, "The Impact of Industrialization in Tsarist Russia on the Socioeconomic Conditions of the Jewish Population," pp. 39–43, and Peled, *Class and Ethnicity in the Pale*, pp. 27–29, 75, 85–87, and 111–118.

73. *IO*, December 2, 1905.

74. Mendelsohn, p. 21.

75. Steklov, *Iz rabochago dvizheniia v Odesse i Nikolaeve*, p. 4; Mendelsohn, p. 21.

76. *Voskhod*, January 16, 1904, p. 31.

77. *KR*, December 9, 1905.
78. Garvi, pp. 127–128.
79. Quoted in Peled, p. 117.
80. Friedgut, *Iuzovka and Revolution*, p. 211.
81. Garvi, p. 127.
82. Herlihy, *Odessa: A History*, p. 276.

3. Labor Organizations and Politics before 1905

1. The following incident illustrates the power that employers and local government officials exerted over these organizations. In the mid-1890s, a delegation of woodworkers presented a charter for a projected mutual-aid society to the Odessa factory inspector who said he would support the petition only if the owners of the woodworking shops were granted control of the governing board. *Rabochee dvizhenie v Odesse (1894–1896 gody)*, p. 21. For a general treatment of mutual aid societies in pre-1905 Russia, see Bonnell, *Roots of Rebellion*, pp. 76–80; Gudvan, *Ocherki po istorii dvizheniia sluzhashchikh v Rossii*, pp. 62–95; Sviatlovskii, *Professional'noe dvizhenie v Rossii* and "Iz istorii kass i obshchestv vzaimopomoshchi rabochikh"; Antoshkin, *Professional'noe dvizhenie v Rossii* and *Ocherk dvizheniia sluzhashchikh v Rossii*; Kolokol'nikov and Rapaport, *1905–1907 gg. v professional'nom dvizhenii*; Kolokol'nikov, *Professional'noe dvizhenie v Rossii*; Grinevich, *Professional'noe dvizhenie rabochikh v Rossii*; Milonov, *Kak voznikli professional'nye soiuzy v Rossii*; Ainzaft, *Pervyi etap professional'nogo dvizheniia v Rossii (1905–1907 gg.)*; Prokopovich, *K rabochemu voprosu v Rossii*.

2. The membership data on sales-clerical organizations do not include Poland, the Baltic region, and Finland. Bonnell, *Roots of Rebellion*, p. 76; Kolokol'nikov and Rapaport, p. 126, *Ocherk za 50 let*, p. 5; *Iuzhno-russkii al'manakh* (1897), p. 183; Prokopovich, pp. 12 and 19; Sviatlovskii, "Iz istorii kass i obshchestv vzaimopomoshchi rabochikh," p. 38 and *Professional'noe dvizhenie v Rossii*, p. 228; *Otchet Odesskago obshchestva vzaimopomoshchi moriakov torgovago flota za 1904–1905 gody*, p. 19; Sh., "Vospominaniia o soiuze kontorshchikov g. Odessy," p. 185.

3. *Iuzhno-russkii al'manakh* (1899), pp. 68–69; *Otchet truzhenikov pechatnago dela*, p. 6.

4. Gudvan, *Prikazchichii vopros*, pp. 55–56.

5. The best work on salesclerks in Odessa is by A. M. Gudvan; the following discussion on the working and living conditions of Odessa salesclerks is based on his works listed in the bibliography. See also the article in *Voskhod*, February 12, 1904, pp. 8–13.

6. The results of the survey can be found in Gudvan, *Prikazchiki v Odesse* and *Prikazchichii vopros*.

7. Karmen, *Zhizn' odesskikh prikazchikov*.

8. For a fuller history of the OMASJS, see *Ocherk za 50 let*, pp. 5–14, *Obzor za 35 let*, pp. 10–11, and *Odesskii vestnik*, June 29, 1863, pp. 317–318.

9. Tarnopol, *Ocherk ego deiatel'nosti*.

10. The Mutual Aid Society of Printers also attracted the most highly skilled and well paid members of the trade: only typesetters, lithographers, engravers, and type-founders could afford the high dues and fees and consequently constituted the bulk of the organization's membership. *Otchet truzhenikov pechatnago dela*, p. 6; *Voskhod*, December 23, 1899.

11. *Ocherk za 50 let*, p. 14.

12. For a general overview of consumer and credit cooperatives, see Kayden and Antsiferov, *The Cooperative Movement in Russia during the War*.

13. *Otchet Odesskago kreditnago tovarishchestva remeslennikov za 1906 g.*

14. Solomonov, "Ocherk razvitiia torgovo-promyshlennykh firm g. Odessy," pp. 267–268.

15. *KR*, February 10, 1905.

16. *KR*, February 27, 1905, March 29, 1905 and April 17, 1905; *IO*, February 27, 1905 and March 25, 1905; *ON*, March 29, 1905; *Remeslennaia gazeta*, no. 18, 1905.

17. *Trudy pervago vserossiiskago s"ezda po remeslennoi promyshlennosti*, vol. 2, p. 296.

18. *Iskra*, February 1901.

19. *Voskhod*, May 17, 1901, pp. 13–14, June 14, 1901, p. 11, January 24, 1902, pp. 16–18, and September 26, 1902, pp. 3–6; *Budushchnost'*, May 12, 1900 and November 2, 1901, p. 865; *KR*, January 29, 1905.

20. *Voskhod*, May 17, 1901, pp. 13–14 and January 24, 1902, pp. 16–17.

21. *Voskhod*, January 24, 1905, p. 18.

22. *Voskhod*, January 16, 1903, p. 23, January 16, 1904, p. 32 and September 5, 1906; *ON*, March 1, 1903.

23. *Voskhod*, February 7, 1902, pp. 1–5, September 19, 1902, pp. 7–11, September 26, 1902, pp. 3–6, and January 16, 1904, p. 32; *Iskra*, February 1901.

24. *Budushchnost'*, December 13, 1902, pp. 994–995; Atlas, "Pervye obshchestva narodnykh universitetov v Odesse," pp. 44–49; *Otchet o deiatel'nosti lektsionnago komiteta*, pp. 16, 45 and 52–57.

25. *Otchet o deiatel'nosti lektsionnago komiteta*, pp. 28, 30 and 45.

26. *Budushchnost'*, December 13, 1902.

27. *Perepis'*, p. xiv.

28. Brower, "Urban Revolution in the Late Russian Empire," p. 343.

29. Lipchenko, "90-ye gody. Probuzhdenie," p. 64.

30. Chemeriskii, "Vospominaniia o 'evreiskoi nezavisimoi rabochei partii'," p. 319.

31. Steklov, *Iz rabochago dvizheniia v Odesse i Nikolaeve*, p. 16.

32. For other accounts of radical and revolutionary activities and labor strife in nineteenth-century Odessa, see Herlihy, *Odessa: A History*, pp. 283–289 and "The Ethnic Composition of the City of Odessa in the Nineteenth Century," p. 59; Borovoi, "Odessa v period promyshlennogo kapitalizma," pp. 70–72; Zagoruiko, vol. 2, 85–86; Adamov, pp. 33–36 and 42; Parasun'ko, pp. 283, 300, 391, and 560–561; and Skinner, "Odessa and the Problem of Urban Modernization," pp. 231–232.

33. The most comprehensive treatment of the South Russian Workers' Union is provided in Itenberg, *"Iuzhnorossiiskii soiuz rabochikh."* See also Pankratova, *Rabochee dvizhenie v Rossii v XIX veke*, 2, pt. 2: 97–163; Venturi, *Roots of Revolution*, pp. 516–517; Skveri, *Pervaia rabochaia sotsialisticheskaia organizatsiia v Odesse (1875 god)*.

34. For a review of revolutionary activity in Odessa from 1875 to 1882, see Pankratova, *Rabochee dvizhenie v Rossii v XIX veke*, 2, pt. 2: 496–502. See also Naimark, *Terrorists and Social Democrats*, pp. 50–53 and 95–96; Zagoruiko, vol. 2: 89–90; Borovoi, "Odessa v period promyshlennogo kapitalizma," pp. 76–77; Pershina, "Nachalo rabochego dvizheniia," pp. 17–20.

35. On contacts between Odessa socialists and Blagoev's organization, see Pershina, "Nachalo rabochego dvizheniia," p. 22.

36. On Gol'dendakh and his activities, see "Pokazaniia D. B. Riazanova"; Polevoi, *Zarozhdenie marksizma v Rossii, 1883–94.*, pp. 477–479; *OPIRKP*, 289–291; TsGAOR, f. 124, op. 6, d. 20, 1897, p. 103 ob.; Naimark, *Terrorists and Social Democrats*, p. 210.

37. Steklov, "Iz vospominanii o sotsial-demokraticheskom dvizhenii," pp. 232–233.

38. Ibid., pp. 234–238 and 248–249.

39. Ibid., p. 249. See Glickman, *Russian Factory Women*, p. 178, for a discussion of women's fears of their husbands' participation in the revolutionary underground.

40. The following discussion on the circles formed by Okol'skii and Boreisha relies heavily on material found in police files preserved in TsGAOR, f. 102, 3rd delopr., d. 856, 1893, pp. 52–98 and 7th delopr., d. 168, 1895.

41. TsGAOR, f. 102, 3rd delopr., d. 856, 1893, p. 59 and 7th delopr., d. 168, 1895, pp. 151 ob. and 155–155 ob.

42. TsGAOR, f. 102, 7th delopr., d. 168, 1895, pp. 120 and 161.

43. The exceptions are Nevskii, who writes that the circles of Okol'skii and Boreisha were of a mixed nature—"half social democratic, half socialist revolutionary"—and V. V. Straten, who states that the circles were "properly called socialist revolutionary but with social democratic coloring." See *OPIRKP*, p. 353; Straten, "'Iuzhno-russkii rabochii soiuz' v Odesse do 1896 goda," p. 193.

44. Naimark, *Terrorists and Social Democrats*, pp. 229–238.

45. TsGAOR, f. 102, 3rd delopr., d. 856, 1893, p. 56 ob. and f. 102, 7th delopr., d. 168, 1895, pp. 64–66 ob. and 68–74 ob.; V. Okol'skii, "Iz epokhi 'mogil'noi tishinoi'," pp. 91–100; B. Okol'skii, "Nesostoiavsheesia pokushenie," pp. 86–94; Konovalov, *Barometr pokazyvaet buriu*, p. 23.

46. Straten, p. 193; Steklov, "Iz vospominanii o sotsial'demokraticheskom dvizhenii," pp. 221–222; Valk, "Pervomaiskie rechi v Odesse v 1895 g.," p. 204.

47. See Valk for the texts of the speeches and information on the May Day events. On the breakup of the South Russian Workers' Union, see Steklov, *Iz rabochago dvizheniia v Odesse i Nikolaeve*, p. 8. Details on the strike fund can be found in TsGAOR, f. 102, 3rd delopr., d. 856, 1893, pp. 52 ob. and 63 and f. 102, 7th delopr., d. 168, 1895, p. 95. ob.

48. Ts. Dargol'ts, p. 119.

49. For discussions of mass agitation, see Mendelsohn, pp. 45–81 and Wildman, *The Making of a Workers' Revolution*, chap. 2.

50. One exception is Mishkinski, "Regional Factors in the Formation of the Jewish Labor Movement in Czarist Russia," pp. 41–42.

51. On the role of Vilna activists in Odessa and the creation of strike funds among Jewish workers, see *OPIRKP*, pp. 515–519, M. Dargol'ts, "Sotsial-demokraticheskaia rabota v gorodakh iuga," p. 103, *Rabochee dvizhenie v Odesse (1894–96 gody)*, and Ts. Dargol'ts, pp. 119–121. Rich material on strike funds and social democratic activity in Odessa during 1895–1897 can be found in TsGAOR, f. 124, op. 6, d. 20, 1897 and op. 7, d. 31, 1898, Pankratova, *Rabochee dvizhenie v Rossii v XIX veke.*, 4, pt. 1: 174–176, and Mel'nik and Filatova, "Sozdanie sotsial-demokraticheskoi organizatsii v Odesse," pp. 32–35.

52. TsGAOR, f. 124, op. 6, d. 20, 1897, pp. 111 ob–120; Konovalov, p. 27; Mel'nik and Filatov, pp. 32–35; Shcherbakov, "Deiatel'nost' revoliutsionnykh sotsial-demokraticheskikh organizatsii Ukrainy," p. 142; Nevskii, *"Iuzhnorusskii rabochii soiuz"*.

53. TsGAOR, f. 124, op. 6, d. 20, 1897, p. 104 ob.

54. *OPIRKP*, pp. 516–517; Mendelsohn, pp. 53 and 64–65; TsGAOR, f. 124, op. 6, d. 20, 1897, pp. 26–27, 29 ob., 33 ob., and 105 ob.–110.

55. Frankel, *Prophecy and Politics*, pp. 196 and 201.

56. Wildman, "Russian and Jewish Social Democracy," p. 84. Frankel, p. 201, seconds Wildman's conclusion when he writes: "For those who left the northwest in order to work in St. Petersburg, Ekaterinoslav, or Odessa, the central element in the Vilna program was seen not as the national concept . . . but the tactic of economic agitation. . . ."

57. Garvi, pp. 30–31 and 47; Mishkinski, p. 41.

58. See, for example, the 1905 letter of a Bolshevik organizer to Lenin in "Perepiska N. Lenina i N. K. Krupskoi s Odesskoi organizatsiei," *PR*, no. 7(42) (1925), p. 35. See also Piatnitskii, *Zapiski bol'shevika*, pp. 76–77.

59. Tobias, *The Jewish Bund in Russia*, 117.

60. One estimate places the number of arrested revolutionaries at 150 in 1895 alone. *Doklad o russkom sotsial'demokraticheskom dvizhenii*, p. 34. See also *OPIRKP*, pp. 353–354 and 517–518; M. Dargol'ts, p. 101.

61. On Trotsky's activities in Odessa and the debate over strategy, see his *My Life*, p. 111, TsGAOR, f. 124, d. 27, ch. 88, 1898, pp. 92–135 ob. and op. 6, d. 20, 1897, pp. 1–135 ob, op. 7, d. 31, 1898, pp. 76 ob–77 ob., 80 ob.–81, 82 ob., and 84 ob.–85, M. Dargol'ts, pp. 104–108, *OPIRKP*, pp. 520–524, Straten, pp. 207 and 210–213,

Weinberg, "Social Democracy and Workers in Odessa," pp. 11–15, Shcherbakov, p. 142, and Ts. Dargol'ts, p. 130.

62. Garvi, pp. 24 and 31.

63. Shapiro, "Iz istorii rabochego dvizheniia," *Professional'naia zhizn'*, no. 30(117) (1924), p. 53.

64. Steklov, *Iz rabochago dvizheniia v Odesse i Nikolaeve*, p. 12.

65. Another assessment of SD activity in Odessa for the years 1898–1900 emphasizes that they had "solid ties" with artisans. *Doklad o russkom sotsial'demokraticheskom dvizhenii*, p. 33; *Iuzhnyi rabochii*, no. 4 (February 1901), pp. 37–38 in Pankratova, *Rabochee dvizhenie v Rossii v XIX veke.*, 4, pt. 2: 635–637. See also the comments by Godlevskii, "Kishinev, Odessa, Nikolaev," no. 2(7) 1924, p. 129.

66. For a more detailed examination of this issue, see Weinberg, "Social Democracy and Workers in Odessa," pp. 16–22.

67. Los', *Pod"em revoliutsionnogo dvizheniia na Ukraine*, p. 272; TsGAOR, f. 102, OO, d. 850, vol. 12, 1901, pp. 40–47 and d. 825, ch. 1, 1901, pp. 62–63 ob., d. 340, 1902, pp. 42, 51–51 ob., 66, 88, and 101–102 ob., and f. 124, op. 11, d. 431, 1902, p. 4; Konovalov, pp. 93–109; Mel'nik, *V. I. Lenin*, pp. 14–24.

68. Novomirskii, "Iz istorii odesskogo podpol'ia," p. 184.

69. TsGAOR, f. 124, op. 10, d. 147, 1901, p. 41 and f. 102, OO, d. 820, vol. 2, 1901, p. 76; Novomirskii, "Iz istorii odesskogo podpol'ia," pp. 194–200; Garvi, pp. 192–197; *Iskra*, March 10, 1902 and August 1, 1902; Lapin, "S.-D. organizatsii Ukrainy i II s"ezd RSDRP," p. 12.

70. TsGAOR, f. 102, OO, d. 5, ch. 19, lit. G, vol. 2, 1898, pp. 11–12 and f. 124, op. 10, d. 149, 1901, pp. 1–2. See also *Iskra*, February 1902; Garvi, pp. 106 and 113–116; TsGAOR, f. 124, op. 10, d. 147, 1901, p. 178 ob. For a more general discussion of the efforts of some Russian SDs to ally with the liberal and radical-democratic opposition, see Zelnik, "Russian Workers and the Revolutionary Movement," pp. 226 and 228, and Wildman, *The Making of a Workers' Revolution*, pp. 213–218.

71. *Iskra*, April 15, 1903.

72. TsGAOR, f. 124, op. 10, d. 147, 1901, pp. 137 and 171–174; Bortnikov, *Iiul'skie dni 1903 g. na iuge Rossii*, p. 34; Degot', *Pod znamenem bol'shevizma*, p. 42; *Iskra*, April 18, 1904; *Perepiska V. I. Lenina i rukovodimykh im uchrezhdenii RSDRP*, 2, bk. 1: 135–136, 239 and 265–266. See also "Perepiska N. Lenina i N. K. Krupskoi s Odesskoi organizatsiei," *PR*, nos. 6(41) (1925), p. 48, 7(42) (1925), p. 24, 11(46) (1925), pp. 37–39, and 12(47) (1925), pp. 25–29; *Vpered*, April 21/7 1905; Shreiber, "Partiinaia rabota v Odesse," p. 141.

73. TsGAOR, f. 124, op. 11, d.. 492, 1902, p. 1, f. 102 OO, d. 5, ch. 19, lit. E, vol. 3, 1898, p. 66 and d. 5, ch. 19, lit. G, vol. 2, 1898, pp. 46 and 60–60 ob.; Fabrichnyi, "Nakanune pervoi revoliutsii," pp. 85–90; Garvi, pp. 107–112; *Iskra*, October 15, 1903; *Rabochee dvizhenie v Rossii v 1901–1904 gg.*, p. 291; Wildman, *The Making of a Workers' Revolution*, pp. 241–245; Schneiderman, *Sergei Zubatov and Revolutionary Marxism*, pp. 295 and 329–330; TsGIA, f. 1405, op. 530, d. 87, p. 233; *Vtoroi S"ezd RSDRP*, pp. 11–12.

74. 1905 Bundist leaflet from Odessa in the B. I. Nicolaevsky Collection, Box 28, Folder 8 at the Hoover Institution Archives. See also Mikhalevich, *Zikhroynes fun a yidishen sotsialist*, 2:133; *Posledniia izvestiia*, January 28/13, 1903, p. 3, April 10/March 28, 1903, p. 3, March 9/February 25, 1904, pp. 1–2, and June 3/May 21, 1904, p. 2; *Piatyi s"ezd Vseobshchago evreiskago rabochago soiuza v Litve, Pol'she i Rossii*, p. 27; *Avtonomiia ili federatsiia*; Gurevich, "Doklady o deiatel'nosti Bunda za 1904–1905 gg.," p. 71 at Bund Archives of the Jewish Labor Movement; *Vopros o predstavitel'stve na mezhdunarodnom sotsialisticheskom kongresse v Amsterdame: Otchet delegatsiia Bunda*, p. 2; Tobias, p. 240; Mishkinski, pp. 27–52; Rafes, *Ocherki istorii evreiskogo rabochego dvizheniia*, pp. 22, 33–35, and 62–63; *Vtoroi s"ezd RSDRP, iiul'–avgust 1903 goda: Protokoly*, pp. 63–64; Konovalov, p. 36.

75. Melancon, "The Socialist Revolutionaries from 1902 to 1907" and "'Stormy Petrels.'"

76. TsGAOR, f. 102, OO, d. 850, vol. 2, 1901, p. 47.

77. *RR*, November 1902, p. 14, February 1, 1903, p. 15, April 1, 1903, p. 11, May 15, 1903, p. 14, June 1, 1903, pp. 16–17 and 22–23, July 1, 1903, pp. 19–20, and January 1, 1904, p. 14; Garvi, pp. 104–105; TsGAOR, f. 102, OO, d. 4, ch. 68, 1898, p. 21 ob. and f. 124, op. 43, d. 2616, 1905, passim; TsGIA, f. 23, op. 30, d. 45, pp. 174–177; TsGIA, f. 1405, op. 530, d. 110, pp. 21–22; "Boevye stranitsy. Odesskie pekari," p. 20; Rice, *Russian Workers and the Socialist-Revolutionary Party through the Revolution of 1905–07*, pp. 47–48.

78. Novomirskii, "Anarkhicheskoe dvizhenie v Odesse," pp. 246–250; Avrich, *The Russian Anarchists*, pp. 61–62, 78, 89, 102–106, and 111; "Ocherk anarkhicheskago dvizheniia v Odesse," *Buntar'*, December 1, 1906, pp. 30–31; *Burevestnik*, November 1907, pp. 10–11; Garvi, p. 105.

79. The most comprehensive work on Zubatovism is Schneiderman, *Sergei Zubatov and Revolutionary Marxism*. See also Bonnell, *The Roots of Rebellion*, pp. 80–86; Engelstein, pp. 59–62, 79–81, 156, 173–174, and 232–233; McDaniel, *Autocracy, Capitalism, and Revolution in Russia*, pp. 64–89.

80. Bukhbinder, "O zubatovshchine," p. 303; Shlosberg and Shul'man, "Vseobshchaia zabastovka v Odesse," p. 115; Schneiderman, pp. 297 and 304; Piontkovskii, "Novoe o zubatovshchine," p. 301; TsGAOR, f. 124, op. 12, d. 546, 1903, p. 124.

81. Chemeriskii, p. 319.

82. Bronevich, "Tiazhelyi put'," p. 53. For two accounts that reach the same conclusion, one from the Odessa city governor, the other from a revolutionary, see TsGAOR, f. 124, op. 12, d. 546, p. 123 ob. and Lepeshinskii, "Ot kruzhkovshchiny k partii," p. 103.

83. A similar state of affairs occurred in Minsk when SDs, in this case the Bund, deemphasized the workers' economic struggle and turned instead to politics, thereby enhancing the appeal of Zubatovism and facilitating their recruitment drives. See Schneiderman, pp. 251–252.

84. Chemeriskii, p. 319.

85. Piontkovskii, p. 301.

86. Schneiderman, pp. 304–305; Chemeriskii, pp. 319–320; Bukhbider, "Nezavisimaia evreiskaia rabochaia partiia," p. 281; TsGAOR, f. 124, op. 12, d. 1546, 1903, pp. 123 ob.–124; TsGIA, f. 1405, op. 530, d. 88, p. 10 and d. 87, p. 187, and f. 23, op. 30, d. 45, p. 208; *Soiuz metallistov*, pp. 12–15; Filinskii, "Za sem' let," p. 158.

87. TsGIA, f. 1405, op. 530, d. 88, p. 10.

88. Schneiderman, p. 298.

89. *Soiuz metallistov v Odesse*, pp. 12–14 and 17–20; Schneiderman, 305–313; TsGIA, f. 23, op. 30, d. 45, pp. 189–223; TsGAOR, f. 102, OO, d. 4, ch. 10, lit. G, vol. 1, 1898, p. 6.

90. TsGIA, f. 23, op. 30, d. 45, pp. 189–223.

91. Schneiderman, pp. 308–309; TsGIA, f. 23, op. 30, d. 45, p. 193 ob.

92. TsGIA, f. 23, op. 30, d. 45, pp. 204 and 208.

93. Piontkovskii, p. 301.

94. See Schneiderman, chaps. 12 and 13, for a detailed account of the general strike.

95. Ibid., p. 314.

96. *Iskra*, August 1903.

97. TsGIA, f. 1405, op. 530, d. 88, p. 154.

98. "Boevye stranitsy," p. 20; Iris, "22 goda bor'by karamel'shchikov," p. 28; Liusternik, "1905 god na tabachnoi fabrike Popova," p. 177; Degot', *Pod znamenem bol'shevizma*, pp. 13, 19 and 50.

99. TsGIA, f. 23, op. 30, d. 45, p. 205.

4. First Stirrings

1. TsGAOR, f. 102, OO, d. 4, ch. 19, lit. A, 1905, pp. 1, 3, 7, 8, and 23, d. 5, ch. 4, lit. A, 1905, pp. 48–50 and 55 and op. 5, d. 975, vol. 2, 1905, p. 23; TsGIA, f. 1328, op. 2, d. 2, pp. 16 and 28 and f. 1405, op. 530, d. 194, p. 49; *IO*, January 13, 1905.

2. Ascher, *The Revolution of 1905*, p. 138.

3. For example, workers in Voronezh did not strike or protest in the aftermath of Bloody Sunday. See Prevo, "Voronezh in 1905," p. 51.

4. TsGAOR, f. 102, OO, op. 5, d. 975, vol. 2, 1905, p. 23 ob. and d. 4, ch. 19, lit. A, 1905, p. 10 ob.; Rogov, "Cherty iz zhizni odesskoi organizatsii bol'shevikov v 1905 godu," pp. 56–57.

5. *VOG*, January 13, 1905; *KR*, January 14, 1905; Dzhervis, "9-oe ianvaria i rabochie massy Odessy," p. 70; *RR*, August 15, 1905, p. 21.

6. Achkanov's assessment seconded one made the year before by an SR who wrote that the war effort dampened the party's appeal to dockworkers during the first months of the hostilities. TsGAOR, f. 102, OO, d. 4, ch. 19, lit. A, 1905, p. 8; *IO*, January 14, 1905; Neizvestnyi, "1905 god v Odesse sredi zheleznodorozhnikov," p. 105; F. Achkanov, "Nasha rabota v glavnykh zheleznodorozhnykh masterskikh," p. 100; *RR*, June 15, 1904, p. 18.

7. TsGAOR, f. 102, OO, d. 1360, 1905, p. 47 ob.

8. Reichman, p. 149.

9. *Iskra*, March 3, 1905; TsGAOR, f. 102, OO, d. 5, ch. 4, lit. Zh, 1905, p. 11 and d. 1350, ch. 30, lit. A, 1905, p. 3; Pankratova, *1905: Stachechnoe dvizhenie*, p. 299.

10. TsGAOR, f. 102, OO, d. 4, ch. 19, lit. A, 1905, p. 18 and d. 5, ch. 4, lit. A, 1905, p. 23.

11. See, for instance, V. Gorelov, "Rabochee dvizhenie Odessy v 1905 godu," p. 15.

12. *VOG*, February 20, 1905.

13. The best accounts of the moderate and liberal opposition movements are Manning, *The Crisis of the Old Order in Russia*, pp. 45–88, Emmons, *The Formation of Political Parties*, chaps. 1 and 2 and "Russia's Banquet Campaign," and Galai, *The Liberation Movement in Russia*.

14. For accounts of the meeting, see *Vpered*, January 14/1, 1905, *PI*, December 15/2, 1904, pp. 1–2, and *Iskra*, December 1, 1904.

15. Emmons, "Russia's Banquet Campaign," p. 63.

16. *Vpered*, January 14/1, 1905; *PI*, December 15/2, 1904, pp. 1–2; *Iskra*, December 1, 1905; Berezhnoi, "Studencheskoe dvizhenie na iuge Ukrainy," pp. 293–294.

17. Emmons, "Russia's Banquet Campaign," p. 63; *Iskra*, December 1, 1904; *PI*, December 15/2, 1904, pp. 1–2.

18. Mebel', *1905 g. na Ukraine*, p. 296; Nekrasov, "Odesskii universitet v 1905 godu," p. 108.

19. TsGAOR, f. 102, OO, op. 5, d. 3, ch. 49, 1905, p. 1; Nekrasov, p. 98.

20. TsGAOR, f. 102, OO, op. 5, d. 3, ch. 49, 1905, p. 5; *Iskra*, February 27, 1905; Mebel', p. 296; Nekrasov, pp. 99–101.

21. TsGAOR, f. 102, OO, op. 5, d. 3, ch. 49, 1905, p. 10; Nekrasov, pp. 100–101; *Iskra*, February 27, 1905; Lysenkov, "E. N. Shchepkin i odesskii universitet (1902–1905)," pp. 28–29; Mebel', p. 302.

22. Nekrasov, pp. 102–103; *Revoliutsionnoe gnezdo*, pp. 5–6, 53, 80, and 97.

23. TsGAOR, f. 102, OO, d. 1350, ch. 30, lit. A, 1905, p. 9 ob.

24. TsGAOR, f. 102, OO, op. 5, d. 975, vol. 2, 1905, pp. 112–113 ob.

25. On other lectures and meetings of professional societies during the early spring, see TsGAOR, f. 102, OO, op. 5, d. 975, vol. 2, 1905, pp. 131, 203, 206–206 ob., and 214 ob.–215 and d. 1350, ch. 30, lit. A, 1905, 1905, pp. 1 ob., 7 ob. and 9 ob., *Iskra,* February 24, 1905, March 6, 1905, April 18, 1905, and April 23, 1905, *Vpered,* February 28/15, 1905, and *IOGD,* April 1905, pp. 1079–1081.

26. *IOGD,* January 1905, p. 151, February 1905, pp. 471–472 and April 1905, p. 898.

27. Bogomolets, "Peresypskoe sanitarnoe popechitel'stvo," passim.

28. Iaroslavskii, "Pervaia polovina 1905 g. v Odesse," p. 13.

29. For information on the ukase and rescript, see Harcave, pp. 36–37.

30. *Rabochii vopros v komissii V. N. Kokovtsova v 1905 g.,* pp. 31–33 and 43–49; TsGAOR, f. 102, OO, d. 4, ch. 19, lit. A, 1905, pp. 43–47; TsGIA, f. 1405, op. 530, d. 194, p. 125; *IO,* April 9, 1905; *Iskra,* April 5, 1905.

31. TsGIA, f. 23, op. 29, d. 80, p. 17.

32. For a general discussion of working and living conditions among pharmacy workers on the eve of 1905, see Sanders, "Drugs and Revolution," pp. 354–358.

33. Zil'berg, pp. 3–6; Sanders, "Drugs and Revolution," p. 354.

34. Sanders, "Drugs and Revolution, p. 361; TsGIA, f. 1328, op. 2, d. 2, p. 93; Mebel', pp. 38–39; Zil'berg, p. 23.

35. TsGAOR, f. 102, OO, d. 4, ch. 19, lit. A, 1905, pp. 22–22 ob., 32–32 ob., 48, 51–52, and 57–60 and d. 5, ch. 4, lit. A, 1905, pp. 41–41 ob.; TsGIA, f. 1328, op. 2, d. 2, p. 189 ob.; Pankratova, *1905: Stachechnoe divizhenie,* pp. 298–299 and 301–302; *Iskra,* February 24, 1905, March 3, 1905 and March 25, 1905; Minovich, "Na odesskikh probochnykh zavodakh," pp. 171–172; Zanchevskii, *Rost proletarskogo samosoznaniia v Odesse,* pp. 4–5; Mebel', pp. 41–44 and 68–69; *ON,* February 17, 1905 and February 21, 1905.

36. Pushkareva, *Zheleznodorozhniki Rossii v burzhuazno-demokraticheskikh revoliutsiiakh,* pp. 94–95.

37. Ibid., pp. 96–98.

38. Sanders, "Lessons from the Periphery," p. 243. See also Reichman, passim and Engelstein, pp. 97–109.

39. *ON,* February 15, 1905.

40. *ON,* February 15, 1905 and February 25, 1905; *IO,* February 16, 1905; Mebel', p. 42; Reichman, pp. 85–89; *PD,* September 22, 1905, p. 4; *Istoriia gorodov i sel,* p. 106.

41. On Raikh, see TsGAOR, f. 102, d. 2409, 1903, pp. 122–126.

42. TsGAOR, f. 102, OO, d. 4, ch. 10, lit. G, vol. 2, 1898, pp. 92–92 ob.; TsGIA, f. 1405, op. 530, d. 88, p. 52.

43. On the nature of the production process, composition of the work force in railway workshops, and pay scales, see Reichman, pp. 58–64 and 78–82. For a general discussion of metalworkers and their special position in Russian industry, see Bonnell, chap. 1 and Hogan, "Labor and Management in Conflict."

44. Reichman, pp. 64 and 85–89.

45. *Istoriia zavodu imeni sichnevoho postannia v Odesi,* p. 62; *KR,* February 10, 1905.

46. *Odesskie glavnye masterskie,* pp. 9–50.

47. TsGIA, f. 1405, op. 530, d. 194, p. 81; TsGAOR, f. 102, OO, d. 5, ch. 4, lit. A, 1905, p. 26.

48. TsGIA, f. 1405, op. 530, d. 194, p. 81; *Istoriia zavodu imeni sichnevoho postannia v Odesi,* p. 65; TsGAOR, f. 102, OO, d. 4, ch. 19, lit. A, 1905, pp. 28 and 34–35. See *ON,* March 10, 1905 and *IO,* March 8, 1905 for newspaper accounts.

49. TsGAOR, f. 102, OO, d. 4, ch. 19, lit. A, 1905, p. 36; Mebel', p. 67.

50. TsGAOR, f. 102, OO, d. 4, ch. 19, lit. A, 1905, pp. 30–30 ob., 34 and 36 ob.

51. Ibid., pp. 30 ob.–31.

52. Another indication that railway workers were now more politically engaged than at the beginning of 1905 was the collection of money for the victims of Bloody Sunday. Although this gesture probably had little real effect, it nonetheless signified a change in the attitude of some Odessa workers toward political events. See *IO*, March 7, 1905 and April 2, 1905.

53. Tim McDaniel, p. 284, writes that "little distinction was made between these two spheres" by workers. See also Surh, *1905 in St. Petersburg*, pp. 58–64, for a first-rate discussion of this matter, as well as Smith, "Workers and Civil Rights in Tsarist Russia, 1899–1917," Edmondson, "Was there a Movement for Civil Rights in Russia in 1905?" and Read, "Labour and Socialism in Tsarist Russia," pp. 177–178.

54. As Diane Koenker and William Rosenberg, *Strikes and Revolution in Russia, 1917*, p. 16, write: "at one level all strikes were (and are) struggles over power, whether inside the factory or out. Hence in one sense, the distinction between political and economic has little meaning."

55. *KR*, March 14, 1905.

56. *KR*, February 27, 1905.

57. On the movement to standardize the workday of salesclerks through petitions, legislation and voluntary compliance, see Gudvan, *Prikazchiki v Odesse*, pp. 47–55 and *Ocherki po istorii dvizheniia sluzhashchikh v Rossii*, pp. 199–226, *Prikazchichii vopros, Trudy pervago s"ezda predstavitelei obshchestv vspomozheniia chastnomu sluzhebnomu trudu*, and *Trudy vtorago s"ezda predstavitelei obshchestv vspomozheniia chastnomu sluzhebnomu trudu*.

58. *KR*, January 13, 1905, January 14, 1905 and March 1, 1905; *ON*, April 30, 1905.

59. *Ocherk za 50 let*, p. 14; Gudvan, *Ocherki po istorii dvizheniia sluzhashchikh v Rossii*, pp. 87–95, 202–204 and 207–208; Lupinskii, "Soiuz prikazchikov Odessy (1905–1907 g.)," pp. 65–67, 76 and 85–90; *Otchet pravleniia Odesskago obshchestva vzaimnago vspomoshchestvovaniia prikazchikov-evreev za 1903*, p. 15.

60. *KR*, January 13, 1905, January 16, 1905 and January 19, 1905.

61. *KR*, January 16, 1905, May 5, 1905 and May 31, 1905.

62. *KR*, January 15, 1905; *Ocherk za 50 let*, p. 15; Lupinskii, p. 74; *ON*, May 21, 1906.

63. *KR*, March 8, 1905 and March 13, 1905.

64. *KR*, March 30, 1905.

65. *KR*, March 6, 1905 and March 11, 1905.

66. *KR*, March 3, 1905, March 8, 1905, March 16, 1905, March 30, 1905, and April 26, 1905. See also the letter from an unemployed salesclerk which stresses that all shop assistants must unite with other workers and struggle to liberate themselves from the "oppression of exploitation" since they, like all proletarians, sell their labor. *KR*, May 25, 1905.

67. *KR*, July 13, 1905, July 17, 1905 and July 31, 1905. Gudvan, *Ocherki po istorii dvizheniia sluzhashchikh v Rossii*, pp. 85–86, makes a similar point.

68. Lupinskii, pp. 65–67, 76 and 85–90; *RR*, May 15, 1905, p. 12; Gudvan, *Ocherki po istorii dvizheniia sluzhashchikh v Rossii*, pp. 202, 204 and 207.

69. Lupinskii, p. 74; Bonnell, *Roots of Rebellion*, p. 161.

70. *IO*, April 10, 1905.

71. *IO*, March 23, 1905.

72. *KR*, March 28, 1905.

73. *Voskhod*, June 2, 1905, p. 20; *Iuzhnye zapiski*, June 12, 1905, pp. 28–30; *IO*, May 3, 1905.

74. *KR*, March 19, 1905. See also *Otchet pravleniia obshchestva vzaimnago vspomozheniia prikazchikov g. Odessy za 1905–1906 gody*, pp. 83–101.

75. *Otchet pravleniia obshchestva vzaimnago vspomozheniia prikazchikov g. Odessy za 1905–1906 gody*, pp. 83–90; *Iuzhnye zapiski*, June 12, 1905.

76. Some confusion exists regarding the organization's name. Some accounts refer to it as a union, while others call it a mutual aid society. The fact that the organization was renamed a "union" in late 1905 suggests that its founders intended it be a mutual aid society. See *IO*, April 23, 1905; *KR*, January 13, 1905, April 21, 1905 and April 22, 1905; *Kontorshchik*, January 5, 1906; *Golos prikazchika*, April 23, 1906, p. 9; *ON*, April 23, 1905.

77. *Golos prikazchika*, April 23, 1906, p. 9.

78. *ON*, April 23, 1905.

79. *Golos prikazchika*, April 23, 1906, pp. 9–10; *IO*, April 20, 1905; *KR*, April 21, 1905 and April 22, 1905; *Kontorshchik*, January 5, 1906; *ON*, April 23, 1905; *Zhizn' prikazchikov*, December 16, 1906.

80. Sviatlovskii, "Iz istorii kass i obshchestv vzaimopomoshchi rabochikh," p. 46. For more discussion, see Weinberg, "The Politicization of Labor in 1905."

81. *IO*, April 23, 1905; *KR*, April 22, 1905.

82. See *Rabochii vopros v komissii V. N. Kokovtsova v 1905 g.*; Ascher, *The Revolution of 1905*, pp. 121–122.

83. TsGIA, f. 1405, op. 530, d. 194, p. 125.

84. TsGAOR, f. 102, OO, d. 5, ch. 4, lit. Zh, 1905, pp. 14–16; TsGIA, f. 1405, op. 530, d. 194, p. 125; *RR*, May 15, 1905, p. 12.

85. TsGIA, f. 95, op. 5, d. 733, pp. 251–251 ob.

86. TsGIA, f. 107, op. 1, d. 1679, pp. 145–145 ob.; TsGAOR, f. 102, OO, d. 4, ch. 19, lit. A, 1905, pp. 63–63 ob.; Mebel', p. 82.

87. TsGAOR, f. 102, OO, d. 4, ch. 19, lit. A, 1905, p. 62 ob.

88. TsGAOR, f. 124, d. 2550, 1905, pp. 1–1 ob. and f. 102, OO, d. 4, ch. 19, lit. A, 1905, pp. 65–65 ob.

89. TsGIA, f. 95, op. 5, d. 733, p. 111 ob. and f. 107, op. 1, d. 1679, pp. 125–125 ob.; TsGAOR, f. 124, d. 2550, 1905, p. 1 ob. and f. 102, OO, d. 4, ch. 19, lit. A, 1905, p. 67.

90. TsGIA, f. 107, op. 1, d. 1679. p. 125 ob.

91. TsGIA, f. 107, op. 1, d. 1679, pp. 125 ob. and 147; TsGAOR, f. 124, d. 2550, 1905, pp. 2–3 and f. 102, OO, d. 4, ch. 19, lit. A, 1905, p. 67.

92. TsGAOR, f. 102, OO, d. 4, ch. 19, lit. A, 1905, pp. 65–65 ob.

93. TsGIA, f. 95, op. 5, d. 733, p. 112 ob.; TsGAOR, f. 124, d. 2550, 1905, p. 4 and f. 102, OO, d. 4, ch. 19, lit. A, 1905, p. 88 ob.

94. The SR newspaper *Revoliutsionnaia Rossiia* (May 15, 1905, p. 12) claimed that SR sailors wrote the demands.

95. TsGIA, f. 95, op. 5, d. 733, pp. 112–113 ob.; *Otchet Odesskago obshchestva vzaimopomoshchi moriakov torgovago flota za 1904–1905 gody*, p. 20; *RR*, May 15, 1905, p. 12.

96. TsGAOR, f. 102, OO, d. 4, ch. 10, lit. G, vol. 2, 1898, p. 93; "Boevye stranitsy," p. 20; *RR*, April 1, 1903, p. 11 and June 1, 1903, pp. 22–23.

97. Journeymen bakers earned 25 rubles a month for workdays that averaged eighteen hours. See *KR*, April 14, 1905 and *RR*, April 1, 1903, p. 11.

98. *Listok bulochnikov i konditerov*, April 15, 1906; Mebel', p. 44; *RR*, April 25, 1905, p. 15 and May 15, 1905, p. 12.

99. On the negotiations and work stoppage, see *ON*, February 24, 1905 and March 1, 1905, TsGAOR, f. 102, OO, d. 4, ch. 19, lit. A, 1905, p. 54, *NPRR*, p. 476, Mebel', pp. 68–69, *IO*, March 24, 1905 and April 5, 1905, and TsGIA, f. 23, op. 17, d. 332, pp. 12–16.

The Bund correspondent reported, "Not one of the local SD organizations had ties with the bakers, and the strike arose without their influence." TsGAOR, f. 102, OO, d. 4, ch. 19, lit. A, 1905, p. 85; *ON*, April 21, 1905; Mebel', pp. 44 and 83–84; *PI*, July 10/June 27, 1905, p. 1.

100. TsGAOR, f. 102, OO, d. 4, ch. 19, lit. A, 1905, pp. 86–87; TsGIA, f. 1405,

op. 530, d. 194, p. 132; *ON*, April 21, 1905; *KR*, April 22, 1905 and April 23, 1905; *IO*, April 22, 1905; *RR*, May 15, 1905, p. 12.

101. *KR*, April 27, 1905; *IO*, April 27, 1905; TsGIA, f. 23, op. 17, d. 332, pp. 12–16; *VOG*, April 23, 1905.

102. *KR*, April 27, 1905, April 29, 1905, April 30, 1905, and May 1, 1905; Mebel', pp. 85–87; *ON*, April 29, 1905.

103. TsGAOR, f. 102, OO, d. 4, ch. 19, lit. A, 1905, pp. 93–95 and d. 5, ch. 4, lit. B, pp. 1–2; Mebel', pp. 86–87; *KR*, April 28, 1905 and April 29, 1905; *ON*, April 27, 1905 and April 29, 1905; *IO*, April 27, 1905.

104. Galili, *The Menshevik Leaders in the Russian Revolution*, pp. 72–73.

105. TsGAOR, f. 102, OO, d. 4, ch. 19, lit. A, 1905, pp. 116–116 ob.

106. Neidhardt was following the lead of former city governor Petr Shuvalov. In his annual report for 1900, Shuvalov suggested that city officials "concern themselves with the improvement of workers' conditions" and provide assistance to workers suffering from unemployment, illness and disability. He also advocated opening a Red Cross hospital for factory workers, a labor exchange, and two bakeries that would sell bread at subsidized low prices. Shuvalov hoped to undercut the appeal of revolutionary propaganda to workers with these measures. See TsGIA, f. 23, op. 30, d. 45, p. 148. On Neidhart's actions, see TsGIA, f. 23, op. 20, d. 1, p. 173 ob., f. 1284, op. 194, d. 53, 1905, pp. 2–2 ob. and op. 24, d. 1230, pp. 78–79; TsGAOR, f. 102, OO, d. 106, ch. 2, 1905, p. 18 ob. and d. 4, ch. 19, lit. A, 1905, pp. 85, 90–92 and 116–116 ob.; *Otchet Odesskoi obshchei remeslennoi upravy za 1902–1904 gg.*, pp. 5–6; Mebel, pp. 84–85; Zanchevskii, p. 7; *KR*, April 30, 1905, May 1, 1905, May 10, 1905, and May 13, 1905; *ON*, April 29, 1905.

5. First Confrontation

1. *ON*, May 1, 1905; *IO*, April 26, 1905 and April 30, 1905.

2. *ON*, May 1, 1905.

3. Ibid.

4. Ibid.

5. The following account is based on material in *Iskra*, 101, June 1, 1905 and "Biulleten' Odesskago Komiteta o stachke po 7 maia," p. 305.

6. These figures undoubtedly understate the actual number of strikes and strikers since available information refers to only work stoppages recorded by the Factory Inspectorate. Accounts of the May strikes and workers' demands are preserved in TsGIA, f. 23, op. 17, d. 332, pp. 18–60 and op. 29, d. 80, pp. 28–127 and TsGAOR, f. 102, OO, d. 4, ch. 19, lit. A, 1905, pp. 100–119. See also *RDVL*, pp. 245–252; *RBNU*, pp. 217–218; Mebel', pp. 106–117.

7. TsGIA, f. 23, op. 29, d. 80, p. 54; TsGAOR, f. 102, OO, d. 4, ch. 19, lit. A, 1905, p. 99; Shklovskii, "Vospominaniia ob Odesse 1905 goda," p. 258; Subda, "Zabastovka 1905 g. na zavode I. I. Gena v Odesse," p. 158.

8. Perrot, *Workers on Strike*, p. 16.

9. TsGAOR, f. 102, OO, d. 4, ch. 19, lit. A, 1905, pp. 104–105; TsGIA, f. 107, op. 1, d. 1679, pp. 151–155 and f. 23, op. 29, d. 80, pp. 28–127 and op. 17, d. 332, pp. 18–60; Pankratova, *1905: Stachechnoe dvizhenie*, p. 315; *ON*, May 14, 1905; Mebel', pp. 106–117; *RDVL*, pp. 249–250, 460–461n. 152 and 462n. 158.

10. TsGAOR, f. 102, OO, d. 4, ch. 19, lit. A, 1905, p. 188; Dzhervis, "K istorii professional'nogo dvizheniia v Odesse," p. 27; *SD*, June 24, 1905, p. 5.

11. *KR*, May 25, 1905; Mebel', p. 113.

12. *ON*, May 22, 1905.

13. Buzhor and Bereshchagina, *Imeni 50-letiia Sovetskoi Ukrainy*, p. 41; "Biulleten' odesskago komiteta o stachke po 10 maia," p. 307; *KR*, May 12, 1905, May 19, 1905

and May, 20, 1905; TsGAOR, f. 102, OO, d. 4, ch. 19, lit. A, 1905, p. 105; *IO,* May 11, 1905; *ON,* May 11, 1905 and May 15, 1905.

14. TsGAOR, f. 124, d. 2552, 1905, p. 1 and f. 102, OO, d. 4, ch. 19, lit. A, 1905, pp. 114, 116 ob. and 117; *Proletarii,* June 3/May 21, 1905, p. 5; *KR,* May 12, 1905 and May 22, 1905; *IO,* May 11, 1905; *ON,* May 11, 1905; *Khronika,* p. 38.

15. TsGAOR, f. 102, OO, d. 4, ch. 19, lit. A, 1905, pp. 116–116 ob. and d. 5, ch. 4, lit. B., 1905, p. 13; *KR,* April 30, 1905, May 1, 1905, May 10, 1905, and May 13, 1905; "Biulleten' odesskago komiteta o stachke po 10 maia," p. 307; *ON,* April 29, 1905; Pankratova, *1905: Stachechnoe dvizhenie,* p. 310; *VOG,* May 4, 1905.

16. "Biulleten' odesskago komiteta o stachke po 10 maia," pp. 306–307; "Biulleten' odesskago komiteta o stachke po 7 maia," pp. 302–305; Dzhervis, "Professional'noe dvizhenie v Odesse v 1905 godu," p. 254; Khain, "Etapy bor'by mukomolov," p. 23; Bronevich, "Tiazhelyi put'," p. 54; *Proletarii,* June 3/May 21, 1905, p. 16 and July 3/June 20, 1905, p. 16; Subda, p. 158; *SD,* April–May 1905, p. 11; TsGAOR, f. 102, OO, d. 4, ch. 19, lit. A, 1905, pp. 99, 102, 106, and 109 ob.

17. *RBNU,* p. 232; Minovich, "Na odesskikh probochnykh zavodakh," pp. 171–172.

18. *PI,* 240, July 10/June 27, 1905, p. 1. *RR,* August 15, 1905, p. 21 and September 1, 1905, p. 16.

19. Novomirskii, "Iz istorii odesskogo podpol'ia," p. 250.

20. Degot', *Pod znamenem bol'shevizma,* p. 14. See also the comments in Shreiber, "Partiinaia rabota v Odesse," pp. 137 and 141.

21. *PI,* July 10/June 27, 1905, pp. 1–2.

22. See the comments of Rogov, p. 57; Shapovalov, *V podpol'e,* p. 133; Avdeev, "Vosstanie na bronenostse 'Potemkin'," p. 196; *Iskra,* June 1, 1905; Pershina, *Imeni ianvarskogo vosstaniia,* p. 35, and Vorobei and Kovbasiuk, "Odesskaia bol'shevistskaia organizatsiia v gody pervoi russkoi revoliutsii," p. 62.

23. "Perepiska N. Lenina i N. K. Krupskoi," no. 11(46), pp. 9–10; Gusev, "Odessa v 1905 godu," p. 167.

24. On the state of affairs among the SDs, especially their relations with workers and the strike movement, see Novomirskii, "Iz istorii odesskogo podpol'ia," p. 250, "Biulleten' odesskago komiteta o stachke po 7 maia," "Biulleten' odesskago komiteta o stachke po 10 maia," "Perepiska N. Lenina i N. K. Krupskoi," nos. 6(41) and 7(42), Shklovskii, pp. 258–259, Shapovalov, pp. 123–133, Mebel', p. 318, Shreiber, pp. 137, 140–141 and 144, Pankratova, *1905: Stachechnoe dvizhenie,* pp. 307–308, *Iskra,* May 15, 1905 and June 1, 1905, *Proletarii,* July 10/June 27, 1905, p. 10, *PI,* July 10/June 27, 1905, pp. 1–2 and July 25/12, 1905, p. 3, Avdeev, p. 196, Subda, p. 163, Berezovskii, *Odinnadtsat' dnei na Potemkine,* p. 69, and Degot', *Pod znamenem bol'shevizma,* pp. 19 and 40–41.

25. *PI,* July 10/June 27, 1905, p. 1; *Iskra,* June 1, 1905; Mebel', pp. 106 and 109–112; Nevskii, "Rabochee dvizhenie v ianvarskie dni," pp. 17–18; Pankratova, *1905: Stachechnoe dvizhenie,* p. 307; *Proletarii,* June 9/May 27, 1905, p. 13 and July 3/June 20, 1905, p. 16.

26. *PI,* July 10/June 27, 1905, pp. 1–2.

27. The police substantiated this conclusion, reporting that, despite the efforts of SDs to stir up the workers, "the revolutionary organizations did not play a direct role in the strikes." Revolutionary parties, according to the police, were not prepared organizationally or financially to assist striking workers due to factional squabbles and police harassment. See TsGAOR, f. 102, OO, d. 4, chl. 19, lit. A, 1905, pp. 106 and 109 ob.–110.

28. TsGIA, f. 23, op. 29, d. 80.

29. TsGIA, f. 23, op. 29, d. 80, pp. 28–127 and d. 78, p. 49 and op. 17, d. 332, pp. 18–60; "Biulleten' odesskago komiteta o stachke po 7 maia," p. 305; Bronevich, p. 55. See also *Kommercheskaia Rossiia* for the second half of May.

30. TsGAOR, f. 102, OO, d. 4, ch. 19, lit. A, 1905, p. 119 ob. and f. 124, d. 2550, p. 5; *ON,* June 2, 1905 and June 12, 1905; *Soiuz metallistov v Odesse,* p. 29.

31. *KR,* May 13, 1905.

32. *ON,* June 2, 1905; TsGAOR, f. 102, OO, d. 4, ch. 19, lit. A, 1905, pp. 119–119 ob. and f. 124, d. 2550, p. 5.

33. TsGAOR, f. 102, OO, op. 5, d. 975, vol. 1, 1905, p. 111 ob. and d. 4, ch. 19, lit. A, 1905, pp. 119–119 ob; *KR,* May 24, June 1, 1905 and June 3, 1905; *ON,* May 29, 1905 and June 4, 1905; *IO,* June 1, 1905; Almazov, *Nasha revoliutsiia,* pp. 379–381; *Iskra,* July 1, 1905.

34. *IOGD,* May 1905, pp. 1250–1255; *IO,* June 12, 1905; *Obzor deiatel'nosti gorodskoi vrachebno-sanitarnoi organizatsii v Odesse za 1905 god,* p. 30; Vel'shtein, "Stachki rabochikh na Peresypi," pp. 626–631.

35. *Soiuz metallistov v Odesse,* p. 26.

36. *ON,* June 2, 1905; Subda, pp. 161–162; *Revoliutsiia 1905–1907 rokiv na Ukraini,* p. 110; *PD,* August 15, 1905.

37. *Khronika,* pp. 41–42; TsGAOR, f. 102, OO, op. 5, d. 975, vol. 1, p. 111 ob.; Avdeev, p. 197.

38. Sources differ regarding the date of this incident and the number of workers arrested. With the exception of Berezovskii, who says the arrests occurred on June 10, all other accounts date the incident on June 8. Although archival sources state that thirty-three persons were arrested, Mebel' reports only thirty arrests. *Iskra,* July 1, 1905; Berezovskii, p. 69; Subda, pp. 161–162; Mebel', p. 144; TsGAOR, f. 102, OO, op. 5, d. 975, vol. 1, 1905, pp. 111 ob.–112.

39. *RR,* August 15, 1905, pp. 21–24 and September 1, 1905, pp. 16–18.

40. TsGAOR, f. 102, OO, op. 5, d. 975, vol. 1, 1905, p. 112; Avdeev, pp. 197–198; *Iskra,* July 15, 1905.

41. TsGAOR, f. 102, OO, op. 5, d. 975, vol. 1, 1905, pp. 112–113 and d. 4, ch. 19, lit. A, 1905, pp. 121–124.

42. Subda, pp. 156–157 and 164–165; *Revoliutsiia 1905–1907 rokiv na Ukraini,* pp. 112–113.

43. *Revoliutsiia 1905–1907 rokiv na Ukraini,* pp. 112–114; TsGAOR, f. 124, d. 3115, 1905, pp. 29–30.

44. *Revoliutsiia 1905–1907 rokiv na Ukraini,* pp. 113–114; TsGAOR, f. 124, d. 3115, 1905, pp. 29–29 ob.; *ON,* June 16, 1905; *Iuzhnye zapiski,* June 19, 1905.

45. *KR,* June 14, 1905.

46. TsGAOR, f. 124, d. 3115, 1905, p. 31 and f. 102, 7th delopr., d. 3769, 1905, p. 21.

47. TsGAOR, f. 124, d. 3115, 1905, pp. 2, 30, 43 ob., and 121 and f. 102, OO, d. 4, ch. 19, lit. A, 1905, pp. 131 ob. and 135 and d. 108, ch. 2, 1905, p. 102; *Revoliutsiia 1905–1907 rokiv na Ukraini,* pp. 111–112; *PI,* July 4/June 21, 1905, p. 3.

48. TsGAOR, f. 124, d. 3115, 1905, pp. 30 and 110; Almazov, pp. 388–389; *Iskra,* July 1, 1905; *Proletarii,* July 10/June 27, 1905, p. 10; *PI,* July 17/4, 1905, pp. 2–3 and August 2/July 20, 1905, p. 6.

49. TsGAOR, f. 124, d. 3115, 1905, pp. 6A ob., 30–32, 40 ob., and 110, f. 102, 7th delopr., d. 3769, 1905, pp. 21 and 23 ob. and OO, d. 1350, ch. 30, lit. A, 1905, p. 17; TsGIA, f. 23, op. 29, d. 80, pp. 67–68; Berezovskii, pp. 76–80; Subda, p. 162; *Khronika,* p. 46; *RDVL,* p. 463n. 161; *Iuzhnye zapiski,* June 19, 1905; Pankratova, *1905: Stachechnoe dvizhenie,* pp. 317 and 319–320; *PI,* July 25/12, 1905, p. 4; Mebel', p. 147.

50. TsGAOR, f. 124, d. 3115, 1905, pp. 3, 14, 30, 32 ob., 40 ob.–42, 44, 47, 52–54, 89–90, 96–109, 119, and 121–122 and f. 102, OO, d. 1350, ch. 30, lit. A, 1905, pp. 17–18 and 24; *Iskra,* 103, June 21, 1905 and July 1, 1905; *PI,* July 17/4, 1905, pp. 1–2 and July 25/July 12, 1905, p. 4; *PD,* August 15, 1905; Pankratova,

1905: Stachechnoe dvizhenie, pp. 317–318; Novomirskii, "Iz istorii odesskogo podpol'ia," p. 252; Almazov, pp. 387–390; *RDVL,* pp. 258–259, 268–269 and 463n. 162; *RBNU,* pp. 228–230; "Iiunskie dni v Odesse," pp. 30–31.

51. The Bundist account in *Posledniia izvestiia* held that the Bolsheviks considered a general strike inopportune because the workers were unarmed; the pro-Menshevik *Iskra* correspondent stated that Bolsehviks urged workers to prepare for an armed uprising but not to engage in open protest, since "the appointed day of revolution had not yet arrived." Pankratova, *1905: Stachechnoe dvizhenie,* p. 330; Gerasimov, *Krasnyi bronenosets,* p. 38; "Iiunskie dni v Odesse," pp. 33–35; Shapovalov, p. 139; *PD,* August 15, 1905; *PI,* July 17/4, 1905, p. 1 and July 25/12, 1905, p. 4; Hertz, "Di ershte russlender revolutsie," p. 211; *Proletarii,* July 10/June 24, 1905, pp. 10 and 19 and August 29/16, 1905, pp. 17–18; *Iskra,* June 21, 1905 and July 15, 1905; *SD,* July 7, 1905, p. 6; Avdeev, p. 199; Konovalov, pp. 216–217.

52. TsGIA, f. 1101, op. 1, d. 1033, p. 1 ob.; Berezovskii, p. 81; *PD,* August 15, 1905; *RR,* August 15, 1905, pp. 22–24.

53. For a general discussion, see Bushnell, *Mutiny amid Repression,* pp. 61–65 and Ascher, *The Revolution of 1905,* pp. 170–174. See also Weinberg, "Worker Organizations and Politics," p. 230n. 62 for bibliographic information.

54. TsGAOR, f. 102, OO, d. 106, ch. 2, 1905, p. 43.

55. *Iskra,* July 1, 1905.

56. TsGAOR, f. 124, d. 3115, pp. 3A–4A ob., 5–6 and 33 ob. and f. 102, 7th delopr., d. 3769, 1905, p. 3 ob.; Berezovskii, p. 95; TsGVIA, f. 400, op. 3, d. 2639, 1905, p. 75; Inozemtsev, "Bronenosets 'Kn. Potemkin Tavricheskii' v Odesse," p. 77; *Iskra,* June 21, 1905; *PI,* July 25/12, 1905, p. 5.

57. TsGAOR, f. 102, 7th delopr., d. 3769, 1905, p. 9 and OO, d. 106, ch. 2, pp. 50–51; TsGIA, f. 1101, op. 1, d. 1033, pp. 2 ob.–4 ob.; TsGVIA, f. 400, op. 15, 16th otd., d. 2641, 1905, pp. 15–17 and op. 3, d. 2639, 1905, p. 19; Inozemtsev, pp. 77–78.

58. TsGVIA, f. 400, op. 15, 16th otd., d. 2641, 1905, pp. 17–17 ob.; TsGIA, f. 1101, op. 1, d. 1033, p. 4; Inozemtsev, pp. 78–80 and 93.

59. TsGAOR, f. 102, 2nd delopr., d. 41, ch. 3, 1905, pp. 18–22 and 46; TsGIA, f. 1329, op. 1, d. 966, p. 54; *Proletarii,* no. 7, July 19/June 27, 1905, p. 10; Inozemtsev, p. 83.

60. Avdeev, p. 203.

61. Grishin, *Uroki "Potemkina"*; Berezovskii, pp. 97–131; Genkin, *Vosstanie na bronenostse,* pp. 17–18; Avdeev, pp. 203–205; Rostotskaia, *Potemkinskie dni v Odesse,* pp. 26–27; Egorov, "'Potemkin Tavricheskii' i 1905 god," pp. 10–11; *Proletarii,* July 10/June 27, 1905, pp. 11–12 and August 29/15, 1905, pp. 12–14; *Iskra,* July 15, 1905; Shapovalov, p. 140; "Perepiska N. Lenina i N. K. Krupskoi," no. 12(47), p. 12.

62. Platonov, *Vosstanie v chernomorskom flote,* p. 5. See also the evaluations of Rostotskaia, p. 8, Nevskii, *Sovety i vooruzhennoe vosstanie v 1905 godu,* p. 181, Grishin, p. 28, Shreiber, pp. 143–144, Vorobei and Kovbasiuk, p. 67, and Shapovalov, pp. 140–160. Shapovalov writes that the SDs spent too much time engaged in "fruitless discussions," such as debating whether the Bund should be called simply the "Bund" or the "General Jewish Workers' Union".

63. Rogov, p. 63.

64. TsGIA, f. 1101, op. 1, d. 1033, p. 3 ob.–4; TsGAOR, f. 102, OO, d. 106, ch. 2, 1905, p. 50 ob. and 124, d. 3115, 1905, pp. 10, 64–65, 68, and 93; Osipovich, "V grozovye gody," pp. 57–58; *RDVL,* p. 465n. 173; Mebel', p. 49.

65. TsGAOR, f. 102, OO, d. 106, ch. 2, 1905, p. 15 ob.; TsGIA, f. 1101, op. 1, d. 1033, p. 4; TsGVIA, f. 400, op. 3, d. 2639, 1905, p. 14; *Proletarii,* July 10/June 27, 1905, p. 12; *Iskra,* June 21, 1905, July 1, 1905 and July 15, 1905; *PI,* July 17/4, 1905, p. 3; "Perepiska N. Lenina i N. K. Krupskoi," nos. 11(46) p. 28 and 12(47) p. 13; Genkin, p. 19; Avdeev, pp. 205–206; *OL,* July 2, 1905; Inozemtsev, p. 93; *Revoliutsiia 1905–1907 rokiv na ukraini,* p. 121; Mebel', p. 147; *RR,* July 1, 1905, p.

14; Kuzminskii Report, pp. cxlvii and cl; Ovsiannikov, "Revoliutsionnoe dvizhenie v voiskakh kievskogo i odesskogo voennykh okrugov," p. 202.

66. K. Gorelov, "Iiunskie dni v portu," p. 135.

67. In one right-wing account, the *bosiaki* participated in the plundering, but the author blames revolutionaries for starting the fire. See Lender, *Potrevozhnaia Rossiia*, pp. 211–212. Some accounts suggest that the police, with the help of right-wing extremists such as the Black Hundreds, deliberately put crates of vodka at the port in order to encourage drunkenness and trigger a pogrom, while others even assert that the police were responsible for setting the fires. While the best evidence and common sense do not warrant such a conclusion—for example the warehouses were already full of liquor—officials did not permit fire brigades to respond promptly to the fire, possibly because it was too dangerous to try to extinguish the blaze. On the destruction of the port and accusations of police involvement, see TsGIA, f. 1101, op. 1, d. 1033, pp. 4 ob.–5, TsGVIA, f. 400, op. 15, 16th otd., d. 2641, 1905, pp. 17–18 and op. 3, d. 2639, 1905, p. 75, TsGAOR, f. 124, d. 3115, 1905, p. 33 ob., *Iskra*, June 21, 1905 and July 15, 1905, Osipovich, "Novye materialy o pozhare," pp. 218 and 226–227, Inozemtsev, p. 95, *Proletarii*, July 10/June 27, 1905, p. 12, *PI*, July 17/4, 1905, p. 3 and July 25/12, 1905, p. 5, Avdeev, pp. 205–206, Genkin, p. 19, *RR*, July 1, 1905, p. 14, and F. Achkanov, "Pervye etapy revoliutsii piatogo goda v Odesse," p. 55.

68. Inozemtsev, pp. 81 and 94–95; TsGAOR, f. 124, d. 3115, 1905, pp. 64–65; Kuzminskii Report, pp. cx–cxii.

69. The number of fatalities ranges from the low of ten, given in one official count, to the more reasonable but perhaps too high 2,000. Port authorities stated that approximately 1,200 perished in the fire. Given the intensity of the fire and shooting, the concentration of people in the port, and the tendency of Odessa officials to underestimate the number of victims in other incidents of unrest, I am inclined to accept as reasonable a larger body count, that is, approximately 1,000 casualties. Bushnell, p. 62; TsGAOR, f. 102, OO, d. 106, ch. 2, 1905, pp. 43–43 ob., f. 102, 7th delopr., d. 3769, 1905, pp. 16 and 79, f. 102, OO, d. 1350, ch. 30, lit. A, 1905, p. 24, and f. 124, d. 3115, 1905, pp. 52 and 64; TsGIA, f. 1101, op. 1, d. 1033, pp. 5–5 ob.; TsGVIA, f. 400, op. 15, 16th otd., d. 2641, 1905, p. 18 ob. and op. 3, d. 2639, 1905, pp. 76–76 ob.; Avdeev, p. 206; "Iiunskie dni v Odesse," p. 41; *RBNU*, p. 245; *Iskra*, July 15, 1905; Inozemtsev, pp. 81–82 and 93–94; Ia. Shternshtein, *Morskie vorota Ukrainy*, p. 36; Kuzminskii Report, p. cxi.

70. TsGAOR, f. 124, d. 3115, 1905, pp. 6A ob., 17 and 67 ob. and f. 102, OO, d. 106, ch. 2, 1905, p. 51; TsGIA, f. 1101, op. 1, d. 1033, p. 7; "Iiunskie dni v Odesse," pp. 47–48; Sher, "Pokhorony Vakulenchuka," pp. 88–89; *RDVL*, pp. 264 and 466nn. 174–176; Inozemtsev, p.84; *Iskra*, July 1, 1905.

71. Berezovskii, p. 130; Ovsiannikov, p. 202; Sher, pp. 89–90; TsGIA, f. 23, d. 45, 1898–1905, pp. 343–345; TsGAOR, f. 124, d. 3115, 1905, p. 2A and f. 102, OO, d. 106, ch. 2, 1905, p. 51; "Iiunskie dni v Odesse," pp. 47–48; Egorov, pp. 10–11; "Krasnyi flot," in *Iskra*, July 15, 1905.

72. TsGAOR, f. 102, OO, d. 4, ch. 19, lit. A, 1905, p. 163, d. 106, ch. 2, 1905, pp. 80–82, 7th delopr., d. 3769, 1905, p. 64, op. 5, d. 975, vol. 1, p. 115 ob. and f. 124, d. 3115, 1905, pp. 19–27; *Khronika*, pp. 50 and 55–56; Harcave, p. 157; Inozemtsev, pp. 85–90; *Iuzhnye zapiski*, June 26, 1905; *ON*, June 28, 1905.

73. TsGAOR, f. 124, d. 3115, 1905, pp. 80 and 85.

74. TsGAOR, f. 102, 7th delopr., d. 3769, 1905, p. 120 and OO, d. 4, ch. 19, lit. A, 1905, pp. 164–181; *KR*, June 21, 1905 and July 1, 1905; *ON*, June 22, 1905, June 26, 1905 and June 28, 1905; Filinskii, "Za sem' let," p. 159; *Pechatnyi vestnik*, July 24, 1905.

75. *VOG*, March 1, 1905; *Voskhod*, February 5, 1904, pp. 26–27, March 17, 1904, pp. 25–26 and January 22, 1905, p. 20; *PI*, December 3/November 20, 1903, p. 4,

December 17/4, 1903, pp. 2–3, April 6/March 24, 1904, p. 1, and June 3/May 21, 1905, pp. 1 and 6; *Iskra*, February 10, 1904, May 1, 1904 and March 10, 1905; Mebel', p. 303; TsGIA, f. 1284, op. 194, d. 69, pp. 2–2 ob., d. 53, 1905, p. 5 and f. 1405, op. 530, d. 110, pp. 60–61 ob.

76. The National Committee of Self-Defense first appeared in 1904, along with the self-defense group called "An Eye for An Eye" and others set up by the Zionists and revolutionaries. TsGAOR, f. 124, op. 43, d. 298, 1905, pp. 1–2 and f. 102, OO, d. 5, ch. 4, lit. B, pp. 3 ob., 5 and 7–8 ob.; Kuzminskii Report, p. 102; *PI*, May 5/April 22, 1904, p. 1, March 11/February 26, 1905, p. 6 and July 10/June 24, 1905, p. 1; *KhEZ*, April 10, 1905, p. 24 and May 8, 1905, pp. 25–27; *Iskra*, May 15, 1905; Hertz, p. 74; Mebel', p. 83; *VOG*, April 28, 1905.

77. *PI*, July 17/4, 1905, p. 2 and July 25/12, 1905, pp. 4–5; *Iskra*, July 1, 1905; TsGAOR, f. 102, OO, d. 106, ch. 2, 1905, p. 50 ob.; *RR*, July 1, 1905, p. 14; *Proletarii*, July 10/June 27, 1905, p. 12 and July 3/June 20, 1905, p. 11.

78. *Odesskie dni* can be found in the Bakhmeteff Archive at Columbia University.

79. See *Otvet na odesskie dni i g.g. Odessity* (also in the Bakhmeteff Archive) for one attempt to refute *Odesskie dni*.

80. Among those government officials who believed Jews were responsible for the disorders was the British Consul in Odessa, who wrote: "All persons implicated in bomb crimes and in attempts on the lives of the police are Jews." Quoted in Hough, *The Potemkin Mutiny*, p. 100. One exception was Levchenko, procurator of the Odessa circuit court. He wrote that the disorders were due to hostility harbored by "a significant portion of the Odessa populace" toward the police and government. TsGAOR, f. 102, 7th delopr., d. 3769, 1905, pp. 16 ob. and 24 and f. 124, d. 3115, p. 80; TsGIA, f. 1101, op. 1, d. 1033, p. 4.

81. Ascher, *The Revolution of 1905*, p. 139.

82. Degot', "Odesskie pechatniki v revoliutsionnom dvizhenii," p. 237.

83. *KR*, May 18, 1905.

84. TsGIA, f. 23, op. 29, d. 80.

85. Charles Tilly, Louise Tilly, and Richard Tilly, *The Rebellious Century, 1830–1930*, pp. 248–249.

6. Breathing Spell and Renewed Confrontation

1. Ascher, p. 138.

2. Avdeev, "Vosstanie na bronenostse 'Potemkine'," p. 206, places the damage at 50 million rubles, but others estimate much less. See TsGAOR, f. 102, OO, d. 106, ch. 2, 1905, pp. 43 ob. and 67–67 ob.

3. *ON*, June 21, 1905.

4. *VOG*, September 20, 1905.

5. *IO*, June 26, 1905; *KR*, August 13, 1905.

6. *IO*, June 26, 1905 and July 23, 1905; *KR*, July 3, 1905; *ON*, July 20, 1905; *OOG za 1905 g.*, pp. 3–4; *OOKTM za 1903–1905 gg.*, p. 14.

7. *KR*, August 20, 1905, August 25, 1905, September 8, 1905, September 10, 1905, and September 14, 1905.

8. *KR*, July 9, 1905 and July 13, 1905; *OL*, July 8, 1905 and July 24, 1905; *ON*, September 22, 1905; *IO*, June 25, 1905.

9. TsGAOR, f. 102, 2nd delopr., d. 41, ch. 3, 1905, pp. 60, 62–63 and 67–68.

10. *PD*, October 10, 1905; TsGAOR, f. 102, OO, d. 4, ch. 19, lit. A, 1905, pp. 188–188 ob.; *Proletarii*, August 16/3, 1905, pp. 10–11; *KR*, August 8, 1905; *ON*, July 21, 1905.

11. TsGAOR, f. 124, d. 3115, 1905, pp. 80–81.

12. TsGAOR, f. 102, OO, d. 4, ch. 19, lit. A, 1905, p. 190.

13. TsGAOR, f. 102, 7th delopr., d. 2, ch. 37, 1904, p. 123. Kakhanov's report can also be found in TsGAOR, f. 102, 2nd delopr., d. 41, ch. 3, 1905, p. 65 ob.

14. TsGAOR, f. 102, 2nd delopr., d. 41, ch. 3, 1905, pp. 87 and 89–90.

15. TsGAOR, f. 102, 2nd delopr., d. 41, ch. 3, 1905, pp. 46, 66 ob., 91 ob.–92 ob., 95–96 ob., and 102, OO, d. 4, ch. 19, lit. A, 1905, p. 190, and OO, d. 106, ch. 2, 1905, pp. 52–52 ob.; Kuzminskii Report, pp. 45–46 and 88. For a general discussion of the statutes governing martial law, see Pipes, *Russia under the Old Regime*, pp. 306–307.

16. TsGAOR, f. 102, OO, d. 106, ch. 2, 1905, pp. 81–81 ob. and 83 and f. 102, 2nd delopr., d. 41, ch. 3, p. 66 ob.; *KR*, August 2, 1905; *PI*, September 8/August 26, 1905, p. 6; *Khronika*, p. 71; *VOG* for July and August.

17. TsGAOR, f. 102, OO, op. 5, d. 975, vol. 3, pp. 101–101 ob.; Mebel', pp. 332–33.

18. *Proletarii*, October 17/4, 1905, pp. 24–25. For similar accounts by other SDs, see *Proletarii*, August 16/3, 1905, p. 10, August 29/16, 1905, pp. 17–18, and October 24/11, 1905, p. 18, Gusev, "Odesskaia partorganizatsiia 1905 g. posle 'Potemkina'," pp. 9–12 and 47, *Perepiska V. I. Lenina i rukovodimykh im zagranichnykh partiinykh organov*, pp. 714, 743, 745–746, and 757, and *PI*, September 8/August 26, 1905, p. 6.

19. TsGIA, f. 1405, op. 530, d. 195, p. 80; Mebel', p. 333; *KR*, July 26, 1905; *VOG*, July 24, 1905.

20. TsGAOR, f. 102, OO, d. 4, ch. 19, lit. A, p. 196 ob.

21. Walkouts occurred among some salesclerks, tailors, masons, jewelers, dockworkers, tramway conductors, carpenters, railway workers, and shoemakers. TsGAOR, f. 102, OO, d. 4, ch. 19, lit. A, 1905, pp. 191, 192–192 ob., 196, and 205; *Khronika*, pp. 68, 70 and 78; Zanchevskii, pp. 11–12; Mebel', pp. 170, 184–185 and 198; Lupinskii, p. 67; *PI*, October 30/17, 1905, pp. 11–12.

22. TsGAOR, f. 102, OO, d. 4, ch. 19, lit. A, 1905, p. 198 ob.

23. *KR*, July 3, 1905 and July 5, 1905; *Proletarii*, August 26/19, 1905, p. 18; *Pechatnyi vestnik*, no. 4, July 24, 1905.

24. *KR*, July 3, 1905 and July 5, 1905; *ON*, July 6, 1905.

25. Mebel', pp. 197–198; TsGAOR, f. 102, OO, d. 4, ch. 19, lit. A, 1905, pp. 200–200 ob. On the efforts of the employees of the Russian Steam Navigation and Trading Company to win permission to elect deputies, see *KR*, July 22, 1905. Workers of the South West Railroad also demanded the establishment of a workers' commission to manage the fund of 400,000 rubles that had been deducted from their pay checks as contributions to the war effort. They suspected the railway's management of pilfering some of the money. See *OL*, August 30, 1905; *IO*, August 11, 1905.

26. TsGIA, f. 95, op. 5, d. 733, pp. 253–263 and op. 5, d. 734; Ivanov, "Bor'ba moriakov torgovogo flota Odessy v 1905–1906 gg.," pp. 185–187; *IO*, July 17, 1905 and September 16, 1905; Gusev, *Vodniki v professional'nom dvizhenii*, pp. 36–40; Mebel', p. 186.

27. TsGAOR, f. 102, OO, d. 824, 1906, pp. 2 ob. and 74 ob.; *ON*, October 9, 1905; *IO*, August 6, 1905; *Khronika*, p. 79.

28. Kuzminskii Report, p. cxviii; TsGAOR, f. 124, op. 49, d. 294, 1911, p. 4.

29. Nekrasov, pp. 105–109; TsGAOR, f. 124, op. 49, d. 294, 1911, pp. 190–191.

30. TsGAOR, f. 102, OO, op. 5, d. 3, ch. 49, 1905, pp. 99 ob. and 152 ob.; Nekrasov, p. 107; *Revoliutsionnoe gnezdo*, p. 15; *ON*, October 5, 1905 and October 6, 1905.

31. TsGAOR, f. 102, OO, op. 5, d. 3, ch. 49, 1905, p. 152; Kuzminskii Report, p. cxviii.

32. TsGAOR, f. 124, op. 49, d. 294, 1911, p. 17 ob.

33. TsGAOR, f. 102, OO, op. 5, d. 3, ch. 49, 1905, pp. 21 and 52; *ON*, October 11, 1905.

34. *Iuzhnye zapiski*, September 25, 1905; TsGIA, f. 733, op. 153, d. 160, p. 13; *KR*, September 21, 1905; Nekrasov, p. 111.

35. TsGAOR, f. 102, OO, op. 5, d. 3, ch. 49, 1905, p. 42.

36. *ON*, October 5, 1905; TsGAOR, f. 102, OO, op. 5, d. 3, ch. 49, 1905, pp. 36 ob.–37 ob.

37. TsGAOR, f. 102, OO, op. 5, d. 3, ch. 49, 1905, pp. 43–43 ob. and 100 ob.; *Mebel'*, pp. 339–340.

38. TsGAOR, f. 102, OO, op. 5, d. 3, ch. 49, 1905, pp. 46–47.

39. TsGAOR, f. 102, OO, op. 5, d. 975, vol. 3, 1905, p. 200 ob.; op. 5, d. 1877, ch. 6, 1905, pp. 13–13 ob.; op. 5, d. 3, ch. 49, 1905, pp. 44 and 101 ob.–102.

40. TsGAOR, f. 102, OO, op. 5, d. 3, ch. 49, 1905, p. 45.

41. TsGIA, f. 733, op. 153, d. 160, pp. 15–16; TsGAOR, f. 102, OO, op. 5, d. 3, ch. 49, 1905, pp. 102–105 and 7th delopr., d. 2, ch. 37, 1904, p. 167; *ON*, October 5, 1905, October 6, 1905, October 7, 1905, and October 8, 1905; *KR*, October 4 and October 5, 1905; *IO*, October 7, 1905 and October 8, 1905; *Voskhod*, October 13, 1905, pp. 19–20.

42. TsGAOR, f. 124, op. 49, d. 294, 1911, p. 207.

43. TsGAOR, f. 102, OO, op. 5, d. 3, ch. 49, 1905, pp. 52–52 ob. and 106, d. 5, ch. 4, lit. Zh, 1905, pp. 64–65 and d. 1350, ch. 30, lit. A, 1905, p. 29.; *ON*, October 11, 1905; *IO*, October 11, 1905.

44. For accounts of the railway strike, see TsGIA, f. 1405, op. 530, d. 193, pp. 99–100 and 102–102 ob., TsGAOR, f. 102, OO, d. 4, ch. 19, lit. A, 1905, p. 205 ob., op. 5, d. 3, ch. 49, 1905, p. 108, and d. 2555, 1905, pp. 289–289 ob., 293 and 296, *KR*, October 14, 1905 and October 15, 1905, *OL*, October 15, 1905, *IO*, October 13, 1905, October 14, 1905 and October 15, 1905, *ON*, October 13, 1905, October 14, 1905 and October 15, 1905, Lender, *Potrevozhnaia Rossiia*, pp. 220–221, Neizvestnyi, pp. 111–115, *Khronika*, p. 84, *RBNU*, pp. 408–409, and *Revoliutsiia 1905–1907 rokiv na Ukraini*, pp. 226–227.

45. TsGAOR, f. 102, OO, d. 4, ch. 19, lit. A, p. 205 ob. and d. 2555, 1905, p. 289 ob.; *KR*, October 15, 1905; *OL*, October 15, 1905; Neizvestnyi, pp. 113–115.

46. TsGAOR, f. 102, OO, op. 5, d. 3, ch. 49, 1905, pp. 108 ob.–109.

47. TsGAOR, f. 102, OO, op. 5, d. 3, ch. 49, 1905, pp. 109 ob.–110 ob., op. 5, d. 3, ch. 56, 1905, p. 4 and d. 1350, ch. 30, lit. A, 1905, pp. 82–82 ob.; Neizvestnyi, p. 114; *ON*, October 15, 1905.

48. Early reports that two students had been killed were apparently false, since later accounts do not mention any deaths. Bobrov and Kuzminskii stated that the students were only injured. TsGAOR, f. 102, OO, op. 5, d. 3, ch. 49, 1905, pp. 110–110 ob.; Kuzminskii Report, pp. cxx–cxxi, 131–135 and 142–143. See TsGAOR, f. 102, OO, d. 1350, ch. 30, lit. A, 1905, p. 55 and op. 5, d. 3, ch. 56, 1905, p. 4 for reports on the deaths.

49. *Proletarii*, November 7/October 25, 1905, p. 2; TsGAOR, f. 102, OO, op. 5, d. 3, ch. 49, 1905, pp. 52 ob., 56 and 111; Kuzminskii Report, p. cxx; *Revoliutsionnoe gnezdo*, p. 15.

50. TsGAOR, f. 102, OO, op. 5, d. 3, ch. 49, 1905, pp. 111–111 ob.; Kuzminskii Report, p. cxxii; *Revoliutsionnoe gnezdo*, pp. 15–16; *ON*, October 15, 1905.

51. TsGAOR, f. 102, OO, op. 5, d. 3, ch. 49, 1905, p. 117.

52. TsGAOR, f. 102, OO, op. 5, d. 3, ch. 49, 1905, p. 58; Kuzminskii Report, pp. 143 and 164; Neizvestnyi, p. 114; Zanchevskii, p. 12; *ON*, October 15, 1905 and October 26, 1905; *IO*, October 15, 1905 and October 26, 1905; Mezhberg, *Zhovtnevi podii 1905 r. v Odesi*, p. 16; *KR*, October 14, 1905.

53. TsGAOR, f. 102, OO, op. 5, d. 3, ch. 49, 1905, pp. 112 ob.–118; Kuzminskii

Report, pp. 141 and 163; *Revoliutsiia 1905–1907 rokiv na Ukraini,* pp. 227–228; *Revoliutsionnoe gnezdo,* pp. 16, 116–117, and 144.

54. TsGAOR, f. 102, OO, op. 5, c. 3, ch. 49, 1905, pp. 113–114 and 116–117 ob.

55. Ibid., pp. 115–118. One report did state that clashes resulting in injuries and deaths did occur on October 15. See *Proletarii,* November 7/October 25, 1905, pp. 6–7.

56. Kuzminskii Report, p. 182; see also p. 50.

57. The precise dating of Neidhardt's order for the removal of ammunition from gun stores is unclear. In a report to the Ministry of Internal Affairs, dated October 25, Neidhardt stated that he issued the order on the evening of October 15. In later reports he stated that he gave the command on October 16. Other evidence reveals that Neidhardt gave the order on October 15. TsGAOR, f. 102, OO, d. 1350, ch. 30, lit. A, 1905, pp. 32 and 82 ob.; Kuzminskii Report, pp. cxxiii, 163, 195, and 201.

58. TsGAOR, f. 102, OO, d. 1350, ch. 30, lit. A, 1905, pp. 54 and 82 ob. and op. 5, d. 3, ch. 49, 1905, pp. 57 and 119 ob.; Kuzminskii Report, pp. cxxii–cxxiii, 144 and 195.

59. TsGAOR, f. 102, OO, op. 5, d. 3, ch. 49, 1905, pp. 62 and 119 ob.; Kuzminskii Report, pp. cxxiv, 53 and 144; *Novaia zhizn',* October 29, 1905.

60. TsGAOR, f. 102, OO, op. 5, d. 3, ch. 49, 1905, pp. 57 and 120, and d. 1350, ch. 30, lit. A, 1905, pp. 39A ob.–39 ob. and 83; Kuzminskii Report, pp. 50–56, 76–81, 145–147, 165, 176, 183–184, and 196; *RBNU,* pp. 409–410; Kurts, "Oktiabr' 1905 goda," pp. 229–230; Frenk, "Voennaia organizatsiia pri ob"edinennom komitete RSDRP v Odesse v 1905–06 gg." p. 78.

61. TsGAOR, f. 102, OO, d. 1350, ch. 30, lit. A, 1905, pp. 35 and 40; Kuzminskii Report, pp. cxxiv–cxxv, 50–56, 107, 145–147, and 183.

62. TsGAOR, f. 102, OO, op. 5, d. 3, ch. 49, 1905, p. 63; Kuzminskii Report, pp. 55 and 196.

63. Kuzminskii Report, p. 196.

64. *Revoliutsionnoe gnezdo,* pp. 16–18 and 83; TsGAOR, f. 124, op. 49, d. 294, 1911, p. 56; TsGIA, f. 733, op. 153, d. 160, pp. 55–56; Kuzminskii Report, p. 125.

65. TsGAOR, f. 102, OO, d. 1350, ch. 30, lit. A, 1905, pp. 82 ob.–83 and op. 5, d. 3, ch. 49, 1905, p. 153 and f. 124, op. 49, d. 294, 1911, pp. 56–61; Kuzminskii Report, pp. cxxv, 107 and 166; *Revoliutsionnoe gnezdo,* pp. 25–26 and 98; *Golos farmatsevta,* no. 1 (1906), pp. 9–10.

66. Kuzminskii Report, p. 184.

67. TsGAOR, f. 124, op. 49, d. 294, 1911, p. 160 ob.; *Revoliutsionnoe gnezdo,* p. 16.

68. Kuzminskii Report, p. 184.

69. Ibid., pp. cxxvii–cxxviii.

70. Kuzminskii Report, pp. cxxv–cxxvii and cxxix; Kurts, p. 231; *IOGD,* February 1905, pp. 310–311.

71. TsGAOR, f. 102, OO, d. 1350, ch. 30, lit. A, 1905, pp. 36, 40 and 42 ob. and op. 5, d. 3, ch. 49, 1905, pp. 63 and 123; TsGIA, f. 1405, op. 530, d. 193, pp. 96 ob.–97; Kuzminskii Report, p. 58: *RBNU,* p. 410.

72. TsGAOR, f. 102, OO, d. 1350, ch. 30, lit. A, 1905, p. 40; Kuzminskii Report, pp. cxxviii–cxxix; *Revoliutsionnoe gnezdo,* p. 16.

73. TsGAOR, f. 102, OO, d. 3, ch. 49, 1905, p. 122; Kuzminskii Report, p. cxxxii.

74. *IOGD,* February 1906, pp. 310–311; Kuzminskii Report, pp. cxxxiii, clxxvii and 148.

75. TsGAOR, f. 102, OO, op. 5, d. 3, ch. 49, 1905, p. 63 and d. 1350, ch. 30, lit. A, 1905, p. 36.

76. Kuzminskii Report, pp. 184 and 196.

77. Lender, *Potrevozhnaia Rossiia,* p. 231.

78. Kuzminskii Report, p. 97.
79. *Collier's,* December 9, 1905, p. 13.
80. The incident about the dogs is disputed in Linden, *Die Judenpogrome in Russland,* 2: 115.
81. TsGAOR, f. 102, op. 5, d. 3, ch. 49, 1905, pp. 122–122 ob.; Kuzminskii Report, pp. cxxxii–cxxxiii, 116–117, 148–149, and 166–167; *Revoliutsionnoe gnezdo,* p. 231.
82. Kuzminskii Report, pp. cxxxvi and 185.
83. TsGAOR, f. 102, OO, d. 1350, ch. 30, lit. A, 1905, pp. 42–42 ob. and op. 5, d. 3, ch. 49, 1905, p. 64; Kuzminskii Report, pp. cxxxvi–cxxxvii, ccvi, 156, 168, and 186–187; *Revoliutsionnoe gnezdo,* pp. 134–135.
84. Piatnitskii, *Memoirs of a Bolshevik,* pp. 84–85; TsGAOR, f. 102, OO, d. 1350, ch. 30, lit. A, 1905, pp. 42, 45 ob. and 83, op. 233, d. 1350, ch. 30, 1905, pp. 60–61 and op. 5, d. 3, ch. 49, 1905, pp. 63 ob. and 123 ob.–124, and f. 124, op. 49, d. 294, 1911, pp. 36–36 ob. and 165–165 ob.; Kuzminskii Report, pp. cxlii, cxxxiv–cxxxv, cxlv, clxi, 110–111, 126, 138–139, 186, 196, and 198; Tanin, "Partzhizn' Odessy v oktiabre–dekabre 1905 goda," p. 151; *Revoliutsionnoe gnezdo,* p. 83 and 134; Gusev, "Odessa v 1905 g." pp. 171–172; Srednev, *Odesskii konvent v oktiabr'skie dni 1905 g.,* p. 24.
85. *IOGD,* October 1905, pp. 2334–2335, November 1905, pp. 2607–2610 and February 1906, pp. 312 and 316–318; TsGAOR, f. 124, op. 49, d. 294, 1911, pp. 167–167 ob. and f. 102, OO, op. 5, d. 3, ch. 49, 1905, p. 119; Kuzminskii Report, pp. cxxix, cxxxviii, cxliv–cxlvi, clxii, cxlvi, ccxi, and 173–175; *OL,* October 25, 1905; *IO,* October 25, 1905.
86. TsGAOR, f. 102, OO, d. 1350, ch. 30, lit. A, 1905, p. 45 ob.; Kuzminskii Report, pp. 126, 168, 177–180, and 198.
87. Kuzminskii Report, p. 126.

7. Politics and Pogrom

1. Treatments of the late 1905 pogroms can be found in Lambroza, "The Pogrom Movement in Russia, 1903–1906," Maevskii, "Obshchaia kartina dvizheniia," pp. 96–104, Linden, *Die Judenpogrome in Russland,* 2 vols., Löwe, *Antisemitismus und reaktionäre Utopie,* pp. 87–103, Thompson and Mehlinger, *Count Witte and the Tsarist Government in the 1905 Revolution,* pp. 57–65, Wynn, *Russian Labor in Revolution and Reaction,* chap. 7, and the Archives of the Alliance Israélite Universelle.
2. On these and other estimates of casualties and property damage, see Linden, vol. 2, 130, *Voskhod,* November 11, 1905, p. 16, Kuzminskii Report, pp. clxvi–clxvii and 201, Witte, *Vospominaniia,* vol. 3, p. 615, Vinaver, "La situation à Odessa," and Obninskii, *Polgoda russkoi revoliutsii,* p. 44.
3. This viewpoint is developed more fully in Rogger, "The Jewish Policy of Late Tsarism: A Reappraisal," p. 33.
4. *Collier's,* November 18, 1905, p. 14.
5. See, for example, Greenberg, *The Jews in Russia,* vol. 2, pp. 76–78.
6. TsGAOR, f. 102, OO, d. 1350, ch. 30, lit. A, 1905, p. 42 ob.; Kuzminskii Report, pp. cxlvii, 104, 151, and 187–188; *IOGD,* February 1906, p. 312.
7. On the large number of dockworkers, day laborers, and vagrants in the procession, see Lender, "Revoliutsionnye buri na iuge," p. 894, Kuzminskii Report, pp. cxlvii–cxlviii, cl, 119, 128, and 158, *KR,* November 25, 1905, and Semenov, "Evreiskie pogromy v Odesse i Odesshchine v 1905 g.," pp. 119–120.
8. Kuzminskii Report, p. 105.
9. Kuzminskii Report, pp. cxlvi–cl, 39, 47, 105, 111, 129, 185, and 188; TsGVIA, f. 400, 16th otd., op. 15, d. 2641, 1905, pp. 35–35 ob.; TsGAOR, f. 102, OO, op. 5, d. 3, ch. 49, 1905, pp. 59 and 64 ob., op. 233, d. 1350, ch. 30, 1905, pp. 60 ob.–61 and d. 1350, ch. 30, lit. A, 1905, p. 47; *KhEZ,* November 11, 1905, p. 19.

10. Kuzminskii Report, pp. 129 and 158; Shapovalov, p. 122; TsGAOR, f. 102, OO, op. 233, d. 1350, ch. 30, 1905, pp. 60 ob.–61.

11. See the reports of Kaul'bars and the head of the Odessa *Okhrana.* TsGVIA, f. 400, 16th otd., op. 15, d. 2641, 1905, p. 35 ob.; TsGAOR, f. 102, OO, op. 5, d. 3, ch. 49, 1905, p. 125 ob. and f. 124, op. 49, d. 294, 1911, p. 58 ob.; Kuzminskii Report, pp. cl–cli, 152–153 and 170–171; *Odesskii pogrom i samooborona,* pp. 46–47.

12. For this incident and other atrocities, see Semenov, pp. 115–135, Hurvits, *Der blutiger pogrom in Odessa,* Malavich, *Odesser pogrom, KhEZ,* October 28, 1905, pp. 11–14 and November 11, 1905, p. 20, *Voskhod,* October 27, 1905, p. 29, November 11, 1905, pp. 16–29 and February 9, 1906, pp. 14–15, and *Odesskii pogrom i samooborona.*

13. *Odesskii pogrom i samooborona,* pp. 36–38.

14. TsGAOR, f. 102, 7th delopr., d. 7195, 1905, p. 32 and f. 124, op. 49, d. 294, 1911, pp. 56 and 74–76; Kuzminskii Report, pp. cxli–cxlii and 130; Malavich; Hurvits; *Odesskii pogrom i samooborona,* pp. 49–62; *Revoliutsionnoe gnezdo,* pp. 57–58 and 83; Neizvestnyi, pp. 116–117; Gusev, "Odesskaia partorganizatsiia 1905 g. posle 'Potemkina'," p. 51; G. Achkanov, "Odesskie rabochie v 1905 g.," p. 48; A. M. Shternshtein, "V. I. Lenin i bol'shevistkaia organizatsiia Odessy v 1905 godu," p. 105.

15. "1906 g. Nekotorye statisticheskie dannye o boevykh otriadakh pri mestnykh organizatsiiakh bunda vremeni ego 7-go s"ezda," Bund Archives of the Jewish Labor Movement; TsGAOR, f. 124, op. 49, d. 294, 1911, pp. 10, 36–36 ob., 58–61, 72–72 ob., 78–79, and 165–167 ob.; G. Achkanov, "Vospominaniia o revoliutsii 1905 goda," p. 199; Maleev, *Odessa v 1905 godu,* p. 41; *Golos farmatsevta,* no. 1 (1906), p. 10; Nekrasov, pp. 115–116; *Proletarii,* November 16/3, 1905, p. 11; Kuzminskii Report, pp. 104–105, 107 and 118–119.

16. TsGAOR, f. 124, op. 49, d. 294, 1911, pp. 165–165 ob. and 170–172 ob.

17. *Doklad Internatsional'nomu sotsialisticheskomu kongressu v Amsterdame,* p. 7; Gusev, "Odesskaia partorganizatsiia 1905 g. posle 'Potemkina'," p. 51; Osipovich, "V grozovye gody," pp. 67–68; Hertz, p. 460; *Odesskii pogrom i samooborona,* pp. 42 and 55–62; G. Achkanov, "Odesskie rabochie v 1905 g.," p. 48 and "Vospominaniia o revoliutsii 1905 g.," pp. 199–201; Tanin, p. 152; Shternshtein, "V. I. Lenin i bol'shevistkaia organizatsiia Odessy v 1905 godu," p. 109; Pleskov, "V revoliutsionnom podpol'e," pp. 69–70 and "V Odesse posle 'Potemkina'," pp. 79–80; Lambroza, "The Pogrom Movement in Russia, 1903–1906," pp. 287–288; TsGAOR, f. 124, op. 49, d. 294, 1911, pp. 192–192 ob.

18. Aronson, *Troubled Waters,* pp. 82–83.

19. Kuzminskii Report, pp. cliii–clvi, 4, 10, 112, 115, and 137; Osipovich, "V grozovye gody," p. 66; TsGVIA, f. 400, 16th otd., op. 15, d. 2641, 1905, p. 38; Semenov, pp. 118 and 123; TsGAOR, f. 102, OO, d. 2540, 1905, p. 94; Forre, "Vospominaniia sestry miloserdiia ob oktiabr'skikh dniakh," pp. 233–234; *Odesskii pogrom i samooborona,* pp. 64–65; *Collier's,* December 9, 1905, p. 13.

20. TsGAOR, f. 102, OO, op. 5, d. 3, ch. 49, 1905, pp. 65–65 ob.

21. TsGAOR, f. 102, OO, d. 2540, 1905, p. 90, d. 1350, ch. 30, lit. A, 1905, p. 85 and op. 5, d. 3, ch. 49, 1905, p. 65; TsGVIA, f. 400, 16th otd., op. 15, d. 2641, 1905, p. 35 ob.; *Pravitel'stvennyi vestnik,* November 12, 1905; Kuzminskii Report, pp. cxciv and 191; *OL,* December 21, 1905; *VOG,* October 21, 1905.

22. TsGAOR, f. 124, op. 49, d. 294, 1911, p. 58 ob.

23. Rogger, "The Jewish Policy of Late Tsarism"; Löwe, *Antisemitismus und reaktionäre Utopie,* pp. 87–103.

24. *The Memoirs of Sergei Witte,* pp. 473–474.

25. *ON,* November 2, 1905, November 16, 1905 and November 17, 1905; *Voskhod,* December 1, 1905, p. 39 and December 30, 1905, pp. 25–27; Greenberg, vol. 2, pp. 76–88; *KhEZ,* November 11, 1905, pp. 19–20 and 22 and December 23, 1905, p. 44; Kuzminskii Report, pp. cxlv, clxi and clxxi; G. Achkanov, "Vospominaniia o revoliutsii

1905 goda," p. 198 and "Odesskie rabochie v 1905 godu," pp. 47–48; Nekrasov, p. 114; Zanchevskii, pp. 13–14; Semenov, p. 130; *Odesskii pogrom i samooborona*, p. 19; Maevskii, pp. 96–104; *IOGD*, March 1906, p. 768.

26. In 1906, Neidhardt was appointed governor of Nizhnii Novgorod, but his appointment was cancelled after local residents registered their protest in a petition campaign. But because Nicholas II liked Odessa's former city governor, under whom he served as a battalion commander in the Preobrazhensky Guards before becoming tsar, Neidhardt was soon appointed to the Senate. Fallows, "The Zemstvo and the Bureaucracy, 1890–1914," pp. 186 and 231n. 25; *The Memoirs of Count Witte*, p. 684.

27. Kuzminskii Report, pp. cxlviii–cxlix, clxxi and 3–4.

28. Ibid., pp. 100–101. An American correspondent reported recognizing "a police inspector in plain clothes" engaged in "Jew-baiting." *Collier's*, December 9, 1905, p. 13.

29. Kuzminskii Report, pp. cliii–cliv and 112; *KhEZ*, November 11, 1905, p. 22.

30. *KhEZ*, November 11, 1905, p. 22; G. Achkanov, "Vospominaniia o revoliutsii 1905 goda," pp. 199–200; Semenov, pp. 116–117.

31. Aronson, *Troubled Waters*, p. 144.

32. Kuzminskii Report, pp. 3–4, 39, 47, and 189–190; *VOG*, October 19, 1905.

33. See NPRR, pp. 474–475.

34. TsGIA, f. 23, op. 20, d. 1, p. 174 and f. 1284, op. 194, d. 53, 1905, pp. 3 ob. and 5–5 ob.; TsGAOR, f. 102, OO, d. 106, ch. 2, 1905, pp. 17–17 ob. and 19.

35. *VOG*, March 1, 1905; *Voskhod*, February 5, 1904, pp. 26–27, March 17, 1904, pp. 25–26 and January 22, 1905, p. 20; *PI*, December 3/November 20, 1903, p. 4, December 17/4, 1903, pp. 2–3, April 6/March 24, 1904, p. 1, and June 3/May 21, 1904, pp. 1 and 6; *Iskra*, February 10, 1904, May 1, 1904 and March 10, 1905; Mebel', p. 303; TsGIA, f. 1284, op. 194, d. 69, pp. 2–2 ob., d. 53, 1905, p. 5 and f. 1405, op. 530, d. 110, pp. 60–61 ob.

36. Dimanshtein, "Ocherk revoliutsionnogo dvizheniia sredi evreiskikh mass," p. 171.

37. During the pogrom Neidhardt reportedly said that he removed the police at the request of Professor Shchepkin, who promised that the student militia would maintain order. Kuzminskii Report, pp. cxxxviii, cxli, cxliii, clxxv–clxxvii, clxxxviii–clxxxix, cxcv–cxcvi, 7, 40, 42, 121, 128–130, 170, 172, 182–183, 185–186, and passim; TsGAOR, f. 124, op. 49, d. 294, 1911, pp. 81 ob. and 167–167 ob.

38. Kuzminskii Report, pp. cxxxviii–cxl, clxxiv–clxxvii, clxxxix–cxc, cxcvi–cci, 6–13, 18–22, 40–44, 120–121, 169–170, and 177. See also TsGAOR, f. 124, op. 49, d. 294, 1911, p. 81 ob.

39. Kuzminskii Report, pp. 123 and 156–157.

40. Kuzminskii Report, p. 155.

41. TsGIA, f. 23, op. 20, d. 1, p. 174; Kuzminskii Report, pp. cxlv–clxvi, 69–71, 74, 128, and 186; Herlihy, *Odessa: A History*, p. 290; *VOG*, October 25, 1905.

42. "Kaul'bars," *ES*, pp. 768–769; "Kaul'bars," *Novyi entsiklopedicheskii slovar'*, pp. 304–305; "Kaul'bars," *The Modern Encyclopedia of Russian and Soviet History*, pp. 72–73.

43. TsGVIA, f. 400, 16 otd., op. 15, d. 2641, 1905, p. 38.

44. Kuzminskii Report, pp. 175–176 and 190.

45. Robbins, *The Tsar's Viceroys*, pp. 196–197. See also Fuller, *Civil-Military Conflict in Imperial Russia*, pp. 77–81.

46. TsGAOR, f. 102, OO, d. 1350, ch. 30, lit. A, 1905, p. 71; TsGVIA, f. 400, 16th otd., op. 15, d. 2641, 1905, p. 37; Semenov, pp. 125 and 130; Kuzminskii Report, pp. clvi–clix, clxi–clxii, clxxix, clxxxi, cci, 9–12, 27, 31, 39, 43–44, 47, 68, 82–90, 115, 123–124, 175–176, 189–192, and passim.

47. Kuzminskii Report, pp. 43–44.

48. Kuzminskii Report, pp. clxv and 123–125; Fuller, p. 211; Vinaver.

49. For the views of Neidhardt, Kuzubov and Bobrov, see TsGAOR, f. 102, OO, op. 5, d. 3, ch. 49, 1905, pp. 66 ob. and 124 ob., and Kuzminskii Report, p. 17.

50. One notable dissenting view was offered by the Archbishop of Odessa and Kherson. In a leaflet distributed on October 22, he wrote that the pogrom was "a disgrace and embarrassment" for a city that considers itself "European." Although the Archbishop believed that Russians had the right to defend the tsar's honor, he nonetheless condemned pogromist actions as not only illegal and disorderly but also as misdirected, since not all Jews are enemies merely because they are "nonbelievers." Moreover, he stressed that existing evidence does not permit precise determination of who fired first on October 19, the celebrants of the Manifesto or the patriotic processionists. See *Vossvanie k Khristianam goroda Odessy,* Bakhmeteff Archives at Columbia University.

51. TsGAOR, f. 102, OO, op. 5, d. 3, ch. 49, 1905, pp. 66 ob. and 124 ob. and d. 1350, ch. 30, lit. A, 1905, p. 85 ob.; TsGVIA, f. 400, 16th otd., op. 15, d. 2641, 1905, p. 35; Kuzminskii Report, pp. cv–cvi, cxlviii, ccxv, and 4. Neidhardt received the backing of several right-wing journalists and public activists, who publicly proclaimed the city governor innocent of any wrong-doing. So did the State Senate, which absolved Neidhardt of any criminal activity. Izgoev, "K istorii odesskago pogroma," pp. 9–13; Elishev, *Oktiabr'skoe vooruzhennoe vosstanie v Odesse*; Srednev, *Evreiskaia revoliutsionnaia samooborona v Odesse* and *Odesskii konvent v oktiabr'iaskie dni 1905 g.*. Neidhardt's spirited defense of his behavior can be found in the Kuzminskii Report, passim and *Pravitel'stvennyi vestnik,* November 12, 1905.

52. Lambroza, "Jewish Responses to Pogroms in Late Imperial Russia," pp. 258 and 268.

53. So stated *Okhrana* chief Bobrov in his report on the pogrom, TsGAOR, f. 102, OO, op. 5, d. 3, ch. 49, 1905, p. 124 ob. See also the comments of gendarme chief Kuzubov in TsGAOR, f. 102, OO, op. 5, d. 3, ch. 49, 1905, p. 66 ob. For a journalistic assessment, see Srednev, *Evreiskaia revoliutsionnaia samooborona v Odesse* and *Odesskii konvent v oktiabr'iaskie dni 1905 g.*

54. At the Empire-wide level, Jews constituted 30 percent of persons arrested for political crimes by 1900. See the 1986 University Lecture at Boston University by Norman Naimark, "Terrorism and the Fall of Imperial Russia," p. 4. Of the seventy-seven persons deemed politically unreliable by the authorities after June, about thirty-eight were Jews; Jews comprised approximately twenty-eight of the sixty-three individuals exiled from Odessa. TsGAOR, f. 102, OO, d. 106, ch. 2, 1905, pp. 54–61, 68–69 ob., 76–78 ob., and 80–81, d. 4, ch. 19, lit. A, 1905, p. 7 ob., op. 5, d. 975, vol. 3, p. 129 ob., and op. 5 d. 1800, ch. 18, 1905, pp. 1–80; *KR,* July 26, 1905; *Iuzhnye zapiski,* July 17, 1905, pp. 61–62.

55. Kuzminskii Report, pp. cxvii, cxxv, cxxxiv–cxxxv, cliii, 4, 100, and 108.

56. Almazov, pp. 586–587; Elishev, p. 19.

57. *KR,* October 30, 1905.

58. In another violent incident, dockworkers during a work stoppage in 1886 attacked strikebreakers with rocks. Matasova, "Materialy dlia istorii russkogo rabochego dvizheniia-1886 god," p. 251; *Iskra,* December 1900; "Khronika vnutrennei zhizni," *Russkoe bogatstvo,* August 1900, pp. 159–162.

59. Mebel', p. 113; TsGAOR, f. 102, OO, d. 4, ch. 19, lit. A, 1905, pp. 213–214; *KR,* November 27, 1905 and December 1, 1905; TsGIA, f. 1405, op. 530, d. 400, p. 52; *IO,* June 29, 1906 and July 9, 1906; Elishev, p. 37.

60. The first quote is from Godlevskii, no.2(8), 1924, p. 131; and the second one is from TsGAOR, f. 102, OO, op. 233, d. 1350, ch. 30, 1905, pp. 60–61.

61. *Collier's,* December 9, 1905, p. 13.

62. *KR,* November 13, 1905.

63. Kuzminskii Report, pp. 130–131; Neizvestnyi, p. 116; *KR,* October 28, 1905, October 30, 1905, November 1, 1905, November 3, 1905, November 5, 1905, November 8, 1905, November 13, 1905, and December 6, 1905; *OL,* October 29, 1905,

November 18, 1905 and November 26, 1905; *ON,* November 2, 1905, November 3, 1905, November 6, 1905, December 2, 1905, and December 6, 1905; *IO,* October 30, 1905 and November 11, 1905; *Istoriia zavodu imeni sichnevoho postannia v Odesi,* p. 70.

64. *OL,* November 2, 1905.

65. Wynn, chap. 7.

66. *KR,* October 30, 1905 and November 2, 1905; *Otchet Odesskago evreiskago tsentral'nago komiteta po okazaniiu pomoshchi postradavshim ot pogromov 1905 goda; OOKTM za 1903–1905 gg.,* pp. 211–213; *OL,* November 6, 1905; Kuzminskii Report, p. 71.

67. "Report of the Central Jewish Committee to Assist Pogrom Victims," at Archives of the Alliance Israélite Universelle.

68. Ibid.

69. *IO,* October 26, 1905; *The Maccabaean* no. 5 (1905), p. 260; *KhEZ,* November 11, 1905, p. 22; *OL,* October 27, 1905; *Voskhod,* December 1, 1905, p. 45; Lambroza, "The Pogrom Movement in Russia, 1903–1906," p. 278.

70. *KR,* October 28, 1905, October 30, 1905, November 1, 1905, November 8, 1905, and November 13, 1905; *IO,* October 30, 1905; *OL,* October 27, 1905 and October 29, 1905; *ON,* November 2, 1905 and November 3, 1905; *IOGD,* October 1905, pp. 2333 and 2337 and February 1906, pp. 315, 321 and 367; *Novaia zhizn',* October 27, 1905 and October 28, 1905; *Obzor deiatel'nosti gorodskoi vrachebno-sanitarnoi organizatsii za 1905 godu,* p. 37.

71. *KR,* November 3, 1905 and November 5, 1905; *ON,* November 6, 1905; *IO,* November 11, 1905.

72. *KR,* November 5, 1905, November 13, 1905 and December 6, 1905; *IO,* November 11, 1905; *ON,* December 2, 1905.

73. Levichev, "Vospominaniia rabochego," p. 179.

74. *OL,* November 18, 1905 and November 26, 1905; *ON,* December 6, 1905.

75. For other views that the forces of reaction enlisted the support of unwitting workers, especially day laborers, see TsGAOR, f. 102, OO, op. 5, d. 3, ch. 49, 1905, p. 113 ob. and *KR,* November 25, 1905. On the pronouncements of workers from Shpolianskii and the Russian Steam Navigation and Trading Company, see *KR,* October 30, 1905 and November 13, 1905. See also G. Achkanov, "Vospominaniia o revoliutsii 1905 goda," p. 202.

8. Final Confrontation

1. Marshall, "Citizenship and Social Class," pp. 1–85.

2. Bonnell, *Roots of Rebellion,* p. 3.

3. *KR,* November 10, 1905 and November 13, 1905; Bronevich, p. 55.

4. Bronevich, p. 55; *KR,* March 1, 1905, March 4, 1905, November 4, 1905, November 10, 1905, November 17, 1905, and November 19, 1905.

5. *KR,* November 9, 1905.

6. *KR,* November 5, 1905.

7. *ON,* November 16, 1905; *KR,* November 13, 1905.

8. *KR,* November 4, 1905; Filinskii, p. 159. See also the comments of a tinsmith who stated that Odessa tinsmiths lost their strike in June because they lacked the "possibility to assemble." But the October Manifesto created a new situation: "the inviolability of person and freedom to assemble and organize." *KR,* November 16, 1905. A salesclerk echoed these sentiments when he wrote that after October 1905 salesclerks now could meet freely. *KR,* November 17, 1905. Similarly, teapackers also hesitated to join a union prior to October because they feared the loss of their jobs.

9. See Surh, *1905 in St. Petersburg,* pp. 274 and 284 for a view that downplays the political significance of the trade union movement in 1905.

10. The quote is from the report of the Odessa delegation to the Second All-Russian Conference of Trade Unions, held in St. Petersburg in February 1906. See Kolokol'nikov and Rapoport, *1905–1907 gg. v professional'nom dvizhenii*, p. 288.

11. I have excluded unions formed by professional workers such as teachers, writers, journalists, lawyers, doctors, draftsmen, and dental technicians. Kolokol'nikov and Rapoport, p. 289; Dzhervis, "K istorii professional'nogo dvizheniia v Odesse," p. 10; *KR*, November 3, 1905; Kats and Milonov, *1905: Professional'noe dvizhenie*, pp. 206–208 and 378. For an overview of union formation in 1905, see *Iuzhnyi professional'nyi listok*, July 16, 1906, *Rabochee delo*, August 15, 1906, and *Soiuz*, September 1906.

12. Kats and Milonov, p. 208; *KR*, November 30, 1905, December 10, 1905 and December 22, 1905; *ON*, November 29, 1905.

13. Bonnell, *Roots of Rebellion*, p. 136; Kats and Milonov, p. 209; *KR*, November 22, 1905, November 23, 1905, November 30, 1905, December 6, 1905, and December 9, 1905.

14. *KR*, November 11, 1905; *OL*, November 2, 1905.

15. *KR*, November 9, 1905.

16. *OL*, November 27, 1905.

17. *Golos prikazchikov*, April 23, 1906; *Zhizn' prikazchikov*, December 16, 1905; Lupinskii, pp. 65–94; Sh., "Vospominaniia o soiuze kontorshchikov g. Odessy," pp. 185–194; *KR*, November 9, 1905, November 11, 1905, November 12, 1905, November 20, 1905, November 23, 1905, November 25, 1905, November 26, 1905, and November 29, 1905; *IO*, November 24, 1905.

18. Dzhervis, "Profsoiuzy Odessy v revoliutsii 1905–06 gg.," p. 242.

19. Zanchevskii, p. 15; *"Osvobozhdenie truda"*, pp. 73–121; *KR*, November 5, 1905.

20. Bel'for, p. 42.

21. *KR*, November 8, 1905.

22. G. Achkanov, "Soiuz mashinostroitel'nykh rabochikh g. Odessy 1905–1906 gg.," p. 222; *Soiuz metallistov v Odesse*, p. 37; Kolokol'nikov, *Professional'noe dvizhenie v Rossii*, p. 40; *KR*, December 4, 1905; Dzhervis, "K istorii professional'nogo dvizhenia v Odesse," p. 6

23. Dzhervis, "Professional'noe dvizhenie v Odesse v 1905 godu," p. 261; *KR*, November 2, 1905, November 23, 1905 and November 27, 1905.

24. Ascher, *The Revolution of 1905*, pp. 150–151.

25. For a discussion of the role of SDs in Odessa unions, see Bagatskii, "Revoliutsionnaia deiatel'nost' bol'shevikov v profsoiuzakh," 53–70. On COTU see Bel'for, p. 39 and Dzhervis, "Professional'noe dvizhenie v Odesse v 1905 godu," p. 260 and "K istorii professional'nogo dvizheniia v Odesse," pp. 9 and 27. For a copy of the model union charter, see *KR*, November 15, 1905.

26. See "Perepiska N. Lenina i N. K. Krupskoi s Odesskoi organizatsiei," *PR*, no. 7(42) (1925), p. 35; *KR*, November 18, 1905 and November 23, 1905.

27. *Istoriia zavoda imeni sichnevoho postannia v Odesi*, pp. 85–88; G. Achkanov, "Vospominaniia o revoliutsii 1905 goda," p. 202; "Perepiska N. Lenina i N. K. Krupskoi s Odesskoi organizatsiei," *PR*, no. 12(47) (1925), p. 19; *Revoliutsionnoe dvizhenie v Rossii v dokladakh ministra Murav'eva 1894–1905*, pp. 153–154; Pershina, p. 35.

28. TsGAOR, f. 102, 7th delopr., d. 7195, 1905, pp. 31–34; Dzhervis, "Profsoiuzy Odessy v revoliutsii 1905–06 g.g.," p. 241.

29. Klimovitskii, "Pervyi soiuz portnykh v Odesse," p. 41.

30. Dzhervis, "Profsoiuzy Odessy v revoliutsii 1905–06 gg.," p. 242.

31. *ON*, November 16, 1905.

32. *IO*, November 9, 1905; *KR*, November 10, 1905, November 15, 1905 and November 29, 1905; Bel'for, p. 43; K. K. "Za 20 let," p. 31; TsGAOR, f. 102, OO, d. 106, ch. 2, 1905, p. 116.

33. Whereas the Bund opposed the establishment of a separate Jewish national territory, both Labor Zionists (also known as *Poale Zion*) and Socialist Zionists advocated the acquisition of a Jewish homeland where a socialist society could be built under conditions of political and national autonomy. The Labor Zionists, unlike the Socialist Zionists, insisted that the territory be Palestine.

34. Bundist organizations in southern Russian tended to advocate neutral unions, a tactic that went against the general line of party-affiliated unions. Kirzhnits, *Evreiskoe rabochee dvizhenie*, p. 283; Tobias, p. 334; Dimanshtein, p. 176.

35. *IO*, December 10, 1905; TsGAOR, f. 102, OO, d. 106, ch. 2, 1905, p. 116; *KR*, November 13, 1905 and November 30, 1905.

36. *KR*, November 15, 1905.

37. *IO*, December 6, 1905; *KR*, November 19, 1905; TsGAOR, f. 124, op. 49, d. 294, 1911, p. 58 ob.

38. The charters are of the unions of metalworkers and machine builders, printers, salesclerks, woodworkers, office workers and bookkeepers, groundskeepers, bakers, and railway workers. They can be found in TsGAOR, f. 102, OO, 1st otd., op. 6, d. 5, ch. 10, 1906, pp. 165–169 ob.; *KR*, November 6, 1905, November 13, 1905, November 16, 1905, November 25, 1905, and December 6, 1905; TsGAOR, Kollektsiia listovok i nelegal'nykh izdanii, no. 30391; *Ustav professional'nago soiuza sluzhashchikh i rabochikh iugo-zapadnykh zh.d.*

39. Dzhervis, "Professional'noe dvizhenie v Odesse v 1905 godu," p. 260.

40. *Ustav professional'nago soiuza sluzhashchikh i rabochikh iugo-zapadnykh zh.d.*, p. 8. These demands were similar to those of the economic program-minimum adopted at the 1903 RSDWP party congress and advocated by Menshevik labor activists in the fall of 1905. In addition to demands for an eight-hour workday and abolition of overtime and night work, the program-minimum addressed other issues related to working conditions, including factory inspection, labor exchanges, child and female labor, and labor-management industrial courts to adjudicate workplace grievances. See Bonnell, *Roots of Rebellion*, p. 156; Harcave, pp. 263–268.

41. *KR*, November 15, 1905.

42. A separate but related matter that underscores the independent stance workers frequently adopted vis-à-vis SDs was whether craft-masters and workshop owners could join unions. This was a divisive issue, since some union activists, especially those affiliated with the SDs, maintained that unions should be comprised of workers and not "exploiters." In heated exchanges at union meetings, workers debated whether workshop owners who worked alone and did not employ any assistants were entitled to union membership. This issue, for example, was the subject of discussion at a meeting of the housepainters and roofers' union, with members rejecting the claim of an SD activist that even workshop owners laboring alone were exploiters and a "reactionary element." The union members disagreed, welcoming into their organization those who fit their definition of workers, namely "those who do not exploit anyone." *KR*, November 23, 1905, December 6, 1905 and December 9, 1905.

43. For descriptions of these gatherings, see *KR*, November 16, 1905, November 19, 1905, November 24, 1905, and December 4, 1905, *OL*, November 12, 1905, *IO*, November 20, 1905, and *ON*, November 12, 1905 and November 25, 1905.

44. *KR*, November 22, 1905; *IO*, November 19, 1905; Nekrasov, pp. 121–122.

45. *KR*, November 29, 1905.

46. *OL*, November 12, 1905.

47. *KR*, December 4, 1905; *ON*, November 12, 1905.

48. Dzhervis, "Professional'noe dvizhenie v Odesse v 1905 godu," p. 262; *KR*, November 23, 1905; Zanchevskii, p. 17; *IO*, November 29, 1905.

49. *KR*, November 6, 1905, November 8, 1905, November 11, 1905, November 23, 1905, November 27, 1905, and December 6, 1905; *OL*, December 1, 1905; *ON*,

December 10, 1905; G. Achkanov, "Odesskie rabochie v 1905 godu," p. 49; *Soiuz metallistov v Odesse,* p. 37.

50. Ascher, chaps. 9–11; Surh, *1905 in St. Petersburg,* chap. 8.

51. *KR,* November 22, 1905, November 24, 1905, November 26, 1905, November 30, 1905, December 1, 1905, December 3, 1905, December 6, 1905, and December 10, 1905; *IO,* November 9, 1905, November 24, 1905, November 26, 1905, November 29, 1905, and December 6, 1905; *ON,* November 24, 1905; Zanchevskii, p. 17; Buzhor and Vereshchagina, p. 48; Ivanov, "Bor'ba moriakov odesskogo torgovogo flota v 1905–1906 gg.," pp. 187–188; TsGAOR, f. 102, OO, d. 824, 1906, p. 76 ob.

52. *KR,* November 10, 1905.

53. Smith, "Workers and Civil Rights in Russia in 1905," p. 158.

54. See Portugeis's two-part article in *KR,* November 27, 1905 and November 30, 1905. On Portugeis, see "Pamiati S. Portugeisa (S. O. Ivanovicha)," pp. 394–395, Zhezmer, *Odes'ka Rada robitnychykh deputativ 1905 roku,* p. 46, and *KR,* November 24, 1905.

55. Bendix, "Tradition and Modernity Reconsidered," p. 340.

56. *KR,* November 17, 1905.

57. *KR,* May 18, 1905.

58. Harcave, p. 154. For an excellent discussion of the Assembly, see Ascher, pp. 144–150.

59. *Novaia zhizn',* November 29, 1905. The new column made its appearance in the November 3 issue of *Odesskie novosti.*

60. *ON,* November 6, 1905 and November 20, 1905; *OL,* November 2, 1905; *IO,* November 1, 1905, November 2, 1905 and November 20, 1905.

61. *ON,* November 1, 1905, November 6, 1905 and November 15, 1905.

62. *ON,* November 2, 1905.

63. *OL,* November 1, 1905. On rumors of a pogrom, see *KhEZ,* November 11, 1905, p. 22.

64. *OL,* November 3, 1905 and November 12, 1905; *KheZ,* November 18, 1905, p. 28; *ON,* November 6, 1905.

65. *The Maccabaean,* no. 5 (1905), p. 261; *Novaia zhizn',* November 8, 1905.

66. *IOGD,* April 1905, p. 1079.

67. *IOGD,* October 1905, pp. 2415–2416.

68. *IOGD,* November 1905, pp. 2611–2629 and March 1906, pp. 749–756 and 764–767; *ON,* November 3, 1905, November 6, 1905 and November 11, 1905; TsGAOR, f. 102, OO, d. 1350, ch. 30, lit. A, 1905, p. 88 ob.; *VOG,* November 6, 1905.

69. *ON,* November 4, 1905 and November 6, 1905; *IOGD,* February 1906, pp. 486–497.

70. *ON,* November 9, 1905, November 11, 1905 and November 29, 1905; *OL,* November 8, 1905, November 13, 1905 and December 10, 1905; *IO,* December 10, 1905; TsGAOR, f. 102, OO, d. 1350, ch. 30, lit. A, 1905, p. 97.

71. Kormich, "Bor'ba bol'shevikov Ukrainy za sozdanie Sovetov," p. 57; Zhezmer, "Odes'ka Rada robitnychykh deputativ 1905 r.," p. 152; *KR,* November 3, 1905; Demochkin, *Sovety 1905 goda,* p. 67.

72. Bonnell, *Roots of Revolution,* p. 176.

73. Nevskii, *Sovety i vooruzhennoe vosstanie v 1905 godu,* p. 137; Mel'nik, *V. I. Lenin i odesskaia partiinaia organizatsiia,* pp. 57–58.

74. *KR,* November 3, 1905; *ON,* November 6, 1905.

75. *IO,* November 8, 1905; G. Achkanov, "Vospominaniia o revoliutsii 1905 goda," p. 204; *KR,* November 6, 1905. For the unification of the Bolsheviks and Mensheviks, see Piatnitskii, *Memoirs of a Bolshevik,* pp. 90–92, G. Achkanov, "Vospominaniia o revoliutsii 1905 goda," pp. 205–208, *KR,* November 9, 1905, Gusev, "Odesskaia partiinaia organizatsiia posle 'Potemkina'," pp. 52–53, and Tanin, pp. 152–153.

76. *IO,* November 8, 1905.

77. For elections to the district soviets, see *IO,* November 9, 1905, *KR,* November 10, 1905, November 22, 1905 and November 23, 1905, and Zhezmer, *Odes'ka Rada robitnychykh deputativ 1905 roku,* pp. 11–17. For meetings of the district soviets, see *KR,* November 16, 1905, November 23, 1905, November 29, 1905, November 30, 1905, and December 1, 1905, *IO,* November 26, 1905 and November 30, 1905, and TsGAOR, f. 102, OO, d. 38, 1905, p. 12.

78. Information on the composition and structure of the Soviet is based on the following: Anweiler, *The Soviets,* p. 53; Dzhervis, "Professional'noe dvizhenie v Odesse v 1905 godu," p. 263; G. Achkanov, "Odesskie rabochie v 1905 godu," p. 49; *KR,* December 1, 1905; *ISRD,* December 12, 1905 and January 9, 1906; Kormich, p. 57; Zhezmer, "Odes'ka Rada robinychykh deputativ 1905 r.," p. 157; Nevskii, "Sovety v 1905 godu" p. 65, *Sovetskaia pechat' i literatura o sovetakh,* p. 402, and "Sovet Rabochikh Deputatov v Odesse v 1905 g.," p. 209; Riabinin-Skliarevskii, "Sovet rabochikh deputatov g. Odessy v 1905 godu," pp. 253–267.

79. See Zhezmer, *Odesk'ka rada robitnychykh deputativ 1905 roku,* pp. 45–53.

80. Because it has been impossible to learn the first names of most of the known deputies, I have determined the number of Jewish deputies by the admittedly imprecise method of counting Jewish-sounding surnames. This method risks underestimating the total since Jews sometimes adopted Russian names. I ascertained the number of women deputies by relying on full first names (when provided) and feminine endings of both surnames and reported occupations.

81. N. N. Demochkin, writing in the 1960s and also relying on incomplete data, found that at the November 28 plenary session of the Soviet there were ninety-eight workers, ten white-collar employees, and five teachers. Of these delegates, twenty-four were Bolsheviks, five Mensheviks and four SRs. See "Pod flagom menshevistskikh idei," p. 168.

82. *IO,* November 8, 1905; *KR,* November 6, 1905, November 16, 1905, November 29, 1905; *ON,* November 30, 1905.

83. *KR,* November 30, 1905.

84. *IO,* November 8, 1905.

85. For a copy of the statutes approved at the November 28 plenum, see *KR,* December 1, 1905.

86. *KR,* November 26, 1905.

87. *KR,* December 1, 1905.

88. For a similar assessment of the situation in St. Petersburg, see Surh, *1905 in St. Petersburg,* p. 409.

89. Mel'nik, "Odesskii Sovet rabochikh deputatov v 1905 g.," pp. 106–107; Vorobei and Kovbasiuk, "Odesskaia bol'shevistskaia organizatsiia," p. 84; Dzhervis, "Professional'noe dvizhenie v Odesse v 1905 godu," p. 264.

90. Mel'nik, "Odesskii Sovet rabochikh deputatov v 1905 g.," p. 196; *ISRD,* December 25, 1905; *ON,* December 2, 1905.

91. *ISRD,* December 13, 1905; *IO,* December 8, 1905; *KR,* December 11, 1905.

92. *KR,* December 11, 1905; *IO,* December 8, 1905.

93. *ISRD,* December 25, 1905.

94. TsGIA, f. 23, op. 29, d. 80, p. 25 ob.; *KR,* November 19, 1905 and December 9, 1905; *ON,* November 10, 1905 and December 4, 1905.

95. TsGAOR, f. 102, OO, op. 5, d. 3, ch. 49, 1905, p. 72 ob.

96. *KR,* December 11, 1905; *IO,* December 8, 1905; *ON,* December 8, 1905.

97. *KR,* December 6, 1905 and December 8, 1905; *IO,* December 8, 1905.

98. *KR,* December 6, 1905, December 8, 1905 and December 11, 1905; *IO,* December 8, 1905; *ON,* December 6, 1905; *Revoliutsiia 1905–1907 rokiv na Ukraini,* p. 249; TsGAOR, f. 102, OO, d. 5, ch. 4, lit. B, 1905, p. 53; *VOG,* December 6, 1905, p. 258.

99. A copy of the Executive Committee's statement appeared in *KR*, December 6, 1905. On *Russkaia rech'*, see TsGAOR, f. 102, OO, d. 5, ch. 4, lit. B, p. 48 ob.

100. *IO*, December 8, 1905; TsGAOR, f. 102, OO, d. 5, ch. 4, lit. B, 1905, pp. 50 and 52; *ON*, December 8, 1905.

101. *KR*, December 8, 1905.

102. The government, fearing another general strike on its railways, dropped the death sentences. See Reichman, pp. 262–263.

103. *KR*, November 23, 1905, November 26, 1905 and December 6, 1905; *IO*, November 24, 1905.

104. *KR*, December 8, 1905.

105. *KR*, December 2, 1905; Buzhor and Vereshchagina, p. 48.

106. *IO*, November 26, 1905; *KR*, November 29, 1905; Vorobei and Kovbasiuk, p. 84.

107. *ISRD*, December 13, 1905.

108. *IO*, December 8, 1905.

109. *IO*, December 8, 1905.

110. *ISRD*, December 25, 1905.

111. *ISRD*, December 15, 1905; *IO*, December 11, 1905; *ON*, December 11, 1905; *KR*, December 11, 1905.

112. *ON*, December 11, 1905; V. Gorelov, "Rabochee dvizhenie Odessy v 1905 godu," p. 30.

113. *ISRD*, December 15, 1905.

114. *KR*, December 8, 1905; Mel'nik, "Odesskii Sovet rabochikh deputatov v 1905 g.," p. 113; *ISRD*, December 25, 1905.

115. *ISRD*, 1, December 13, 1905; Gorin, *Ocherk po istorii Sovetov rabochikh deputatov v 1905 g.*, p. 253.

116. TsGAOR, f. 102, 7th delopr., d. 7195, 1905, pp. 1 and 31–33 ob., OO, d. 2080, 1905, pp. 6–6 ob., and OO, d. 2540, vol. 2, 1905, p. 95.

117. TsGAOR, f. 102, 7th delopr., d. 7195, 1905, p. 34 and OO, d. 2540, vol. 2, 1905, p. 95.

118. *ISRD*, December 13, 1905.

119. TsGAOR, f. 102, OO, d. 2540, vol. 2, 1905, p. 132 and op. 233, d. 1350, ch. 30, 1905, p. 86; *IO*, December 9, 1905, December 11, 1905 and December 20, 1905; *ISRD*, December 13, 1905 and December 25, 1905.

120. Piatnitskii, *Memoirs of a Bolshevik*, p. 93.

121. *ISRD*, December 15, 1905 and December 25, 1905.

122. *KR*, December 20, 1905 and December 21, 1905; *ON*, December 20, 1905; TsGAOR, f. 102, OO, op. 233, d. 1350, ch. 30, 1905, p. 94; Gurshtein, "Kak my pechatali pervyi nomer 'Izvestiia Odesskogo Soveta Rabochikh Deputatov'," pp. 152–158; *VPR*, p. 535.

123. TsGAOR, f. 102, OO, op. 233, d. 1350, ch. 30, 1905, p. 87 ob.

124. TsGAOR, f. 102, OO, d. 4, ch. 19, lit. A, 1905, p. 216 and op. 233, d. 1350, ch. 30, 1905, p. 86; *KR*, December 20, 1905.

125. Another indication that the Executive Committee wanted to avoid violence is found in the financial report covering its activities from December 8 to December 22. Although the soviet had over 7,000 rubles in its treasury, it spent a paltry 54 rubles on weapons and ammunition. This failure to spend money strongly suggests that they never seriously intended to lead an armed uprising or even to assist in the arming of workers. See *ISRD*, December 25, 1905.

126. *ISRD*, December 25, 1905; Buzhor and Vereshchagina, p. 52.

127. Abraham Ascher, p. 312, writing about similar events in Moscow, argues that the difference between calling for an armed struggle and preparing for one was illusory.

128. *ISRD*, December 13, 1905, December 15, 1905 and December 25, 1905; *KR*, December 11, 1905; TsGAOR, f. 102, 7th delopr., d. 7194, 1905.

129. *KR*, December 20, 1905; *IO*, December 20, 1905; *ISRD*, December 25, 1905.

130. *ISRD*, December 25, 1905.

131. *VPR*, pp. 535–536.

132. Galili, *The Menshevik Leaders in the Russian Revolution*, pp. 275–277.

133. See, for example, Gorin, pp. 198–203 and 252–255. Nevskii also condemned the Executive Committee for failing to adopt more militant measures during the December strike. See his "Sovet rabochikh deputatov v Odesse v 1905 g.," p. 208. For more recent assessments reiterating the views of Gorin and Nevskii, see Mel'nik, *V. I. Lenin i odesskaia partiinaia organizatsiia*, pp. 61–62, Kormich, pp. 157–159, and A. M. Shternshtein, "V. I. Lenin i bol'shevistskaia organizatsiia Odessy v 1905 godu," pp. 112–129 and 165.

134. TsGAOR, f. 102, OO, d. 4, ch. 19, lit. A, 1905, p. 216 ob.

135. For a similar, though not identical view, see V. Gorelov, "Rabochee dvizhene Odessy v 1905 godu," pp. 31–33. He writes that the December strike failed because a "revolutionary mood among workers did not crystallize." Although he acknowledges that workers were not willing to engage in open conflict, he condemns the soviet for not pursuing "the battle to the end."

136. "Letuchii listok," January 6, 1906, located in TsGIA, f. 1405, op. 530, d. 401, pp. 13–14.

137. TsGAOR, f. 102, OO, d. 4, ch. 19, lit. A, 1905, p. 216 ob.

138. TsGAOR, f. 102, OO, d. 2540, vol. 2, 1905, p. 132 ob.

139. TsGAOR, f. 102, OO, d. 4, ch. 19, lit. A, 1905, p. 217.

140. For an account of the activities of the Executive Committee, see *ISRD*, December 25, 1905.

141. *ISRD*, December 13, 1905 and December 15, 1905; *KR*, December 21, 1905; *ON*, December 22, 1905.

142. *IO*, December 20, 1905; *KR*, November 25, 1905, December 11, 1905, December 21, 1905, and December 22, 1905; *ON*, November 4, 1905, November 27, 1905 and December 20, 1905; Kormich, p. 59; *ISRD*, December 15, 1905 and January 9, 1906; F. Achkanov, "Nasha rabota v glavnykh zhelezno-dorozhnykh masterskikh," pp. 102–103; TsGIA, f. 23, op. 17, d. 332, p. 73; Zhezmer, *Odes'ka Rada robitychkh deputativ 1905 roku*, p. 16.

143. The diary entry appears in *KR*, December 22, 1905.

144. *KR*, December 20, 1905.

145. On the bombing, see TsGAOR, f. 102, OO, d. 106, ch. 2, 1905, pp. 135–126 and d. 2540, vol. 2, 1905, p. 163 ob., *KR*, December 20, 1905, Avrich, pp. 61 and 67–68, and Novomirskii, "Anarkhicheskoe dvizhenie v Odesse," pp. 254–255.

146. *ON*, December 23, 1905; TsGIA, f. 1405, op. 520, d. 195, p. 134; *KR*, December 22, 1905. The reactions of workers, the soviet, and SDs to the Café Libman bombing are unknown.

147. Nevskii, "Sovet rabochikh deputatov v Odesse v 1905 g.," p. 208.

148. *ISRD*, December 15, 1905; Nekrasov, p. 118; *Revoliutsionnoe gnezdo*, p. 17; Bushnell, p. 107; *VPR*, pp. 502, 530 and 555–560; TsGAOR, f. 102, OO, d. 4, ch. 19, lit. A, 1905, p. 216. For short overviews of socialist agitation in the garrison, see Pleskov, "V revoliutsionnom podpol'e," pp. 64–75; Frenk, pp. 76–84; A. Riabinin-Skliarevskii, "Revoliutsionnaia rabota v voiskakh Odesskogo garnizona v 1904–5–6 g.g.," pp. 155–175.

149. *VtPR*, pp. 145 and 648–649(n. 63).

150. TsGAOR, f. 102, OO, op. 233, d. 1350, ch. 30, 1905, p. 94 and d. 824, 1906, pp. 2 ob. and 75 ob–76; TsGIA, f. 95, op. 5, d. 733, p. 270 ob.; *IO*, December 25, 1905; Ivanov, "Bor'ba moriakov torgovogo flota Odessy v 1905–1906 gg.," p. 187.

151. TsGAOR, f. 102, OO, d. 2540, vol. 3, 1905, pp. 36 and 40 ob.; *VtPR*, p. 156.

152. Vorobei and Kovbasiuk, p. 85; Piatnitskii, *Memoirs of a Bolshevik*, p. 94; TsGAOR, f. 102, OO, d. 2540, vol. 3, 1905, p. 61.

Conclusion

1. V. Gorelov, "Rabochee dvizhenie Odessy v 1905 godu," p. 16.

2. Smith, "Workers and Civil Rights in Tsarist Russia," p. 164 and passim; Edmondson, "Was there a Movement for Civil Rights in Russia in 1905?," p. 284.

3. Scott, *The Glassworkers of Carmaux*, p. 116.

4. *Bol'shevistskie listovki 1905*, pp. 65–67.

5. Alexis de Tocqueville, *The Old Regime and the French Revolution*, p. 177.

6. Zelnik, "Passivity and Protest in Germany and Russia," pp. 499 and 503–505.

7. Ascher, *The Revolution of 1905*, p. 219.

8. Surh, "Workers in 1905," pp. 527–528. See also Surh's assessment in *1905 in St. Petersburg*, pp. 409–410 and the following statement by Laura Engelstein, p. 222, about SD influence on Moscow workers: "the parties never controlled the form and direction of popular involvement . . . the working class demonstrated a remarkable degree of autonomy."

9. TsGIA, f. 23, op. 29, d. 78, p. 55 ob.

BIBLIOGRAPHY

Archives

Alliance Israélite Universelle. Paris.
    Dossier: URSS IC-1. M. Vinaver, "La situation à Odessa."
    Dossier: URSS VII B: Odessa. File 5715/2. "Report of the Central Jewish
    Committee to Assist Pogrom Victims."
Bakhmeteff Archive of Russian and East European History and Culture.
    Columbia University. Zosa Szajkowskii Collection. Oversized Folders. *Odesskie dni,*
    Otvet na odesskie dni i g.g. Odessity, and *Vossvanie k Khristianam goroda Odessy.*
Bund Archives of the Jewish Labor Movement. New York.
    File MG 10, no. 5. M. S. Gurevich, "Doklady o deiatel'nosti bunda za 1904–
    1905 gg."
    File MG 10, no. 7. "1906 g. Nekotorye statisticheskie dannye v boevykh
    otriadakh pri mestnykh organizatsiiakh bunda vremeni ego 7-go s"ezda."
Hoover Institution on War, Revolution and Peace. Stanford University.
    B. I. Nicolaevsky Collection. Box 28. Folder 8, Bund Pamphlet. Odessa. 1905.
Tsentral'nyi gosudarstvennyi arkhiv oktiabr'skoi revoliutsii SSSR (TsGAOR)
    fond 102—Departament politsii Ministerstva vnutrennikh del. Osobyi Otdel
    (OO).
    fond 124—Vremennaia kantseliariia po proizvodstvu osobykh ugolovnykh del i
    ugolovnye otdeleniia I departamenta Ministerstva iustitsii.
    Kollektsiia listovok i nelegal'nykh izdanii.
Tsentral'nyi gosudarstvennyi istoricheskii arkhiv SSSR (TsGIA)
    fond 23—Ministerstvo torgovli i promyshlennosti.
    fond 95—Otdel torgovogo moreplavaniia i torgovykh portov Ministerstva tor-
    govli i promyshlennosti.
    fond 107—Russkoe obshchestvo parokhodstva i torgovli.
    fond 1101—Dokumenty lichnogo proiskhozhdeniia ne sostovliaiushchie
    otdel'nykh fondov.
    fond 1284—Departament obshchikh del Ministerstva vnutrennikh del.
    fond 1328—Upravlenie dvortsovogo komendanta.
    fond 1405—Ministerstvo iustitsii.
Tsentral'nyi gosudarstvennyi voenno-istoricheskii arkhiv SSSR (TsGVIA)
    fond 400—Glavnyi shtab Voennogo ministerstva.

Newspapers and Journals

Budushchnost' (St. Petersburg)
Buntar' (Paris-Geneva)
Burevestnik (Paris)
Golos farmatsevta (St. Petersburg)
Golos prikazchika (St. Petersburg)
Iskra (Munich-London-Geneva)
Iuzhnoe obozrenie (Odessa)
Iuzhno-russkii al'manakh (Odessa)
Iuzhnye zapiski (Odessa)
Iuzhnyi professional'nyi listok (Odessa)

Izvestiia Odesskoi gorodskoi dumy (Odessa)
Izvestiia Soveta rabochikh deputatov g. Odessy (Odessa)
Kandal'nyi zvon (Odessa)
Khronika evreiskoi zhizni (St. Petersburg)
Knizhki 'Voskhoda' (St. Petersburg)
Kontorshchik (St. Petersburg)
Krasnaia letopis' (Moscow-Leningrad)
Krasnyi arkhiv (Moscow)
Kommercheskaia Rossiia (Odessa)
Letopis' revoliutsii (Kharkov)
Listok bulochnikov i konditerov (St. Petersburg)
Nedel'naia khronika 'Voskhoda' (St. Petersburg)
Novaia zhizn' (St. Petersburg)
Odesskie novosti (Odessa)
Odesskii listok (Odessa)
Odesskii vestnik (Odessa)
Pechatnyi vestnik (St. Petersburg)
Peterburgskii listok (St. Petersburg)
Posledniia izvestiia (London-Geneva)
Pravitel'stvennyi vestnik (St. Petersburg)
Professional'naia zhizn' (Odessa)
Proletarii (Geneva)
Proletarskaia revoliutsiia (Moscow)
Proletarskoe delo (Odessa)
Puti revoliutsii (Odessa)
Rabochee delo (Odessa)
Revoliutsionnaia Rossiia (Paris-London)
Russkoe bogatstvo (St. Petersburg)
Shveinik (Odessa)
Soiuz (Odessa)
Sotsial-demokrat (Geneva)
Vedomosti Odesskago gradonachal'stva (Odessa)
Vestnik truda (Moscow)
Voskhod (St. Petersburg)
Vpered (Geneva)
Zhizn' prikazchikov (Moscow)

Books and Articles

Achkanov, F. "Nasha rabota v glavnykh zheleznodorozhnykh masterskikh." In *1905 god*, vol. 2, pp. 91–103. Odessa, 1926.
———. "Pervye etapy revoliutsii piatogo goda v Odesse." In *1905 god*, vol. 1, pp. 42–59. Odessa, 1925.
Achkanov, G. "Odesskie rabochie v 1905 g." *Vestnik truda* no. 12(61) (1925), pp. 44–51.
———. "Soiuz mashinostroitel'nykh rabochikh g. Odessy 1905–1906 gg." *Vestnik truda* no. 8(45) (1924), pp. 221–224.
———. "Vospominaniia o revoliutsii 1905 goda." In *1905 god*, vol. 2, pp. 192–208. Odessa, 1926.
Adamov, I. A. "Rabochie i moriaki odesskogo porta v revoliutsionnom dvizhenii XIX i nachala XX stoletii." Candidate of Historical Science dissertation, Odessa University, 1940.
Adamovich, M. (K. Arl'). *Chernomorskaia registratsiia*. Moscow, 1929.

Adres-kalendar' Odesskago gradonachal'stva na 1898 god. Odessa, 1897.

Ainzaft, S. S. *Pervyi etap professional'nogo dvizheniia v Rossii (1905–1907gg.)*. Moscow and Gomel, 1924.

Aleichem, Sholom. *From the Fair*. Translated and edited by Curt Leviant. New York: Viking/Penguin Inc., 1985.

Aleksandrovskii, I. V. "Artel'nye rabochie v g. Odesse." *Otchet o deiatel'nosti Petropavlovskago sanitarnago popechitel'stva v g. Odesse za 1898 i 1899 gg.*, pp. 232–287. Odessa, 1900.

Almazov, P. *Nasha revoliutsiia (1902–1907)*. Kiev, 1908.

Alymov, V. "K voprosu o polozhenii truda v remeslennom proizvodstve." *Narodnoe khoziaistvo*, bk. 6 (November-December 1904), pp. 1–27.

———. "Remeslennye fabriki v Odesskom gradonachal'stve." In *Otchet Odesskago komiteta torgovli i manufaktur za 1901 g., prilozhenie* 17. Odessa, 1902.

Anderson, Barbara A. *Internal Migration during Modernization in Late Nineteenth-Century Russia*. Princeton: Princeton University Press, 1975.

Antoshkin, D. V. *Ocherk dvizheniia sluzhashchikh v Rossii so vtoroi poloviny XIX-go veka*. Moscow, 1921.

———. *Professional'noe dvizhenie v Rossii*. 3rd ed. Moscow, 1925.

Anweiler, Oskar. *The Soviets: The Russian Workers, Peasants and Soldiers Councils, 1905–1921*. Translated by Ruth Hein. New York: Random House, 1974.

Aronson, G., Dubnow-Erlich, S., and Hertz, J. Sh., eds. *Di geshikhte fun Bund*. 3 vols. New York, 1960–1966.

Aronson, I. Michael. *Troubled Waters: The Origins of the 1881 Anti-Jewish Pogroms in Russia*. Pittsburgh: University of Pittsburgh Press, 1990.

Ascher, Abraham. *The Revolution of 1905: Russia in Disarray*. Stanford: Stanford University Press, 1988.

Atlas, G. "Pervye obshchestva narodnykh universitetov v Odesse." In *Chto takoe narodnyi universitet? Sbornik statei*, pp. 44–56. Odessa, 1917.

Avdeev, N. "Vosstanie na bronenostse 'Potemkin'." In *1905: Istoriia revoliutsionnogo dvizheniia v otdel'nykh ocherkakh*, edited by M. K. Pokrovskii. Vol. 2, *Ot ianvaria k oktiabriu*, pp. 180–224. Moscow-Leningrad, 1925.

Avdenko, I. K. *Noveishii putevoditel' po Odesse i ee okrestnostiam*. Odessa, 1907.

Avrich, Paul. *The Russian Anarchists*. Princeton: Princeton University Press, 1967.

Avtonomiia ili federatsiia. London, 1903.

Bagatskii, V. V. "Revoliutsionnaia deiatel'nost' bol'shevikov v profsoiuzakh v pervoi russkoi revoliutsii v 1905–1907 gg. (Na materialakh Ukrainy)." Candidate of Historical Science dissertation, Odessa University, 1980.

Balaban, Ia. S. "Usloviia fabrichnago truda v Odesse." *Iuzhno-russkii al'manakh*, pp. 29–42. Odessa, 1902.

Bel'for, D. S. "Profsoiuzy Odessy v revoliutsii 1905–1907 godov." *Trudy odesskogo gosudarstvennogo universiteta: Sbornik posviashchennyi 50-letiiu pervoi russkoi revoliutsii 1905–1907 gg.* 146 (1956): 29–52.

Bendix, Reinhard. "Tradition and Modernity Reconsidered." *Comparative Studies in Society and History* 9 (April 1967): 292–346.

Berezhnoi, I. S. "Studencheskoe dvizhenie na iuge Ukrainy v kontse XIX-nachale XX vekov." Candidate of Historical Science dissertation, Institute of History of the Academy of Sciences of the Ukrainian SSR, Kiev, 1964.

Berezovskii, A. P. (Kirill). *Odinnadtsat' dnei na Potemkine*. St. Petersburg, 1907.

Bernshtein, S. G. *Odessa: Istoricheskii i torgovo-ekonomicheskii ocherk Odessy v sviazi s Novorossiiskim kraem*. Odessa, 1881.

"Biulleten odesskago komiteta o stachke po 10 maia." In *1905 god*, vol. 2, pp. 306–310. Odessa, 1926.

"Biulleten odesskago komiteta o stachke po 7 maia." In *1905 god*, vol. 2, pp. 302–306. Odessa, 1926.

Bliumenfel'd, G. "Torgovo-promyshlennaia deiatel'nost' evreev v Odesse." *Voskhod* nos. 4 (April 1884), pp. 1–14 and 5 (May 1884), pp. 1–14.

"Boevye stranitsy: Odesskie pekari." In *Pishchevik: Iubileinyi sbornik*, p. 20. Odessa, n.d.

Bogomolets, M. A. "Fabriki spichek g. Brodskago na Peresypi." *Izvestiia Odesskoi gordoskoi dumy* no. 5–6 (March 1905), *prilozheniia*, pp. 127–130.

———. "Peresypskoe sanitarnoe popechitel'stvo v 1904 godu." *Izvestiia Odesskoi gorodskoi dumy* no. 1–2 (January 1905), *prilozheniia*, pp. 1–29.

Bol'shevistskie listovki 1905. Moscow, 1955.

Bonnell, Victoria. *Roots of Rebellion: Workers' Politics and Organizations in St. Petersburg and Moscow, 1900–1914.* Berkeley and Los Angeles: University of California Press, 1983.

———. *The Russian Worker: Life and Labor under the Tsarist Regime.* Berkeley and Los Angeles: University of California Press, 1983.

Borovoi, A. A. *Mikhailu Bakuninu, 1876–1926.* Moscow, 1926.

Borovoi, S. Ia. "Ekonomicheskoe polozhenie trudiashchegosia naseleniia Odessy nakanune pervoi narodnoi revoliutsii v Rossii." *Nauchnye zapiski odesskogo kreditno-ekonomicheskogo instituta* 9 (1957): 171–203.

———. "Odessa v period promyshlennogo kapitalizma." In *Odessa: Ocherk istorii goroda-geroia*, edited by S. M. Kovbasiuk, pp. 53–78. Odessa, 1957.

———. "Polozhenie rabochego klassa Odessy v XIX i nachale XX v." In *Iz istorii rabochego i revoliutsionnogo dvizheniia*, edited by A. M. Pankratova, pp. 308–318. Moscow, 1958.

Bortnikov, I. V. *Iiul'skie dni 1903 g. na iuge Rossii.* Odessa, 1953.

Bradley, Joseph. *Muzhik and Muscovite: Urbanization in Late Imperial Russia.* Berkeley and Los Angeles: University of California Press, 1985.

Brodovskii, I. *Evreiskaia nishcheta v Odesse.* Odessa, 1902.

Bronevich, G. "Tiazhelyi put': Iz zhizni mel'nichnykh rabochikh." In *Pishchevik: Iubileinyi sbornik*, pp. 53–55. Odessa, n.d.

Bronshtein, D. S. *Mery k uluchsheniiu fabrichnoi i zavodskoi promyshlennosti g. Odessy.* Odessa, 1885.

Brower, Daniel, et al. "Labor Violence in Russia in the Late Nineteenth Century." *Slavic Review* 41, no. 3 (Fall 1982): 417–453.

———. *The Russian City between Tradition and Modernity, 1850–1900.* Berkeley and Los Angeles: University of California Press, 1990.

———. "Urban Revolution in the Late Russian Empire." In *The City in Late Imperial Russia*, edited by Michael Hamm, pp. 319–353. Bloomington: Indiana University Press, 1986.

Brutskus, B. D. *Statistika evreiskago naseleniia.* St. Petersburg, 1909.

Bukhbinder, N. A. "Nezavisimaia evreiskaia rabochaia partiia (Po neizdannym arkhivnym dokumentam)." *Krasnaia letopis'* no. 2–3 (1922), 208–284.

———. "O zubatovshchine (Po neizdannym arkhivnym materialam)." *Krasnaia letopis'* no. 4 (1922), pp. 289–335.

Bushnell, John. *Mutiny amid Repression: Russian Soldiers in the Revolution of 1905–1906.* Bloomington: Indiana University Press, 1985.

Buzhor, Iu. I. and Bereshchagina, V. G., eds. *Imeni 50-letiia Sovetskoi Ukrainy.* Odessa, 1973.

Chemeriskii, A. "Vospominaniia o 'evreiskoi nezavisimoi rabochei partii.'" *Krasnyi arkhiv* 1 (1922): 315–328.

Chivonibar, A. (A. Rabinovich). *Bosiaki. Zhenshchiny. Den'gi.* Odessa, 1904.

———. "Chistil'shchik sapog." In Chivonibar, *Bosiaki. Zhenshchiny. Den'gi*, pp. 54–62. Odessa, 1904.

———. "Dikari." In Chivonibar, *Bosiaki. Zhenshchiny. Den'gi*, pp. 32–47. Odessa, 1904.

Chto takoe narodnyi universitet? Sbornik statei. Odessa, 1917.

Coquin, François-Xavier and Gervais-Francelle, Céline, eds. *1905: La Première*

Révolution Russe. Paris: Publications de la Sorbonne et l'Institut d'études slaves, 1986.

Crisp, Olga and Linda Edmondson, eds., *Civil Rights in Imperial Russia*. Oxford: Clarendon Press, 1989.

Dargol'ts, M. G. "Sotsial'demokraticheskaia rabota v gorodakh iuga, sviazannykh s Kievom." In *K dvadstatipiatiletiiu pervogo s"ezda partii (1898–1923)*, pp. 95–115. Moscow-Petrograd, 1923.

Dargol'ts, Ts. I. "Beglye zametki o sostoianii odesskoi organizatsii k momentu I-go partiinogo s"ezda." In *K dvadstatipiatiletiiu pervogo s"ezda partii (1898–1923)*, pp. 116–135. Moscow-Petrograd, 1923.

Degot', V. A. "Odesskie pechatniki v revoliutsionnom dvizhenii." In *Materialy po istorii professional'nogo dvizheniia v Rossii*, vol. 3, pp. 236–245. Moscow-Leningrad, 1925.

———. *Pod znamenem bol'shevizma: Zapiski podpol'shchika*. Moscow, 1927.

Demochkin, N. N. "Pod flagom menshevistskikh idei: Zametki o sovremmennoi burzhuaznoi istoriografii Sovetov 1905 goda." *Istoriia SSR* no. 5 (1966), pp. 164–182.

———. *Sovety 1905 goda: organy revoliutsionnoi vlasti*. Moscow, 1963.

Derenkovskii, G. M., ed., *Vtoroi period revoliutsii, 1906–1907 gody: ianvar'-aprel' 1906 goda*. Pt. 1, bk. 2. Moscow, 1959.

Diatroptov, P. N. *Narodnoe zdravie i sanitarnye uchrezhdeniia Odessy v 1894 godu*. Odessa, 1894.

Dimanshtein, S. "Ocherk revoliutsionnogo dvizheniia sredi evreiskikh mass." In *1905: Istoriia revoliutsionnogo dvizheniia v otdel'nykh ocherkakh*, edited by M. N. Pokrovskii, vol. 3, *Ot oktiabria k dekabriu. Revoliutsionnoe dvizhenie natsional'nostei i okrain*, pp. 105–182. Moscow-Leningrad, 1927.

Doklad Internatsional'nomu sotsialisticheskomu kongressu v Amsterdame: Deiatel'nost' bunda posle ego V-go s"ezda s iiunia 1903 do iiulia 1904 g. Geneva, 1904.

Doklad o russkom sotsial'demokraticheskom dvizhenii mezhdunarodnomu sotsialisticheskomu kongressu v Parizhe v 1900 g. Geneva, 1901.

Doklad Odesskago birzhevago komiteta otnositel'no preprovozhdennoi komitetu Vysochaishe uchrezhdennym Osobym Soveshchaniem o nuzhdakh sel'skokhoziaistvennoi promyshlennosti: Zapiski po voprosu o merakh k uporiadocheniiu khlebnoi torgovli. Odessa, 1902.

Dzhervis, M. "9-oe ianvaria i rabochie massy Odessy." *Professional'naia zhizn'* no. 65 (1925), pp. 69–71.

———. "K istorii professional'nogo dvizheniia v Odesse v 1905 godu." In *Materialy po istorii professional'nogo dvizheniia v Rossii*, vol. 5, pp. 5–44. Moscow, 1927.

———. "Professional'noe dvizhenie v Odesse v 1905 godu." *Vestnik truda* no. 6(55) (1925), pp. 253–265.

———. "Profsoiuzy Odessy v revoliutsii 1905–06 g.g." In *1905 god*, vol. 1, pp. 238–252. Odessa, 1925.

———. *Russkaia tabachnaia fabrika v XVIII i XIX vekakh*. Leningrad, 1933.

Edmondson, Linda. "Was there a Movement for Civil Rights in Russia in 1905?" In *Civil Rights in Imperial Russia*, edited by Olga Crisp and Linda Edmondson, pp. 263–285. Oxford: Clarendon Press, 1989.

Egorov, I. "'Potemkin Tavricheskii' i 1905 god." *Morskoi sbornik* no. 6–7 (1925), pp. 3–16.

Elishev, A. I. *Oktiabr'skoe vooruzhennoe vosstanie v Odesse*. Moscow, 1908.

Elwood, Ralph Carter. *Russian Social Democracy in the Underground: A Study of the RSDRP in the Ukraine, 1907–1914*. Assen, The Netherlands: Van Gorcum and Company, 1974.

Emmons, Terence. *The Formation of Political Parties and the First National Elections in Russia*. Cambridge: Harvard University Press, 1983.

————. "Russia's Banquet Campaign." *California Slavic Studies* 10 (1977): 45–86.
Engelstein, Laura. *Moscow, 1905: Working-Class Organization and Political Conflict.* Stanford: Stanford University Press, 1982.
Erazul'skii, M. A. *Organizatsiia meditsinskoi pomoshchi pri upravlenii rabot v Odesskom porte.* Odessa, 1906.
Evdomikov, I. "90-ye gody. Kak my bastovali." In *60 let ianvarskikh masterskikh: Iubileinyi sbornik. 1863–1923,* pp. 64–66. Odessa, 1923.
Fabrichnyi, A. A. "Nakanune pervoi revoliutsii." In *1905 god,* vol. 2, pp. 85–90. Odessa, 1926.
Fallows, Thomas. "The Zemstvo and the Bureaucracy, 1890–1904." In *The Zemstvo in Russia,* edited by Terence Emmons and Wayne Vucinich, pp. 177–241. Cambridge: Cambridge University Press, 1982.
Fedorov, I. "O polozhenii rabochago klassa v Odesse." *Pamiatnaia knizhka Odesskago gradonachal'stva na 1870 g.* Pt. 2, pp. 89–106. Odessa, 1869.
Fel'dman, K. "Potemkinskoe dvizhenie (14–25 iiunia 1905 g.): Vospominaniia uchastnika." In *Vosstanie na bronenostse "Kniaz' Potemkin Tavricheskii": Vospominaniia, materialy i dokumenty,* edited by V. I. Nevskii, pp. 37–209. Moscow-Petrograd, 1924.
Filinskii, S. "Za sem' let Ocherk profdvizheniia rabochikh pechatnago dela v Odesse." *Russkoe bogatstvo* no. 7 (1914), pp. 157–178.
Forre, T. "Vospominaniia sestry miloserdiia ob oktiabr'skikh dniakh 1905 goda." In *1905 god,* vol. 2, pp. 233–234. Odessa, 1926.
Fox, David J. "Odessa." *Scottish Geographical Magazine* 79, no. 1 (1963): 5–22.
Frankel, Jonathan. *Prophecy and Politics: Socialism, Nationalism, and the Russian Jews, 1862–1917.* Cambridge: Cambridge University Press, 1981.
Frenk, L. B. "Voennaia organizatsiia pri ob"edinennom komitete RSDRP v Odesse v 1905–06 gg." In *1905 god,* vol. 2, pp. 76–84. Odessa, 1926.
Friedgut, Theodore. *Iuzovka and Revolution.* Volume 1. *Life and Work in Russia's Donbass, 1869–1914.* Princeton: Princeton University Press, 1989.
Fuller, William C., Jr. *Civil-Military Conflict in Imperial Russia, 1881–1914.* Princeton: Princeton University Press, 1985.
Galai, Shmuel. *The Liberation Movement in Russia.* Cambridge: Harvard University Press, 1973.
Galili, Ziva. *The Menshevik Leaders in the Russian Revolution: Social Realities and Political Strategies.* Princeton: Princeton University Press, 1989.
Gard, William G. "The Party and the Proletariat in Ivanovo-Voznesensk, 1905." *Russian History* 2, no. 2 (1975): 101–123.
Garvi, P. A. *Vospominaniia sotsial-demokrata.* New York, 1946.
Genkin, I. *Vosstanie na bronenostse "Potemkin Tavricheskii": K dvadtsatiletiiu vosstaniia.* Moscow-Leningrad, 1925.
Gerasimov, A. *Krasnyi bronenosets: Vooruzhennoe vosstanie v 1905 godu na bronenostse "Potemkin Tavricheskii".* Leningrad, 1925.
Glickman, Rose. *Russian Factory Women: Workplace and Society, 1880–1914.* Berkeley and Los Angeles: University of California Press, 1984.
Godlevskii. "Kishinev, Odessa, Nikolaev. (Iz istorii s.-d. dvizheniia 1895–1903 g.g.) Vospominaniia." *Letopis' revoliutsii* no. 2(7) (1924), pp. 113–135, no. 3(8) (1924), pp. 122–137 and no. 4(9) (1924), pp. 95–109.
Gorelov, K. "Iiunskie dni v portu." In *1905 god,* vol. 1, pp. 133–140. Odessa, 1925.
Gorelov, V. "Rabochee dvizhenie Odessy v 1905 godu." In *1905 god,* vol. 1, pp. 12–33. Odessa, 1925.
Gorin, P. O. *Ocherk po istorii Sovetov rabochikh deputatov v 1905 g.* Moscow, 1925.
Goroda Rossii v 1910 godu. St. Petersburg, 1914.
Gorokhovskaia, E. "Zhenshchiny v revoliutsionnom dvizhenii 1905 goda v Odesse." *Puti revoliutsii* no. 2–3(5–6) (1926), pp. 82–90.

Greenberg, Louis. *The Jews in Russia: The Struggle for Emancipation.* 2 vols. New York: Schocken Books, 1978.

Grinevich, V. *Professional'noe dvizhenie rabochikh v Rossii.* St. Petersburg, 1908.

Grishin, P. P. *Uroki "Potemkina" i taktika vooruzhennogo vosstaniia.* Moscow-Leningrad, 1932.

Gudvan, A. M. *Ocherki po istorii dvizheniia sluzhashchikh v Rossii.* Pt. 1, *Do revoliutsii 1905 goda.* Moscow, 1925.

———. *Prikazchichii vopros (Zhizn' i trud prikazchikov).* Odessa, 1905.

———. *Prikazchiki v Odesse.* Odessa, 1903.

Gurshtein, P. "Kak my pechatali pervyi nomer 'Izvestiia Odesskogo Soveta Rabochikh Deputatov'." *Proletarskaia revoliutsiia* no. 10(45) (1925), pp. 152–158.

Gusev, S. "Odessa v 1905 godu." *Proletarskaia revoliutsiia* no. 2(49) (1926), pp. 162–176.

———. "Odesskaia partorganizatsiia 1905 g. posle 'Potemkina'." In *1905 god,* vol. 2, pp. 39–54. Odessa, 1926.

———. *Vodniki v professional'nom dvizhenii.* Moscow, 1928.

Halevy, Zvi. *Jewish Schools under Czarism and Communism: A Struggle for Cultural Identity.* New York: Springer Publishing Co., 1976.

Hamburg, Gary. *Politics of the Russian Nobility, 1881–1905.* New Brunswick: Rutgers University Press, 1984.

Hamm, Michael, ed. *The City in Late Imperial Russia.* Bloomington: Indiana University Press, 1986.

———, ed. *The City in Russian History.* Lexington: University Press of Kentucky, 1976.

———. "The Modern Russian City: An Historiographical Analysis." *Journal of Urban History* 4, no. 1 (1977): 39–76.

Harcave, Sidney. *The Russian Revolution of 1905.* London: The Macmillan Company, 1964; rpt. 1970.

Herlihy, Patricia. "Greek Merchants in Odessa in the Nineteenth Century." *Harvard Ukrainian Studies* 3/4, pt. 1 (1981): 399–420.

———. *Odessa: A History, 1794–1914.* Cambridge: Harvard University Press, 1987.

———. "Odessa: Staple Trade and Urbanization in New Russia." *Jahrbücher für Geschichte Osteuropas* 21, no. 2 (1973): 184–195.

———. "The Ethnic Composition of the City of Odessa in the Nineteenth Century." *Harvard Ukrainian Studies* 1, no. 1 (1977): 53–78.

Hertz, J. Sh. "Di ershte russlender revolutsie." In *Di geshikhte fun Bund,* edited by G. Aronson, S. Dubnow-Erlich, and J. Sh. Hertz, vol. 2, pp. 7–482. New York, 1962.

Hogan, Heather. "Labor and Management in Conflict: The St. Petersburg Metal Working Industry, 1900–1914." Ph.D. dissertation, University of Michigan, 1979.

Hough, Richard. *The Potemkin Mutiny.* New York: Pantheon Books, 1960.

Hunt, Lynn. "Charles Tilly's Collective Action." In *Vision and Method in Historical Sociology,* edited by Theda Skocpol, pp. 244–275. Cambridge: Cambridge University Press, 1984.

Hurvits, D. *Der blutiger pogrom in Odessa.* Odessa, 1905.

Iaroslavskii, E. "Pervaia polovina 1905 g. v Odesse." In *1905 god,* vol. 2, pp. 9–38. Odessa, 1926.

Inozemtsev, M., ed. "Bronenosets 'Kn. Potemkin Tavricheskii' v Odesse." *Krasnyi arkhiv* 69–70 (1935): 72–100.

Iris. "22 goda bor'by karamel'shchikov." In *Pishchevik: Iubileinyi sbornik,* pp. 28–30. Odessa, n.d.

Istoriia gorodov i sel Ukrainskoi SSR. Odesskaia oblast'. Kharkov, 1978.

Istoriia zavodu imeni sichnevoho postannia v Odesi (Zbirka dokumentiv 1876–1920 rr.). Odessa, 1932.

Itenberg, B. S. *"Iuzhnorossiiskii soiuz rabochikh": pervaia proletarskaia organizatsii v Rossii.* Moscow, 1954.

"Iiunskie dni v Odesse." In *Revoliutsionnyi Bronenosets. Vosstanie v chernomorskom flote. (Po materialam "Iskry" i "Sotsialdemokrata"),* pp. 29–35. Geneva, 1905.

Iushkevich, S. S. *Prolog: Povest'.* Munich, 1903.

Ivanov, L. M. "Bor'ba moriakov torgovogo flota Odessy v 1905–1906 gg." *Uchenye zapiski Moskovskogo gosudarstvennogo universiteta: Kafedra istorii,* vyp. 167 (1954), pp. 179–154.

Izgoev, A. S. "K istorii odesskogo pogroma." *Russkaia mysl'* no. 6 (1912), pp. 9–13.

Johnson, Christopher. "Economic Growth and Artisan Discontent: The Tailors' History, 1800–1848." In *Revolution and Reaction,* edited by Roger Price, pp. 87–114. London: Croom Helm, 1975.

Johnson, Robert. *Peasant and Proletarian: The Working Class of Moscow in the Late Nineteenth Century.* New Brunswick: Rutgers University Press, 1979.

K dvadtsatipiatiletiiu pervogo s"ezda partii (1898–1923). Moscow-Petrograd, 1923.

"K 40-letiiu 'Iskry'." *Krasnyi arkhiv* no. 6(103) (1940), pp. 34–44.

K. K. "Za 20 let. Miasniki-rubal'shchiki i kolbasniki." In *Pishchevik: Iubileinyi sbornik,* pp. 30–32. Odessa, n.d.

Kahan, Arcadius. "The Impact of Industrialization in Tsarist Russia on the Socioeconomic Conditions of the Jewish Population." In Arcadius Kahan, *Essays in Jewish Social and Economic History,* edited by Roger Weiss, pp. 1–69. Chicago: University of Chicago Press, 1986.

Karmen, L. O. *V rodnom gnezde.* Odessa, 1900.

———. *Zhizn' odesskikh prikazchikov.* Odessa, 1903.

Kats, A. and Milonov, Iu., eds. *1905: Professional'noe dvizhenie.* In *1905: Materialy i dokumenty,* edited by M. N. Pokrovskii. Moscow-Leningrad, 1926.

Katznelson, Ira and Zolberg, Aristide R., eds. *Working-Class Formation: Nineteenth-Century Patterns in Western Europe and the United States.* Princeton: Princeton University Press, 1986.

"Kaul'bars." *Entsiklopedicheskii slovar'.* Vol. 14., pp. 768–769. St. Petersburg, 1897.

———. *Novyi entsiklopedicheskii slovar'.* Vol. 21, pp. 304–305. St. Petersburg, 1911–1916.

———. *The Modern Encyclopedia of Russian and Soviet History*, edited by Joseph L. Wieczynski, vol. 16, pp. 72–73. Gulf Breeze: Academic International Press, 1980.

Kayden, Eugene and Alexis N. Antsiferov. *The Cooperative Movement in Russia during the War.* New Haven: Yale University Press, 1929.

Keep, John L. H. *The Rise of Social Democracy in Russia.* Oxford: Oxford University Press, 1963.

Khain, I. "Etapy bor'by mukomolov." In *Pishchevik: Iubileinyi sbornik,* pp. 51–53. Odessa, n.d.

Khronika revoliutsionnykh sobytii na Odesshchine v gody pervoi russkoi revoliutsii, 1905–1907. Odessa, 1976.

"Khronika vnutrennei zhizni." *Russkoe bogatstvo* no. 8 (1900), pp. 159–162.

Kir'ianov, Iu. I., and Prorina, P. V., eds. *Polozhenie proletariata Rossii: Ukazatel' literatury.* 2 vols. Moscow, 1972.

Kirzhnits, A. D. *Evreiskoe rabochee dvizhenie.* In *1905: Materialy i dokumenty,* edited by M. N. Pokrovskii. Moscow-Leningrad, 1928.

Kitanina, T. M. *Khlebnaia torgovlia Rossii v 1875–1914 gg.* Leningrad, 1978.

Kleinbort, L. M. *Istoriia bezrabotitsy v Rossii.* Moscow, 1925.

Klimovitskii (Shmerel'). "Pervyi soiuz portnykh v Odesse." *Shveinik* no. 1 (1922), pp. 40–41.

Knuzhevitskii, S. A. *Obzor kommercheskoi deiatel'nosti iuzhno-russkikh portov.* Kharkov, 1910.

Koenker, Diane and Rosenberg, William. *Strikes and Revolution in Russia, 1917.* Princeton: Princeton University Press, 1989.

Kogan, D. "Pervye desiatiletiia evreiskoi obshchiny v Odesse i pogrom 1821 goda." *Evreiskaia starina* 3 (1911): 260–267.

Kokol'nikov, P. N. *Professional'noe dvizhenie v Rossii.* Petrograd, 1918.

Kolokol'nikov P. and Rapoport, S., eds. *1905–1907 gg. v professional'nom dvizhenii: I i II Vserossiiskie konferentsii professional'nykh soiuzov.* Moscow, 1925.

Kon, F. Ia. *V tsarskoi kazarme. Soldaty i matrosy v pervoi revoliutsii.* Moscow, 1929.

Konovalov, V. G. *Barometr pokazyvaet buriu.* Odessa, 1980.

Kormich, A. I. "Bor'ba bol'shevikov Ukrainy za sozdanie Sovetov i prevrashchenie ikh v organy vooruzhennogo vosstaniia v period pervoi revoliutsii v Rossii." Candidate of Historical Science dissertation, Odessa University, 1979.

Kovalenko, A. "Odinnadtsat' dnei na bronenostse 'Kniaz' Potemkin Tavricheskii'." *Byloe* nos. 1(13) (1907), pp. 88–113, 2(14) (1907), pp. 124–141 and 3(15) (1907), pp. 46–68.

Kovalenko, K. S., ed. *Iz istorii odesskoi partiinoi organizatsii: Ocherki.* Odessa, 1964.

Kovbasiuk, S. M. ed., *Odessa: Ocherk istorii goroda-geroia.* Odessa, 1957.

Kristalovskii, I. "Iz istorii zarozhdeniia i razvitiia bol'shevizma v Odesse (Vospominaniia)." *Letopis' revoliutsii* no. 2(7) (1924), pp. 136–155.

Kurts, A. "Oktiabr' 1905 goda." In *1905 god*, vol. 2, pp. 229–232. Odessa, 1926.

Lambroza, Shlomo. "Jewish Responses to Pogroms in Late Imperial Russia." In *Living with Antisemitism: Modern Jewish Responses*, edited by Jehuda Reinharz, pp. 253–274. Hanover and London: University Press of New England, 1987.

———. "The Pogrom Movement in Russia, 1903–1906. Ph.D. dissertation, Rutgers University, 1981.

Lapin, V. "S.-D. organizatsii Ukrainy i II s"ezd RSDRP." *Letopis' revoliutsii* no. 5(32) (1928), pp. 7–53.

Lazarovich, S. "Ekonomicheskaia zhizn' g. Odessy." *Iuzhno-russkii al'manakh*, pp. 2–12. Odessa, 1900.

———. "Ekonomicheskie usloviia g. Odessy." *Iuzhno-russkii al'manakh*, pp. 2–8. Odessa, 1899.

———. "Materialy k voprosu o nochlezhnykh domakh v g. Odessy." *Otchet o deiatel'nosti Petropavlovskago sanitarnago popechitel'stva goroda Odessy za 1898–1899 gg.*, pp. 214–217. Odessa, 1900.

Lender, N. N. (Putnik). *Potrevozhnaia Rossiia.* St. Petersburg, 1908.

———. "Revoliutsionnye buri na iuge: 'Potemkin' i oktiabr'skaia revoliutsiia v Odesse." *Istoricheskii vestnik* 104, no. 6 (1904): 879–901.

Lepeshinskii, P. N. "Ot kruzhkovshchiny k partii (Period staroi 'Iskry')." In *Protokoly vtorogo s"ezda RSDRP*, pp. 5–130. Petrograd, 1924.

Levichev, D. "Vospominaniia rabochego." In *1905 god*, vol. 1, pp. 177–179. Odessa, 1925.

Levin, M. "Krizis i bezrabotitsa (Pis'mo iz Odessy)." *Knizhki 'Voskhoda'* no. 5 (May 1904), pp. 187–193.

Levitats, Isaac. *The Jewish Community in Russia, 1772–1844.* New York: Columbia University Press, 1943.

———. *The Jewish Community in Russia, 1844–1917.* Jerusalem: Posner and Sons Ltd., 1981.

Linden, A. (L. Motzkin), ed. *Die Judenpogrome in Russland.* 2 vols. Cologne and Leipzig, 1910.

Lipchenko, T. "90-ye gody: Probuzhdenie." In *60 let ianvarskikh masterskikh. Iubileinyi sbornik: 1863–1923*, p. 64. Odessa, 1923.

Liusternik, R. "1905 god na tabachnoi fabrike Popova." In *1905 god*, vol. 2, pp. 177–179. Odessa, 1926.

Los', F. E., ed. *Pod"em revoliutsionnogo dvizheniia na Ukraine nakanune pervoi russkoi revoliutsii (1901–1904 gg.).* Kiev, 1955.

———, ed. *Revoliutsionnaia bor'ba na Ukraine v period pervoi russkoi revoliutsii, 1905 g.* Pt. 1. Kiev, 1955.

Löwe, Heinz-Dietrich. *Antisemitismus und reaktionäre Utopie: Russischer Konservatismus um Kampf gegen den Wandel von Staat und Gesellschaft, 1890–1917.* Hamburg: Hoffman und Campe, 1978.

Lupinskii, P. "Soiuz prikazchikov Odessy (1905–1907 g.)." In *Professional'noe dvizhenie sluzhashchikh Ukrainy (1905–1907 gg.)*, edited by I. S. Stepanskii, pp. 65–94. Kharkov, 1927.

Lysenkov, N. K. "E. N. Shchepkin i odesskii universitet (1902–1905)." In *Pamiati professora Evgeniia Shchepkina. Sbornik*, pp. 27–31. Odessa, 1927.

Maevskii, E. "Obshchaia kartina dvizheniia." In *Obshchestvennoe dvizhenie v Rossii*, edited by Iu. Martov, P. Maslov and A. Potresov, vol. 2, pt. 1, pp. 96–104. St. Petersburg, 1909.

Malavich, A. *Odesser pogrom.* London, 1906.

Maleev, A. *Odessa v 1905 godu.* Odessa, 1925.

Manning, Roberta. *The Crisis of the Old Order in Russia: Gentry and Government.* Princeton: Princeton University Press, 1982.

Margolin, S. O. "O evreiskikh remeslakh." *Knizhki 'Voskhoda'* no. 12 (December 1904), pp. 35–56.

———. "Organizatsiia evreiskikh remesl." *Knizhki 'Voskhoda'* no. 3 (March 1905), pp. 72–95.

———. "Organizatsiia evreiskikh remeslennikov." *Knizhki 'Voskhoda'* no. 5 (May 1905), pp. 86–104.

———. "Professional'nye zadachi evreiskikh rabochikh soiuzov." *Knizhki 'Voskhoda'* no. 6 (June 1905), pp. 74–86.

———. "Usloviia truda v remeslennoi i domashnei promyshlennosti." *Vestnik fabrichnago zakonodatel'stva professional'noi gigieny* no. 2 (February 1905), pp. 40–51.

Markevich, A. L. "Zheleznye dorogi, soediniaiushchiia Odessu s ostal'noiu Rossiei." *Iuzhno-russkii al'manakh*, pp. 6–28. Odessa, 1900.

Marshall, T. H. "Citizenship and Social Class." In *Citizenship and Social Class and Other Essays* by T. H. Marshall, pp. 1–85. Cambridge: Cambridge University Press, 1950.

Matasova, F. "Materialy dlia istorii russkogo rabochego dvizheniia: 1886 god." *Krasnaia letopis'* no. 2(13) (1925), pp. 247–253.

Materialy k istorii russkoi kontr-revoliutsii. Vol. 1, *Pogromy po offitsial'nym dokumentam.* St. Petersburg, 1908.

Materialy po istorii professional'nogo dvizheniia v Rossii. 5 vols. Moscow, 1924–1927.

Mayer, Arno. *Dynamics of Counterrevolution in Europe, 1870–1956.* New York: Harper and Row, Publishers, 1971.

McDaniel, Tim. *Autocracy, Capitalism, and Revolution in Russia.* Berkeley and Los Angeles: University of California Press, 1988.

Mebel', M. I., ed. *1905 g. na Ukraine: Khronika i materialy.* Kharkov, 1926.

Melancon, Michael. "'Stormy Petrels': The Socialist Revolutionaries in Russia's Labor Organizations, 1905–1914," *The Carl Beck Papers in Russian and East European Studies* no. 703 (June 1988).

———. "The Socialist Revolutionaries from 1902 to 1907: Peasant and Workers' Party." *Russian History* 12, no. 1 (September 1985): 2–47.

Mel'nik, S. K. "Odesskii Sovet rabochikh deputatov v 1905 godu." *Nauchnye zapiski odesskogo kreditno-ekonomicheskogo instituta* 8 (1957): 96–119.

———. "Oktiabr'skaia politicheskaia stachka 1905 goda v Odesse." *Nauchnye zapiski odesskogo kreditno-ekonomicheskogo instituta* 5 (1956): 110–128.

————. *V. I. Lenin i odesskaia partiinaia organizatsiia.* Odessa, 1960.

Mel'nik, S. K. and Filatova, N. N. "Sozdanie sotsial-demokraticheskoi organizatsii v Odesse i nachal'nyi period ee deiatel'nosti (1895–1904 gody)." In *Iz istorii odesskoi partiinoi organizatsii: Ocherki*, edited by K. S. Kovalenko, pp. 29–58. Odessa, 1964.

Mel'nikov, N. P. *O sostoianii i razvitii tekhnicheskikh proizvodstv na iuge Rossii.* Odessa, 1875.

Mendelsohn, Ezra. *Class Struggle in the Pale: The Formative Years of the Jewish Workers' Movement in Tsarist Russia.* Cambridge: Cambridge University Press, 1970.

Mezhberg, M. *Zhovtnevi podii 1905 r. v Odesi.* Kharkov-Odessa, 1931.

Mikhalevich, B. *Zikhroynes fun a yidishen sotsialist.* 3 vols. Warsaw, 1921–1929.

Mikulin, A. A. *Fabrichno-zavodskaia i remeslennaia promyshlennost' Khersonskoi gubernii, Odesskago gradonachal'stva i Nikolaevskago voennago gubernatorstva v 1897 godu.* Odessa, 1898.

————. *Fabrichno-zavodskaia i remeslennaia promyshlennost' Khersonskoi gubernii, Odesskago gradonachal'stva i Nikolaevskago voennago gubernatorstva v 1898 godu.* Odessa, 1899.

————. *Strakhovanie rabochikh ot neschastnykh sluchaev na fabrikakh i zavodakh Odesskago gradonachal'stva (v 1894 i 1895 gg.).* Nizhnii Novgorod, 1896.

Milonov, Iu. *Kak voznikli professional'nye soiuzy v Rossii.* 2nd ed. Moscow, 1929.

Minovich, "Na odesskikh probochnykh zavodakh." In *1905 god*, vol. 2, pp. 168–176. Odessa, 1926.

Mishkinski, Moshe. "Regional Factors in the Formation of the Jewish Labor Movement in Czarist Russia." *YIVO Annual of Jewish Social Science* 14 (1969): 27–52.

Morgulis, M. "Bezporiadki 1871 goda v Odesse." *Evreiskii mir* 2 (December 1910): 42–66.

Moskvich, G. G. *Illiustirovannyi prakticheskii putevoditel' po Odesse.* Odessa, 1904.

Naimark, Norman. "Terrorism and the Fall of Imperial Russia." University Lecture Series. Boston University, 1986.

————. *Terrorists and Social Democrats: The Russian Revolutionary Movement under Alexander III.* Cambridge: Harvard University Press, 1983.

Narkevich, L. O. "K voprosu o polozhenii bezdomnykh rabochikh v odesskom portu." *Trudy Odesskago otdela Russkago obshchestva okhraneniia zdraviia*, vyp. 4 (1904), pp. 103–123.

Neizvestnyi, V. "1905 god v Odesse sredi zheleznodorozhnikov." In *1905 god*, vol. 2, pp. 104–122. Odessa, 1926.

Nekrasov, P. A. "Odesskii universitet v 1905 godu." *Trudy odesskogo gosudarstvennogo universiteta. Sbornik posviashchennyi 50-letiiu pervoi russkoi revoliutsii 1905–1907 gg.* 146 (1956): 97–122.

Nesterenko, A. A. *Ocherki istorii promyshlennosti i polozheniia proletariata Ukrainy v kontse XIX i nachale XX v.* Moscow, 1954.

Nevskii, V. I. *"Iuzhno-russkii rabochii soiuz" v g. Nikolaeve v 1897 g.* Moscow, 1922.

————. *Ocherki po istorii rossiiskoi kommunisticheskoi partii.* Vol. 1, 2nd. ed. Leningrad, 1925.

————. "Rabochee dvizhenie v ianvarskie dni 1905 goda i vosstanie na 'Potemkine'." In *Vosstanie na bronenostse "Kniaz' Potemkin Tavricheskii": Vospominaniia, materialy i dokumenty*, edited by V. I. Nevskii, pp. 3–33. Moscow-Petrograd, 1924.

————. "Sovet rabochikh deputatov v Odesse v 1905 g." *Proletarskaia revoliutsiia* no. 1(24) (1924), pp. 203–238.

————. *Sovetskaia pechat' i literatura o sovetakh.* In *1905: Materialy i dokumenty*, edited by M. N. Pokrovskii. Moscow, 1925.

————. *Sovety i vooruzhennoe vosstanie v 1905 godu.* Moscow, 1931.

————. "Sovety v 1905 godu." In *1905: Istoriia revoliutsionnogo dvizheniia v otdel'nykh ocherkakh*, edited by M. N. Pokrovskii. Vol. 3, *Ot oktiabria do dekabriu: Revoliutsionnoe dvizhenie natsional'nostei i okrain*, pp. 4–73. Moscow-Leningrad, 1927.

———, ed. *Vosstanie na bronenostse "Kniaz' Potemkin Tavricheskii": Vospominaniia, materialy i dokumenty.* Moscow-Petrograd, 1924.

Nikiforchuk, I. P. "Partiinaia organizatsiia Odessy v gody reaktsii i novogo revoliutsionnogo pod"ema (1907–1914 gg.)." Candidate of Historical Science dissertation, Odessa University, 1963.

Novomirskii, D. B. "Anarkhicheskoe dvizhenie v Odesse." In *Mikhailu Bakuninu, 1876–1926*, edited by A. A. Borovoi, pp. 246–278. Moscow, 1926.

———."Iz istorii odesskogo podpol'ia." *Proletarskaia revoliutsiia* no. 4(63) (1924), pp. 181–202.

Obninskii, Viktor. *Polgoda russkoi revoliutsii.* Vyp. 1. Moscow, 1906.

Obzor deiatel'nosti gorodskoi vrachebno-sanitarnoi organizatsii v Odesse za 1905 g. Odessa, 1907.

Obzor deiatel'nosti Odesskago obshchestva vzaimnago vspomoshchestvovaniia prikazchikov-evreev za 35 let. Odessa, 1898.

Obzory Odesskago gradonachal'stva za 1900–1906 gg. Odessa, 1901–1907.

Obzor sanitarnago sostoianiia g. Odessy po sanitarno-statisticheskim dannym za 1903 g. Odessa, 1904.

Ocherk deiatel'nosti Odesskago obshchestva vzaimnago vspomoshchestvovaniia prikazchikov-evreev za 50 let. Odessa, 1913.

"Odessa." *Entsiklopedicheskii slovar'.* Vol. 21, pp. 726–730. St. Petersburg, 1897.

———. *Evreiskaia entsiklopediia.* Vol. 12, pp. 50–68. St. Petersburg, 1910.

———. *The Jewish Encyclopedia.* Vol. 9, pp. 377–385. New York and London, 1905.

Odessa, 1794–1894. Odessa, 1895.

Odesskie glavnye masterskie. Ikh ustroistvo, oborudovanie i proizvoditel'nost'. Kiev, 1896.

Odesskii pogrom i samooborona. Paris, 1906.

Okol'skii, Boris. "Nesostoiavsheesia pokushenie." *Kandal'nyi zvon* no. 1 (1925), pp. 86–94.

Okol'skii, Viktor. "Iz epokhi 'mogil'noi tishinyi'." *Puti revoliutsii* no. 2 (1925), pp. 91–100.

Oliunina, E. A. *Portnovskii promysel v Moskve i derevniakh Moskovskoi i Riazanskoi gubernii: Materialy k istorii domashnei promyshlennosti v Rossii.* Moscow, 1914.

Opisanie odesskikh ulichnykh bezporiadkov v dni sv. Paskhi 1871 goda. Odessa, 1871.

Opisanie odesskago porta. St. Petersburg, 1913.

Orlov, A. *Istoricheskii ocherk Odessy s 1794 po 1803 god.* Odessa, 1885.

Osipovich, N. "Novye materialy o pozhare i vystrele odesskogo porta v iiunskie dni 1905 g." In *1905 god*, vol. 2, pp. 216–228. Odessa, 1926.

———. "V grozovye gody." *Kandal'nyi zvon* no. 3 (1926), pp. 31–87.

"Osvobozhdenie truda": Sbornik statei po rabochemu voprosu. Odessa, 1907.

Otchet o deiatel'nosti lektsionnago komiteta pri Odesskoi gorodskoi auditorii za 1897–1900 uchebnye gody. Odessa, 1901.

Otchet Odesskago evreiskago tsentral'nago komiteta po okazaniiu pomoshchi postradavshim ot pogromov 1905 goda. Odessa, 1906.

Otchety Odesskago komiteta torgovli i manufaktur za 1900–1906 gg. Odessa, 1901–1907.

Otchet Odesskago obshchestva vzaimopomoshchi moriakov torgovago flota za 1904–1905 gody. Odessa, 1906.

Otchet Odesskoi obshchei remeslennoi upravy za 1902–1904 gg. Odessa, 1905.

Otchet pravleniia obshchestva vzaimnago vspomozheniia prikazchikov g. Odessy za 1905–1906 gody. Odessa, 1907.

Otchet pravleniia obshchestva vzaimnago vspomozheniia truzhenikov pechatnago dela g. Odessy za 1890–91 gody. Odessa, 1892.

Otchety pravleniia Odesskago obshchestva vzaimnago vspomoshchestvovaniia prikazchikov-evreev za 1903–1904 gg. Odessa, 1904–1905.

Otchety rasporiaditel'nago komiteta nochlezhnykh priiutov za 1880–1904 gody. Odessa, 1880–1904.

Ovsiannikov, P. I. "Revoliutsionnoe dvizhenie v voiskakh kievskogo i odesskogo voennykh okrugov." In *1905: Materialy i dokumenty*, edited by M. N. Pokrovskii. *Armiia v pervoi revoliutsii. Ocherki i materialy*, pp. 180–223. Moscow-Leningrad, 1927.

"Pamiati S. Portugeisa (S. O. Ivanovicha)." *Novyi zhurnal* 8 (1944): pp. 394–395.

Pankratova, A. M. ed. *Iz istorii rabochego i revoliutsionnogo dvizheniia.* Moscow, 1958.

———., ed. *Rabochee dvizhenie v Rossii v XIX veke: Sbornik dokumentov i materialov.* 4 vols. Moscow-Leningrad, 1950–1963.

———, ed. "1905: Stachechnoe dvizhenie." In *1905: Materialy i dokumenty*, edited by M. N. Pokrovskii. Vol. 2. Moscow-Leningrad, 1925.

Parasun'ko, O. A. *Polozhenie i bor'ba rabochego klassa Ukrainy. Kiev, 1963.*

Pazhitnov, K. A. *Problemy remeslennykh tsekhov v zakonodatel'stve russkogo absoliutizma* (Moscow, 1952).

Peled, Yoav. *Class and Ethnicity in the Pale: The Political Economy of Jewish Workers' Nationalism in Late Imperial Russia.* New York: St. Martin's Press, 1989.

"Perepiska N. Lenina i N. K. Krupskoi s Odesskoi organizatsiei." *Proletarskaia revoliutsiia* nos. 6(41) (1925), pp. 5–63, 7(42) (1925), pp. 5–53, 11(46) (1925), pp. 9–48, and 12(47) (1925), pp. 5–88.

Perepiska V. I. Lenina i rukovodimykh im uchrezhdenii RSDRP s partiinymi organizatsiiami 1905–1907 gg. Sbornik dokumentov v piati tomakh. Moscow, 1979.

Perepiska V. I. Lenina i rukovodimykh im zagranichnykh partiinykh organov s sotsial-demokraticheskimi organizatsiiami Ukrainy (1901–1905 gg.): Sbornik dokumentov i materialov. Kiev, 1964.

Perrot, Michelle. "On the Formation of the French Working Class." In *Working-Class Formation: Nineteenth-Century Patterns in Western Europe and the United States*, edited by Ira Katznelson and Aristide R. Zolberg, pp. 71–110. Princeton: Princeton University Press, 1986.

———. *Workers on Strike: France 1871–1890.* Translated by Chris Turner. New Haven: Yale University Press, 1987.

Pershina, Z. V. *Imeni ianvarskogo vosstaniia.* Odessa, 1963.

———. "Nachalo rabochego dvizheniia. Pervye marksistskie kruzhki v Odesse (1883–1895 gody)." In *Iz istorii odesskoi partiinoi organizatsii: Ocherki*, edited by K. S. Kovalenko, pp. 7–28. Odessa, 1964.

Pervaia maia v tsarskoi Rossii, 1890–1916 g.g. Sbornik dokumentov. Moscow, 1939.

Pervaia russkaia revoliutsiia: Ukazatel' literatury. Moscow, 1930.

Pervaia vseobshchaia perepis' naseleniia Rossiiskoi Imperii, 1897 g. Vol. 47, *Gorod Odessa.* St. Petersburg, 1904.

Piatnitskii, O. *Memoirs of a Bolshevik.* London: 1930.

———. *Zapiski bol'shevika.* Leningrad, 1926.

Piatyi s"ezd Vseobshchago evreiskago rabochago soiuza v Litve, Polshe i Rossii. London, 1903.

Piontkovskii, S., ed. "Novoe o zubatovshchine." *Krasnyi arkhiv* no. 1 (1922), pp. 289–314.

Pipes, Richard. *Russia under the Old Regime.* New York: Charles Scribners' Sons, 1974.

Pishchevik: Iubileinyi sbornik. Odessa, n.d.

Plaksin, S. I. *Kommerchesko-promyshlennaia Odessa i ee predstaviteli v kontse deviatnadtsatago stoletiia i istoriia razvitiia torgovykh firm.* Odessa, 1901.

Platonov, A. P. *Vosstanie v chernomorskom flote v 1905 g. v iiune v Odesse i v noiabre v Sevastopole.* Leningrad, 1925.

Pleskov, V. A. "V Odesse posle 'Potemkina'." In *V tsarskoi kazarme: Soldaty i matrosy v pervoi revoliutsii*, edited by F. Ia. Kon, pp. 65–87. Moscow, 1929.

———. "V revoliutsionnom podpol'e. (Odesskaia voennaia organizatsiia 1905 g.)." In *1905 god*, vol. 2, pp. 64–75. Odessa, 1926.

"Pokazaniia D. B. Riazanova (Gol'dendakha) ot 17–23 dekabria 1891 g." *Istoriko-revoliutsionnyi sbornik 2* (1924): 197–204.

Pokrovskii, M. N., ed. *1905: Istoriia revoliutsionnogo dvizheniia v otdel'nykh ocherkakh*. 3 vols. Moscow-Leningrad, 1925–1927.

———, ed. *1905: Materialy i dokumenty*. 8 vols. Moscow-Leningrad, 1925–1928.

Polevoi, Iu. G. *Zarozhdenie marksizma v Rossii, 1883–94*. Moscow, 1959.

Prevo, Kathleen. "The Revolution of 1905 in Voronezh: The Labor Movement and Political Consciousness in a Russian Provincial City." Ph.D. dissertation, Indiana University, 1979.

———. "Voronezh in 1905: Workers and Politics in a Provincial City." *Russian History* 12, no. 1 (Spring 1985): 48–70.

Prokopovich, S. N. *K rabochemu voprosu v Rossii*. St. Petersburg, 1905.

Protokoly 3-go vserossiiskago s"ezda obshchestv vspomozheniia chastnomu sluzhebnomu trudu i drugikh odnorodnykh po idee i tseli. Moscow, 1906.

Puryear, Vernon J. "Odessa: Its Rise and International Importance, 1815–1850." *Pacific Historical Review 3* (1934): 192–215.

Pushkareva, I. M. *Zheleznodorozhniki Rossii v burzhuazno-demokraticheskikh revoliutsiiakh*. Moscow, 1975.

Putevoditel' po Odesse i ee okrestnostiam. Odessa, 1907.

Rabinowitsch, S. *Die Organizationen des jüdisches Proletariats in Russland*. Karlsruhe, 1903.

Rabochee dvizhenie v Odesse (1894–1896 gody). Geneva, 1903.

Rabochee dvizhenie v Rossii v 1901–1904 gg. Sbornik dokumentov. Leningrad, 1975.

Rabochii vopros v komissii V. N. Kokovtsova v 1905 g. Moscow, 1926.

Rafes, M. G. *Ocherki istorii evreiskogo rabochego dvizheniia*. Moscow-Leningrad, 1929.

Rashin, A. G. *Naselenie Rossii za 100 let (1811–1913 gg.)*. Moscow, 1956.

Read, Christopher. "Labour and Socialism in Tsarist Russia." In *Labour and Socialist Movements in Europe before 1914*, edited by Dick Geary, pp. 137–181. Oxford: Berg Publishers Limited, 1989.

Reardon, Judy. "Belgian and French Workers in Nineteenth-Century Roubaix." In *Class Conflict and Collective Action*. Edited by Louise Tilly and Charles Tilly, pp. 167–183. London: Sage Publications, 1981.

Reichman, Henry. *Railwaymen and Revolution: Russia, 1905*. Berkeley and Los Angeles: University of California Press, 1987.

Remeslenniki i remeslennoe upravlenie v Rossii. Petrograd, 1916.

Revoliutsiia 1905–1907 rokiv na Ukraini: Zbirnykh dokumentiv i materialiv. Kiev, 1949.

Revoliutsionnoe dvizhenie v chernomorskom flote v 1905 godu: Sbornik vospominanii i materialov. Moscow, 1925.

Revoliutsionnoe dvizhenie v Rossii v dokladakh ministra Murav'eva 1894–1905. St. Petersburg, 1907.

Revoliutsionnoe gnezdo: Iz istorii Novorossiiskago universiteta. St. Petersburg, 1909.

Revoliutsionnyi bronenosets: Vosstanie v chernomorskom flote (Po materialam "Iskry" i "Sotsialdemokrata"). Geneva, 1905.

Rezul'taty odnodnevnoi perepisi g. Odessy, 1 dekabria 1892 goda. Odessa, 1894.

Riabinin-Skliarevskii, A. "Revoliutsionnaia rabota v voiskakh Odesskogo garnizona v 1904–5–6 g.g." *Letopis' revoliutsii* no. 5–6(14–15) (1925), pp. 155–175.

———. "Sovet rabochikh deputatov g. Odessy v 1905 godu." In *1905 god*, vol. 1, 253–267. Odessa, 1925.

Rice, Christopher. *Russian Workers and the Socialist-Revolutionary Party through the Revolution of 1905–07*. New York: St. Martin's Press, 1988.

Rieber, Alfred. *Merchants and Entrepreneurs in Imperial Russia*. Chapel Hill: University of North Carolina Press, 1982.

Robbins, Richard G., Jr. *The Tsar's Viceroys: Russian Provincial Governors in the Last Years of the Empire*. Ithaca: Cornell University Press, 1987.

Rogger, Hans. "The Jewish Policy of Late Tsarism: A Reappraisal." In *Jewish Policies and Right-Wing Politics in Imperial Russia* by Hans Rogger, pp. 25–39. Berkeley and Los Angeles: University of California Press, 1986.

Rogov, V. I. (A. Cherniavskii). "Cherty iz zhizni odesskoi organizatsii bol'shevikov v 1905 godu." In *1905 god*, vol. 2, pp. 55–63. Odessa, 1926.

Rostotskaia, N. *Potemkinskie dni v Odesse*. Odessa, 1906.

Sanders, Jonathan. "Lessons from the Periphery: Saratov, January 1905." *Slavic Review* 46, no. 2 (Summer 1987): 229–244.

———. "Drugs and Revolution: Moscow Pharmacists in the First Russian Revolution." *Russian Review* 44, no. 4 (October 1985): 351–377.

Schneiderman, Jeremiah. *Sergei Zubatov and Revolutionary Marxism: The Struggle for the Working Class in Tsarist Russia*. Ithaca and London: Cornell University Press, 1970, 1976.

Schwarz, Solomon. *The Russian Revolution of 1905: The Workers' Movement and the Formation of Bolshevism and Menshevism*. Translated by Gertrude Vakar. Chicago and London: University of Chicago Press, 1967.

Scott, Joan. *The Glassworkers of Carmaux: French Craftsmen and Political Action in a Nineteenth-Century City*. Cambridge: Harvard University Press, 1974.

Semenov, S. "Evreiskie pogromy v Odesse i Odesshchine v 1905 g." *Puti revoliutsii* no. 3 (1925), pp. 115–135.

Sh., Ia. "Vospominaniia o soiuze kontorshchikov g. Odessy: dekabr' 1905 goda-aprel' 1906 goda." In *Professional'noe dvizhenie sluzhashchikh Ukrainy (1905–1907 gg.)*, edited by I. S. Stepanskii, pp. 185–194. Kharkov, 1927.

Shapiro, S. "Iz istorii rabochego dvizheniia v Odesse." *Professional'naia zhizn'* nos. 23(110) (1922), pp. 16–17, 24(111) (1922), pp. 13–14, 25(112) (1922), pp. 59–64, 28–29(115–116) (1923), pp. 65–68, 30(117) (1923), pp. 51–54, and 31–32(118–119) (1923), pp. 70–72.

Shapovalov, A. S. *V podpol'e*, 2nd ed. Moscow-Leningrad, 1931.

Shcherbakov, D. N. "Deiatel'nost' revoliutsionnykh sotsial-demokraticheskikh organizatsii Ukrainy po politicheskomu vospitaniiu proletariata i rukovodstvu rabochim dvizheniem (1894–1904 gg.)." Doctor of Historical Science dissertation, Kiev University, 1979.

Shelgunov, N. *Ocherki russkoi zhizni*. St. Petersburg, 1895.

Sher, I. "Pokhorony Vakulenchuka." *Kandal'nyi zvon* no. 3 (1926), pp. 88–90.

60 let ianvarskikh masterskikh: Iubileinyi sbornik. 1863–1923. Odessa, 1923.

Shklovskii, L. "Vospominaniia ob Odesse 1905 goda." *Proletarskaia revoliutsiia* no. 11(46) (1925), pp. 250–261.

Shlosberg, D. and V. Shul'man. "Vseobshchaia zabastovka v Odesse v 1903 godu i 'nezavisimtsy'." *Letopis' revoliutsii* no. 1(34) (1929).

Shreiber, S. "Partiinaia rabota v Odesse (Sentiabr'-dekabr' 1905). *Letopis' revoliutsii* no. 5–6(14–15) (1925), pp. 132–148.

Shternshtein, A. M. "V. I. Lenin i bol'shevistskaia organizatsiia Odessy v 1905 godu." Candidate of Historical Science dissertation, Kiev University, 1974.

Shternshtein, Ia. M. *Morskie vorota Ukrainy*. Odessa, 1958.

Shuster, U. A. *Peterburgskie rabochie v 1905–1907 gg*. Leningrad, 1976.

Sidorov, A. L., ed. *Vysshii pod"em revoliutsii 1905–1907 gg. Vooruzhennye vosstaniia: noiabr'-dekabr' 1905 goda*. Pt. 3, bk. 1. Moscow, 1956.

Siegelbaum, Lewis. "The Odessa Grain Trade: A Case Study in Urban Growth and Development." *The Journal of European Economic History* 9, no. 1 (1980): 113–151.

Skal'kovskii, A. A. *Istoriko-statisticheskii opyt o torgovykh i promyshlennykh silakh Odessy.* Odessa, 1839.

―――. "Nachalo razvitiia zavodskoi promyshlennosti v Odesse." *Trudy Odesskago statisticheskago komiteta.* Vol. IV, pp. 148–157. Odessa, 1870.

―――. *Pervoe tridtsatiletie istorii goroda Odessy, 1795–1823.* Odessa, 1837.

―――. *Zapiski o torgovykh i promyshlennykh silakh Odessy.* St. Petersburg, 1865.

Skinner, Frederick. "City Planning in Russia: The Development of Odessa, 1789–1892." Ph.D. dissertation, Princeton University, 1973.

―――. "Odessa and the Problem of Modernization." In *The City in Late Imperial Russia*, edited by Michael Hamm, pp. 209–248. Bloomington: Indiana University Press, 1986.

―――. "Trends in Planning Practices: The Building of Odessa, 1794–1917." In *The City in Russian History*, edited by Michael Hamm, pp. 139–159. Lexington: University Press of Kentucky, 1976.

Skocpol, Theda, ed. *Vision and Method in Historical Sociology.* Cambridge: Cambridge University Press, 1984.

Skveri, M. *Pervaia rabochaia sotsialisticheskaia organizatsiia v Odesse (1875 god).* Odessa, 1921.

Smith, S. A. "Workers and Civil Rights in Tsarist Russia, 1899–1917." In *Civil Rights in Imperial Russia*, edited by Olga Crisp and Linda Edmondson, pp. 145–169. Oxford: Clarendon Press, 1989.

Smol'ianinov, K. *Istoriia Odessy.* Odessa, 1853.

Soiuz metallistov (Po vospominaniiam veteranov) 1898–1925. Odessa, 1925.

Solomonov, V. "Ocherk razvitiia torgovo-promyshlennykh firm g. Odessy." *Iuzhno-russkii al'manakh*, pp. 259–268. Odessa, 1900.

"Spravochnye svedeniia po g. Odesse." *Iuzhno-russkii al'manakh*, pp. 143–155. Odessa, 1897.

Srednev, N. *Evreiskaia revoliutsionnaia samooborona v Odesse.* Odessa, 1907.

―――. *Odesskii konvent v oktiabr'skie dni 1905 g.* Odessa, 1908.

Statisticheskoe obozrenie Odessy za 1890 g. Odessa. 1892.

Steklov, Iu. M. *Iz rabochago dvizheniia v Odesse i Nikolaeve.* Geneva, 1900.

―――. "Iz vospominanii o sotsial'demokraticheskom dvizhenii sredi odesskikh rabochikh v 1893–1894 godakh." *Minuvshie gody*, September 1908, pp. 251–252.

Straten, V. V. "'Iuzhno-russkii rabochii soiuz' v Odesse. Sotsial-demokraticheskoe dvizhenie v Odesse do 1896 goda." *Letopis' revoliutsii* no. 2(7) (1924), pp. 192–216.

Subbotin, A. P. *V cherte evreiskoi osedlosti.* St. Petersburg, 1890.

Subda, A. "Zabastovka 1905 g. na zavode I. I. Gena v Odesse." In *1905 god*, vol. 2, pp. 155–167. Odessa, 1926.

Suny, Ronald. "Nationalism and Social Class in the Russian Revolution: The Cases of Baku and Tiflis." In *Transcaucasia: Nationalism and Social Change: Essays in the History of Armenia, Azerbaijan, and Georgia*, edited by Ronald Suny, pp. 239–258. Ann Arbor: Michigan Slavic Publications, 1983.

―――. *The Baku Commune, 1917–1918: Class and Nationality in the Russian Revolution.* Princeton: Princeton University Press, 1972.

Surh, Gerald. "Petersburg Workers in 1905: Strikes, Workplace Democracy, and the Revolution." Ph.D. dissertation, University of California, 1979.

―――. *1905 in St. Petersburg: Labor, Society, and Revolution.* Stanford: Stanford University Press, 1989.

Sushkin, G. G. *Bezvestnye: Zhenskie siluety revoliutsionnogo podpol'ia kanuna 1905 goda.* Moscow, 1930.

Sviatlovskii, V. V. "Iz istorii kass i obshchestv vzaimopomoshchi rabochikh." *Arkhiv istorii truda v Rossii*, bk. 4 (1922), 32–46.

———. *Professional'noe dvizhenie v Rossii*. St. Petersburg, 1907.

Svirskii, A. I. "Iz putevogo dnevnika." *Knizhki 'Voskhoda'* no. 7 (July 1904), pp. 166–172.

———. *Trushchoby*. In A. I. Svirskii, *Polnoe sobranie sochinenii*. Vol. 9. Moscow-Leningrad, 1928–1929.

Tanin, Ia. "Partzhizn' Odessy v oktiabre-dekabre 1905 goda." *Letopis' revoliutsii* no. 5–6(14–15) (1925), pp. 149–154.

Tarnopol, G. A. *Ocherk ego deiatel'nosti kak predsedatelia obshchestva vzaimnago vspomoshchestvaniia prikazchikov-evreev g. Odessy*. Odessa, 1890.

Teziakov, N. I. *Rynki sel'sko-khoziaistvennykh rabochikh na iuge Rossii v sanitarnom otnoshenii i vrachebno prodovol'stvennom punkte*. Vyp. 2. St. Petersburg, 1902.

———. *Sel'sko-khoziaistvennye rabochie i organizatsiia za nimi sanitarnago nadzora v Khersonskoi gubernii*. Kherson, 1896.

———. "Sel'sko-khoziaistvennye rabochie voobshche i prishlye, v chastnosti v Khersonskoi gubernii v sanitarnom otnoshenii." *Sbornik Khersonskago zemstva* no. 8 (1891), pp. 8–102.

Thompson, John and Mehlinger, Howard. *Count Witte and the Tsarist Government in the 1905 Revolution*. Bloomington: Indiana University Press, 1972.

Tiazheloispytannyi, Andrei. *Pesni odesskikh bosiakov*. n.p., n.d.

Tilly, Charles. "The Changing Place of Collective Violence." In *Workers in the Industrial Revolution: Recent Studies of Labor in the United States and Europe*, edited by Peter Stearns and Daniel Walkowitz, pp. 117–137. New Brunswick: Transaction Books, 1974.

———, and Tilly, Louise, eds. *Class Conflict and Collective Action*. London: Sage Publications, 1981.

———, Tilly, Louise and Tilly, Richard. *The Rebellious Century, 1830–1930*. Cambridge: Harvard University Press, 1975.

Tobias, Henry. *The Jewish Bund in Russia: From Its Origins to 1905*. Stanford: Stanford University Press, 1972.

Tocqueville, Alexis de. *The Old Régime and the French Revolution*. Translated by Stuart Gilbert. Garden City: Doubleday and Company, 1955.

Trotsky, Leon. *My Life*. New York: Charles Scribners' Sons, 1930.

Trudy pervago s"ezda predstavitelei obshchestv vspomozheniia chastnomu sluzhebnomu trudu. Nizhnii Novgorod, 1897.

Trudy pervago vserossiiskago s"ezda po remeslennoi promyshlennosti. 3 vols. St. Petersburg, 1900.

Trudy vtorago s"ezda predstavitelei obshchestv vspomozheniia chastnomu sluzhebnomu trudu. Moscow, 1900.

Trusova, N. S., ed. *Nachalo pervoi russkoi revoliutsii: ianvar'-mart 1905 goda*. Moscow, 1955.

———, ed. *Revoliutsionnoe dvizhenie v Rossii vesnoi i letom 1905 goda: aprel'-sentiabr'*. Pt. 2, bk. 1. Moscow, 1961.

Tsetterbaum, M. *Klassovye protivorechiia v evreiskom obshchestve*. Kiev, 1905.

1905 god. Revoliutsionnoe dvizhenie v Odesse i Odesshchine. 2 vols. Odessa, 1925–1926.

Ustav professional'nago soiuza sluzhashchikh i rabochikh iugo-zapadnykh zh.d. Kiev, 1905.

V. B. "Stachechnoe dvizhenie na iugo-zapadnykh zheleznykh dorogakh v 1905 godu." *Letopis' revoliutsii* no. 2(29) (1928), pp. 144–173.

Valk, S. N., ed. "Pervomaiskie rechi v Odesse v 1895 g." *Krasnyi arkhiv* no. 6(19) (1926), pp. 203–207.

Vanner, D. I., ed. *Illiustrirovannyi putevoditel' "Odessa."* Odessa, 1900.

Vasil'evskaia, V. K. "Polozheniia portovykh rabochikh v Odesse." *Trudy Odesskago otdela Russkago obshchestva okhraneniia zdraviia*, vyp. 4 (1904), pp. 36–49.

Vasil'evskii, N. *Ocherk sanitarnago polozheniia g. Odessy.* Odessa, 1901.

Vel'shtein, E. P. "Stachki rabochikh na Peresypi." *Izvestiia Odesskoi gorodskoi dumy* no. 19–20 (October 1905), *prilozheniia*, pp. 625–632.

Venturi, Franco. *Roots of Revolution.* New York: Grosset and Dunlap, 1960.

Verner, Andrew. *The Crisis of Russian Autocracy: Nicholas II and the 1905 Revolution.* Princeton: Princeton University Press, 1990.

Volkov, M. I. *Opyt ankety o domashnei zhizni i usloviiakh truda rabochikh kozhevennago proizvodstva g. Odessy.* Odessa, 1909.

Vopros o predstavitel'stve na mezhdunarodnom sotsialisticheskom kongresse v Amsterdame: Otchet delegatsiia Bunda. Geneva, 1904.

Vorobei, P. I. and Kovbasiuk, S. M. "Odesskaia bol'shevistskaia organizatsiia v gody pervoi russkoi revoliutsii (1905–1907 gody)." In *Iz istorii odesskoi partiinoi organizatsii: Ocherki,* edited by K. S. Kovalenko, pp. 59–93. Odessa, 1964.

Vtoroi s"ezd RSDRP, iiul'-avgust 1903 goda: Protokoly. Moscow, 1959.

Weinberg, Robert. "The Politicization of Labor in 1905: The Case of Odessa Sales-clerks." *Slavic Review* 49, no. 3 (Fall 1990): 427–445.

———. "Social Democracy and Workers in Odessa: Ethnic and Political Considerations." *The Carl Beck Papers in Russian and East European Studies* no. 504 (1986).

———. "Worker Organizations and Politics in the Revolution of 1905 in Odessa." Ph.D. dissertation, University of California, Berkeley. 1985.

———. "Workers, Pogroms, and the 1905 Revolution in Odessa." *Russian Review* 46, no. 1 (July 1987): 53–75.

Wildman, Allan K. "Russian and Jewish Social Democracy." In *Revolution and Politics in Russia: Essays in Memory of B. I. Nicolaevsky,* edited by Alexander and Janet Rabinowitch with Ladis K. D. Kristof, pp. 75–87. Bloomington: Indiana University Press, 1972.

———. *The Making of a Workers' Revolution: Russian Social Democracy, 1891–1903.* Chicago and London: University of Chicago Press, 1967.

Witte, Sergei. *The Memoirs of Count Witte.* Translated and edited by Sidney Harcave. Armonk, New York: M. E. Sharpe, Inc. 1990.

———. *Vospominaniia.* Moscow, 1960.

Wynn, Charters. *Workers, Strikes, and Pogroms: The Donbass to Dnepr Bend, 1870–1905.* Princeton: Princeton University Press, 1992.

Zagoruiko, V. *Po stranitsam istorii Odessy i Odesshchiny.* 2 vols. Odessa, 1957 and 1960.

Zanchevskii, A. *Rost proletarskogo samosoznaniia v Odesse v 1905 g. v sviazi s zabastovkami.* Odessa, 1925.

Zelnik, Reginald. *Labor and Society in Tsarist Russia: The Factory Workers of St. Petersburg, 1855–1870.* Stanford: Stanford University Press, 1971.

———. "Passivity and Protest in Germany and Russia: Barrington Moore's Conception of Working-Class Responses to Injustice." *Journal of Social History* 15, no. 3 (Spring 1982): 485–512.

———. "Russian Workers and the Revolutionary Movement." *Journal of Social History* 6, no. 2 (1972–1973): 214–236.

Zhezmer, M. "Odesk'ka Rada robitnychykh deputativ 1905 r." *Letopis' revoliutsii* no. 6(45) (193), pp. 149–175.

———. *Odesk'ka Rada robitnychykh deputativ 1905 roku.* Kharkov-Odessa, 1931.

Zil'berg, I. G. *Professional'noe dvizhenie sluzhashchikh farmatsevtov. Period pervoi russkoi revoliutsii.* Moscow, 1930.

Zipperstein, Steven. "Jewish Enlightenment in Odessa: Cultural Characteristics, 1794–1881." *Jewish Social Studies* 44, no. 1 (1982): 19–36.

———. *The Jews of Odessa: A Cultural History, 1794–1881.* Stanford: Stanford University Press, 1985.

Zuev, V. I. "Gorodskoe blagoustroistvo, kak faktor okhraneniia narodnago zdraviia." *Trudy Odesskago otdela Russkago obshchestva okhraneniia zdraviia.* Vyp. 4 (1904), pp. 123–131.

INDEX